Rave Reviews for
Company of Adventurers

"Peter Newman's *Company of Adventurers* is not only essential Canadian history; it's also a great adventure story."
Mordecai Richler

"Author Peter C. Newman tells a thrilling, chilling story of brave explorers who lost fingers, toes and illusions in the chilly wastes of Canada looking for beaver skins and furs for the Hudson's Bay Company."

Daily Express
London, England

"The author's interest in copulation keeps peeping through his vivid, full-bodied history of the Hudson's Bay Co. and its crucial role in shaping Canada. He even describes how beavers do it."

The Gazette
Montreal

"Newman writes with force and elegance. His intimate knowledge of the company's history fills *Company of Adventurers* with wonderful details about the evolving nature of venture capitalism. A picture emerges that is canny, vivid, deeply appreciative and critically astute."

The Washington Post

"I cannot conceal my enthusiasm for the story of the Hudson's Bay Company; here it is very well told. This story of service and endurance, unspoken heroism, restores respect for the human species, when we need some uplift these days."

Financial Times
London, England

"After years of travel and research, Newman has brought to vivid life the men whose adventures guaranteed the future of an improbable nation. Every Canadian reader will be enriched by this splendid book."

Bruce Hutchison

"*Company of Adventurers* is marvelous history and powerful storytelling. It is reminiscent in its grandeur and drama of Samuel Morison's 'The European Discovery of America.' And that, as far as this reviewer is concerned, is the highest compliment one can pay to any work of history."

Daily Press
Virginia

"Newman is a fluent story-teller with a feeling for people . . . at his best when exploring the psychological isolation of the trappers and Company men, the price of whose freedom he sees as cultural disinheritance and social marginality."

Times Literary Supplement
London, England

"In return for unrestricted access to the Bay archives, Newman gave the company nothing. He is sharply critical of the company's parsimony and stodgy management during its first century of business. And in the Bay's current decline, he sees a connection with many earlier, equally despondent times."

Quill & Quire

"Newman is, in a way, the ideal Bay historian. His commitment to Canada as a patriot and nationalist has led him constantly to wonder how we became what we are; as a journalist, he frequently stretches the nation out on a psychoanalytic couch."

The Globe and Mail

"Mr. Newman skillfully blends the fascinating details of daily frontier hardships (the icicles that grew inside the traders' crude outposts, the social and sexual interplay among white Europeans, Indians and Eskimos and the foods they ate, including deer blood soup) with the grander policy designs in London and Paris that sometimes had men-of-war standing off the forts that fur built on that vast, icy bay atop North America."

The New York Times

PENGUIN BOOKS

Company of Adventurers

Peter C. Newman is the author whose pioneering studies of power — how it is used and abused within Canadian society — made the Canadian Establishment a household phrase. Now, he tackles the oldest and most fascinating institution of them all: the Governor and Company of Adventurers of England trading into Hudson's Bay.

Recipient of a dozen of the most coveted awards in North American journalism, Newman has been editor-in-chief of the country's largest newspaper, *The Toronto Star*, and most influential magazine, *Maclean's*. He resigned from *Maclean's* in the spring of 1982, after successfully transforming it into the country's first newsweekly, to concentrate fully on this book. The research took him from the simple dwellings of the Swampy Cree and Inuit who still trade with the HBC's 120 outposts in Northern Canada to the private drawing room offices of the powerful in London's financial district.

As well as continuing his probes of the Canadian Establishment, Newman is currently at work on the second volume of this monumental — and highly unauthorized — history.

Forts of the Hudson's Bay Company

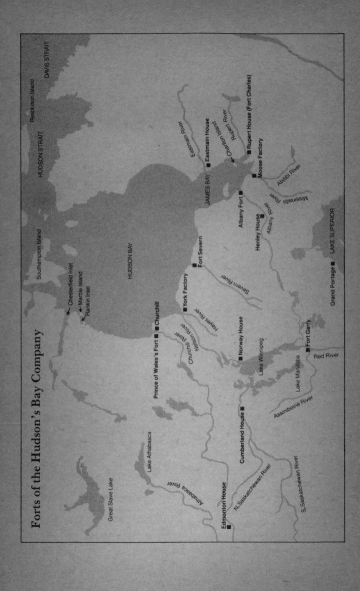

COMPANY
OF
ADVENTURERS

Volume I

PETER C. NEWMAN

Penguin Books

Penguin Books Canada Limited, 2801 John Street, Markham, Ontario, Canada L3R 1B4
Penguin Books Ltd., Harmondsworth, Middlesex, England
Penguin Books, 40 West 23rd Street, New York, New York 10010 U.S.A.
Penguin Books Australia Ltd., Ringwood, Victoria, Australia
Penguin Books (N.Z.) Ltd. Private Bag, Takapuna, Auckland 9, New Zealand

First published by Penguin Books Canada Limited, 1985
Published in this edition, 1986

Copyright © Power Reporting Limited, 1985

All rights reserved.

Manufactured in Canada
Book design by V. John Lee

Canadian Cataloguing in Publication Data

Newman, Peter C. 1929–
  Company of Adventurers

Bibliography: p.
Includes index.
ISBN 0-14-006720-5

1. Hudson's Bay Company — History. 2. Northwest,
Canadian — History — To 1870.* 3. Fur trade —
Canada — History. I. Title.

FC3207.N49 1986   971.2'01   C85-098657-5
F1060.N49 1985

For H. ALBERT HOCHBAUM, a wise diviner
of Arctic lore and painter of its beauty, who knows
that the assaults of technology and bureaucrats
on the Canadian North are not as bad as they seem:
they are worse

and for PROFESSOR RICHARD GLOVER, who unearthed
much of the Hudson's Bay Company's original history
and so generously shared his excitement
with an enquiring chronicler.

I wish also to thank the Hudson's Bay Company
for not even *trying* to influence my judgments
during the research and writing of this book.
Except for granting me unimpeded access to
archives and files, the HBC has had no involvement –
financial or editorial – in this project.
My only debt to the Company of Adventurers
is a slightly overdue department store bill;
the cheque is in the mail.

"We were Caesars, being nobody to contradict us…"

— Pierre-Esprit Radisson

CONTENTS

COMPANY
OF
ADVENTURERS

Foreword

HISTORY IS NO MORE THAN MEMORIES REFINED or, as the great Canadian historian Donald Creighton put it, the record of encounters between character and circumstance. This book – the first of two volumes about the impact of the Hudson's Bay Company on Canada as a nation and as a state of mind – deals as much with lone memories as with documented spans of momentous events. It is an attempt to chronicle the half-remembered genesis of English Canada's corporate and psychic beginnings on the bleak shores of Hudson Bay, more than three centuries ago.

Why spend time and energy rustling through fragile documents? Why bother to resurrect the lives of fur traders who huddled under the polar moon and befuddled explorers who meandered across the continent, certain that the way to China lay around each swampy river bend?

Because in an imported country like Canada, which has so much more geography than history, it is essential to illuminate the past, not backlit by hindsight but as it really was.

The eighteenth century, when most of the events in these pages took place, seems very long ago, yet it is only three memories back. "My grandfather, who was ninety in the mid-1930s, told me of events that happened in the late 1700s, told him by his grandfather," said Albert Hochbaum, the Manitoba artist-naturalist who helped me place the HBC story in its proper context.

Memories dim. They must be refreshed.

ANY AUTHOR OF A COMPANY HISTORY, even one as totally unauthorized as this is, must defend his objectiv-

ity. My lack of bias is genuine in that I set out to popular-
ize this epic without adorning it. It needs no cosmetics.
The characters who populate the pages that follow speak
eloquently enough for themselves. Each document I
examined, even if it was mottled with age, was as new to
me as if it had still been exuding the faint smell of fresh
ink. I took little for granted and held no opinions sacred,
though I did keep in mind Abbé Raynal's stern admonition that "the murmurs of the nation have been excited
against this Company." I discovered plenty of good reasons
why.

The real problem was how to sort out all those
masses of names, dates and faces into a coherent narrative.
I remember feeling a little better about the eight filing
cabinets of facts I had accumulated after reading in *The
Spectator* an interview with the British historian A.J.P.
Taylor, who declared, on his seventy-seventh birthday,
that "history is not a catalogue, but ..., a convincing
version of events." That rang true. All the historians I
admire – Taylor, Francis Parkman, G.M. Trevelyan, Pierre
Berton, Alan Moorehead and, above all, Barbara
Tuchman – have managed to capture on the printed page
the magical enthusiasm of the storyteller, to spin the
web accurately without being swamped by detail. If I
have a literary credo, it is an echo of Tuchman's evocative
declaration in her recent collection of essays, *Practising
History*: "In my mind is a picture of Kipling's itinerant
storyteller of India, with his rice bowl, who tells tales
of ancient romance and legend to a circle of villagers by
firelight. If he sees figures drifting away from the edge of
the circle in the darkness, and his audience thinning out,
he knows his rice bowl will be meagerly filled ... I feel
just as urgent a connection with the reader."

Events happen in sequence or simultaneously, but
never in categories, so it was impossible to fit the HBC
story into any neat set of carefully marshalled revela-

tions. Instead, at each pivotal stage of the Company's evolution, I have chosen one individual as a representative type. This has allowed me, through one character at a time, to freeze-frame the landscape of the HBC's activity at that particular moment. I have attempted to recreate the world in which these animators lived and acted, to discover the way each character was altered by sets of peculiar fates (or the other way round), the weight of collective heritage fighting against individual impulse, the tug of the Company's past competing with the pull of the new continent's future.

This is a journalist's book, a search for the stories, the themes, the personalities who dominated the first century of the Company's long stewardship. I believe it is a valid new approach to an old subject because it is rooted in the writer's own desire to make sense for himself of the tantalizing moments that gave the history of the HBC its meaning and of the beguiling individuals who gave it excitement. The hard-bitten Bay men profiled in this volume are as true to life as I could make them, and I have carefully limited myself to the available evidence.

Many Canadian readers may know by now that I have somewhat unconventional writing habits. I get up about four in the morning, clamp headphones around my brain and, energized by the loud and evocative rhythms of big-band jazz (thank you yet again, Stan Kenton, and all you young'uns who make good, big music), dive into the pages in front of me. I have kept to my crazy schedule during the more than three years of digging through my collected research to write this book, and I swear that I kept hearing the burr of leather-faced Hudson's Bay Company traders chiding me to "turn off that awful music – and make sure you get our story right."

I hope I have.

Acknowledgements

THE HUDSON'S BAY COMPANY is probably the best-documented institution in the world, next to the Vatican.

When the HBC papers, now lodged in the Provincial Archives of Manitoba, had to be valued for insurance purposes before being transferred from London to Winnipeg in 1974, they weighed in at sixty-eight tons – not counting the old muskets, sextants and other paraphernalia that pushed the weight even higher. The six thousand linear feet of journals, ships' logs, minute books, ledgers and personal diaries provide a detailed catalogue of the Company's daily activities all the way back to the 1670s. The sense of physical isolation the early HBC traders suffered on the flat foreign shores of Hudson Bay echoes through their letters and journals, which comprise a superb record of pre-Confederation Canada. One exhilarating moment for me was reading the entry by James Isham of York Factory in the 1730s in which he complains how the swarms of mosquitoes "have visited the plague of Egypt upon us" – and then finding a mosquito carcass, bloated with English blood, squashed right onto the page.

My gratitude to the original authors of these documents and their conscientious keepers is beyond measure. Apart from those archives, mined for me in part by Allan Levine, a talented Ph.D. in Canadian history who now teaches at Winnipeg's St John's Ravenscourt School, many secondary sources were consulted. The matter-of-fact listing of books and articles in the bibliography and the chapter notes hardly does justice to the dedication of this country's many fur-trade scholars. The "moccasin telegraph" that once informally bound together the HBC's outposts still exists, but the information network now wends through academic halls and offices as students and their professors argue the fine points of fur-trade history. My greatest good fortune was to be temporarily admitted to that magic circle, with scholars such as Del Anaquod, Michael Asch, Oliver Brass, Jennifer Brown, Stan Cuthand, Robin Fisher, John Foster, Frits Pannekoek, Ahab Spence, Irene Spry, Blair Stonechild, Adrian Tanner, Sylvia Van Kirk, Mel Watkins and a number of others who generously shared their knowledge with me.

I am equally indebted to those experts in various aspects of the HBC's history and related areas who allowed me to share their insight and experience. Their names are listed in Appendix Seven.

I am particularly grateful to that remarkable group of British governors, deputy governors and directors of the HBC who guided its fortunes during and after the Second World War. I interviewed most of them on a tour of England in 1980 and came to understand at last how the Company's huge domain could be run with such brave results for three hundred years by men who seldom set foot in it. Although their remarks and reminiscences are more relevant to subsequent volumes of this history, I would like to pay special tribute to Lord Adeane, Lord Amory, Lord Cobbold, J.E.H. Collins, Lady Cooper (widow of Sir Patrick Ashley Cooper), James and Anne Cooper, Sir Eric Faulkner, Arthur Frayling, Sir William Keswick, Lord Tweedsmuir and, most of all, to J.G. Links, by royal appointment furrier to the Queen and an HBC director from 1947 to 1975, whose spritely and graceful observations made the Company ethos come alive.

In a series of airborne sweeps across the Canadian Arctic during the winters of 1982 and 1983, my wife Camilla and I talked to the modern successors of the men who people this volume. Their patient willingness to examine their motivations and aspirations did much to explain why it still means a lot to be a Bay man in Canada's North. Despite poor pay, rampant paternalism and bureaucratic frustrations, there remains something splendid about being a part of an enterprise as grand as the Royal Navy and as permanent as a religious order.

AS L.P. HARTLEY NOTED IN THE OPENING LINES of his classic novel of Victorian life, *The Go-Between*: "The past is a foreign country; they do things differently there." On my journey into that foreign land I enjoyed the company of many guides. Nine of them proved to be constant companions, steering my research, correcting the manuscript and unscrambling my sometimes quixotic grammar. They were:

Professor Glyndwr Williams, Head of the Department and Professor of History at Queen Mary College, University of London, who spent a decade as general editor of the Hudson's Bay Record Society.

Professor Richard Glover, distinguished British military historian, who edited many of the original volumes of the Hudson's Bay Record Society, taught history at the University of Manitoba and at Carleton University and later headed the National Museum of Man in Ottawa. He patiently helped me follow Samuel Hearne's epic trek to the Coppermine and became friend as well as tutor. My favourite moment during the sometimes tedious research process occurred when Professor Glover's Gothic features lit up as he confided to me at Rattenbury's, a restaurant in Victoria, B.C. – after first looking around to make sure no one could overhear us – "You know, I really think Hearne might have had a *mistress!*" (Samuel Hearne died in 1792.)

Professor Abraham Rotstein, the University of Toronto political economist and my loyal friend, who allowed me to read and discuss with him at length his unpublished thesis *Fur Trade and Empire*.

Professor Timothy Ball, the University of Winnipeg geographer and climatologist, who recently launched the Rupertsland Society and who may be the most militant guardian of HBC history in the country.

Al Hochbaum, an artist living in Delta, Manitoba, who has been poking around marshes and forests all his life and has made twenty-eight camping trips into the Arctic. A free spirit who makes a fetish of being beholden to no one, he studied zoology at Cornell, fine art at the University of Wisconsin and is the author and illustrator of several naturalist classics including *To Ride the Wind*.

Alastair Sweeny, the diligent author of Sir George Étienne Cartier's biography, who scouted the Public Archives of Canada for me and set down the initial research matrix for this volume.

Martin Lynch, a former assistant news editor of *The Globe and Mail*, and **Janet Craig**, who has deftly improved many a Newman manuscript, have been invaluable critics. Their fanatical dedication to accuracy and to the task of correcting my sometimes exasperating runs at the English language have left me with a greater debt than I can possibly acknowledge.

Camilla Newman, my wife, who provided a healthy chunk of the research, plus the essential day-to-day structural editing, the creative wrangling over the right word or phrase and the loving home environment that made this project feasible. We met when she was an assistant editor at *The Financial Post*, and ever since, I have been blessed with a productive literary partnership and a happy marriage – a rare and treasured combination.

There were many others: George Whitman, the Bay's external affairs director, put on his independent beaver hat and shared the common sense wisdom of his life with me, as I hope he soon will with others in what should be an action-packed autobiography; John Bovey and his staff at the British Columbia Provincial Archives; Jocelyn McKillop and Leslie Hoffman, formerly staff historians of the HBC, who patiently answered so many of my queries; Pat Harding, who kept me out of harm's way and is unflagging in her enlightened secretarial assistance; Ann Nicholas, who has valiantly deciphered the flow of words and deserves a navigator's medal for her intelligence in typing the manuscript – repeatedly – as it took shape; Mary Adachi, for her good-humoured exactness in copyediting; Rick Kleer, who used first-rate initiative on the chapter notes; Chris Blackburn, for his capability in compiling the index; Peter Carson, Penguin's Chief Editorial Director in England, and Cynthia Good, Editorial Director of Penguin Books Canada, who both worked hard and well to marshal the whole project from concept to finished book, and beyond.

Some notes on style. For the sake of clarity, modern place names have been used, and most of the quotations have been transposed into modern English. There are exceptions. How to improve, for example, on one contemporary's description of the accident-prone Hudson Bay explorer Captain Thomas James as a "Heroicke Soule"? The outdated term "Eskimo" has been used instead of the currently more correct "Inuit" because that was the usage of the time. The name "Hudson Bay" for the body of water was a bit of a problem. In the HBC Charter, it is spelled with an *s*, but in 1900 the Geographic Board of Canada established the officially sanctioned form for the topographical feature as "Hudson Bay," and that has been used throughout. The names of the early fur trading posts periodically changed (from Fort Albany to Albany Fort to Albany, for example) but only one appellation was altered entirely. Charles Fort became Rupert House, in honour of the Company's founder.

Like all my previous works, this book owes its existence to many not mentioned here, but the responsibility for its imperfections is fully my own.

P.C.N.

Cordova Bay, B.C.
and Toronto, Ontario
April 1, 1982–July 1, 1985

COMPANY
OF
ADVENTURERS

A PUFF OF ONSHORE WIND *ruffles the low-lying vegetation; nothing else moves. There is no enduring memory of the great events that took place here because there is no one left to remember them. Every so often native trappers wander by, the juice of wild blueberries purpling their faces. The abandoned pastures hum with the liquid accent of the Swampy Cree as*

they circle KICHEWASKAHIKUN, *the now-empty "Big House" still standing on the shores of the Hayes River. They sing as they walk by because they believe the huge depot to be the home of evil spirits.*

This is York Factory, once the Company's great tidewater headquarters on Hudson Bay. The most essential HBC destination, then and now, York Factory is where history and present-day reality come together. This was where the Company first perfected the fur trade as a world-scale enterprise; from here that most of its pathfinders set off to probe its inland empire; and it is here that its vulnerability to change is most dramatically on view.

Formerly the busiest of the HBC's trading posts, the depot building's hundred vacant windows yawn in the silver afternoon, reminding outsiders that here was the centre of North American commerce, the overseas headquarters of the Company of Adventurers.

The first white man to winter near this spot, halfway up Hudson Bay's west coast, was Sir Thomas Button, who searched in 1612 for the doomed explorer Henry Hudson and for a navigable North West Passage. Seven more decades elapsed before an expedition headed by Pierre Radisson, travelling under the French flag, returned to the site; two years later, the HBC built its first permanent trading station and named it York Factory after the Company's Governor, the Duke of York. (It was called a "factory" not because anything was manufactured there but because this was where the factor lived.)

In the next dozen years, York Factory would become a pawn in the tangled wars between the English and the French for control of Hudson Bay, changing hands six times. During the early 1690s it was the only bay post not held by the French. Then Pierre Le Moyne d'Iberville, the most astute military genius Canada has produced, captured the fort for New France in an epic sea battle as the thunder of cannon fire rolled along Hudson Bay's growling cliffs and ships-of-the-line foundered in frigid waters almost as deadly as the combat itself. Returned to English possession by the Treaty of Utrecht in 1713, York Factory was sacked nearly seventy years later by a valiant raiding party of French marines who had dashed north *from the West Indies during the American Revolution. Joseph Colen, the HBC Chief Factor in charge of rebuilding it (and York Factory's first resident intellectual; he moved in with a library of fourteen hundred books), decided to shift operations to their present site. He gave the refurbished post the only name that seemed to fit: "New York."*

The new depot took on an even more essential function when the HBC amalgamated with the Montreal-based North West Company. Virtually all the trade goods going in and the fur harvest going out of the Company's vast territorial holdings moved through York Factory. Here in pompous conclave sat the Council of the Northern Department of Rupert's Land – the body governing the greater part of what is now Canada.

By the mid-1800s the Factory had become a township of thirty buildings laid out in the shape of a great H, with the main depot and guest houses forming the centre bar, its wings including the doctor's house, an Anglican church, a hospital, library, cooperage, smithy, bakehouse, various fur stores, provisions houses and officers' and servants' quarters. "I was much surprised at the 'great swell' the Factory is – it looks beautiful," commented the vivacious Letitia Hargrave, wife of a Chief Factor resident in the 1840s who created a sensation by importing from Vienna a piano of six-and-a-half octaves. North of the fort lay a palisaded powder magazine; to the south, an Indian settlement "alive with children and dogs." The grounds were dominated by a flagstaff of Norway pine with a snapping Company flag and the hexagonal cupola of the depot building.

From that vantage point, hand-wringing clerks sighted the arrival in late summer of the annual supply ship from England, heavy with trade goods and apprehensive recruits. The majestic vessels would ride gently on their anchor chains at Five Fathom Hole, the sandy anchorage seven miles out from the depot, while scurrying Factory sloops exchanged the mother ship's cargo of guns, brandy, textiles, axes, knives and other supplies for the bundles of furs collected from the inland posts.

Down the roaring Saskatchewan, the fast-flowing Winnipeg River and the sluggish Red, from Norway House and Cumberland House and from Fort Edmonton fifteen hundred miles away came the summer fleets of York boats bearing the winter's harvest. York's foreshore was ablaze with campfires as the wild uplanders sang, wrestled, drank and gambled the night away. Inside the garish, yellow-painted Bachelors' Hall, by the glow of tallow candles in tin sconces, the resident York Factory traders gathered to swap friendly insults and the season's inland gossip.

Life at York Factory had its darker moments. Robert Ballantyne, the HBC clerk who wintered here in 1846 and became a popular nineteenth-century adventure novelist, called the trading post "a monstrous blot on a swampy spot, with a partial view of the frozen sea." Writing to his family, Chief Factor Hargrave accurately described the local climate as "nine months of winter, varied by three of rain and mosquitoes." The York Factory journals, numbering nearly twenty thousand pages, are crammed with hints of unhappy endings: the suicide who left a trail of discarded clothes on his way to an ice hole on the river; the apprentice with pockets full of fireworks who accidentally turned himself into a human torch; the desperate men punished in 1791 for stealing the mainsail off the Factory's sloop so they could cut it up into new trousers for themselves.

Apart from the annual rituals of the fur brigades and supply ships, Arctic explorers (Sir John Franklin among them), botanists, missionaries, geologists, misfits and, later, settlers (and the troops to defend them) filtered into the new continent through York Factory.

During the long week between Christmas Eve and New

Year's Day, the wilderness post exploded in a kind of madness, its dour inhabitants indulging in every available excess. Appalled by the carryings-on, the Rev. J.P. Gardiner counted the flasks emptied during the 1861 celebrations and came up with the astonishing total of 104 7/8 gallons of liquor, mostly brandy and rum, that had been consumed by York Factory's Yuletide population of fifty. Other indoor diversions ranged from pillow fights in Bachelors' Hall to Bacchanalian feasts of wild duck and venison to such sexual promiscuity as covert visits to the married quarters or to the Cree village would allow. Letitia Hargrave's attendance at a typical Christmas Ball to which local Indians had been invited was, in her own words, "a humbling affair. Forty squaws old and young with their hair plaited in long tails, nothing on their heads but their everlasting blankets smelling of smoke and everything obnoxious. Babies almost newly born & in their cradles were with their mothers & all nursing them in the face of everyone … I was glad to come home."

Great fires burned in the hearths through the winter but made little difference in a climate where the quicksilver in thermometers froze so solid it could be shot out of muskets and still retain its shape. Ballantyne described how the breath of the revellers at the 1846 Christmas Ball transformed the room: "In consequence of the breathing of so many people in so small a room, for such a length of time, the walls had become quite damp, and ere the guests departed, moisture was trickling down in many places. During the night, this moisture was frozen; and, on rising the following morning, I found, to my astonishment, that Bachelors' Hall was apparently converted into a palace of crystal. The walls and ceiling were thickly coated with beautiful minute crystalline flowers, not sticking flat upon them, but projecting outwards in various directions, thus giving the whole apartment a cheerful light appearance, quite indescribable. The moment our stove was heated, *however, the crystals became fluid, and ere long evaporated, leaving the walls exposed in all their original dinginess."*

FOR 249 YEARS THE HUDSON'S BAY COMPANY *sent supply ships to Five Fathom Hole from its docks in London. Then in 1931, the traffic stopped. From being district headquarters York Factory had been downgraded to just another HBC trading post, but the decline really dated back to the 1870s, when railway construction reached the Red River, providing a new and cheaper method of supplying the Company's western network. The HBC had been experimenting with a southern route since 1858 and was involved in the introduction of steam navigation on the Red River the following year. The trade's headquarters was shifted to the site of present-day Winnipeg. The last brigade of York boats set off from Norway House three years later, and York Factory was reduced to handling local traffic.*

The great seaboard fort fell into disuse. Most of its buildings were pulled down, razed or ravaged by vandals. Nearly seven hundred Cree still followed their ancestors' tradition and came to trade at York Factory in 1936, but twenty years later their total was down to seventy and, in 1957, the HBC abandoned its once-proud headquarters.

Only the great white depot building remains, its door barricaded in a useless gesture against natural and human intruders. For decades the building has withstood the assault of wind, frost and the occasional marauders (mostly American goose-hunters) who rolled old cannon balls along its polished floors at beer-bottle tenpins, smashed mickeys of whisky against its satiny spruce walls, tore off its siding to burn as fuel and used its elegant pantries as pissoirs. The depot is still standing only because its builders placed the structure on top of a complex system of drainage ditches and compensated for permafrost

heave by mounting it on replaceable wooden sills instead of masonry that would inevitably have crumbled.

The Cree who once flocked here have retreated inland to Shamattawa and the reserve at Split Lake. Now and again a polar bear pads around the sacred confines of the depot's courtyard, searching for meat and companionship.

At the hub of a vanished empire, York Factory is an apt example of the Company's penchant for sloughing off past hindrances and expediently renewing itself in other places, other guises. For more than three centuries, the Company has shuttled between splendour and dust, unstoppable momentum and impending collapse.

COMPANY
OF
ADVENTURERS

I DREAMS OF EMPIRE

CHAPTER 1

T HE
BAY
MEN

*The Hudson's Bay Company turned much of the
upper half of North America into a company
town writ large, in which customers displayed
individuality and imagination at their own risk.*

FOR A TIME THEY WERE TRUSTEES of the largest sweep
of pale red on Mercator's map, lording it over a new
subcontinent, building their toy forts and seducing the
Indian maidens they crudely called their "bits of brown."
They were displaced Scots and Englishmen – mostly
gentle Orkney carpenters, ambitious Aberdeen clerks and
black-sheep progeny of Anglican clergymen – toiling for
fur in the service of the Governor and Company of Adventurers of England Trading into Hudson's Bay.

Through the polished-brass telescope of imperial
history, the Hudson's Bay Company appears a majestic,
fiercely patrician enterprise, grandly fielding its own armies
and navies, minting its own coins, issuing its own medals,
even operating according to a calendar dating from its
own Creation. But for the generations of lumpen fur
traders who scratched for a living in the North American
wilderness, the reality was often harsh and disillusioning.
They neither struck metaphorical gold nor found a land

to build a dream on. Yet there was a certain valour in their stand against the vastness of the untamed land. Those who were touched by it hugged the memory of their time on Hudson Bay as they would an extra blanket on a bitter night – glad that they had been there, gladder still to have returned. The men in the little bush forts huddling beneath the pewter sky developed the camaraderie of a lengthy sea voyage, marked forever by their time "on the bay."

ROOTED IN THE NEW WORLD'S NORTHERN SWAMPS, the early HBC was more of an independent beaver republic than a business firm. As John Buchan, First Baron Tweedsmuir and the author-statesman who served as Governor General of Canada in the late 1930s, astutely observed: "The Hudson's Bay is *not* an ordinary commercial company, but a kind of kingdom by itself, and it needs statesmen to administer it." It did not always find them, but during the first two centuries of its dominance, nothing stopped the HBC's march as it commandeered a domain that eventually stretched over a twelfth of the earth's surface. The Company's trading posts reached from the white shores of the Arctic Ocean to the sweaty docks of San Francisco and westward to balmy Hawaii, and its influence spread far beyond that.

HBC's amazing realm eventually encompassed nearly three million square miles – ten times the size of the Holy Roman Empire at its height. When Sir George Simpson, its overseas Governor, attended a civic dinner at Christiania in Norway during his 1841 world tour, he was toasted as "head of the most extended dominion in the known world – the Emperor of Russia, the Queen of England and the President of the United States excepted."

Much of modern Canada emerged from the HBC; it

was the presence of the Hudson's Bay Company's traders that kept the Canadian West out of the grasp of American colonizers pushing northward. It was the 1870 sale of Company territory to the new nation of Canada that let the former colonies fill in their western and northern boundaries, and three of the early HBC trading posts – Fort Garry (Winnipeg), Fort Edmonton and Fort Victoria – grew into provincial capitals. Its officers charted the Arctic coast and mapped the British Columbia interior.

Bearing in mind the fact that the HBC was heir to the Montreal-based North West Company which it absorbed in 1821, the Company's impact on the formation of present-day Canada has been incalculable. The Hudson's Bay Company determined the country's political and physical shape, endowing the new nationality with a mentality that endures to this day. University of Alberta historian John Foster had the HBC in mind when he wrote: "For nearly all regions of Canada, recorded history begins with the fur trade. Its history is a kaleidoscope of experiences, ranging from the demi-heroic achievements of individuals to the machinations of empires headquartered in distant homelands."

All that power prompted resentment. The initials HBC were (and are) just as often defined for the inquiring tenderfoot as "the Hungry Belly Company" as by the more benign "Here Before Christ."*

A pugnacious relic of the high afternoon of Empire and the oldest continuous capitalist corporation still in existence, the HBC is the ultimate example of corporate Darwinism. It has always managed to adapt itself to successive sets of altered circumstances. The Company

---

* A young Inuit girl in the mid-1970s wrote to the editor of *Inuit Today* claiming the initials should really stand for Horny Boys' Club.

has weathered 315 years of war, rebellion, ambush, siege, bumbling bureaucracy and coupon-clipping neglect. Unlike the splendiferous and much more ambitious Cecil Rhodes, Stamford Raffles, Rajah Brooke and the East India nabobs, the HBC has not only endured but, until lately, also prospered. Despite recent years of humiliating financial losses, the Company remains a major economic force as the world's largest private fur auctioneer, Canada's most widespread department store chain and a significant international player in real estate and oil – still stuffing $5 billion in sales into its coffers every year. It has survived by turning nearly every necessity into an opportunity and by never moving too fast. The HBC motto should really have been "Wait and Seize."

"What the HBC gave with one hand, it seemed to take back with the other," French-Canadian novelist Gabrielle Roy has argued, voicing the sentiment of many of its subjects. A more specific *cri de coeur* comes from Blair Stonechild, a full-blood Cree who heads the Department of Indian Studies at the Saskatchewan Indian Federated College in Regina: "The Company takes the view that it treated Indians fairly, using the rationale that it did not attempt to exterminate them, as was done in the U.S. It is the difference between being in the fire and being in the frying pan."

THE HISTORY OF THE HUDSON'S BAY COMPANY has been played out in the vast mysterious hinterland that Canadian poet Al Purdy once described as being "north of summer." Canadians' romance with their North has not been defused by time, even if they themselves seldom venture into latitudes higher than their summer cottages. "Because of our origin in the northern frontier," wrote historian W.L. Morton, "Canadian life to this day is marked by a northern quality. The line which marks the frontier from the farmstead, the wilderness from the baseland, the hinterland from the metropolis, runs through every Canadian psyche." The same resonance of spirit has been caught so evocatively in Canada's unofficial national anthem, Quebec folksinger Gilles Vigneault's *Mon pays, c'est l'hiver*.

It was partly this sense of quintessential northernness that made the Hudson's Bay Company such a subliminally essential element pervading the Canadian consciousness. Imprisoned in paved cities and blinkered by urban impulses, the modern Canadian is barely aware that the geographical centre of the country is at Baker Lake, originally an HBC trading post nuzzling Chesterfield Inlet, west off Hudson Bay.

The Canadian North is usually defined by its size (1.5 million square miles north of 60°), its low temperatures (the cold can be so intense it burns the flesh) and its isolation. Yet what makes life there unique is the quality of the silence – very different from the inert void of space or the foreboding hush of a battlefield. The North is suffused with a tumultuous stillness, almost deafening in its intensity, that conveys a warning to the visitor: this land has entered into only a temporary truce with man's presence. It is not a place to seek or to find tranquillity and will shake pomposity out of anyone's boots. The North is attractive mainly for what Hugh Stewart, an old Arctic hand, has called "the moral alternative it offers."

In winter, the North shines with a dozen recognizably different shades of white; in autumn, the neon-red brilliance of bearberries lights up the countryside for miles around, accented by cloud or hill shadows. Along the treeline, the pastel hues of the land are heightened here and there by a cluster of spruce. In February, the calm radiance of an afternoon can instantaneously vanish in a blizzard so thick that snow-walkers cannot see as far as their feet. At high noon on a sparkling patch of snow, the light can literally blind.

To describe this frozen country as forbidding seems beside the point, yet it is an unfailingly fascinating landscape. An omnivorous Arctic fox, his wise countenance as world-weary as a long-tenured professor's, materializes out of rocky scrub that looks as if it could not sustain a field mouse. Fox fur was used by the natives to wipe babies' bottoms until first Edwardian duchesses and then the fancy high-steppers of Harlem and streetwalkers of Paris adopted white boas as their trademark – and created a market.

The northern furies seldom disturbed the Company's well-moneyed English proprietors. The Governors (roughly equivalent to chairmen of the board), Deputy Governors (presidents) and the Committeemen (the seven directors) who ran the burgeoning enterprise from the City, London's financial district for three centuries, never heard the castanet tail-slap of an alarmed beaver in a wilderness pond or felt the chill of autumn's early frost closing in on Hudson Bay. Nor did they want to.

They were the ultimate absentee landlords. No Governor visited Hudson Bay until 264 years after the Company's incorporation, when Patrick Ashley Cooper, the twenty-ninth man to hold the office, made a brief ceremonial procession through its posts.

The London-based proprietors exercised authority from afar according to the Bertrand Russell definition of power as "the production of intended effects." Fortunately for them, the hardy men at the outposts were resistant enough to interpret London's orders none too literally. Instead, they invested considerable energy trying to educate various governors about the essential contradictions that made life so difficult on the bay. Somehow the long-distance marriage worked, with each side maintaining a mixture of a mutual respect for and proper distrust of one another.

For their part, the London Committeemen were always careful to confine their dispatches to corporate details.* There was little flavour of manifest destiny in their often mundane instructions, for they were creating a merchant empire dedicated strictly to profit. They betrayed scant urge to seek title to its spiritual dimension. At the same time, no money-saving wrinkle was too much trouble to claim the management's attention. A May 29, 1680 directive to John Nixon, then in charge of the bay posts, instructs him on how to economize on food imports by raising his own pigs. "Upon Hay Island where our grand Factory is," it runs, "you may propergate swine without much difficulty, wch is an excellent flesh, and the creature is hardy and will live where some other creatures cannot."

Such irrelevant nonsense (the climate could not possibly sustain forage for pigs to survive, like European wild boars, unsheltered for a winter) tended to fix in the minds of the bay-side traders a stereotype of the London governors as superannuated financiers with abalone-shaped jowls and little common sense. Most of them had indeed simmered up in the lugubrious universe of upper-crust England, where a discreetly arched eyebrow could ruin a man's or a country's credit. But except for the trio of lordly personages who established the Company's original claims (Prince Rupert, the Duke of York and the Duke of Marlborough) the HBC governors were tough-minded City financiers who supported Lord Palmerston's stern edict: "We have no permanent friends nor perpetual enemies: our interests are permanent."

Unlike some of their contemporaries, they did not

---

*The occasional directive was totally misguided, such as the 1784 decision to send 150 copies of *The Country Clergyman's Advice to Parishioners* for distribution among Indians who could not read any printed work, let alone English parochial flummery.

subscribe to the unblushing credo that Providence was the ultimate source of British authority. But if they would not bow to "heaven's command" in spreading British munificence around the world, they most assuredly recognized the connection between harvesting profits overseas and furthering England's diplomatic interests abroad. John S. Galbraith, the California historian who wrote a book (*The Hudson's Bay Company as an Imperial Factor*) to document the thesis that "the expansion of the British Empire has been largely motivated by the energies of the mercantile class," argued that largely unknown merchants were more influential in shaping Imperial policy than the statesmen who got the kudos. It seemed a point beyond contention to the men who directed the affairs of the HBC that their corporate objectives and England's priorities of state were one and the same.

A clue to why the HBC's operational code evolved as it did – the notion that moderation in the conduct of the whole enterprise was not just a safe course between extremes but a secular mandate on how to conduct one's life – was that, as it matured, the Bay came more and more under Scottish influence. Sparse of speech but swift in action, the tight-lipped individualists who came to North America from the distinctive parishes of Scotland had temperaments ideally suited for the fur trade: a meld of persistence and self-sufficiency. Intellectually armed by the Shorter Catechism, they made up in loyalty and moral fibre what they lacked in creativity and exuberance.

Nearly all the great names in the HBC's annals grew up in Scotland; not just Sir George Simpson, Donald Smith and Sir James Douglas, the trio who dominated the Company's nineteenth-century history, but others: Chief Factor Robert Campbell, who spent eleven years fur trading and map making among hostile Indians of the unknown Yukon; Chief Factor Alexander Hunter Murray, who plunked down Fort Yukon in Russian territory and told Imperial Russia to like it; John McLean from the Isle of Mull, who helped unlock the savage land of Ungava; Thomas Simpson, descendant of Duncan Forbes of Culloden, who mapped some of the most forbidding parts of the Arctic coast; James Leith of Aberdeenshire, who left half his estate for the propagation of the Protestant faith among the Indians; John Stuart of Strathspey, who first penetrated the region that became northern British Columbia; and many, many more.

They became citizens of the New Land, in the early years mating with the Indian tribes with whom they traded. When the Scottish Marquis of Lorne, then Governor General of Canada, made his first national tour in 1881 and found himself at Rat Portage in northwestern Ontario, he asked the local HBC Factor to introduce him to a "typical" Indian. The Bay man motioned for the fiercest-looking brave to come forward: "Would ye come here for a minute, Macdonald?"

The introduction of the Scottish strain via the HBC into the complicated weave that makes up the tartan of the Canadian character must be ranked as one of the Company's enduring legacies. "Canadians like to see themselves as the Scots of North America," concluded Ronald Bryden, director of the Graduate Centre for the Study of Drama at the University of Toronto, "canny, sober, frugal folk of superior education who by quietly terrible Calvinist virtue will inherit the 21st century." The residual Calvinism of the early Scots was the real religion of the first Hudson Bay posts: inbred obedience to authority and eagerness to bear the burden of Calvinism's earthly path to salvation – hard work.

On other continents, West European civilization had been spearheaded by devoted missionaries, followed by glory-driven soldiers and flinty-eyed traders. In the Canadian North and West, the order was precisely the reverse – traders, soldiers, then missionaries. The

Company's backhanded attitude towards itinerant men of God was summed up in an 1863 directive from Alexander Grant Dallas, then Governor of Rupert's Land, who allowed that as a general rule the Company ought to be civil to and assist the missionaries, but not allow them to trespass too far upon its resources.*

To take the place of organized religion and to impose its authority, the Company at irregular intervals issued its own commandments prescribing how its men should behave. A typical set of paper tablets, proclaimed on September 26, 1714, directed its men "to live lovingly with one another, not to swear or quarrel, but to live peaceably, without drunkenness or profaneness." The traders were forbidden "to embezzle gunpowder" and neither were they "to meddle, trade or affront any Indians, nor to concern themselves with women – which Frenchmen did, thereby cutting themselves off through jealousy … Men going contrary to be punished before Indians."

Such Company edicts comprised the true gospel. As late as 1921, N.M.W.J. McKenzie wrote in *The Men of*

---

*Just to cover all the eventualities, God was enlisted in the Company's business affairs to the extent that His helping hand was extolled no fewer than three times in the official Bill of Lading forms then in use: "Shipped, by the Grace of God, in good order and well-conditioned by.......... in the Hudson's Bay Company service for and on account of the Honourable Governor and Company of Adventurers of England trading into Hudson Bay, in and upon the good ship.......... now riding at anchor at .... in North America and, by God's Grace, bound for.......... All which goods and merchandise I promise to deliver according to the order of the Governor and Committee of the Honourable Hudson's Bay Company (the dangers of the seas only excepted). And so God send the good ship to her desired port in safety. Amen."

the Hudson's Bay Company, "you might break all the ten Commandments in one clatter, but to break any of the rules of the Company, *that* was quite another thing."

EXCEPT FOR SERVANTS FROM THE ORKNEY ISLANDS, the early Bay men came from no specific social stratum of England or Scotland. Not satisfied to waste their careers serving time in the stultifying occupations then available in a crowded and fluctuating domestic labour market yet not rash enough to volunteer for the military, they signed on with the intention of saving enough money to return, marry well and settle into small-scale but independent pursuits.

But once they found themselves on Hudson Bay – living out their first five-year hitches and having to exist near the limits of human endurance – they were never the same again. Some hurried home on the first supply ship due out after the expiration of their contracts. Most stayed, or came back after a visit home, caught despite themselves in the dream and drama of the Company of Adventurers. They were, one after the other, transmogrified into Company men, faithful to a corporate ethic they perceived as being somehow more alluring than merely a return on investment, even though this was how their efforts were invariably judged. They continued in the trade, braving conditions of life and work beyond the call of duty, firm in their conviction that even when their dreams proved flawed, particular circumstances were at fault rather than the great enterprise itself.

Stoicism was a prized virtue, even at the top. When Colonel John Crofton came to Rupert's Land in 1846 with his 6th Regiment of Foot, the Royal Warwickshires, to help defend the Red River settlement, he travelled up the thirty-four portages from York Factory to Fort Garry with Sir George Simpson, who was by then sixty years old. The daily canoe journey was strenuous enough, but camping on wet ground every night without a tent was far worse. "One night," the Colonel confided to his journal, "when wet and cold, old Sir George turned to me and said: "I wish to heaven you'd say, 'This is dreadful, horrid work'– for I want to grumble, but not to be the first to do so." Neither man voiced a whimper of public complaint.

Despite the drawbacks of climate and the primitive facilities, postings at the forts tended to be viewed as the real world, while sojourns back to England, Scotland or, later, to urban Canada made the HBC traders feel ill at ease and out of place. They would arrive, after a lengthy assignment in the service, to pay their respects to the London Committeemen, shifting restlessly in upholstered armchairs and standing about in Sabbath waistcoats that might have been in vogue a decade or two earlier, giving off a distinctly musty odour. Accustomed to silence and not knowing what to say to whom, they were reduced from knights of the bay to shuffling misfits. No wonder they signed up again, abandoned their patrimonies and rushed back to the new continent where they could stand tall in silent valleys that marched towards the Rocky Mountains or dip their canteens in northern waters that no one else knew.

Yet for all its freedoms, it was a life that imprisoned the soul. With some exceptions, the Bay men became internal exiles in both their homelands, original and adopted. Never part of any society outside the fur trade, they gradually pruned their ancestral roots, becoming bitterly aware of the true nature of any voluntary emigration: that one is exiled *from*, never *to*, and that disinheritance and marginality are all too often the price of freedom. More than one loyal HBC trader faced the end of his days with few close friends or blood relatives he wished to acknowledge and so bequeathed whatever worldly goods he had gathered to the only family he had: the Company. "They were comfortably settled but apparently at a loss what to do with themselves," Sir George Simpson commented about his own retired factors. "They sigh for the Indian Country, the squaws, and skins and savages."

INDENTURED TO THEIR CORPORATE LUST for beaver pelts – the commodity that allowed the HBC traders to produce handsome profits of at least £20 million by 1857 – the Hudson's Bay Company provided ultimate proof of Adam Smith's contention that England was a nation of shopkeepers on an imperial scale.

The HBC was far more interested in making profit than in making history. Once the Treaty of Utrecht had been signed and the Hudson Bay territories were officially tucked beneath England's wing, the vanities of Empire touched the HBC and its proprietors only tangentially. The notion that the Company of Adventurers might be destined for such lofty purposes as colonizing the New World, converting "the savages" or discovering the North West Passage tested the upper limits of its governors' condescension. Such postulations of glory were reserved for early-morning conceits, discarded while toying at breakfast with the silver salvers keeping their devilled kidneys warm. At serious times of the day the proprietors went on doing what they knew best: turning furs into money.

Unlike their competitors in France, they never did seem to feel themselves charged with the concurrent missions of extending their monarch's territorial reach. As private capitalists, they were unhampered by the parasitic aristocrats who haunted their French rivals beholden to the court at Versailles. Operating under the strict discipline of strained balance sheets, the Bay men bent their efforts towards maximum gain quietly enough to avoid stirring up homegrown competitors who might challenge their questionable monopoly. "Throughout the Company's history, we have to remind ourselves that it existed not for the advancement of geographical knowledge nor to win the admiration of later generations, but to make money," K.G. Davies, the British historian, shrewdly noted, "and that an important part of making money is not losing it. This objective, if limited, was legitimate, and was undoubtedly achieved …"

The single-minded drive for greater revenues coloured everything the Company did. For the first two hundred years of its existence, the HBC was dedicated to maintaining its vaunted fur trade monopoly; as soon as that carefully nurtured domain was overrun by floods of immigrants determined to turn the southern portion of the fur preserve into farmland, the Company switched to building up new monopolies devoted to supplying settlers with their goods and to gaining exclusive jurisdiction over water transportation on the Red, Saskatchewan, Athabasca and Mackenzie river systems.

This ability to evolve and thrive without competition was fortified from the beginning by a series of determined attempts to diversify the HBC's economic base. Some commodities that came their way as by-products of occupying the North, such as goose quills, walrus tusks, bear grease, whale oil and sealskins, were traded from the start, but the English governors were endlessly puzzled that the New Land seemed to contain no precious metals. They dispatched Samuel Hearne, James Knight and others on monumental journeys to find and claim non-existent mountains of copper. Except for two coal mines the Company later developed on Vancouver Island near Nanaimo and Fort Rupert, the hunt for minerals proved fruitless.

Exports to England at one time or another included such diverse items as buffalo wool and buffalo tongues, eiderdown from ducks, narwhal tusks, smoked, dried and salted salmon, turpentine distilled from coniferous trees and Labrador tea – the leaves of a local plant that produced a passable beverage but proved much more useful in keeping rats out of granaries, moths out of clothes closets and fleas out of beds. The trade in all these items produced nothing but headaches. A similar result was achieved in 1921, when the HBC decided to breed reindeer on Baffin Island: 550 of the animals were transported from Norway and the Hudson's Bay Reindeer Company was incorporated under the direction of the well-known Arctic explorer Vilhjalmur Stefansson. But the project failed when there proved to be no suitable moss for the animals to chaw, and when the Lapps who had been hired as herders turned out to be fishermen.

The most bizarre HBC sideline was selling ice to Californians during the 1850s. At the time, San Francisco's population had swollen because of the 1848 Gold Rush, and all the available ice had to be shipped around Cape Horn from north of Boston. In 1854, James Douglas, the HBC's Chief Factor on the Pacific coast, leased out for $14,000 a year the ice fields under the Company's jurisdiction to a former U.S. naval captain named W.A. Howard, who represented a group of San Francisco entrepreneurs. Their ice ship, the *Fanny Major*, put into Frederick Sound (in what is now Alaska), where Captain Howard hired five hundred Stikine Indians to cut and load chunks of the blue glacier. The first shipment of three hundred tons sold so quickly that Howard and his backers rushed to buy six more ice ships and decided to share their profitable mode of natural air conditioning and food preservation with Hong Kong and Honolulu. That was a mistake. The ice melted on the way across the Pacific, and the ships arrived with wet, empty holds. The business collapsed in 1856 when the senior San Francisco shareholder embezzled the funds and absconded to China.*

A far more serious and very much more profitable venture was a scheme organized during the stormy stewardship of the British financier Sir Robert Molesworth Kindersley, the HBC's twenty-seventh Governor, to supply France, Russia and Romania with food and munitions during the First World War. (The venture was actually the brainchild of Jean Monnet, who later became the first head of the European Common Market.) Through an elaborate maze of subsidiaries and overseas agencies, the Hudson's Bay Company arranged credits for the French administration and operated a fleet of nearly three hundred merchant ships. The HBC became a massive mover of edibles, fuel, lumber, ammunition and troops. More than thirteen million tons of supplies were delivered to France alone. By the spring of 1918, the private armada was discharging eleven thousand tons of freight daily at French ports. The HBC fleet's captains evaded German submarines whenever possible, but 110 vessels flying the Company's flag were sunk. The HBC applied its northern shipping experience to delivering similar cargoes to Czarist Russia and, at Winston Churchill's request, took charge of supplying the White Russian armies following the Bolshevik Revolution. It was on the Archangel run that the HBC supply ship *Nascopie*'s deck gun sank a German submarine.

---

*In the western Arctic, hosts still advise their guests they will never have a hangover if they use glacial ice in their drinks – implying that the rattle in their glasses has recently been hacked from local glaciers.

Apart from these and many other attempts to diversify,* the HBC has always devoted inordinate, almost obscene energy to trimming costs. One early result of this obsessive penny-pinching was that long after the Age of Steam, the posts around Hudson Bay were still operating on Iron Age technology. "Even a casual observer of fur trade society recognized that as the Nineteenth Century wore on, life in posts like York Factory got more and more out of touch with life in Britain," noted Michael Payne in his social history of York Factory. "In 1844 a Scottish friend of James Hargrave [the resident Chief Factor] wrote him a letter calling York Factory a 'heavy, lumbering, lazy' sort of place quite distinct from the 'velocified' world of Britain ... The world of work at a fur trade post remained essentially 'pre-industrial.'"

Salaries were (and are) kept at a minimum. David Thompson, whose pioneering maps of Western Canada were standard reference works for three-quarters of a century, was casually allowed to join the competing North West Company after twenty-three years of service with the HBC because the London Committeemen thought he was spending too much time shooting the sun instead of trading pelts. Such impersonal cost cutting left no detail untouched. In an official memorandum headed *SAUCES*, Sir George Simpson reprimanded Hargrave at York Factory on March 3, 1843 for spending too much on condiments. "I consider it quite unnecessary," scolded the parsimonious Governor, "to indent [requisition] for Sauces & Pickles on public account ... I never use fish sauce in the

---

*Another was the establishment in 1964 of the U-Paddle Canoe rental service, which allows latter-day *voyageurs* to pick up their boats at one northern HBC store and deposit them at another.

country, and never saw anyone use it or pickles either. From the quantity of Mustard indented for, one would suppose it is now issued as an article of trade with the Indians!"

Simpson also had a nasty habit of inducing his traders to re-engage for as little as three-quarters of the prevailing rates by renewing contracts for officers and men during the winter when they were isolated and could not take advantage of a competitive market.

Few Bay men beat the system. One who tried was John McKay, who invited his rivals from the North West Company to celebrate Christmas in 1799 at Osnaburgh House. "I had the honour of my neighbours company to dinner," he smugly reported. "Your Honours has the honour of bearing the expence." More typical was the pathetic 1789 journal entry of Thomas Stayner, the Factor at Manchester House on the North Saskatchewan River: "This being Christmas Morning, our small stock of flour, afforded us, a cake to eat, with a little tea & chocolate ... No one can know what it is to want bread, but those who experience it – which we here, daily do, in this Wild Country; particular Holidays only excepted."

A twentieth-century version of the Company's single-minded devotion to business that continued into the 1960s was the habit of not heating its northern stores, keeping them so cool, in fact, that inside walls and nailheads would be coated with ice. "The reason was that they didn't want anybody hanging around ... they wanted everybody out trapping," recalls Stuart Hodgson, who served twelve years as Commissioner of the Northwest Territories. "I remember going over to Repulse Bay in 1965 to see old Henry Voisey, and he complained they were going to heat his store the next year. When I told him it was about time, he said: 'What the hell do you mean it's about time? It's going to be terrible. I won't be able to get people out of here to do some work.'" E.J.

(Scotty) Gall, who spent forty-four years with the HBC in the Western Arctic, was proud of the unheated stores he ran for a quarter of a century and considered his hunters good workers only if they were on the trapline or out hunting. "I never encouraged them to hang around."

THE HBC'S REMARKABLE LONGEVITY has been due in no small measure to several lucky geographical accidents.

By choosing to settle the deserted shores of Hudson Bay rather than more attractive landfalls to the south, the early traders appropriated the overwhelming advantage of being able to deliver their goods into the very heart of the new continent, at the mouths of wide rivers that flowed through a fur-rich hinterland stretching back to the foothills of the Rocky Mountains. (An astounding 43 percent of Canada's territory drains into Hudson Bay, compared with only 10 percent into the much more populated St Lawrence.)

The trip from the loading docks on the Thames to the anchorage at Five Fathom Hole off York Factory was equal to the sailing time required to reach Montreal. By the end of the journey up the St Lawrence, however, the goods were still very far from the Lake Winnipeg streams that flowed to the beaver ponds of the northern forests. Hudson Bay's southwestern shore is 1,500 miles closer than the storehouses of Montreal to the Saskatchewan River system, then the richest beaver country. Until the advent of the railways, the Montreal-based fur merchants had to store and finance trade goods for two full years before reaping any harvest. It simply was not possible to make the round trip of thousands of miles inland by canoe during the time needed for the supply ships to arrive, unload and leave the St Lawrence before freeze-up. It was the capital burden of this lengthy overhead period, as much as any other reason, that defeated the

North West Company. Being all too aware of the HBC's geographical advantage, the bold Nor'Westers tried unsuccessfully to negotiate their own access into Hudson Bay, even attempting to buy out the HBC.

The other great geographical advantage that allowed the fur trade to flourish was that most of Canada's huge drainage system is interconnected with relatively short portages – the main exceptions being the nine-mile Grand Portage west from Lake Superior and the twelve-mile Methy Portage into the Mackenzie Basin, first crossed by Peter Pond in 1778. Apart from these twenty-one-mile land barriers, it is possible to cross the upper half of the continent east of the Rockies by canoe.* "Canada's almost total navigability by canoe," noted Eric W. Morse, a modern explorer who has paddled most of the water routes, "is related to the fact that half of its surface lies on the world's oldest land mass, the Precambrian Shield, whose peaks and precipices have in billions of years been ground to gentler gradients. The great contribution of the Shield in making throughways is the chain of vast, connected lakes which it caused to be formed around its edge. Great Bear, Great Slave, Athabasca, Winnipeg, Lake of the Woods, Superior and Huron all have one side, or

---

*Writing in the March 3, 1975 issue of *The New Yorker*, John McPhee documented how easily the continent can be crossed by its water routes: "A friend of mine who grew up in Timmins, a remote community in Ontario, once told me about an Indian friend of his boyhood who developed an irresistible urge to see New York City. He put his canoe in the water and started out. From stream to lake to pond to portage, he made his way a hundred miles to Lake Timiskaming, and its outlet, the Ottawa River. He went down the Ottawa to the St. Lawrence, down the St. Lawrence to the Richelieu, up the Richelieu to Lake Champlain, and from Lake Champlain to the Hudson. At the 79th Street Boat Basin he left the canoe in custody of attendants, and walked into town."

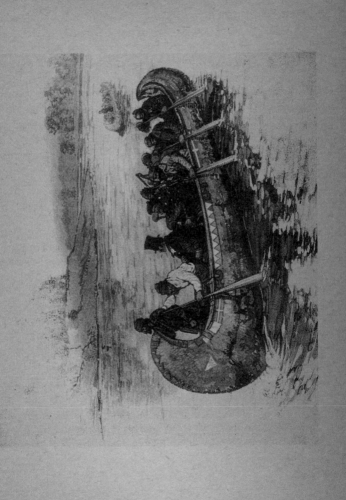

end, in granite. As the rains and ice-melt for thousands of years poured down from the steep edges of the Shield, water courses in softer soil were formed, draining to the sea. In this way were born great arterial rivers such as the Mackenzie, the Churchill, the Winnipeg and the Ottawa."

Three large lakes – Superior, Winnipeg and Athabasca – were all eventually controlled by the HBC as staging areas for the fur trade. During the summer, the Canadian Shield is laced by impatient rivers, some as wide as the Danube yet so remote they have yet to be named, all racing to tidewater at Hudson Bay. Nature could hardly have planned to meet the Company's corporate objectives more effectively: here was a huge subcontinent for the taking with a ready-made, free transportation system; frigid enough that its animals grew thick pelts; fertile enough to sprout an immense boreal forest that provided those animals with shelter; rugged enough to keep out permanent settlers.

It was the fur trade moving up the beaver-choked rivers that determined Canada's political boundaries. As Harold A. Innis noted in his monumental *The Fur Trade in Canada*, "Canada emerged as a political entity with boundaries largely determined by the fur trade ... not in spite of geography but because of it." Such nation building was no altruistic act of statesmanship by the HBC. Except for its inland community at Red River, a bizarre experiment by the utopian-minded Lord Selkirk, the Company was dead set against settlers. They upset the animals. The Company pushed westward not to plant colonies but to control competing traders. By thus exhibiting a highly visible presence west of the Lakehead, it prevented American farmers and mountain men from pushing north and, after amalgamation with the Nor' Westers in 1821, stretched its own version of the Canadian nation from Hudson Bay and the Gulf of St Lawrence to the Pacific.

That sometimes great notion was ultimately nailed

down by the building from Montreal to Vancouver of the transcontinental Canadian Pacific Railway. As Pierre Berton wrote in *The Last Spike*, the second volume of his perceptive study of the CPR: "For the next half century [1880–1930], this single corporation would be the dominant force west of Ottawa. Already its initials, CPR, had entered the national lexicon; soon they would be as familiar to most Canadians as their own. In the decades to follow they would come to symbolize many things to many people – repression, monopoly, daring, exploitation, imagination, government subsidy, high finance, patriotism, paternalism, and even life itself. There were few Canadians who were not in some manner affected by the presence of the Canadian Pacific; indeed, no other private company, with the single exception of the Hudson's Bay, has had such an influence on the destinies of the nation."

Irene Spry, the talented godmother of Canadian fur trade students, has pushed this argument one step further: "There is little doubt that the forces of American manifest destiny would have taken the West into a continental orbit, and if Canada had *not* been coast to coast, the pitiful little settlements in the St. Lawrence Valley would have been absorbed by the Americans long ago."

At the same time, both the CPR and the HBC – those ubiquitous sets of initials that richly earned the scepticism due any externally owned monopoly – ignited the resentment inherent in the master-servant relationship between the Central Canadian and the Western Canadian settlements that has accounted for many of the country's regional conflicts ever since. Too many Central Canadians still view the West as a kind of afterthought, a cranky child of the East. In fact, the fur-trading West was from the beginning politically and economically quite distinct – a different nation altogether from the farms and villages of the St Lawrence Valley, the Atlantic provinces or the nascent manufacturing industries around Lake

Ontario. A proud society that existed on its own terms, this pre-agricultural West saw the birth of many genuine grievances against the metropolitan East.*

"MY COUNTRY HAS NO HISTORY, only a past," complained New Brunswick poet Alden Nowlan. That may be true, if history is thought of as pompous successions of grandiloquent men, rosters of events or attempts to turn back economic tidal waves. But history always adds up to more than the ascertainable facts. The sudden promptings of blind accident or coalitions of individual yearnings that defeat armies – such quixotic forces also drive history's unpredictable chariots.

In the case of the Hudson's Bay Company, history was made by an enterprise of marginal economic and geographical significance that gradually evolved into one of the central formative influences in the founding of a nation – and, equally important, in the profound impact it had on the mentality of its inhabitants.

A loose federation of regions on the cold periphery of world civilization, Canada has always had trouble organizing itself to deal with crises threatening its national integrity, and as a result Canadians feel they are a marginal people with few core values to call their own. But they do share a distinctive mentality that, if often the despair of its more restless animators, has allowed this brave huddle of like-minded survivors to prosper in North America's attic.

It is the original implanting of that special mentality within the Canadian psyche, a combination of creative deference and cautiously progressive pragmatism, that is

---

*How the HBC bore the brunt of that anger and the dramatic consequences that followed is a theme of the second volume in this history.

the Hudson's Bay Company's most pervasive legacy.

This prevailing ethic (ideology is too strong a term, philosophy too pretentious) was very different from the aggressive egalitarianism of the American frontier. Canada had few vigilantes, no Davy Crocketts or Daniel Boones. In sharp contrast to that of the United States, the Canadian experience flowed from the principles of allegiance rather than social contract and was founded on the organic growth of tradition rather than the assertion of revolutionary will. This was why, as historian William Kilbourn has noted, the original British North America Act set down common objectives of peace, order and good government in contrast to the individualistic emphasis in the American Declaration of Independence on life, liberty and the pursuit of happiness.

The fur trade in general and the Hudson's Bay Company in particular exercised a profound influence in the sculpting of the Canadian soul. "The shape of the indigenous Canadian imagination," concluded Abraham Rotstein, the University of Toronto economist who is an expert on both the fur trade and Canada's identity, "took root in the experiences of the fur trade, both for the French period and after the Conquest. Voyageurs, rapids, the outlying frontier, courageous exploration of rivers, long portages, relations with distant Indian tribes, these and other features of the fur trade are echoed today in the Canadian self-image. The vivid response in Canadian public opinion to such issues as pipelines and northern development bears the stamp of this legacy of 'nordicity' … The fur trade, in short, more than virtually any other single experience, is the primary matrix out of which modern Canada emerged."

THE HUDSON'S BAY COMPANY TURNED much of the upper half of North America into a company town writ large, in which customers displayed individuality and imagination at their own risk.

The first HBC forts were the ultimate expression of what Northrop Frye, the eminent Canadian literary critic, dubbed "the garrison mentality." Frye described these small, isolated communities as "surrounded with a physical or psychological 'frontier,' separated from one another and from their American and British cultural sources: communities that provide all that their members have in the way of distinctively human values, and that are compelled to feel a great respect for the law and order that holds them together, yet confronted with a huge, unthinking, menacing, and formidable physical setting ... A garrison is a closely-knit and beleaguered society, and its moral and social values are unquestionable. In a perilous enterprise, one does not discuss causes or motives: one is either a fighter or a deserter."

During the HBC's first half-century, its outposts were garrisons in more than a metaphoric sense, and later, as they began to soften into trading towns, very little changed. The prevailing ethic remained deference to authority inside the ramparts and deference to nature beyond them. This orderly attitude, rooted in collective survival rather than individual excellence, still colours what most Canadians do and, especially, don't do.

Another element injected into the Canadian mentality by the HBC is the notion that monopoly or a mixture of private and public enterprise works better than individual ventures. This concept was derived from the enormous size of the continent, its climatic challenges and the fact that the only alternative to the Indian/Inuit mode of living off the land was to field such a huge economic infrastructure that over the long term only a state enterprise or a monopoly could afford it.

Coming from a mixed English/Scottish tradition, the early HBC traders set out a primitive form of capitalism in the cold-frame latitudes around Hudson Bay. They stressed life's sombre virtues – the notion that there is no feeling more satisfying than a hard day's work well done and that the good man always earns more than his keep. In dramatic contrast to the shotgun individualism of the American West, the idea was to be *careful*, plainly dressed and quiet spoken, close with one's money and emotions. Flashes of pleasure and moments of splendour had to look accidental, never planned.

Such a gloomy credo could have been carved in stone for the Thomson family – Roy, the Scottish-Canadian press potentate who was appointed to the British House of Lords, and his son, Kenneth, who purchased control of the HBC in 1979 for $640 million cash. "They say business is the law of the jungle," Roy Thomson once mused. "I think it is the law of life. If you want to live and you want to prosper, you have to be ambitious. You've got to be ready to sacrifice leisure and pleasure. I was forty years old before I had any money at all. But these things don't happen overnight. How many people are there who will wait that long to be successful, and work all the time? Not very many. Maybe they're right. Maybe I'm a bloody fool. But I don't think I am."

Amen.

VIEWED THROUGH THE SEPIA GLOW OF RETROSPECT, the HBC was a mercantile colossus, straddling oceans, spanning continents and only recently reduced to more modest circumstances. Yet in terms of manpower and gross revenues, the very opposite was true. The Company has always been large in terms of the square miles it controlled, but until the mid-twentieth century it was never very big. At the height of its geographical presence, when its domain covered a quarter of North America, the HBC had fewer than three thousand employees, and as late as 1811 when it was competing head to head with the rambunctious platoons of Nor'Westers fanning out from Montreal, a staff of only 320 manned its seventy-six posts.*

Despite recent setbacks, the Company's exponential fiscal growth occurred not during its historic heyday but in the early 1980s when its personnel roster nudged 50,000 – an army of clerks and generals as large as the late and glorious East India Company at the height of its powers. Gross revenues first exceeded $1 billion in 1977 and the Company's highest profit ($80.3 million) was recorded in 1979. By the end of 1984, the payroll was down to 42,500 people and profits had been replaced by a three-year losing streak of nearly $350 million that saw the control shares Lord Thomson of Fleet had purchased for $37 plummet to as low as $15.†

A decade-and-a-half into its fourth century of business, the Hudson's Bay Company is bleeding, its bond ratings cut to shameful levels, its balance sheet adrift in red ink, its management on edge. The once proud Company of Adventurers threatens to become – in the words of Kevin Fleming, the *National Geographic* photographer who spent most of a year flying around the North, portraying its

---

*The natural tendency to exaggerate the Company's power and size found its most absurd expression in a novel published by Jules Verne in 1873. In *The Fur Country*, the best-selling author of *Twenty Thousand Leagues Under the Sea* assured his readers that the Hudson's Bay Company at that time employed "about a million men in its territories."

†For a record of the Company's dividends from 1670 to 1984, see Appendix Five. In 1970, when the HBC's headquarters was moved from London to Winnipeg, 7 percent of its stock was held in Canada; by Dec. 31, 1984, only 3.8 percent of the shares were still owned in the United Kingdom.

decaying splendour – "little more than a K-mart with a Twin Otter."

Donald McGiverin, the present Governor who has headed the Company in its best and worst years (having force-marched total sales from less than $500 million to nearly $5 billion*), remains philosophical in the face of adversity, blaming the economic recession that hit every merchandiser and the fact that too much debt (a peak of $2 billion in 1982) was acquired for expanding the business. "I regret that the recession took place and I wish Canada were not overstored. But in the tradition of this Company you have to build forts in order to *be* there, even if they are hard to maintain for a while. This is still a great Company. We must be doing something right when we have $5-billion worth of business with the public ... This is not what I had in mind, but the chief executive officer never has a bulletproof vest."

By the winter of 1984–85, McGiverin, a gregarious merchandiser with a kindly disposition, was having private as well as public troubles: his weekend hideaway at Palgrave, deep in the Ontario bush, was being overrun by beavers. "The little buggers keep eating away at my only apple tree," he complained after having tied steel plates around its gnawed trunk. He has defended his domain against the industrious rodents with every avail-

---

*As of the spring of 1985, the modern Hudson's Bay Company had 484 Canadian stores with combined retailing space of more than 31 million square feet, operating 120 outlets in the Canadian North. It is the world's largest fur auctioneer. It controls an oil company (Roxy Petroleum) with five million barrels of oil in reserve and owns Markborough Properties, one of the world's largest real estate firms, which has built forty-six shopping centres, twenty-three warehouses and factories, and thirteen office buildings, hotels and apartment towers in Canada, the U.S. and the United Kingdom.

able weapon, including dynamite to bust their dams. But the beavers, perhaps driven by tribal memory of the millions of their ancestors who gave their all to the Company of Adventurers, will not leave the Governor in peace. Sometimes, late at night while reading in bed, trying to find solace from the brutal competition of the marketplace, McGiverin thinks he hears a tree falling. Those damn beavers will get him yet.

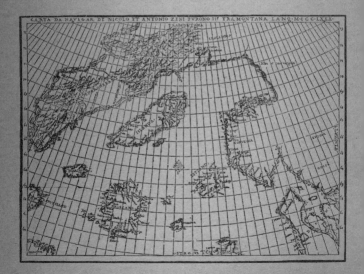

CHAPTER 2

BEYOND THE WESTERING SEA

"Whosoever commands the seas, commands the trade; whosoever commands the trade of the world, commands the riches of the world – and consequently, the world itself."
— *Sir Walter Raleigh*

THEY CAME IN UNGAINLY THREE-MASTED SHIPS with brave bowsprits and shuddering shrouds to claim a New World.

The chimera of a North West Passage had haunted Europeans for most of three hundred years, its discovery eventually becoming as much the pursuit of personal fulfilment as a feat of navigation. In the foreword to *Northwest Passage*, American novelist Kenneth Roberts caught the true nature of this operatic quest: "On every side of us are men who hunt perpetually for their personal Northwest Passage, too often sacrificing health, strength, and life itself to the search; and who shall say they are not happier in their vain and hopeful quest than wiser, duller folks who sit at home, venturing nothing and, with sour laughs, deriding the seekers for that fabled thoroughfare?"

The search took on almost religious overtones, with many ice-bound mariners comforting themselves with the thought that the Creator had placed daunting natural obstacles in the way because the richest reward would go to those who dared and suffered most. In cockleshells of ships more suitable for cruising the relatively benign coastal waters of Europe, they set out to test their souls against the elements. Many never returned. Most of those who wintered on the new continent soon regretted their vows, offering their Deity secret bargains to swap their pretensions to glory for mere survival.

By the dawn of the sixteenth century, nearly every European monarch whose kingdom was washed by the sea had commissioned adventurous captains to seek lucrative landfalls beyond the setting sun.

Their rhumb line was set by the scatter-brained Italian mariner Christopher Columbus, who had crossed the great Western Ocean four times to confirm his conviction that he had found "the islands at the end of the Orient." He mistook Haiti for Japan, was more fascinated by the ornaments "worn in the noses of the natives" than in discovering new territory and, when he found no gold, recommended to Queen Isabella that she encourage the barter of local "cannibal-slaves" for Spanish cattle.

Until the Spanish found silver and gold, Europe's outward-bound mariners were searching not for a new continent but for a fast route to the treasures of India and Cathay. The idea of reaching the Far East by sailing west was still unproved, and for the next three centuries expeditions of varying skill but equal determination would try to butt their way past or through the land barrier blocking access to Asia. A cargo of Oriental silks or cloves from the spice islands of the East Indies could yield tenfold profits for the importer. European tastebuds craved exotic condiments to mask the taste of tainted meat in summer or, even worse, the salted cuts in winter. The land route to China was long, tedious and infested by

Islamic tax collectors, but Magellan's sea alternative past the furies of Cape Horn was estimated to be two thousand leagues (six thousand miles) longer than a direct passage – if there were one.

Determined skippers bent their ships' topgallants, heading due west, hopeful they could find the secret seaway through the cursed land barrier. Every deep cove was thought to be a passage to India. Inevitably, ships heading confidently up some bay, inlet or river would heave-to, as their captains entered in log-books the oft repeated lament: "Once more, we are embayed ..."

"They had not expected to find North America in the first place, impudently lying across their path to the Orient," Daniel Francis has pointed out in *Battle for the West*, "and when they discovered it was not just an over-sized island but an entire continent stretching almost from pole to pole, they were infuriated." Ownership of the New World had originally been claimed by Spain and Portugal, their authority stemming from a series of arrogant papal bulls and the Treaty of Tordesillas (1494), which divided between the Iberian powers the unknown territory along a meridian lying 370 leagues west of the Cape Verde Islands, with a line drawn roughly from Brazil to Newfoundland. This sweeping claim held fast through most of the 1500s, even though it was violated as frequently as it was respected.

THE NOTION OF A NEW WORLD on the far shore of the Atlantic had intrigued European navigators ever since the restless Vikings had probed the western edges of that misty sea. They left little to posterity but a few stone ruins and an anonymous chronicle, *The King's Mirror*, which would forever frame the romantic essence of their journeys. "If you wish to know what men seek in that land, why men journey thither in so great peril of their lives, it is the threefold nature of man that draws him … One part thereof is the spirit of rivalry and the desire for fame; for it is man's nature to go where there is likelihood of great danger, and to make himself famous thereby. Another part is the desire for knowledge; for it is man's nature to wish to know and see those parts of which he had heard … The third part is the desire of gain; for men seek after riches in every place where they learn that profit is to be had, even though there is great danger in it."

For three interminable centuries, brave and otherwise rational men cast common sense aside to embark on improbable voyages into the void. They were lured by the fact that the once nebulous concept of a short route to the Far East had grown increasingly specific, even if little of the rumoured geographical detail was accurate. Brooding savants of the day who themselves seldom ventured to sea postulated that since the amount of the earth's water was bound to be equally divided between the northern and southern hemispheres, the capacity of land masses also had to coincide. Portuguese navigators who had circled Africa to reach the Orient perceived that the Asian coastline veered eastward at its upper extensions, while Spanish galleon captains in the Pacific, tacking north of Panama, reported the American coastline bending steadily westward. From this scanty data flowed the conclusion that the two land masses were joined at the top, and that the new continent was really a giant peninsula jutting out of Asia, with rivers crossing it affording easy access to Cathay.

The magnetism of the North was not limited to the swing of compass needles. Fishermen from St Malo and Bristol had glimpsed the New World while harvesting the profusion of sea life on the shallow Grand Banks. This revived the long-dormant saga of how the Vikings reached Greenland, there to establish Christian settlements prosperous enough to pay tithes to the Pope as well as taxes to the King of Norway and even to dispatch a small contingent to the Crusades.

The first organized voyage to the northern gate of this new land mass was that of John Cabot. A silk-clad Venetian dandy who had immigrated to England in 1495, Cabot was sponsored by Henry VII. Seven years earlier the English king had turned down a plea from Bartholomew Columbus to underwrite his brother Christopher's impending journey, and he was determined not to be outdone by his Spanish rivals again. Henry granted Cabot and his sons the right to govern whatever lands they might find, plus a trade monopoly subject to a 20 percent tax payable to the Crown. An experienced explorer who had already visited Mecca and contemplated caravans winding their solemn way from "Xanadu," Cabot had constructed a magnificent globe of the earth with land masses converging at each pole and the Asian continent bulging obligingly into the Atlantic. He used this fanciful construct, plus the privilege of the royal charter, to extract the necessary financing from Bristol merchants and, after one false start, set off in May 1497 aboard the fifty-ton *Matthew* to seek his fortune. Thirty-five days later he made a landfall, probably on the east coast of either Newfoundland or Cape Breton Island. He claimed the territory for his royal sponsor and a scant two weeks later was back in England.

Hailed as the conqueror of a New World, Cabot was awarded £10 by Henry and became the idol of his day, with crowds of admirers surrounding him on the Bristol docks, aping his every gesture. He enthralled his entourage by describing how, when anchored off the new-found-land, his crew had dipped buckets into the sea and hauled them up brimming with silvery cod, swearing that the fish were so plentiful "that at times they even stayed the ship's passage." Cabot had indeed found treasure; for centuries afterward, Bristol merchants would exploit the fishing grounds fully.

The following summer a convoy of Bristol settlers led by Cabot and reportedly accompanied by a Venetian bishop planned to establish a permanent community in the new territory before sailing the rest of the way to Chipangu (Japan). The five-ship flotilla set off with great fanfare amid all the appropriate blessings but ingloriously sank, except for one vessel that limped back to Ireland. Cabot, safe home, died quietly in England the next year.

Cabot's son Sebastian chose a different path to the Asian mainland by organizing expeditions to search for a North *East* Passage and succeeded in establishing lucrative trade links with Russia through Archangel, on the White Sea. To exploit that commerce, a group of London merchants gathered under the banner of the Muscovy Company and received in 1555 the first English charter granted to an overseas trading company. In return for weapons and other items of relatively advanced technology, the czars agreed to export squirrel, tallow, wax, deerhide, beaver, marten, flax and cordage. (It was Russian rope trimming the sails of Elizabeth I's rampaging navy that helped defeat the Spanish Armada in 1588.) This Russian trade proved so profitable that further exploration was shelved, but the Muscovy Company's prized monopoly was soon threatened, particularly by the belligerent sea-beggars of the Netherlands.

The transatlantic voyages that followed, mainly from France, England and the Netherlands, consisted of a succession of curiosity-driven navigators claiming hesitant outposts on the inhospitable eastern seaboard of the new land. The first northern settlements had been founded by Basque fishermen during the third quarter of the sixteenth century as temporary wintering stations for the fleets of whaling galleons sailing out of Biscay. At about the same time, the Oxford-educated privateer Sir Humphrey

Gilbert planted a short-lived colony in Newfoundland (the first English settlement in North America), but two of his vessels later foundered, and he was last seen aboard his sinking flagship shouting grandly into the wind: "We are as near heaven by sea as by land!"

The saddest early attempt at colonization was the doomed undertaking of the splendidly named Troilus de La Roche de Mesgouez, the first viceroy of New France, who chose to colonize, of all places, the treacherous sands of Sable Island, off Nova Scotia. There he settled his ragged crew of three hundred "vagabonds and beggars," who promptly proceeded to massacre their leaders and one another.

Gradually becoming aware that they were dealing with a separate continent and not a protrusion of Asia, European mariners determined to find an easier passage round the land barrier than the fog-bound and violent Strait of Magellan between the mainland's southernmost tip and the inhospitable Tierra del Fuego islands. Jacques Cartier tacked up the beckoning St Lawrence River, convinced he had found a passage to Cathay.*

One theory current at the time held that the new continent was bisected by three great bays – the Gulf of Mexico on the southeast, the Gulf of California on the southwest and the still unnamed Hudson Bay on the northeast, with the latter two connected in some undetermined fashion. Because both coasts of South America had been avidly explored without discovery of this mythical waterway's outlets, attention turned to the north-

---

*Time did not shake this belief. More than a century later, René-Robert Cavelier, Sieur de La Salle, who later explored the Mississippi to its delta, was granted a site by the Sulpician Fathers at the rapids where the St Lawrence narrows and named the tiny settlement *La Chine* (now Lachine), certain he was on his way to the Orient.

ern continent, and the hunt for the North West Passage started in earnest.

The two qualifications for northern exploration seemed to be courage bordering on the foolhardy and a literary obsession for recording everyday minutiae. Journals proliferated on the shelves of printers in London and on the continent, weighty sagas documenting the adventure and hardship of the search for the elusive Passage. None of these accounts of tragic escapades, which recounted every pang of conscience and twitch of frozen toe, deterred successive waves of nautical speculators from seeking the prize. Sir Walter Raleigh best expressed the sentiment of outward-bound Europeans: "Whosoever commands the seas, commands the trade; whosoever commands the trade of the world, commands the riches of the world – and consequently, the world itself."

Sir Martin Frobisher, a dour fortune hunter who headed three absurd expeditions into the Arctic, voiced another reason for all the fuss when he declared that discovering the North West Passage was "the only thing of the world that was left yet undone." A typical Elizabethan sea-dog and captain of his own ship at twenty, Frobisher never cloaked his appetites in piety, believing that privateering was a fit profession for a gentleman – even if the English geographer Richard Hakluyt described him as "the most infamous for outrageous common and daily piracies." After trying unsuccessfully for fifteen years to obtain the necessary financing, Frobisher presented his scheme for a voyage of discovery to the directors of the Muscovy Company. They at first turned him down, but he caught the interest of a City broker named Michael Lok who had himself captained a merchantman in the Levant Company's trade. Both men had enough friends at court to apply royal pressure on the Muscovy directors and enlist their participation. Elizabeth I herself subscribed £100 to the Frobisher expedition in the full expectation that he would

return with a hoard of silver from Lima and trunks laden with Manila gold. The funds proved adequate to afford Frobisher some unusual comforts, including "duck upholstery for his bedding" and "a bottell of aquavite."

His three ships dropped down the Thames tide on June 7, 1576, firing a smoky cannonade as they passed the royal Palace at Greenwich: "Her Majestie beholding the same, commended it and bade us farewell, with shaking her hand at us out the window." Off Greenland (which Frobisher alarmingly mistook for the mythical "Friesland"), one of his vessels was swamped by a storm, and its captain, unnerved by the ice, turned back. Twenty-eight days later, aboard the ten-ton *Gabriel*, Frobisher sighted land. Convinced that they had discovered the northern equivalent of Magellan's passage round the lower tip of South America, Frobisher's pilot George Best proudly reported: "So this place he named Frobisher's Straits – like as Magellan at the southwest end of the world, we having discovered the passage to the South Sea."

When he returned to London two months later without pursuing his find, Frobisher was carrying a heavy black rock he had picked up during a brief landfall at Hall Island. The wife of Michael Lok, his financial backer, happened to throw a chip of it into the dining-room fire. It burned with a strange flame, and when it was coated in vinegar "glisttered with a bright Marquesset of gold." Lok promptly took samples to London assayers, who just as promptly declared them worthless. But an Italian metallurgical charlatan named John Baptiste Agnello pronounced that the rock fragments contained traces of gold. (When Lok demanded how Agnello had found what his colleagues missed, the alchemist soothingly assured the financier it was "necessary to know how to flatter nature.")

Lok eventually unearthed another imaginative metallurgist who also perceived the "gold," and the Queen granted the prospectors a charter and £1,000 to establish the Cathay Company, naming Lok its first governor. Frobisher was promoted to high admiral and set out the following April with three new ships and twelve dozen Cornish miners. The expedition returned with two hundred tons of ore, making the run home in only twenty days, and reported with mounting excitement that the stones of the islands they passed "glitter in the sun like gold." Assays this time claimed that the rock contained up to £53 of gold per ton. Aboard the fifteen ships of the 1578 expedition that followed were four hundred men (including an Anglican divine, the Reverend Mr Wolfall), heavy tunnelling equipment and a prefabricated bunker designed to winter a hundred miners. After dropping off his supplies on an island in Countess of Warwick Strait, Frobisher sailed 180 miles into what would later be named Hudson Strait, convinced that he was on his way to the South Seas – until the floating ice stopped him cold.

The miners dug up nearly two thousand tons of the ore. Wintering plans were happily abandoned and the flotilla returned in triumph to discharge its cargo at a special smelter built on the Thames. But the ore turned out to contain no gold (the crushed rock was eventually put to use paving the streets of London), and the unfortunate Lok found himself languishing in debtors' prison.* Frobisher nimbly escaped his critics and he was awarded a

---

*The diggings (including a still existing jetty) were revisited by Charles Francis Hall in 1861, the Rawson-MacMillan Sub-Arctic Expedition of 1927 and by Dr Walter Kenyon of the Royal Ontario Museum in 1974. Chemical analyses of the ore showed it to be a combination of amphibolite and pyroxenite, which modern miners call "fool's gold." What glistened turned out to be flecks of biotite mica.

gold chain by Elizabeth I – the only gold he ever found. He presented his sovereign with a narwhal tusk and an Eskimo, complete with kayak. The Queen was so delighted with her new charge that she allowed the Arctic hunter to spear swans along the Avon River, customarily a royal prerogative. Frobisher went on to greater joy, serving as vice-admiral under his friend Sir Francis Drake in privateering ventures off the West Indies, winning rich laurels for his inspiring command of a squadron during the defeat of the Spanish Armada. He died from wounds in 1594 during an assault on the Spanish-held fortress of Crozon, in Brittany. The most enduring legacy of his northern adventures was the maxim credited to George Best, who rose from pilot to command of the *Anne Francis* on Frobisher's third expedition. This wise navigator had good reason to coin a new version of the enduring aphorism: "All is not gold that shineth."

Seven years after Frobisher's anticlimactic return, Elizabeth granted a similar exploration charter to John Davis, a mathematically inclined navigator eager to prove his theories about the precise location of the North West Passage. He staged three modest expeditions, uneventful except that, for once, they turned a tidy profit from the codfish and sealskins brought back. He observed that at the outlet of what is now Davis Strait there was "a furious overfall … like the rage of the waters under London Bridge"– the riptide ebbing out of Hudson Strait.

There followed two brief probes of northern channels by Captain George Weymouth (1602) and John Knight (1606), each sponsored by the newly founded East India Company, anxious to locate a quicker route to the gold of the Philippines and the silks of China.

These desultory forays gave way to methodical exploration in the epic voyages of Henry Hudson, who gave his name (and life) to the inland sea that would eventually yield access to a fortune in furs.

A seasoned mariner who had been hired by the Muscovy Company to reach Cathay via the North Pole, Hudson turned this apparently impossible assignment into a profitable venture by discovering a bay teeming with whales on Spitzbergen, a wind-whipped archipelago off Norway. Hired away by the rival Dutch East India Company, Hudson sailed northward along the American east coast, putting in at what is now New York and sailing 150 miles up the Manna-hata River as far as the site of Albany. That journey led in 1626 to the famous purchase of Manhattan Island from local Canarsee Indians for trinkets and cloth worth twenty-four dollars.

Hudson's successful exploits brought him to the attention of James I, who refused to sanction his return to Amsterdam. A syndicate of English courtiers – the Earl of Northampton, Lord Keeper of the Privy Seal; the Earl of Nottingham, Admiral of England; the Earls of Suffolk, Southampton and Salisbury; Sir Thomas Smith; John Wolstenholme of the new East India Company; and the scholarly Sir Dudley Digges – joined to sponsor Hudson's next trip to map the North West Passage.

The enduring mystery of Hudson, who commanded the most lavishly financed single-ship expedition of his day, was why he deliberately gathered such a devil's brew of ill-assorted malcontents instead of recruiting some of the qualified seamen then readily available for hire on the London docks. Among them were his mate, Robert Juet, a thug who held Hudson in low esteem; John King, the quartermaster, a moody troublemaker; the haberdasher Abacuck Prickett; and a florid young rogue named Henry Greene, who did not board the fifty-ton *Discovery* at St Katharine's Pool along with the others but was mysteriously plucked off a dock at Gravesend, twenty miles down the Thames.

Given this motley assemblage, Hudson might have been able to mould them into an effective crew with determination and discipline. Instead, he went against the prevailing ethic of his age by trying to run the expedition as a floating democracy, seeking mutual consent for major decisions. This only infuriated the crewmen, barely able to conceal their contempt for the vacillating captain. Stuck among the floes of Ungava Bay, Hudson offered to turn back, if that was the will of the majority, but he was interrupted by the need to save the ship from being crushed by a rogue iceberg. After that, Hudson arbitrarily set his course to the northwest, but his authority had been fatally undermined. Once past the islands he named for his backers, Nottingham and Digges, Hudson realized he was in open water again, and his dark spirits lifted. He felt that he had won the Passage. Before him lay an open ocean; scuds of water birds mewed their wild calls, as if to lure him deeper into the beckoning bay.

The *Discovery* ran southward, heeling happily, along four hundred miles of forbidding coastline. Hudson noticed the shore veering to the southwest, then almost due west. He judged himself to be sailing across the top of the continent. The approach to Cathay could be only a few watches away. Past Cape Jones he saw the shore sharply dropping away, first to the south, then to the southwest and finally, worst of all, due north. This was no North West Passage, he realized with dawning horror, but the bottom pocket of a huge bay. Instead of sailing out of this obvious cul-de-sac, Hudson panicked. He criss-crossed what is now James Bay, aware that his food supplies would scarcely last the coming winter, yet unable to break out of his predicament. It was September by then and the early winter gales nearly broached the *Discovery*, her lee scuppers foaming in the rushing waves. Juet rebelled, and Hudson threw the mate in irons, then put him on trial. Some of the crew were preparing to break open the arms locker and assume command. With the prevailing north winds threatening to founder the ship on the wilderness beaches of James Bay, Hudson turned back to find shelter inside what is now Rupert Bay and hauled the ship into shallow water. Philip Staffe, the ship's carpenter, erected a small lean-to of tamarack on the frozen shore, and there they huddled against the winter, emerging only to hunt birds and fill buckets with snow for water.

Because they had been bound for the South Seas, few members of the crew had heavy clothes, and as the furious winter gales buffeted the inadequate shelter, frostbite, scurvy and death became frequent visitors. The first to go was John Williams, the ship's gunner. Instead of following the custom of the sea and auctioning the dead man's clothing, Hudson gave Williams's coat to Henry Greene, the dissolute malingerer who had joined the expedition separately. When Greene failed to show any gratitude, Hudson snatched the garment away from him and awarded it to Robert Bylot, the deckhand he had promoted as his mate. The only interruption to such petty infighting was the appearance of an Indian dragging a sled with two deer and a pair of beaver hides on it. Hudson gave the visitor a knife, a looking-glass and some buttons for the pelts, initiating the bay's fur trade.

By June 18, 1611, the *Discovery* had floated free of ice and the survivors re-embarked, desperate to head home. Instead of rationing the remaining food, Hudson handed out all the maggoty hardtack and mouldy cheese, failing to allay the suspicion that he had retained a hoard of supplies for himself and his favourites. Hudson resumed his wanderings, erratically tacking across James Bay with no apparent destination in mind. He undercut his authority one more time by demoting Bylot and making the

carpenter Philip Staffe, who could neither read nor write, his new mate. At the same time, he confiscated all the navigation equipment aboard so that his crew could only guess the course he was steering. Certain that their captain intended to play out what was left of their lives aimlessly cruising the cursed bay, the crew turned mutinous. Six days out of Rupert, Greene and Juet organized the takeover, bundling a dazed Hudson into the ship's shallop, followed by his young son John and half a dozen scurvy-ridden tars. Only Staffe, the loyal carpenter, volunteered to join the doomed party.

The *Discovery* towed the lifeboat into clear water. Then, as the ship's mainsail ballooned under a following sou'wester, the dinghy was cut loose. Hudson raised his own sail and caught up with his disloyal crew who were busy looting the ship and gorging on his hidden cache of beer and biscuits. Guilty at the reappearance of their commanding officer, the mutineers trimmed the *Discovery*'s sails and raced away as if fleeing from the devil himself.

Henry Hudson and his eight companions perished without hope.* The history-book image of Hudson is the Collier portrait of him surrounded by icebergs, his bearded

---

*The only clue to Henry Hudson's final resting place is an obscure entry in the log of Captain Thomas James, the Bristol sailor who wintered on Charlton Island in James Bay in 1631–32. On nearby Danby Island, he found "some stakes driven into the ground." They were "about the bigness of my arms and had been cut sharpe at the ends with a hatchet." This could only have been the work of Europeans, and history records no unaccounted-for presence except that of Henry Hudson and his sad remnant of loyalists. Historian Richard Glover remembers several HBC men telling him about the first white man the Eskimos saw on Hudson Strait. He was dead, but in the boat with him was a live white boy. They did not know what to do with him, so they tied him up in dog harness, outside their tent. And that was that. No more was recalled.

countenance downcast, his hand on the tiller of his tiny shallop, his haunted eyes gazing into the blank distance, overwhelmed by the self-pity of knowing he is facing certain death on the unknown coast of a merciless sea.

The conspirators aboard the *Discovery* hacked their way home, stopping off at Digges Island to hunt for provisions before they were chased away by local Eskimos. Rations were so short that the starving sailors were reduced to chewing candles and sucking picked-over gulls' bones dipped in vinegar. They had ceased to care "which end of the ship went forward." It was only the stamina and navigational instincts of Robert Bylot, Hudson's erstwhile mate, that brought them back to England. Tried for murder instead of mutiny, the crewmen were acquitted.

The *Discovery* was back in Hudson Bay the following summer, under the command of Sir Thomas Button, a Welsh sea captain who enlisted the most distinguished patrons for any northern voyage. The charter signed by James I for the "Company of Merchants, Discoverers of the North West Passage" enjoyed the supreme protection of Henry, Prince of Wales, and included among its investors the Archbishop of Canterbury, Sir Francis Bacon (then Solicitor General), the mathematician Henry Briggs and the geographer Richard Hakluyt, as well as six dozen assorted lords and knights plus one lady. Button's commission was to find the source of the strange tides ebbing from the west that the Hudson expedition's survivors reported as certain evidence of the Passage's existence. Enlisting Bylot as his navigator, Button sailed straight across Hudson Bay only to sight its western shore just above the estuary of what was later called the Churchill River. He then veered south and anchored off a great stream he named the Nelson, after one of his officers who died there. Button and his crew thus became the first white men to winter anywhere near the future site of York

Factory. After spring breakup, Button nosed north on the bay, tracing the shoreline of Southampton Island before heading for England. His faith was undiminished. "I do confidently believe there to be a Passage," he declared, "as there is one between Calais and Dover." During the next two decades, nine plucky explorers followed Button, all but one of them English.

The exception was the Danish pathfinder Jens Munk, who had already tried to locate a North East Passage, fought pirates in the North Sea, commanded an Arctic whaler and served in the Royal Danish Navy in several senior capacities. Ordered by King Christian IV to plot the exact Mercator projections of the Passage westward out of Hudson Bay, he rounded up an able-bodied crew of sixty-three aboard two naval ships, the *Unicorn* and *Lamprey*, and set off on May 30, 1619 for what turned out to be one of the most harrowing epics of survival in the history of northern exploration. The party landed without incident at the mouth of the Churchill River and dug in for the winter. At first, the profusion of wild berries, ptarmigan, the beluga whales, visiting polar bears and plentiful firewood made it seem a perfect landfall. Then the Hudson Bay winter set in, with ice "forty fathoms deep" and the wind biting exposed skin. "I gave the men wine and strong beer," Munk noted in his log, "which they had to boil afresh, for it was frozen to the bottom." The Danes were soon writhing with scurvy, that dreaded disease of early maritime expeditions caused by the lack of ascorbic acid (Vitamin C). It loosened men's teeth, stiffened their joints and if unchecked caused internal bleeding and death. Munk described the "peculiar illness" as causing "great pains in the loins, as if a thousand knives had been thrust there. At the same time the body was discoloured as when someone has a black eye, and all the limbs were powerless; all the teeth were loose, so that it was impossible to eat."* By summer only Munk and two crewmen were still alive. Sixty-one sailors had died, and no one had the strength to bury them. Below decks, the Danish captain recorded his awful plight: "As I could no longer stand the bad smell of the dead bodies that had remained on the ship so long, I managed to crawl out of my berth. For surely it would not matter where I died ... I spent the night on deck, wrapped in the clothing of those who were already dead." In spring Munk crawled over the rotting bodies to munch a few blades of grass. By mid-July, with the two other survivors, he refloated the *Lamprey*, and in an astounding feat of seamanship and navigation the three emaciated Danes managed to sail safely to Copenhagen, 3,500 miles away. Munk's log book, published in 1624, remains a classic epic of endurance. In one chilling entry the stalwart captain, who had been cajoling his men to hang on to life longer than their bodies would allow, finally saluted his own mortality: "Herewith, good-night to all the world – and my soul into the hand of God ..."

BEING A PRACTICAL PEOPLE, the Danes opted to surrender to others the honour of charting the North West Passage, but English sailors could not bear to leave the prize unclaimed. They were driven by that combination of curiosity and stubbornness that Napoleon would later brand the rarest form of audacity – the courage of the early morning.

---

*That so many men perished from scurvy, when fresh meat was available, has been the Munk expedition's unsolved mystery. It has been suggested that while some scurvy did indeed occur, most of the men died of trichinosis, from improperly cooked polar bear meat. The key to the puzzle may be Munk's off-hand comment that his own meat was more thoroughly cooked than that of the others because he liked it well done.

Next in line for the northern prize was the duo of Luke Foxe and Thomas James, whose nearly parallel tracks through Hudson Bay lent their voyages a strange echo effect. They copied each other in equipment – the *Charles* and the *Henrietta Maria*, both eighty-ton pinnaces with twenty-man crews, provisioned for eighteen months – and both captains carried letters of introduction from Charles I to the Emperor of Japan. They left their home ports of London and Bristol within days of each other during the spring of 1631 and headed for identical destinations. But the two captains themselves were very different. Foxe was all dash and daring, a rough self-educated mariner who picked up most of his knowledge of the new continent by visiting local globemakers' shops. James, on the other hand, was a cultivated Welshman, a barrister-at-law educated at London's Inner Temple, who had his personal quadrant fashioned of pearwood and spent as much effort polishing the entries in his log book as searching for the Passage. Well schooled in what was then the art (rather than the science) of navigation, James was described by a contemporary as "a heroicke soule," yet he was surprisingly accident-prone for an explorer. He once, for instance, almost managed the difficult act of self-immolation while up a tree on Charlton Island.

With a lilt of language that presaged the cadence of the Welsh songster Dylan Thomas, James began his chronicle: "Many a Storme, and Rocke and Mist, and Wind, and Tyde, and Sea, and Mount of Ice, have I in this Discovery encountred withall; Many a despaire and death had, almost, overwhelmed mee...."* In his writings, the icy wind became "Satan's malice," and when James observed a storm overtaking his ship, he rushed below to

---

*Samuel Taylor Coleridge, more than a century later, used the James chronicle as inspiration for some of the more lurid imagery in *The Rime of the Ancient Mariner*.

rhapsodize: " … there came a great rowling sea out of the NNE and by eight a clock it blew very hard at SE…. the sea was all in a breach; and to make up a perfect tempest, it did so lighten, snow, rain and blow, all the night long, that I was never in the like … nor I, nor any that were then with me, ever saw the sea in such a breach. Our ship was so tormented, and did so labour; with taking it in on both sides, and at both ends; that we were in a most miserable distress, in this so unknown a place…. the sea, indeed, so continually over-rackt us, that we were like Jonas in the Whales-Belly."

Not to be outdone, Foxe in his terser log entries painted his version of the evocative landscape. "This delicate morning," a typical notation begins, "the sun rose clear, and so continued all this cold virgin day … This evening the sun set clear; the air breathed gentle from the east. We lay quietly all night amongst the ice …" Foxe, gulping down polar bear steaks or gaping awestruck at the gaudy gossamer of the Northern Lights, exulted in the natural wonders of his environment. "So long as I am sailing," he wrote, expressing the prayer of all good sailors, "I bless God and care not." One warm day, while coasting down the bay's wooded western shore on a broad reach with the life-giving sun glinting on the water around him, Foxe recorded a prayerful gasp of satisfaction: "God, hold it."

When they were not preoccupied with their literary pursuits, the two navigators followed each other from Churchill down as far as Cape Henrietta Maria, so named by James, who continued sailing southward. Foxe veered due north and after poking his bow past the Arctic Circle into what is now Foxe Basin, sailed for home, icicles hanging from his rigging. Despite the publication of his memoirs in which he billed himself as "North-West Foxe," the London navigator soon lapsed into obscurity.

His Bristol compatriot decided to winter on Charlton

Island in the part of the great bay that would be named after him. James realized that the only way to save his vessel from being pounded to bits by the winter surf and ice was to sink it. Taking his auger down to the ship's bilges, he drilled holes to allow the vessel to settle on the sandy bottom from which it might be deballasted and refloated after breakup. The winter on Charlton was the usual dismal nightmare, with four men dying of scurvy and James noting: "I caused the surgeon to cut the hairs of my head short, and to shave away all the hair of my face; for that it was become intolerable, that it would freeze great with icicles."

By spring the crew was able to refloat the *Henrietta Maria*, but James almost missed sailing home. On June 25 he scrambled up the island's tallest pine and told one of his seamen to set a neighbouring evergreen afire as a signal to attract any well-disposed Indians who might be nearby. Not surprisingly, the branches under James's feet also caught fire, as did most of the island, very nearly roasting the captain. Four months later, the *Henrietta Maria* was welcomed back to Bristol. James received more acclaim than Foxe because he and his crew had stayed to suffer through the long sub-Arctic winter. The exuberant memoir that followed (*The Strange and Dangerous Voyage of Captain Thomas James*) outsold Foxe's inferior effort. It was notable for identifying the potential of Hudson Bay's shores and the islands as "the home of many of the choicest fur-bearing animals in the world." James went on to battle privateers off the English coast in command of the saucily christened *Ninth Whelp of the Lion*. The two navigators died within weeks of each other in 1635.

They had recorded no dramatic discoveries, but their paths had made known the bay's uncharted western shore, providing conclusive evidence that it hid no seaway to the Orient. "Even if that merely imaginary passage did exist,"

James flatly predicted, "it would be narrow, beset by ice, and longer than the route to the east by the Cape." Another century would go by before the search for the North West Passage was resumed, but now the dimensions of Hudson Bay had been mapped and its fur potential recognized. The commercial exploitation of that great inland sea was about to begin.

LA CACCIA DEI CASTORI.

CHAPTER 3

A BOUNTY OF BEAVER

"The beaver, by its defencelessness, no less than by its value, was responsible for unrolling the map of Canada."

— *Eric W. Morse*

SELDOM HAS AN ANIMAL exercised such a profound influence on the history of a continent. Men defied oceans and hacked their way across North America; armies and navies clashed under the polar moon; an Indian civilization was debauched – all in quest of the pug-nosed rodent with the lustrous fur. In the conduct of this feverish enterprise, which stretched from the early 1650s to the late 1850s, the cartography of world trade routes was filled in and the roots of many a dynastic fortune were planted.

There was nothing genteel about the hunt. Beaver became the breathing equivalent of gold. Men risked their lives and reputations for a scramble at the bonanza, caught up in a trade that transformed one of nature's gentlest creatures into a *casus belli*.

Paradoxically, the beavers themselves, peering myopically from the portcullises of their mud-and-twig castles, led the interlopers ever deeper into North America's hinterland. As the streams draining into the St Lawrence Valley were trapped out, the traders and their

Indian middlemen were obliged to keep pressing westward and northward: the best pelts were always round the next bend of the river. The beaver is a non-migratory animal which needs relatively large spaces to keep it happy, so that once a creek was "beavered out," the hunters had to move on, deeper and farther into the New Land. Just as the stalking of elephants for their ivories lured white hunters into the heart of Africa, so the pelts of the beaver drew the traders from both Hudson Bay and the St Lawrence towards the snow-capped Rocky Mountains and eventually to the shores of the bottle-green Pacific.

It was the confluence of three separate trends that transformed a marginal barter for furs by sixteenth-century seamen into an important export. First, there was the undiminishing supply of beaver provided by an immense drainage system containing nearly half the world's fresh water; second, the flourishing and astonishingly durable demand for the products of the beaver's coat in the European market; and third, the availability of an inexpensive and willing labour force – Indians with an insatiable passion for the cornucopia of European trade goods.

Without anyone being particularly aware of it, the hunt for beaver turned into the quest for a nation. As the modern explorer Eric W. Morse noted in his classic study of fur trade canoe routes: "The beaver, by its defencelessness, no less than by its value, was responsible for unrolling the map of Canada."

Basque and Iberian fishermen had already swapped furs informally, but the first documented beaver-pelt transaction took place in the summer of 1534, when Jacques Cartier, the St Malo navigator, tacked into the Baie de Chaleur, a narrowing inlet between the present-day provinces of Quebec and New Brunswick. There the French explorer encountered a beached fleet of fifty Micmac canoes, their owners enjoying a picnic on the strand. "They made frequent signs to us to come on shore, holding up some furs on sticks," Cartier noted in his ship's log. The ensuing bargaining grew so spirited that the Indians traded even the robes off their backs for European beads and knives.

Fur-trade biologist W.A. MacKay relates that as the ships pulled away accompanied by the fleet of gesticulating Indians, Cartier observed that his satisfied if naked customers were leaping and dancing in their canoes – and parenthetically noted that they were a small tribe. This prompted MacKay to comment wryly: "Any tribe that practises dancing in canoes is bound to be small."

EVER SINCE ADAM AND EVE, ejected from Eden, first donned the skins of wild beasts, fur has been a spectacular talisman. In the delicate interplay between sensibility and fashion, practicality and luxury, the wearing of furs has retained a savage symbolic undercurrent of potency, success and brute strength – bestowing on its wearer an aura of wild beauty, magic powers and social cachet. In Sung times, Chinese emperors decapitated courtiers churlish enough to wear sea otter robes without imperial permission. In the original French fairy tale, Cinderella's slipper was made of squirrel fur (*vair*) and not glass (*verre*), contrasting the sensuality of the medieval image with its brittle modern version.

Fur was, of course, worn for warmth, but its varieties were inextricably bound up with social distinctions, in the belief that each pelt perpetuated the essence of its original animal nature. A coat fashioned of rabbit or polecat skins might be just as warm but lacked the metaphysical zap of lion, leopard or fox. At Troy, Agamemnon wore a lion skin while Paris preferred leopard, but that great prince of Israel, the wise King Solomon, stuck to beaver.* Medieval edicts governed precisely who could wear what skin. The Westminster Church Council proclaimed in 1127 that abbesses and nuns could not wear winter garments any more precious than lamb or black cat. By 1337, edicts were passed stating that only nobles (and clerks earning more than £100 annually) could adorn themselves with certain furs. But a thriving black market in second-hand furs obliterated these official barriers and many a grandee was heard to complain that it was becoming impossible to distinguish an innkeeper's wife from a gentlewoman. By the middle of the fifteenth century, the once-plentiful beaver was extinct in England; mayors and sheriffs were permitted to sport marten and squirrel. Edward III decreed that rare furs, such as ermine and sable, should be restricted to royalty, the nobility and persons who gave at least £100 a year to the Church. Ladies wearing furs had to be of blameless or at least noble birth.

Yesterday's velvety beavers were nothing like today's Disneyfied replicas of Davy Crockett's coonskin cap, with the ringed tail bobbing down the back. The true beaver hat was made not from the glossy long-haired pelt but from the fine thick underhair, shaved and sheared from the skin. Unlike that of most animals, the beaver's undercoat is covered with tiny barbs that allow the downy fibres to be matted and beaten, then shellacked and shaped into a lustrous, wonderfully soft and durable felt.

The production of felt from fur is an ancient human

---

*Fur trade historians lament that there is no mention of beavers on the Ark but console themselves with the fact that when scouring the Black Sea, Jason and the Argonauts took time out to exchange Greek pottery for beaver pelts.

technology, its discovery credited to central Asian nomads such as the Scythians, whose descendants roof their tents and wagons with heavy waterproof felt made by combing out sheep's wool, wetting it, rolling and beating it with sticks and, finally, pressing it flat between reed mats. Felt was used by the Greeks and Romans for waterproof cloaks and as padding under metal armour. Its manufacture eventually became a specialty of the back-alley artisans of Constantinople. The Crusaders picked up the technique and took it back to Europe, mainly to France, where felt making flourished. The Turkish artisans were themselves driven into Russia, but after the sacking of Kiev by Tartars in 1240, escaped to Western Europe and joined their fellow felt makers in France. There, the finest felt hats were turned out at Rouen, Caudebec and other towns in Normandy, largely by Huguenots. But increasing prejudice against them and the heresy of their pragmatic faith culminated in the St Bartholomew's Day massacre in Paris and other towns, so that scores of the Protestants fled to Holland and England. The Edict of Nantes, which allowed Huguenots freedom of conscience, ended these conflicts in 1598. To protect themselves, Protestant towns were permitted to have their own armed forces and assemblies, and walled Atlantic towns, such as La Rochelle, became home ports for roaming privateers. But the Edict of Nantes was revoked in 1685 and up to half a million Huguenots emigrated, including an estimated ten thousand hatters, so that by 1701 France was forced to import its fashionable hats from England. Samuel Smiles, who chronicled the sorry exodus, concluded that "Hat-making was one of the most important manufactures brought to England by the Huguenots, who alone possessed the secret of the liquid composition which served to prepare rabbit, hare and beaver skins ... After the Revocation, most of the hatmakers went to London, and took with them the secret of their art, which was lost

"CONTINENTAL."
COCKED HAT.
(1776)

"NAVY"
COCKED HAT.
(1800)

ARMY. (1837)

CLERICAL.
(Eighteenth Century)

(THE WELLINGTON.)
(1812)

CIVIL.

(THE PARIS BEAU.)
(1815)

(THE D'ORSAY.)
(1820)

(THE REGENT.)
(1825)

MODIFICATIONS OF THE BEAVER HAT.

to France for about forty years.* During this period, the French nobility, and all persons making pretensions to dress, wore none but English hats. Even the Roman cardinals got their hats from the celebrated manufactory at Wandsworth, established by the refugees."

Before the invention of the umbrella, beaver headgear provided an elegant way to keep dry, but there was much more to the fashion than mere practicality. It was more mania than swank. Men and women could be instantly placed within the social structure according to their hats; meticulous etiquette prevailed about how the headpieces were worn and the sweeping gesture with which they were removed and parked so that they would mark their owners' station in life. The precise technique used in doffing a beaver expressed minute shadings of deference. "To own a fine beaver was to prove one's standing as a man – or woman – of the beau monde," U.S. historical writer Walter O'Meara has pointed out. "To appear without one was to be quite hopelessly out of style – and there was only one kind of fur out of which a beaver hat could be made, and that, quite naturally, was the beaver's."

Beaver hats became the rage in Stuart England, the fashion having been copied from the superb beaver bonnets worn by the victorious Swedish cavalrymen in the Thirty Years' War. Beavers assumed a variety of shapes and meanings, from plumed ceremonial models to tricorner pointed toppers.† So valuable did the beaver headpieces become

---

*The mercury fumes inhaled during the felt-making process drove practitioners of the art into early senility; thus the saying, "mad as a hatter."

†The fur "muff", an outgrowth of the beaver-edged angel sleeve, became a popular fashion item for both men and women. This led to the breeding of tiny "muff dogs," personal pets small enough to be carried along as one's (presumably "muff-broken") canine companion.

that they were willed by fathers to eldest sons. Samuel Pepys boasted in one of his 1662 diary entries that he had paid eighty-five shillings for his beaver hat. It was such a precious object that he kept a spare rabbit version for bad weather.

Styles varied not only according to the wearer's social schedule and station but with changing political regimes. During the reign of the first two Stuarts, the elaborate, blocky, wide-brimmed "Spanish Beaver" was in vogue, but with the beheading of Charles I and the austere stewardship of Oliver Cromwell, the severely unadorned conical beaver came into its own. This Puritan headgear was followed, during the Restoration, by the adoption of the feathered fedora-like slouch adapted from the French court. "Every major political upheaval," noted Murray G. Lawson, who traced fashion's erratic patterns, "brought in its train a corresponding change in hat styles."

In France the hat gained such status that generous trade-ins were given for worn models on new purchases. They were sold in Spain, then trimmed of the most worn parts for resale in Portugal. Finally, a little the worse for wear, they were swapped for ivory in Africa.

NORTH AMERICA'S RIVERS, flowing under succulent clumps of aspen, willow and white birch, were progressively denuded of animals, as Indians rushed to swap pelts for trade goods. "The beaver does everything perfectly well," marvelled a Montagnais chief. "He makes us kettles, axes, swords, knives, and gives us drink and food without the trouble of cultivating the ground …"

Beaver became such a valued commodity that it was literally turned into money. For a century and a half, the standard of currency was not cash but beaver skins. "Made-beaver" (M-B), a prime quality skin from an adult beaver or its equivalent in other furs or goods, was the fixed unit of barter.* At the fur-gathering end of the commerce, all goods were quoted in terms of their beaver equivalents, so that two otter skins, eight pair of moose hooves or ten pounds of goose feathers each equalled one made-beaver. A moose hide or the fur of a black bear would fetch goods worth the equivalent of two made-beavers. Indians could get an impressive array of goods for their catch, as shown in this tally taken from the standard of trade as it existed at the Hudson's Bay Company post at Albany Fort in 1733:

Coloured beads	3/4	pound	for	1	Made-Beaver
Kettles, Brass	1	"	"	1	"
Lead, black	1	"	"	1	"
Gun-Powder	1½	"	"	1	"
Shot	5	"	"	1	"
Sugar	2	"	"	1	"
Tobacco, Brazil	2	"	"	1	"
Ditto Leaf	1½	"	"	1	"
Ditto Roll	1½	"	"	1	"
Thread	1	"	"	1	"
Vermilion	1½	ounce	"	1	"
Brandy	1	gallon	"	1	"

---

*"Made-beaver" constituted the money of the new frontier, not in the sense of a medium of exchange but in the sense of a unit of account. When coins were eventually introduced to facilitate the fur trade, they were made-beaver tokens. Minted of brass or stamped out of the copper bindings of kegs shipped to the bay from London, they were imprinted with whatever fraction of a made-beaver they represented and could be spent like cash inside HBC stores. A prime quality beaver usually represented a dozen tokens; a bear skin, twenty. The last tokens were aluminum pieces for use in the white fox trade, issued in the eastern Arctic by the HBC in 1946. The standard fluctuated from time to time and from factory to factory, depending on the trading circumstances.

Broad Cloth	2	yard	for	1	Made-Beaver
Blankets	1		,,	1	,,
Flannel	2	,,	,,	1	,,
Gartering	2	,,	,,	1	,,
Awl Blades	12		,,	1	,,
Buttons	12	dozen	,,	1	,,
Breeches	1	pair	,,	1	,,
Combs	2		,,	1	,,
Egg Boxes	4		,,	1	,,
Feathers, red	2		,,	1	,,
Fish-Hooks	20		,,	1	,,
Fire Steels	4		,,	1	,,
Files	1		,,	1	,,
Flints	20		,,	1	,,
Guns	1		,,	10, 11, 12 M-B	
Pistols	1		,,	4	M-B
Gun-Worms	1		,,	1	,,
Gloves, Yarn	1		,,	1	,,
Goggles	2		,,	1	,,
Handkerchiefs	1		,,	1	,,
Hats, laced	1		,,	1	,,
Hatchets	2		,,	1	,,
Hawk Bells	8		,,	1	,,
Ice Chisels	2		,,	1	,,
Knives	8		,,	1	,,
Looking-Glasses	2		,,	1	,,
Mocotagans [Curved knives]	2		,,	1	,,
Needles	12		,,	1	,,
Net-Lines	2		,,	1	,,
Powder Horns	2		,,	1	,,
Plain Rings	6		,,	1	,,
Stone Rings	3		,,	1	,,
Scrapers	2		,,	1	,,
Sword Blades	2		,,	1	,,
Spoons	4		,,	1	,,

Shirts	2	for	1	Made-Beaver
Shoes	1	,,	1	,,
Stockings	1	,,	1¼	,,
Sashes, Worsted	2	,,	1	,,
Thimbles	6	,,	1	,,
Tobacco Boxes	2	,,	1	,,

ANOTHER PART OF THE BEAVER that sparked dreams of fortune in men's eyes was its pear-shaped perineal scent glands located in the anal region of both sexes. They contain a bitter orange-brown alkaloid substance called *castoreum*, which proved to be a surprisingly effective medicine. It cured headaches, helped reduce fever and possessed many other magical healing qualities.*

Solomon was reported to have used Spanish castoreum for his migraines, Hippocrates mentioned it favourably in 500 B.C. and Pliny recommended it for allaying hysteria. It was used as a nostrum for mental illness, an anti-spasmodic by anxious midwives and a palliative for epilepsy and tuberculosis. Joanne Franco, an early enthusiast of the medical sciences, confided in 1685 that "Castoreum does much good to mad people, and those who are attacked with pleurisy give proof of its effect every day, however little may be given to them. Castoreum destroys fleas; is an excellent stomachic; stops hiccough; induces sleep; strengthens the sight, and taken up the nose it causes sneezing and clears the brain.… A Jew of my acquaintance who visited me occasionally,… communicated to me a secret which he had learnt from his ancestors, who themselves got it from Solomon who had proved it. He assured me that in order to acquire a prodigious memory

---

*There is a strong basis for this in fact. Modern chemical analysis has shown castoreum to contain acetylsalicylic acid, the main component of Aspirin and other headache remedies.

and never to forget what one had once read, it was only necessary to wear a hat of the beaver's skin, to rub the head and spine every month with that animal's oil, and to take, twice a year, the weight of a gold crown-piece of castoreum."

From the very beginnings of the fur trade, the pear-shaped "beaver stones" were treasured almost as much as the furs. Between 1808 and 1828, the HBC exported nearly ten tons of castoreum out of the Athabasca district alone. Because of the gooey substance's proven curative powers, the prosaic beaver became an object of folk fantasy. The *Latin Bestiary of the Twelfth Century* claimed that when the beaver notices it is being pursued by a hunter, "he removes his own testicles with a bite, and casts them before the sportsman, and thus escapes by flight. What is more, if he should again happen to be chased by a second hunter, he lifts himself up and shows his members to him. And the latter, when he perceives the testicles to be missing, leaves the Beaver alone … The creature is called a Beaver (Castor)* because of the castration."

There are no accurate calculations of how many beavers sacrificed their glands or became hats, but in 1854, when the fashion in beaver hats had already passed its height,† 509,000 pelts were auctioned off in London

---

*The word comes from the old Sanskrit word *Kasturi* meaning "musk"; "beaver" is likely derived from the Sanskrit word for "brown."

†Beaver felt declined in value after the mid-nineteenth century when silk velour was found to be a less expensive and socially acceptable substitute. When Prince Albert, Queen Victoria's consort, appeared in public in a silk topper, the industry seemed doomed. But in 1843, Archibald Barclay, the Hudson's Bay Company's London-based secretary, had a brilliant suggestion. "We have been trying some experiments on the beaver," he informed the Committeemen confidentially, "with a view of testing the article to be used as … *fur!*"

alone, and HBC accountants calculated from 1853 to 1877 they had sold three million skins. The beaver had once colonized nearly every river bed from the Rio Grande to the Arctic Ocean, with estimates of the rodent's original North American population ranging between sixty million and four hundred million. Robert J. Naiman, a biologist with the Woods Hole Oceanographic Institution in Massachusetts, believes that in 1670 there were at least ten million beavers within the boundaries of present-day Canada.

What changed the odds against the beaver was the perfecting of the steel trap by Sewell Newhouse at Oneida, N.Y., in 1823. Instead of lashing ice chisels to sticks and trying to spear the animals as they repaired the holes in their lodges, hunters could now set dozens of traps, bait them with castoreum and collect the carcasses. The record catch was made by Alexander Ross, a canny Scots trapper who in 1824 led a twenty-man expedition into the Bitterroot Mountains along what is now the Montana-Idaho border. The group caught as many as 155 beavers in a single day and came back with five thousand pelts.

While it was an uneven contest, most Indians respected the beaver's intelligence and believed the animal had sacred origins. According to Ojibway legend, the Great Spirit sent the beaver to dive beneath the waters then covering the surface of the earth to dredge up mud to form land surfaces. The Algonquin believed that it was the clapping of the beavers' tails that made thunder and the Crow venerated the animals, convinced they would be reincarnated as beavers. There were tales of marriages between beavers and Indian women, and lively legends of beaveroid offspring.

Among the Ojibway, a young man might ask for a daughter's hand in marriage by saying to her father: "I love your daughter. Will you give her to me, that the roots of her heart may entangle with mine, so that the strongest wind that blows shall never separate them?" If the father approved, he would throw a beaver robe over the couple. That act marked them as man and wife.

Indian legends relate that beavers had originally been endowed with the power of speech, but exhibited so many other noble qualities that the Great Spirit took away this gift to prevent them from becoming superior in understanding to mankind. None of this veneration stopped the slaughter, but after skinning and eating a beaver, Indian families took care not to feed its bones to the dogs, depositing them instead in the pond that had been the beaver's home.

Invading fur traders dismissed such spiritual ritual as flummery – and added the beaver to their menus. The early trappers pounded the beaver meat with wild fruit, then dipped the mixture into tallow and packed it into hot deer bladders for a delicious repast. It was the scaly stern appendage that popularized the beaver among Catholic missionaries and their converts. In 1704, Michel Sarrazin, Louis XIV's chief physician in New France, sent a petition to the *Académie Royale des Sciences* in Paris, which conveniently decreed that the beaver's hairless tail was really a fish. This ruling, later approved by the Faculty of Divinity at the University of Paris, guaranteed the beaver's inclusion as a proper dish on Friday dinner or Lenten menus.

Early naturalists fantasized that the paddle-tailed animals lived in multi-storey condominiums in which "their republics are well governed," and there were engravings of beavers officiously marching around, lugging smoothly planed wooden boards on their shoulders to build their dams. In his *Universal Dictionary of Trade and Commerce* (1751), Malachy Postlethwayt postulated that beavers eat only fish – except those he accused of being "lazy beavers" which lived on land and went near water only to drink. The aquatic variety, according to Postlethwayt,

The Cataract of NIAGARA. some make
this Water-Fall to be half a League while
others reckon it no more than
a hundred Fathom.

gathered every spring, "and, walking two by two, they go in a body to hunt for animals of their own species; and all those they can catch they lead into their dams, where they make them work like slaves."

Samuel Hearne, the young Royal Navy seaman who became one of the HBC's most daring explorers, contemptuously dismissed the notion of such a hierarchy within the beaver world, pointing out that some animals found with hairless backs got that way because of the mange, not by carrying heavy boards on their shoulders. "I cannot refrain from smiling," he wrote in his *Journey to the Northern Ocean*, "when I read the accounts of different authors who have written on the economy of those animals, [as]... Little remains to be added beside a vocabulary of their language, a code of their laws, and a sketch of their religion ... Their plaistering the inside of their houses with a composition of mud and straw, and swimming with mud and stones on their tails, are still more incredible.... It would be as impossible for a beaver to use its tail as a trowel, except on the surface of the ground on which it walks, as it would have been for Sir James Thornhill to have painted the dome of St. Paul's cathedral without the assistance of scaffolding."

One of the few fur traders who took the trouble to domesticate beaver kits thoroughly enough so that they answered to their names, Hearne was fascinated by the playful creatures. He studied even what he called their dunging habits. "In respect to the beaver dunging in their houses, as some persons assert, it is quite wrong, as they always plunge into the water to do it ... I had a house built for them, and a small piece of water before the door, into which they always plunged when they wanted to ease nature; and their dung being of a light substance, immediately rises and floats on the surface then separates and subsides to the bottom. When the Winter sets in so as to freeze the water solid, they still continue their custom of coming out of their house, and dunging and making water on the ice; and when the weather was so cold that I was obliged to take them into my house, they always went into a large tub of water which I set for that purpose; so that they made not the least dirt."

Except for Grey Owl, an eccentric Englishman named Archie Belaney, who masqueraded as an Indian and shared his living quarters with a family of beavers, few people have successfully tamed the little beasts. Dr John Knox, Danish ambassador to Canada in the 1950s, spent most of his spare time in the Gatineau Hills north of Ottawa patiently observing beavers, with mixed results: "Anxious to learn more about their ways when confined to the lodge and the waters under the ice, I called on my forest friends one Saturday in December, when the pond was icebound and the cold was biting my fingers," he related. "It was obvious that in two places the beavers had, until recently, managed to keep openings in the ice. I broke the ice at one of these places and waited patiently for a beaver to come out. Though I could hear one moving around under the ice, he appeared only after I had moved to the other hole on the far shore of the pond. Aided by a sixth sense, he came out of hole number one when I was watching hole number two. Sitting up on his haunches, scratching his belly, he sniffed against the wind and directed a sly look in my direction across the pond. That entire afternoon he would invariably choose the better hole of the two – where I would not be at that moment."

Beavers are difficult to domesticate partly because they must spend most of their waking hours chewing wood. Maud Watt, wife of the HBC factor at Rupert House on James Bay, kept a beaver kit in her house in the 1920s. After it chewed through most of the family's furniture, the Watts decided to deport the offending creature to Akimiski Island. During the short trip, the little passenger chewed right through its wooden cage and gnawed a hole in the bottom of the boat. The craft just made it to shore before sinking.

The saddest and all too frequent use for the beaver's magnificent teeth is to chew off its own leg to escape old-fashioned steel traps.

A touching instance of how the animals look after one another was the observation by Dan McCowan, a Canadian naturalist, of two beavers swimming in a small lake near Banff, Alberta. The hindmost swam touching the leader's tail with its nose; once, when the rear beaver swam abreast, it bumped into a rock and quickly realigned itself in the nose-to-tail position. Having reached shore, the duo started munching contentedly, but when McCowan walked up to have a look, the leading beaver swished back into the lake. The other stayed stock-still, unable to flee. It was blind.

The beaver's brainpower has not been tested, but its instincts and behaviour certainly seem more advanced than those of most rodents, and it is one of the few animals that manipulates the environment so explicitly to suit its needs. "It does act intelligently," concluded E.R. Warren in *The Beaver and Its Works*, "not with the human intelligence some writers would ascribe to it, but it does things in which it is guided by something more than instinct alone."

A nocturnal animal that passes more than half its waking life tucked away in its underwater lodge, the beaver is deceptively unimpressive looking, with a dumpy figure, webbed feet, no neck to speak of and squinty little eyes.* Its weight varies between 40 and 60 pounds, though

---

*Although they lack obvious star quality, they have been celebrated in various art forms, such as *The Revolt of the Beavers*, a play presented by Washington's Federal Theater Project in 1937, and Stan Kenton's dam-busting *Eager Beaver*, a rhythmical riff first recorded on November 19, 1943.

Vernon Bailey of the U.S. Biological Service once caught a 110-pounder on the Iron Ore River in Wisconsin.*

The beaver's broad, scaly tail, about a foot long, six inches wide and three-quarters of an inch thick, is useful for submerged steering, for propping the animal up while it is cutting trees and for slapping the water as a warning of approaching danger. It also acts as a radiator, allowing beavers to disperse excess body heat. But it is not, as some early naturalists maintained, used as a trowel during dam construction or as a punt for ferrying kits ashore. The rudder-like appendage can be manoeuvred with considerable dexterity, so that when the beaver is towing a leafy branch, for example, it angles its tail to overcome the torque of its forward motion.

The animal is an eating machine, even if it is not always hungry. It *must* chaw continually with its chisel-like teeth or it will perish. Its four self-sharpening incisors, coated with bright orange enamel, can grow up to a length of seven inches and if not worn down by constant gnawing will eventually pierce the beaver's skull. The incisors can chop their way through a six-inch tree in five minutes. Trees up to forty-two inches in diameter have been felled by these determined lumber-rats, their heads tilted as they chew against the grain, spitting out the chips.

The naturalist Ernest Thompson Seton has observed

---

*That was a midget compared with pre-history's giant beavers (*Castoroides ohioensis*), which walked tall during the Pleistocene epoch. These Brobdingnagian rodents were up to nine feet long and weighed as much as a full-grown grizzly. Samples of the giant beaver's lower incisors measure 9.69 inches. Dr Richard Harrington, chief of the paleobiology division of the National Museum of Natural Sciences in Ottawa, recently discovered remains of these behemoths in the Old Crow Basin of the Yukon. Their incisors were highly prized as cutting tools by the first North American Indians.

that a beaver can cut down a tree as fast as a man with a dull hatchet. The beaver squats on its tail at the foot of the tree and, clasping the trunk with its forepaws, cuts two horizontal grooves three inches apart with its incisors, then pries out the wood between cuts. The animal then positions itself at the opposite side of the tree and connects up to the previous trench at a slightly higher level. Seton estimates that the average beaver fells 216 trees a year.*

When beavers are not eating, they are grooming. As soon as it wades to shore, the beaver will raise itself erect on its tail, scratch its belly and shake its ears dry by hopping from side to side. Then it waterproofs its fur, tuft by tuft, by smearing it with the greasy discharge of special oil glands stored in pockets near the anus. It dips its forepaws into the glandular excretion and spreads the musky substance over its fur. Then, using the second and third toes of its hind feet, which are split to form a primitive comb, it fastidiously preens its coat until it is smooth and glossy. This grooming not only produces an oiled pelage so essential to aquatic animals, but it helps get rid of annoying beetles snuggling in the underhair.

When on land the beaver walks with an awkward gait but undergoes a metamorphosis under water, becoming as sleek as a seal and fast as a torpedo. It can remain submerged under water without a breath for as long as fifteen minutes, a feat made possible by relatively large

---

*The myth persists that beavers are intelligent enough to determine the direction in which their chosen trees will fall. The reason most shore trees tumble into the stream where they can be towed to the dams is that their upper branches, reaching for sunlight, tend to grow faster on the water side. Top-heavy, they usually topple in the direction most convenient for the beaver, but occasionally the tree falls the wrong way, once in a while right on top of the dumpy little lumberjack.

lungs and an oversize liver that allow the beaver to extend oxygen storage. The animal's respiratory system tolerates high doses of carbon dioxide, and when under ice, the beaver will sometimes wait while an exhaled breath-bubble is oxygenated by the water, then re-inhale it to extend time under water. With its thick fur and layers of fat that insulate better than a diver's wet suit, the beaver comes very close to being nature's scuba diver. Its webbed hind paws act like flippers; valvular ears and nose close off automatically beneath the surface and transparent goggle-like eyelids permit underwater vision. Tight folds of skin behind the incisors shut water out of the mouth, allowing the beaver to chew tree bark while under the surface. It has its own sonar: the animal's auditory nerves are so finely tuned it can detect threatening vibrations through the water. The beaver's sense of smell is acute but, just to make sure, it will always feed on the lee side of potential enemies.

Beavers mate for life, and the ladies seem to rule the roost. According to Lars Willson, a zoologist who has studied their behaviour, the female beaver initiates the relationship by beating off stray males who waddle into her territory, testing their vigour to make sure she chooses the strongest. Once set to raise a family, the couple never quarrels again. After pairing takes place, the male defends his pond, his lodge and his mate against randy strangers. If he is killed, the female scurries off to a neighbouring lodge, ferrying her kits in her teeth to the new location. Beavers communicate through auditory signals such as whines, bellows and tail whacks, as well as complicated paw-mark messages on the soft mud pies they leave on the sides of canals.

Alexander Henry, the elder (a fur trader captured by Ojibway in 1763), reported that "the beaver is much given to jealousy. If a strange male approaches, a battle immediately ensues. The female remains an unconcerned spectator, careless to which party the law of conquest may assign her ... The male is as constant as he is jealous, never attaching himself to more than one female, while the female, on her side, is always fond of strangers."

In the mated pair, amatory foreplay is quickly resolved because beaver sex leaves little time for diversionary antics. Beavers make love face to face, *vis-à-vis* and *ventre-à-ventre*, swimming on their sides while spiralling through the water in an aquatic ballet that requires total concentration and commendable technique.*

Kits weigh a pound at birth, arriving in litters of up to nine, and can manage a basic dog-paddle the day after they are born. The mother makes a nursery for her brood by splitting aspen and birch sticks into long fibres that allow the moving water beneath to cleanse the cradles. The newcomers enjoy their youth, cavorting in the water, chasing each other and learning to slap their tails for protection. Daily gnawing lessons are a compulsory part of the cycle.

But at the age of two, everything changes. The young beavers are driven out of the lodge, forced to strike out on

---

*Beavers have seldom been observed in the sex act. One exception was the commentary of Frank Kahan, an Arlington, Washington researcher who reported in the *American Journal of Mammology* (vol. 21, 1940): "While the female was swimming the male clasped her above the hips with his fore limbs and turned on his side, hanging on while the female swam slowly for a moment. Then they churned the water and dived with a splash. Upon coming to the surface they swam to shore, climbed out and sat side by side combing themselves. A few minutes later the female entered the water, the male followed and the same performance was repeated." In both males and females, sexual organs are enclosed within a cloacal chamber, so that it is impossible to tell one from another, even with the beaver in hand. The beavers themselves have no such problem.

their own to build lodges downstream from their parents. Reluctant to face the wet, cruel world, the befuddled adolescents sometimes try sneaking back into the nest but are rebuffed, and if they persist, they are killed. With more kits on the way and food supplies limited, the whole colony would be endangered by their continued presence.

The beaver has been called the only animal besides man that can manufacture its own environment. The snug lodges where the beavers live are marvels of animal architecture, the protective dams as much as a mile long and forty feet thick. Their foundations are twigs stuck into the river bottom, anchored down with stones and mud; the self-supporting structure may rise to twelve feet or more. The outer walls of the lodges are intricately interlaced branches and trimmed tree trunks, insulated with tufts of grass patiently patted into place by beaver snouts. The miracle of the beaver lodge is how its builders know precisely where to locate exits and breathing chimneys; how they sense exactly how thick the ice will be each winter so that they can place their living platforms above it. The members of a beaver colony put up caches of poplar and willow to feed on during freeze-up. The sides of the colony's lodge are plastered with mud, which washes into the cracks between branches and twigs. When it freezes, the mixture congeals into a wall solid enough to keep out predators, except for man. Their secret is the network of peripheral dams the beavers erect up- and downstream from their lodges to control water levels to the nearest inch. The dams can be as much as six feet high, eighteen feet wide and consist of 250 tons of material. They hold water at five-foot level differentials, and the total effect is of miniature castles complete with moat, underwater entrances and dry, well-ventilated sleeping chambers along passageways sometimes twenty feet long.

Beavers sleep on mats made from patted-down twigs and wide blades of grass; bedding is regularly changed when it gets fouled by mud.

The original explorers brought back tales of beaver lodges three storeys high, complete with windows, balconies and distinctively separate sleeping lairs and rooms for dining or nesting. Contemporary research proves them at least partly correct. Frank Conibear, inventor of a more humane trap, spent thirty years in the Canadian north and examined the interior of many beaver lodges. In his book, *The Wise One*, he wrote: "In my youth the Indians who were my companions along the trap-line told much of the ways of beaver. In speaking of the beaver lodges, they described the larger ones as containing usually three rooms, a room for sleeping, a room for eating in, and a smaller [underwater] room where the beaver passed their excrement, which was cleaned out at regular intervals. In addition to these rooms, the mother of the family in the spring hollowed out for herself an additional small room in the thick part of the partition, in which to have her young. In my own observations of beaver I have never found anything which caused me to doubt the genuineness of either of these items of information. On the contrary, I have seen what I believe to be proof that the Indians, with centuries of beaver lore behind them, were, as always, right."

The beaver's most sophisticated engineering feat is the canal system that supports the colony. Intricately designed ditches divert water, collect seepage from swamps and help the beaver float food supplies homeward. Canals six feet wide and more than six hundred feet long have been found, some elaborately controlled by spillways and crude locks. "These canals," the naturalist A. Radclyffe Dugmore has noted, "are a demonstration of the highest skill to be found of any animal below man

... It is doubtful whether man in his lowest form does such extraordinary work and with such remarkable success."

"THE HISTORY OF CANADA," noted H.A. Innis in his classic *The Fur Trade in Canada*, "has been profoundly influenced by the habits of an animal which very fittingly occupies a prominent place on her coat of arms. The beaver was of dominant importance in the beginnings of the Canadian fur trade. It is impossible to understand the characteristic developments of the trade or of Canadian history without some knowledge of its life and habits."

A glorified water rat with a flat tail, *Castor canadensis* has richly earned its pride of place as Canada's national emblem.

CHAPTER 4

MESSRS RADISHES & GOOSEBERRIES

*"Glib, plausible, ambitious, supported by
unquestionable physical courage, they were the
completely equipped fortune hunters."*
— Douglas MacKay

MOUNTING GEOGRAPHICAL EVIDENCE TO THE CONTRARY, the settlers in the St Lawrence Valley who made up the colony of New France still believed it would eventually be possible to reach China overland from Montreal. An explorer named Jean Nicollet, who discovered Lake Michigan in the 1630s, spent a decade trekking through the wilderness of America's Northwest with a robe of Chinese damask carefully packed in his knapsack so that he would be properly attired to greet the mandarins of Cathay.*

Successive French officials resident in Quebec confirmed the existence of Hudson Bay, firmly believing it was connected to an unspecified Oriental sea. The century-old dream of Jacques Cartier was still alive, and it did not really end until 1742, when Louis-Joseph and François

---

*At Green Bay in what is now Wisconsin, Nicollet finally put on his damask robe. He struck such terror in the gathered Winnebagos that they thought he was a god and promptly concluded a peace treaty.

La Vérendrye brought back Cree reports of a great mountain range blocking the continent's western gate.

Of the many fur traders, missionaries, confidence men and royal emissaries sent inland from New France to take the measure of *le pays d'en haut*, two men stood out among the rest: Pierre-Esprit Radisson and Médard Chouart, Sieur Des Groseilliers. Every Canadian schoolchild knows them as "Radishes and Gooseberries"* though few grasped the full impact of their exploits. This astute pair of *coureurs de bois* were the first Europeans to penetrate deep into the forest belt of the North, first to negotiate treaties with the Cree, first to explore the upper reaches of the Mississippi and Missouri and first to establish the durable trading pattern responsible for creation of the Hudson's Bay Company. The frontier historian Agnes Laut refers to Radisson and Groseilliers slipping nimbly "between the Sun King and His Britannic Majesty, between Jesuit camp and Recollect clique, between New England and Old England, between New France and Old France, between Catholicism and Protestantism, giving merry chase to the wits of monarchs, fur-trading barons, governors, and churchmen."

The two are invariably mentioned in tandem, but they were very different in age (Radisson was twenty-two years the junior), temperament (Groseilliers was the steadfast organizer, Radisson the mercurial merchandiser) and

---

*The members of Charles II's court could not or would not pronounce the two men's names correctly and the HBC minutes contain eight different spellings of "Groseilliers," with the record keepers eventually settling on "Gooseberries." In Radisson's case, the problem was with his first name – which was cited so often as Peter that in his will, written in his own hand, dated July 17, 1710, he refers to himself as Peter Radisson. The only posthumous mention of his widow (his third wife), in the HBC minutes on January 2, 1732, refers to her as Elizabeth Radiston.

outlook (Radisson wanted to make history, his confrère to forget it).

If Radisson is inevitably ranked as the more prominent of the two, it is mainly because he left behind jovial jottings of his journeys, colouring valid geographical detail with tales of birds so fat they could scarcely fly and Indians who could shoot three ducks with one arrow.* It was he who issued the famous boast: "We were Caesars, being nobody to contradict us." While it is unwise to accept Radisson at his word, the lives and times of the two men provided the essential link between the trapping of animals as a subsistence activity and the exploitation on a grand scale of the furry riches of North America's streams and lakes. "A more daring pair of intentional promoters cannot be found in the history of commerce," wrote Douglas MacKay in *The Honourable Company*. "Glib, plausible, ambitious, supported by unquestionable physical courage, they were the completely equipped fortune hunters."

MÉDARD CHOUART ARRIVED IN QUEBEC during his late teens from the Marne country in north-central France, where his parents managed a farm known in the surrounding villages as *Les Groseilliers* (Gooseberry Bushes). By 1646, the youngster had become a disciple of the Jesuit fathers and was serving as a lay assistant at their Huron mission near Georgian Bay. Back in Quebec, he married Hélène, the daughter of a river pilot named Abraham Martin (whose land would achieve historical fame a century later as the Plains of Abraham) and settled down in a

---

*The original copy in French of Radisson's *Voyages* was lost, but one contemporary translation survived in the papers of Samuel Pepys. It was discovered by chance, just before being sold to a fish-and-chip shop as wrapping paper, and now reposes in the Bodleian Library at Oxford.

seigneury near Trois-Rivières. Better educated than most of the other *coureurs de bois* who populated the young colony, he was a natural leader, resentful of imagined injustice and proud enough of his sliver of land to call himself Sieur Des Groseilliers, attaching the name of his parents' farm to his new estate. After his first wife's death, he married Marguerite Hayet, half-sister of a local roustabout named Pierre Radisson.

Radisson served a more savage apprenticeship. At the age of fifteen while out on a duck shoot, he was ambushed by a band of roving Mohawks who took him to their village on Lake Champlain. Adopted by the family of a warrior who had nineteen white scalps to his credit, Radisson quickly learned the Mohawk language and ways of hunting. He began to understand the psychology of being Indian that would later help him act as an effective interlocutor for the fur traders. Going along on Mohawk war parties pillaging the villages of hostile tribes, he became, in effect, a white Indian. But the memories of life in New France were too sweet to forget. While hunting with three Mohawks and a captive Algonquin, he and the prisoner escaped after crushing the skulls of their sleeping companions. They were tracked down and quickly recaptured. The Algonquin was executed on the spot while Radisson was placed on the village scaffold. His soles were seared with heated irons and a red-hot sword was driven through one of his feet. His fingernails were pulled out, each one more slowly than the last; then the raw fingertips were dipped into canisters of live coals. Children were beginning to chew his tortured hands when he was rescued by his adopted family. But the nightmare of that ordeal never left him. After two more years of life as a Mohawk slave, he escaped to Fort Orange, the Dutch trading post on the site of modern Albany, New York, where he acted as an interpreter until he returned to Trois Rivières. Though still less than twenty-one years old, Radisson was toughened beyond his years and fully primed for his travels inland.

Groseilliers had meanwhile paddled into the land of the Huron to persuade them to bring more pelts down to the St Lawrence. In the Green Bay area, he picked up stories about a legendary Eldorado of untouched beaver preserves north of Lake Superior. It was into this country that the two "brothers," as they started to call each other, ventured in the early spring of 1659. During the winter that followed, in the long evenings around campfires with the Huron, and later with the Sioux and the Cree, the two traders heard tales of the wealth of beaver ponds between Lake Superior and Hudson Bay's southwestern shore.* Visiting Cree from that mysterious region had collected the glossiest pelts Radisson and Groseilliers had ever seen, claiming they came from massive rivers rising beyond the nearby divide of ice-scoured granite that flowed north into an inland sea.

Although the rich bales of fur the two brought back to Quebec probably saved the colony's struggling economy, the governor, the Marquis d'Argenson, arbitrarily confiscated most of the pelts and briefly jailed Groseilliers for trading without a licence. Concerned that exploration of the Hudson Bay route might shift the focus of the fur trade away from the St Lawrence, the French governor refused to grant the *coureurs de bois* permission to reconnoitre the distant territory, which left them little choice but to try their luck in New England. That switch in loyalties was to have momentous consequences, the first of a long chain of sometimes unconnected events that reached its climax a

---

*Radisson claimed in his reminiscences written a decade later that they had actually travelled to the shores of Hudson Bay, but the time sequence involved makes this highly unlikely, since they did not leave Superior until breakup in late April and were back in Quebec by August 19.

century later with the British conquest of New France.

During the next three years the pair persuaded several Boston punters to sponsor voyages into Hudson Bay – though only one (in 1663, under the command of Capt. Zachariah Gillam) actually made it into Hudson Strait, before being forced back by ice. This abortive attempt caught the attention of Colonel George Cartwright, a commissioner sent by Charles II to enlist support from the truculent New Englanders and extract taxes from the new colony. The colonel persuaded the two renegades to sail with him to England, planning to introduce them to his influential friend Sir George Carteret in the hope of enlisting royal support for exploration of what he visualized as a beaver-packed passage to the South Seas. Like nearly every other enterprise involving young Radisson, their transatlantic voyage turned out to be high adventure: the *Charles*, which was supposed to carry the party smartly back to England, was captured by Dutch privateers, and her passengers were unexpectedly put ashore in Spain, so that it took almost twice the usual time to reach London.

THE LONDON THAT RADISSON AND GROSEILLIERS EN-COUNTERED in the autumn of 1665 was a grotesque caricature of Dante's Inferno, devastated by the bubonic plague that had already carried off one-sixth of its half-million citizens.* Normal life had been disrupted by the horror of

---

*The plague was carried by lice and fleas which fed on rats, slowly killing them. As the rodents died, the insects fled the cooling bodies and transferred their attentions to humans, feeding on their blood and causing fatal infections. There was no immunity to the plague except escape, but according to street gossip, its effects could be ameliorated by catching a pox of almost equal ferocity, such as syphilis. The rumour was false, but that did not discourage a run on London's bawdy houses.

carts collecting the daily dead.

As Cartwright accompanied the visitors on the boat voyage up the Thames to Oxford, where the court had temporarily fled, they passed through a chilling landscape of lifeless streets and looted houses. There were smoke-wreathed barges anchored in mid-stream, crowded with families trying to avoid the pestilence. As their shallop passed under the arches of London Bridge, they were given perfumed handkerchiefs to cut the stench of putre-faction coming from the "plague pits" where victims were dumped. They could see the wild-eyed prophets of doom parading on the empty streets, with scrawled signs pro-claiming even more horror in the offing.* One lunatic, wearing only a loincloth and carrying a brazier of hot coals on his head, ran about Westminster shouting: "Oh, the great and dreadful God!"

The two woodrunners were about to meet a king of England who deftly balanced his roles as a debauched playboy and as an enlightened statesman. Charles II has deservedly been credited with resurrecting the Royal Navy and reviving English theatre and science. He not only restored the Crown but with his talented advisers moved England towards a constitutional monarchy without a revolution, yet he headed the most blasé court of voluptu-aries in Europe and was himself absorbed in endless hori-zontal rendezvous with his round of thirty-nine frisky

---

*They were right. Within a year, on September 2, 1666, a fire that started in the king's bakery shop in Pudding Lane engulfed London. It raged for five days, razing an estimated thirteen thousand wooden houses and eighty-eight churches. That catas-trophe was followed in 1667 by the humiliation of a Dutch fleet sneaking up the Thames, sailing to Chatham harbour and sink-ing half a dozen Royal Navy ships at their moorings, then towing the flagship, *Royal Charles*, back to Holland.

mistresses.* The Earl of Rochester, a notorious court wag of the period, summed up the king with the appropriate comment that he was a monarch "who never said a foolish thing, nor ever did a wise one" – to which Charles riposted: "My sayings are my own, but my actions are my ministers." Although he regularly attended Privy Council sessions and demonstrated a lively instinct for politics as the art of making the necessary possible, he had a remarkably small tolerance for ennui. He spent more time egging on the mischief of his courtiers than delving into serious affairs of state, depending on his natural charm and highly developed survival instinct to preserve the Stuart dynasty.

Charles's other ruling passion was money; he could never get enough. Although Parliament voted him an annual stipend of £1,200,000 and he received a dowry worth £800,000 when he married the pious Portuguese Infanta, Catherine of Braganza, his costs ran very high. He even returned Dunkirk to the French in exchange for £400,000

---

*When asked about this precise total of his amours, Charles replied that it reminded him of the 39 Articles of the Church of England. How he had time or energy to spare for governing after dealing with these devouring Restoration beauties is a mystery. Their portraits picture them as remarkably interchangeable, nearly all sharing the round faces, pouting mouths and flaxen curls so fashionable in those circles at the time. But at least two women stood out in the crowd. Barbara Villiers, Lady Castlemaine, a hot-tempered nymphomaniac who enjoyed royal favour longer than any of her rivals, had no hesitation in taking other lovers, among them Jacob the Rope Dancer, whose gymnastics inspired in her the urge to know "how he might be under his tumbling clothes." The other was Nell Gwyn, an actress with bouncy breasts and wit to match, who was not quite, according to Charles II's biographer Antonia Fraser, "the golden-hearted prostitute of popular imagination. Or rather, she may have had a heart of gold, but she also liked the stuff for its own sake." But Charles really loved her. When she died he

and finally accepted a secret £2,000,000 bribe from Louis
XIV. Not only did he have to provide for his mistresses
(who could not always be fobbed off with titles) but the
royal purse also had to absorb most of the cost of the
Royal Navy and the upkeep of Whitehall, then Europe's
most commodious palace.*

Charles II was the first English monarch to maintain
close personal connections with London's City financiers
and waged war against Holland mainly for commercial
reasons. Mercantile concerns became national interests,
and very much a part of that trend was the expansion of
English trade into the colonies of Africa, India and North
America. This was one reason Radisson and Groseilliers –
who brought with them a novel scheme for exploiting the
assets of the new continent across the Atlantic that did not
call for heavy financial outlays to establish large permanent
colonies – were guaranteed a receptive audience even before
the details of their plan were known. The other reason
their timing fitted in so well with the mood of the English
court was that, despite the plague and other distractions,

---

ordered that there never again be flowers in the park where
they walked together – and it is Green Park to this day. The
King publicly acknowledged fourteen children from these and
other liaisons, prompting the saying that he was truly the father
of his people.

*The compound was an agglomeration of galleries, courtyards,
gardens, public service buildings and regal dwellings sprawling
over twenty-three acres. (The Vatican at the time covered less
than fourteen, Versailles only seven.) One visiting diplomat
complained that of Whitehall's more than two thousand rooms,
not one was really cozy or comfortable. Its architecture, a jumble of Dutch brick, Tudor stone and Elizabethan half-timber,
was dominated by Inigo Jones's great Banqueting Hall with its
magnificent Rubens ceiling. Stretching half a mile along the
Thames and reaching to the present site of No. 10 Downing
Street, the original Whitehall, or most of it, burned in 1698.

King Charles II

the Restoration of Charles II had aroused in England's ruling circles a spirit of commercial innovation perfectly attuned to the impending exploitation of Hudson Bay.

The Restoration was the green end to England's hardest winter – a freeing of the spirit after a decade of Cromwellian suppression, when even amusements as innocent as maypoles were pulled down, theatres were closed and stained glass and stone church carvings sledgehammered. It was judged illegal to go walking on Sundays except to a religious service in one's own parish. Without a king, a proper Parliament or a functioning Church of England to channel or deflect popular emotions, the prevailing Puritanism became a source of bitterness rather than of enlightenment. The euphoria of the Restoration led to outbursts of creativity everywhere, among its main agents of change being Sir Christopher Wren (architecture), Grinling Gibbons (ornamental wood carving), Henry Purcell (music), Sir Isaac Newton (gravity), Edmund Halley (comets), William Congreve (theatre), Robert Boyle (chemistry) and Samuel Pepys (honest gossip). The most profound economic change that accompanied this renascence in science and the arts was the renewed emphasis on royal charters for overseas trading monopolies.

It was the confluence of these new attitudes, plus new technologies in shipbuilding, navigation and felting, that set the stage for the arrival of the two *coureurs de bois* at the English court.

At the time, the expanding fortunes and recently liberated energies of the land-owning class were being reflected in their search for private investment that would marry trade and profit. The East India Company, which was sending its thirty ships around the Cape on lucrative voyages of ten thousand miles, provided a sterling example of what might be achieved. The new Hudson Bay project, it was rumoured, would yield not only fabulous wealth in fur and copper but offer easy entry to the long-sought

North West Passage that would dramatically shorten the costly journeys to Cathay and the Spice Islands.

It is not clear whether it was Robert Boyle (then secretary of the Royal Society) or Sir George Carteret (the king's most trusted financial adviser) who actually introduced Radisson and Groseilliers to Charles II, and there is no record of their conversation among the dreaming spires of Oxford. But talk they did, on October 25, 1666, and from that exchange flowed the royal prerogatives that made the Company of Adventurers possible. Intrigued by glowing rhetoric about "the Bay of the North" and by Radisson's testimony that he had travelled a river that discharged "North West into the South Seas," into which they went and returned "North East into Hudson Bay," Charles II detected in the visitors' flowery description how a new pattern in fur trading might be developed for England's benefit. Peaceful Indians might be enticed to paddle their pelts down the many rivers to Hudson Bay, where they would be met by ships coming from the northern waters with goods to trade.

The immediate effect of the encounter was that Radisson and Groseilliers were granted royal protection and a weekly pension of forty shillings, and were placed in the care of a young banker named Sir Peter Colleton. The king began to discuss the idea of outfitting a royal ship for a voyage into Hudson Bay, and in the process, piqued the interest of the Duke of Cumberland, Earl of Holderness and Count Palatine of the Rhine – better known to history as Prince Rupert.

II ASSUMPTION OF EMPIRE

CHAPTER 5

A PRINCELY UNDERTAKING

"A soldier's life is a life of honour, but a dog would not lead it."

— *Rupert of the Rhine*

THE LAST OF THE CLASSIC KNIGHTS ERRANT, Prince Rupert of the Rhine buoyed the frail fortunes of the Hudson's Bay Company during the first dozen years of its existence, providing the royal patronage and the romantic impulse without which the tiny enterprise would have foundered.

A latter-day Renaissance man, the dark and handsome prince earned distinction as a cavalry leader, king's admiral, freebooting pirate, chemist, metallurgist, inventor, artist and entrepreneur. Rupert was accurately described by Lord Tweedsmuir, a former Governor General of Canada, as having had "one of the most varied careers that ever fell to the lot of man." Never popular in the raffish Restoration court because he was neither by birth nor inclination an Englishman and because his unquiet but disciplined spirit made his hedonist peers uncomfortable, the prince remains a puzzling historical figure, not as prominent or as widely understood as he deserves to be. Oliver Cromwell, who broke Rupert's cavalry at Marston Moor, dismissed him as a man who had his hands very deep in the blood of many innocent people and the Lord Protector's fellow Roundheads sanctimoniously condemned him as the most diabolical of the Cavaliers. Typical of the times was the lambasting by the anonymous 1644 pamphleteer who, after accusing the "Robber Prince" of every evil there was, demanded: "How many towns hast thou fired? How many virgins hast thou ruined? How many Godly ministers hast thou killed?"

Such denunciations bothered Rupert not one whit. Sensitive to his inner drives and passions but outwardly impervious to his legions of detractors, the Bohemian prince was a military genius who marched to his own drum corps. Preferring to be feared rather than loved, he was scornful of court intrigues and thus very often their victim. "A man of intense loyalties but few friends, proud, reserved and morose, uncompromising, unpolitical, undiplomatic, single-minded in his chosen craft of war, which he saw as a personal adventure, such was Prince Rupert of the Rhine," asserted British historian Hugh Trevor-Roper. "Though he lived long in England, he seems never to have understood it, or loved it, or its people: only his uncle, Charles I, and – to a lesser extent – his cousin Charles II who, on his Restoration, would reward his services with offices and revenues. For the rest, he lived to himself, in a private world, with his blackamoors and his poodles, his books, his laboratory and his instruments of art."

An incongruous pastiche of Galahad and Cyrano, the Bohemian prince enlisted his panache in the unpredictable causes of his cousins, the English Stuart kings, drawing his sword to defend the divine right of Charles I yet devoting himself equally to the preservation of Parliament under Charles II. Driven out of his father's adopted land when he was less than a year old and forced to flee his British uncle's kingdom a quarter-century later, Rupert spent more than half his life in exile, searching for familiar touchstones that might grant his restless soul the solace of hearth and home. Deprived of a natural sanctuary, he opted for a nomadic existence fighting for (or against) various armies and navies manned by the English, the French, the Dutch and the Italians. He was never a ruler, always the prince.

A streak of stubbornness was developed early in Rupert's character. One of his tutors recalled that the teenage prince, while out hunting with his dog, had chased a fox into its burrow and then become stuck. After considerable effort, the teacher succeeded in pulling out Rupert, dog and fox – all three still firmly attached to each other.

One of those rare warriors at home in the world of ideas, Rupert found no sequestered oasis away from the battle zones but took on the status-quo thinkers of his time with all the dramatic dash of his cavalry charges. "Because he was abreast of contemporary thought," noted biographer George Edinger, "he was ahead of contemporary opinion. He is perhaps the only leader of men, certainly the only royal prince, whose views advanced with his years. He began life, the champion of causes lately lost; and ended it, the protagonist of others yet to be won."

During the last decade and a half of his life, while actively pursuing the business of the Hudson's Bay Company, Rupert set up a laboratory and metal forge in his lodgings at Windsor Castle. His inventions and innovations add up to an impressive tally. He is credited with fashioning the first primitive torpedo, the forerunners of the modern revolver and machine gun, a new method of manufacturing hail-shot, a useful new alloy of copper and zinc still called "Prince's Metal," tear-shaped glass globules known as "Rupert's Drops" that led to the making of bulletproof glass, a new means of boring cannon to ensure truer aim, a naval quadrant that made it possible to take observations at sea in rough weather, and a "diving engine" successfully used to retrieve pieces-of-eight from the sunken Spanish treasure ship *Nuestra Señora de la Concepcion* off Hispaniola. In the autumn of 1667, faced by a brain operation to ease his agonizing migraines, the prince put his ingenuity to work designing and forging the surgical instruments used to relieve the pain under his periwig.

In his alternate incarnation of artist, Rupert worked out a new means of drawing buildings in perspective and a technique for painting on marble; his best-known marble "canvas" is an erotic depiction on the theme of *The Woman Taken in Adultery*. His main artistic coup involved importing into England the art of mezzotint, a method of engraving on copper achieved by scraping away parts of the roughened surface, first taught him by the German artist Ludwig von Siegen. Rupert's prints and etchings reveal a fine hand, and according to P.H. Hulton, Assistant Keeper of Prints at the British Museum, his mezzotints are among the finest ever produced.

Considered the scientific equal of Sir Isaac Newton or Sir Christopher Wren and a founding Fellow of the Royal Society, Rupert took his experiments so seriously that he became the butt of royal jests. Charles II and the Duke of Buckingham would often pay surprise visits to his laboratories to torment the prince, his soot-covered face knotted in concentration as he bent over his fire with vials and beakers. To rid himself of these and less majestic intruders, Rupert kept handy a supply of sulphur powder to throw into his forge-fire; the resultant cloud of noxious fumes drove out the curious interlopers, and the king vowed never again to enter that "alchemist's hell."

GENEALOGISTS HAVE TRACED RUPERT'S LINEAGE back to Attila, Charlemagne and William the Silent, one of the "Sea Beggars" who founded the Netherlands. His father was Frederick V, Elector Palatine, one of the seven German rulers entitled to choose the Holy Roman Emperor; his mother was Elizabeth, the daughter of James I of England and VI of Scotland. Responding to the call of the Protestant nobles of Bohemia (later part of Czechoslovakia), the young couple became the little kingdom's monarchs in 1619, and only six weeks after their coronation, Elizabeth gave birth to a son. The first royal prince to be born in Bohemia for more than a century, he was swaddled in Cambrai lace and rocked in a cradle of ivory filigreed with gold. The young prince was named Ruprecht von Wittelsbach, and the christening was a grand state occasion. The Russian ambassador presented the Bohemian crown with fifty carriages, each bearing gifts of red leather chests brimming with valuable furs, while the homage of other plenipotentiaries was borne in coaches drawn by trained polar bears and tame black stags. The arrival of each well-wisher was heralded by flourishes of trumpets and kettledrums, harmonizing with the peal of bells from the Lower Town. The court attracted Moravian hawkboys, young nobles who carried birds of prey in upraised salutes as a symbol of the kingdom's new vitality, their aristocratic gaze translated onto canvas by the great Czech painter Wenceslas Brožik.

Despite the seamless joy of the celebrations, local Jesuits, loyal to Rome and aware of the political momentum gathering outside Bohemia's borders, coined a disquieting title for Rupert's father, referring to him as "The Winter King" who would vanish as surely as the snow. The Jesuits were secretly in league with the Habsburg emperor in Vienna who was plotting to bind his Bohemian subjects closer to his crown.

The Bohemians and Austrians clashed that autumn along the White Mountains stretching behind Hradčany Castle, and the Habsburg mercenaries overwhelmed the brave defenders in an hour. While loyal Moravian Calvinists and the Palatine royal guard fought a courageous rearguard action on the castle grounds, a quick-witted chamberlain remembered the baby Rupert and hid him in the last of the royal carriages clanking and lurching across the Charles Bridge. And so the dream of Bohemian independence had been crushed – not for the last time – only three days before a blizzard that might have bogged down the Austrian invaders. The savage Thirty Years' War that followed reduced a generation of Central Europeans to terror as hired gangs of pikemen, indiscriminately waving crosses and swords, committed the most brutish slaughters, all in the name of a distant god.

Rupert and his fleeing parents found temporary refuge with the queen's brother-in-law, the mean-spirited Elector George of Brandenburg, who reluctantly permitted the exiles to occupy an empty castle at Kustrin. Three years later, the family found refuge in Amsterdam, where Rupert was first officially recognized by England when he was granted a royal "pension" of £300 by his uncle, Charles I. The youngster studied at the University of Leyden, specializing in mathematics, military architecture and draughting. He spent much of his spare time in rough canvas clothes haunting the Dutch docks and taverns where sailors congregated at big oak tables, smoking their clay churchwardens and spinning yarns about palmy faraway landfalls.

The *émigré* family threw itself on the fiscal mercies of its royal relatives, and in 1636 Rupert and his brother Carl Louis were invited to visit London. Even at sixteen, Rupert impressed the English court with his sense of adventure and strength of character. Much fuss was made over the handsome young hotspur, and he was even offered the chance to lead an expedition to Madagascar, off Africa's east coast, with the promise that he could be king of the island should he succeed in conquering it. That quixotic notion was vetoed by his mother, and he reluctantly returned to Holland, where he joined the Life Guards of that enlightened military strategist, the Prince of Orange. Dispatched under Swedish patronage to besiege the Austrians at Vlotho in Westphalia, Rupert was captured and spent the next three years imprisoned in the brooding

Danube fortress of Linz.

Here the Rupert saga slips into steamy soap opera. The prison's governor, Count von Kuefstein, had a dark-eyed daughter named Susanne who was asked to minister to the prisoner, and she promptly fell in love with him. Their mutual crush quickly spun into an intense but short-lived romance, consummated in Rupert's non-monastic cell above the rolling Danube. Alas! The young prince was ransomed by his uncle and recalled to England to help fend off the king's enemies, but he never forgot his sweet sojourn in Linz.

It was in prison that Rupert also acquired the first of his many pets, a dog he referred to as "my rare bitch Puddle" and a tame hare that could open the prince's interior cell door with its snout at his bidding.

WHEN CHARLES I RAISED HIS STANDARD at Nottingham in 1642, he vowed that he would return to London on his own terms and named the twenty-two-year-old Bohemian prince his General of Horse, with a command independent of the other royal military and political advisers. The young warrior became a master of the lightning cavalry charge, coaching his men to hold their fire until the most propitious instant. He drove back the Parliamentary forces at every encounter, briskly capturing Bristol, England's second-largest city, raising arms and money, enforcing his military priorities and extending his influence in every direction. A grateful Charles soon appointed him his commander-in-chief. An extraordinary marksman (on one occasion he hit the weathercock on the church steeple at Stratford with one musket shot) Rupert pioneered many of the tactics of modern-day guerrilla fighting, living off the land and striking at the most unexpected moments. He was particularly known for his unorthodox manner of obtaining first-hand intelligence about his enemy's strength and intentions.

Just before the battle of Warwick he disguised himself as a cabbage vendor and drove a cart into the town to examine the fortifications and troop deployments.

Mounting court intrigue and Rupert's own insensitivity to the political dimensions of the situation in which he found himself gradually undermined his prestige and authority. As the war's most audacious and most successful commander, he attracted the blame for its savagery, and like most other military potentates blinded by the hubris of too many easy victories, he eventually overstepped himself. Rupert had rashly promised Charles he could hold Bristol against any odds, but once typhus started and an outlying fortress was captured, he pronounced the city indefensible and surrendered in four days. "I have no stomach for sieges," the chastened cavalry commander confessed in a rare display of introspection into both his tactics and personality, when he was reprimanded by the king.

Prince Rupert was to serve the Stuart family's cause with undiminished loyalty for another thirty-six years, first as commander of the royal fleet during the Second Civil War, and later as a blue water pilot gathering spoils for the court of the exiled Charles II in daring raids across the Mediterranean and Caribbean seas. Recalled to England at the time of the Restoration by a grateful king, Rupert was granted an annual pension of £2,000, appointed to the Privy Council, named Admiral of the Fleet and for six years held the important portfolio of First Lord of the Admiralty. He fought the Dutch in three minor wars and helped restore discipline to the Royal Navy – in one instance by throwing two mutineers over the side of his flagship with his own hands. He was tolerant of drinking at sea as long as it inflamed rather than dulled the fighting spirit, and when there were complaints about excessive liquor consumption, he scoffed at the charges, replying with the memorable riposte: "God damme, if they will turn out every man that will be drunk, they must turn out all the commanders in the fleet."

STILL IN HIS EARLY FORTIES, Rupert appeared an out-moded figure to the City and within the Restoration court, an all too visible reminder of wars best forgotten, an embarrassment to a society trying to compromise its recent past. The martial magic was gone, and the garlands of war that trailed his name had been won against too many of his current compatriots. There was a tragic tinge to his demeanour. Here was a man who had validated both his physical courage and his social prestige, yet he had always been a prince without a principality, a grandee of empire without a hectare to call his own.

Although something of a recluse, Rupert did join the royal court in the giddy frolics at the summer resort of Tunbridge Wells. There he met and wooed Margaret Hughes, a spirited and beautiful actress who had commenced her career with the opening of the Drury Lane Theatre in 1663. He eventually purchased for her a magnificent country seat near Hammersmith and had a daughter (appropriately named Ruperta) by her, but they never married. He had also formed a passionate liaison in his Continental days with Francesca Bard, daughter of an Irish peer, and had a son by her named Dudley, but neither in that case had a wedding followed.*

---

* The only scandal caused by Rupert's social life was the dispute that arose at court as to whether his mistress, Peg Hughes, was more beautiful than the king's favourite, Nell Gwyn. When one of Peg's brothers, who was in Rupert's service, took his sister's side in the dispute, he was killed in a duel by a champion of the king. Rupert's sister, the Duchess Sophia, noted that the Danish ambassador had thought the actress Hughes to be very modest, adding in her caustic way: "I was going to say the most modest of the court, but that would be no great praise."

After these infatuations had exhausted themselves, Rupert settled permanently into moody bachelorhood as Governor of Windsor Castle. He concentrated on his art and scientific experiments, but an inadequate personal income and his dreams of empire found him devoting more time and energy to the prospect of overseas trade. Fur-pelt was becoming a strategic staple because its water-resistant qualities were valuable to soldiers trying to keep their powder dry.

The rise of the Dutch commercial empire, based on maritime security and the attendant decline of the Hanseatic League in the Baltic, had driven up fur prices, forcing England to look elsewhere not only for cheaper pelts but also for a more secure and controllable supply of vital timber, copper and cordage for the Royal Navy.

Rupert's meetings at his Windsor apartments with Radisson and Groseilliers ignited his determination to wrest the lucrative North American fur trade from the French. Closely questioning the renegade traders from New France about Indian reports of gold and copper, Rupert (then also Governor of the Mines Royal) was excited by the prospect that the back country beyond Hudson Bay might yield not only fur but as much mineral wealth to the Stuart dynasty as the mines of Mexico and Peru had produced for the kings of Spain. He took the visitors at their word, listening with rapt attention as Radisson described the fur harvest and the copper outcrops he had seen north of Lake Superior, and set about organizing a private syndicate to finance an exploratory journey to Hudson Bay.

The original ledgers have been lost, but the earliest subscribers are known to have included at least half a dozen of the Adventurers who later congealed as the Hudson's Bay Company. Using cash advanced by Charles's banker, Sir Robert Vyner, Customs Commissioner Francis Millington and Admiralty Paymaster John Fenn, Rupert's group envisioned a voyage to North America in the spring of 1667, but the first vessel lent to the expedition proved inadequate, and the journey was postponed for a season. "The full complement of original investors," according to Fulmer Mood, a University of California historian, "grew in almost organic fashion from a rudimentary nucleus into a financial entity that was, in social, political and religious composition, and functions, fairly complex … The process is not unlike that which happens when a crystal, in suitably prepared mother liquid, grows from a small to a great size by progressive accretions."

The syndicate had been recruited by Rupert, but it was his personal secretary, Sir James Hayes, who fleshed out the details. The prince had persuaded Charles to lease the associates a two-masted ketch, the *Eaglet*, for a nominal £6 2s.6d. The even smaller forty-five-ton *Nonsuch** was purchased for £290 from Sir William Warren, a wealthy London timber merchant who had repossessed the vessel

---

*Royal Navy records list the *Nonsuch* as having had a beam of fifteen feet, a draft of six feet six inches and an overall deck length of fifty-three feet. This would be about half the size of the *Mayflower* (1620) and slightly shorter than the sixteen-oared knoors used by the Vikings. In modern terms, the *Nonsuch* was not as long as the twelve-metre sloops in the America's Cup races. A *Nonsuch* replica, built by the HBC to celebrate the Company's three hundredth anniversary in 1970, was authentic enough except for a 90-h.p. diesel engine and some electronic equipment. After sailing around the United Kingdom, the vessel was loaded on a merchant ship at Bristol for the Atlantic crossing. She toured twenty-eight ports along the St Lawrence and the Great Lakes as well as the waters of Puget Sound and the coast of British Columbia. A truck then took her to a permanent concrete berth at the Manitoba Museum of Man and Nature in Winnipeg, moored to a re-creation of London's Deptford docks.

from the Royal Navy the previous autumn.*

By May 1668 the ships had been outfitted; grocers, chandlers, sailmakers, ropemakers, vintners, butchers, haberdashers, timber merchants and ironmongers furnished the *Eaglet* and *Nonsuch* as floating department stores. Into the little ships were stowed hundreds of items, including hatchets, spears, scrapers, muskets, blunderbusses, pistols, gunpowder, eighteen barrels of shot, paper, quills, ink, thirty-seven pounds of tobacco, compasses, flags, lanterns, ropes, pitch, tar, axes, saws, hammers, anchors; "shirts, socks and mittens and other slopsellers' wares"; four dozen pairs of shoes; malt for ship's beer, eight gallons of lemon

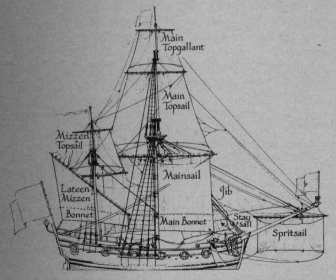

*The original *Nonsuch* had been built as a merchant vessel at Wivenhoe, Essex in 1650. It was purchased by the Royal Navy four years later, captured by the Dutch and eventually recaptured by the English.

juice to ward off scurvy, five thousand needles; food such as biscuits, raisins, prunes, peas, oatmeal, salt beef and pork; wines and brandy; fifty-six pounds of cork; and a trumpet. Both vessels also carried necklaces of wampum, the standard currency of the Indian trade, consisting of small shell beads that had been brought to England by Groseilliers. Radisson was instructed by the associates to sail on the *Eaglet* with Captain William Stannard and to winter on Hudson Bay; Groseilliers, aboard the *Nonsuch* with their old shipmate Captain Zachariah Gillam, was to bring home the pelts from the first summer's trade and return again with provisions. The captains were enjoined to treat the Frenchmen "with all manner of civility and courtesy, they being the persons upon whose credit we have undertaken this expedition." The sailing instructions, drafted by Rupert's secretary, Sir James Hayes, covered every contingency: "We do also declare that if by accident you meete with any Sea Horse or Mors teeth [narwhal horn] … it is to be made good to our account." As the expedition's British commanders, the captains were ordered to build fortifications, trade cautiously, hunt whales, prospect for minerals and, as an afterthought, to remember "the discovery of the passage into the South Sea, and attempt it as occasion shall offer." The *Nonsuch* also carried a French surgeon named Pierre Romieux* and a crew of eight.

After a farewell banquet in his Spring Gardens home, Rupert and the syndicate members were rowed down the Thames to see the ships off at Gravesend. On the misty morning ebb-tide of June 3, 1668, the *Eaglet* and *Nonsuch* were piloted out of the river by Isaac Marychurch for a fee of £5. By evening they had reached the open sea and turned north in a fresh breeze; ten days later they rounded the Orkneys and headed due west

---

*He is referred to in the ship's roster as Peter Romulus, while Chouart Sieur Des Groseilliers is reduced to Mr Groselyer.

towards the New World. Four hundred leagues off Ireland, they were struck by a storm that nearly broached the low-waisted *Eaglet*, forcing her to turn back.

Six weeks later, Gillam sighted the coast of Labrador and turned north, navigating the *Nonsuch* skilfully under clouds of seabirds over the "furious overfall" into Hudson Strait. The tiny ketch sailed past the Belchers and found refuge in the same river mouth where Henry Hudson had wintered more than half a century before. It was promptly named Rupert River, after the expedition's Royal sponsor. The crew chopped down scores of spruce trees and cleared a site; the *Nonsuch*, its keel grating on the gravel of the river bed, was hauled up and careened on the river bank; a stockade and house were built of vertical logs chinked with moss and a roof fashioned from local thatch. A twelve-foot-deep cellar was dug below the frost line to store the beer, pike were gill-netted in the river and hundreds of geese and ptarmigan were killed and hung for the winter.

The long season that followed was cold and monotonous, but Groseilliers had experienced far worse, and his bush-honed talents, as well as the shipmaster skills of Gillam, made their survival more pleasant and possible. The men developed only a touch of scurvy of the gums, helped along by Groseilliers's bitter-tasting concoctions of spruce beer and by the lemon juice brought along on the voyage. That spring nearly three hundred James Bay Indians came to trade. Advised by Groseilliers, Gillam made a "League of Friendship" with the chief and "formally purchased" the land. Although there was some pilfering from the stockade and the ship, the British muskets, hatchets, scrapers, needles and trinkets were easily and profitably traded for valuable prime-coat beaver – that is, fur the Indians had worn so that the guard hairs were loosened and the inner down could be combed out more easily for feltmaking. "This visit," historians Toby Morantz and Daniel Francis noted in *Partners in Furs*, "was different from earlier ones. Now the white man came, not in search of a passage to China, but rather intent on establishing trading settlements, claiming ownership of the land and bartering for furs. The James Bay Indians accepted the newcomers, not because they were naive or helpless, but because the Europeans brought rare and useful items to trade for the most common of New World commodities, furs."

On June 14, 1669, pursued by millions of ravenous mosquitoes, the crew of the *Nonsuch* fled Rupert River. Gillam sailed quickly north, but ice at the top of the bay slowed his passage and it was not until mid-August that he reached open water. Two uneventful months later, the *Nonsuch* cast anchor back in the Thames, and Groseilliers, glad to find Radisson still alive, welcomed his partner warmly.

The return of the fur-loaded little ketch caused minimal stir; its cargo, bartered for goods originally purchased for £650, brought £1,379 on the London fur market, and the ship was resold for £152. Wages of £535 plus the required startup investments, customs duties, the damage to the *Eaglet* and other expenses had failed to make the voyage profitable. But the backers were pleased. The thesis that Radisson and Groseilliers had been expounding for more than a decade had been proved correct: it was entirely practicable to sail into Hudson Bay, winter on its shores and return with a profitable cargo of fur.

Rupert led the delighted backers in obtaining from Charles II the loan of another, larger ship, the pink* *Wivenhoe*, and commissioned construction of a seventy-five-ton frigate especially for the new trade, christened the *Prince Rupert*. To promote further shareholding in the Company, the early Adventurers paid out £34 for hats made from some of the hundred pounds of best Hudson Bay beaver fur kept back from sale, both as trophies for

---

*A pink is a flat-bottomed, narrow-sterned three-master with a triangular sail as mizzen.

themselves and as gifts for prominent patrons and suppliers who might be interested in financing the Company.

At the age of fifty-one the Bohemian soldier-scientist was becoming such a hero to London commerce that a few months after the return of the *Nonsuch* Rupert was invited to lay the cornerstone of London's new Royal Exchange. The stage was now set to exploit the commercial opening pioneered by the *Nonsuch* voyages. What the Adventurers trading into Hudson Bay really wanted was a royally approved monopoly over the kingdom of fur they had so daringly discovered.

ON FRIDAY, MAY 2, 1670 IN WHITEHALL PALACE, they got their wish. Charles II awarded Rupert and his fellow Adventurers a charter as "true lords and proprietors" of all the sea and lands of Hudson Bay and its entire drainage system.

By any standard, the royal declaration in favour of his cousin that established history's oldest continuing capitalist company was an extraordinary document.* The HBC charter was one of the most generous gifts ever presented by a monarch to his subjects, but its benefits are more visible in retrospect than they were at the time.

It was a fairly routine (and inexpensive) grant for the king to bestow. Its purposes fitted in precisely with the

---

*The claim that the Hudson's Bay Company is the world's oldest continuing commercial enterprise requires some qualification. Several business partnerships, such as the Lowenbrau brewery in Munich (1383), the Banco di Napoli (1539) and Joseph Travers & Sons Ltd. in Singapore (1666) are older, but they have not maintained an unbroken operation under the same name or form of organization. The only real rival for the claim is the Swedish concern Stora Kopparberg, established in 1288 – but it altered its business from copper mining to iron manufacturing, the development of water power and making chemicals. Probably the first recorded example of joint stock company (in that it

objectives of the English mercantilism of the day: to direct trade policies in a way that would allow private investors to minimize their risks and maximize their profits. They, and not the state, would bear the costs of developing markets for British goods in barely accessible colonies with inhospitable climates and independently minded natives. Similar gifts had been granted to slave traders and gold hunters of West Africa, and only two years earlier Charles II had transferred the Indian island of Bombay (part of the dowry received when he married Catherine of Braganza) to the East India Company for an annual rental of £10.

What made Charles II hesitate for most of a year before actually approving the document requested by Rupert and his impatient associates was the possible effect this particular grant might have on his friendship with Louis XIV of France, who was not only an ally but was also the provider of the pension that allowed the English sovereign to act independently of Parliament. Charles had recently bound himself to the French court by the Treaty of Breda, which returned most of the Cromwellian conquests in America to France. Apart from the northward claims of New France, Louis XIV had himself, on April 27, 1670, granted a charter over roughly the same territory as Rupert's to an obscure Dutch mariner, Jan Van Heemskerk. That claim was based on the exploits of the captain's great-

---

existed as an independent business unit apart from its owners), Stora Kopparberg issued negotiable share certificates in 1888; its 1,200 medieval lots in the Great Copper Mountain were exchanged for stock certificates worth 1,000 Swedish crowns each. The first printed share certificates were issued by the Dutch East India Company in 1606. The HBC was a joint-stock company, which meant that transfer by investors had to be made in the Company's London office where a ledger was kept of the proprietors and their claims. Printed share certificates were not issued until 1863.

uncle, a confused navigator claiming to have made "a voyage for Holland to the East Indies, entering by way of Formosa in the South Sea and departing to the north of California, reaching Holland by way of Hudson Bay."*

Royal assent was finally granted on the second day of May, partly because Rupert could justifiably claim that this was the only reward he had requested from Stuart monarchs despite his life-long dedication to their cause. Another reason, not sufficiently documented, may be that the king was promised a monetary reward for signing the Hudson's Bay Company charter.†

The contents of the HBC charter itself, at least as far as its provisions for a monopoly were concerned, differed hardly at all from those of many similar royal grants.‡ Because capital gains from overseas voyages were at best uncertain and investments had to be secured over the often lengthy period between the launching of an enterprise and its payoff, it was not unusual for merchants of the day to demand monopolistic protection for their ventures so that potential rivals and interlopers could be kept

---

*Van Heemskerk sailed from Brest with three vessels on August 14, 1670, determined to copy his great-uncle's remarkable geographical manoeuvre in reverse. His quandary was resolved when the little fleet sank during a storm in the Bay of Biscay.

†In her authoritative *Conquest of the Great North-west*, Agnes C. Laut quotes a Company minute to the effect that in 1684, Sir James Hayes, then Deputy Governor of the HBC, was ordered to present Charles II "his dividend in gold in a faire embroidered purse."

‡Other, earlier enterprises that received similar sanctions included the East India Company, chartered by Elizabeth I on Dec. 31, 1600; the Dutch East India Company (1602); the Danish East India Company (1634); and the French East India Company (1664). None survived past 1858. Scores of smaller enterprises were chartered to exploit the Antilles, Bermuda, Senegal, the West Indies, Cape Verde and Virginia.

away. "The granting of such wide territory and such rich resources was no mere favouritism," Arthur S. Morton noted in his *History of the Canadian West*. "It carried with it the obligation first of all to put out the private capital to make the natural resources available, and then to use these to establish settlements and to govern the colony."

Apart from its leathery durability, what set the HBC charter apart from similar documents was the formidable dimension of the estate it unknowingly granted. By setting the geographical limits of the territory at the sources of the streams that drain into Hudson Bay, the grant enclosed a virtual subcontinent of 1.5 million square miles, its eastern boundary extending back to the height of land in the unexplored reaches of Labrador, its southern extremities stretching along a huge territory just above the headwaters of the St Lawrence's many tributaries. Then it swept into the Red River Valley, south past the 49th parallel, vaulting west to the very peaks of the Rocky Mountain divide. Only the wild lands around the great streams gushing northward (the Coppermine and the Mackenzie), the rivers flowing westward into the Pacific (the Columbia, the Fraser, the Skeena, the Yukon and the Milk River basin draining to the Missouri) were excluded.

Named Rupert's Land, this huge freehold was the equivalent of nearly 40 percent of modern Canada: all of northern Ontario and Quebec; all of Manitoba; southern Saskatchewan and Alberta; a huge chunk of the eastern portion of the Northwest Territories; plus much of the American states of Minnesota and North Dakota. Even these gargantuan boundaries did not entirely accommodate the limits set out in the document. Because it was open-ended in defining the outer limits of the Company's trade, the charter in effect granted a monopoly over trade originating anywhere west of Hudson Bay, so that if the North West Passage had actually existed where navigators

of that day thought it did, the HBC would have possessed control of trade rights, based on discovery, all the way to the shores of Cathay.*

The commercially minded Adventurers had no intention of disturbing their monopoly by sponsoring the discovery of a North West Passage. But the charter's preamble did praise "Our Deare and entirely Beloved cousin Prince Rupert" and his associates, who had "at theire owne great cost and charge undertaken an expedicion for Hudsons Bay in the North west part of America for the discovery of a new Passage into the South Sea and for the finding of some Trade for Furrs Mineralls and other considerable Commodityes and by such theire undertakeing have already made such discoveryes as doe encourage them to proceed further in pursuance of theire said designe by meanes whereof there may probably arise very great advantage to us and our Kingdome."

Nor was the document particularly clear on how strenuous an effort at colonization was required of its recipients. The HBC staunchly resisted admitting anyone other than its own traders into Rupert's Land for another 142 years – the first real settlers being the ragged band of Red River immigrants brought by Lord Selkirk in 1812 – but in any case there were no sanctions applied or available to spur the Company to create a more hospitable haven.†

Unlike some of the joint-stock charters of the time, the HBC grant makes no mention of any religious obligations,

---

*No explorer from the east found his way across the continent until Alexander Mackenzie did it in 1793. Because he was in the employ of the North West Company at the time, he carefully noted that he had come "from *Canada* [not Hudson Bay] by land."

†This was partly a matter of climate. Alternative destinations for would-be colonists were available in the Carolinas, Bermuda, Antigua and Barbados. At the same time, British policy was

although a set of accompanying instructions drawn up by Charles II's Colonial Office did contain this injunction: "You are to consider how the Indians and slaves may be best instructed in and united to the Christian religion; it being both for the honour of the Crown and of the Protestant religion itself, that all persons within any of our territories, though never so remote, should be taught the knowledge of God, and be made acquainted with the mysteries of salvation."

But again, there was no enforcing clause accompanying this mandate, and except for one chaplain sent out for a three-year stint in 1683 and another one-season experiment in 1693, the notion of spreading Christianity to the natives or anyone else remained a dead letter. From the very outset, the whole business of the Company was business, not the dissemination of the British way of life or the proclamation of the gospel of Christ.

Quite apart from Charles II's cavalier dismissal of French claims in granting the Charter, the English monarch omitted any reference to the well-established occupancy of the Indian inhabitants. The only proviso was that the Company not make war against another Christian monarch without his permission and that territory claimed by any other Christian Prince be excluded from the grant. Although the document clearly recognized that the fur trade depended on the continuing presence of the indigenous peoples, no attempt was made to draw them into any

---

directed to preventing Newfoundland from having a settled population until well into the nineteenth century. To ensure sufficient naval personnel, the West Country fishermen were required to return to England after each season. Even Newfoundland, which had a settled population, was refused the status of a colony partly because of the rigours of its weather and the infertility of its soil. The Commissioners for Trade and Plantations ruled in 1675 that "all inhabiting in that country must be discouraged."

"league of friendship" as informal treaties were then known. The HBC was, in effect, being handed a vast hunting preserve, to dispose of and exploit at will.

Certainly, the price exacted by the Charter for these considerable privileges amounted to a bit of Restoration hokum. In return for his splendid gift, Charles II required the Company merely to yield and pay two elks and two black beavers "whensoever and as often as wee our heires and successors shall happen to enter into the said Countryes Territoryes and Regions hereby granted."* This bizarre bit of bounty was actually paid only four times. The royal rent ceremony was first performed in 1927 when the Prince of Wales (the future Edward VIII) visited his ranch in Alberta; the second time in 1939 for George VI; the third time in 1959 for Queen Elizabeth II; and the last time in 1970 for the Queen and Prince Philip. The 1970 ceremony was unique in that live black beavers were presented for the first (and last) time.†

---

*The ceremonial fee amounted to a puckish codicil by Charles II. But ever conscious of its precious charter, the HBC took its "rent" payment deadly seriously. "We kept stuffed elk's heads and beaver pelts in most of our western stores, just in case the Queen should put down somewhere, because the continuation of our Charter depended on making the presentation," Sir Eric Faulkner, former Deputy Governor of the HBC, recalled in 1981. "In case she put down in Saskatoon or Winnipeg, somebody was always ready to rush out and present the items to her, otherwise our Charter was forfeit and enemies of the Company would damn well see that it *was* forfeited. So my recollection is that there were some rather moth-eaten pelts in some of the stores. But this only applied to Rupert's Land. She could slip into Toronto or Vancouver and that was all right. It was only if she set foot in what was formerly Rupert's Land that we were in trouble."

†The ceremony, held on the rainy afternoon of July 14, 1970, on a dais outside Lower Fort Garry near Winnipeg, was unique in

Despite the inclusion of subsequently discovered weak spots, the charter had been drafted with a great deal of thought and attention to legal tradition, and even though the circumstances surrounding its land grant changed drastically, the validity of the document was never successfully challenged.* This was a remarkable achievement in view of the fact that the authority bestowed on the Company was almost feudal in its prerogatives. No British subject (much less anyone else) was allowed to trade within the Company's territory, and if that regulation was violated, all the goods of the trespasser would be confiscated, with half going to the king and half to the Company. The HBC had the absolute right to administer law and to judge all cases, civil or criminal, on the spot. It was empowered to employ its own armies and navies, erect forts and generally defend its fiefdom in any way it chose.

The original Adventurers who came to possess this remarkable document certainly had no doubt about its worth. The five sheepskin parchment sheets bearing its seven thousand words of text were locked away in an iron-bound chest kept in Rupert's apartments at Windsor

---

another respect. The animals were feeling particularly perky in their presentation tank that day, and just as the Queen bent over to accept the symbolic rent, the beavers, not versed in court etiquette, released their tensions by first having a tussle and then by making love. "Whatever are they doing?" Her Majesty demanded of Lord Amory, the HBC governor, who was presiding over the ceremony. "Ma'am, it's no good asking me," intoned the Governor, peering down at his coupling charges with undisguised disgust. "I am a bachelor." The Queen assumed her customary mid-distance gaze and murmured, "I *quite* understand."

*Between 1690, when the privileges were confirmed by Act of Parliament, and 1870, when the Company gave up its monopoly, the Charter was formally recognized in five major international treaties and at least nine Commons bills at Westminster.

Castle.* In the context of its time, the HBC charter's provisions conformed to the purposes of both its sponsors and its recipients. But even at its granting it was an important document, easily ranking, as Canadian historian Barry M. Gough has observed, with "the passing of the Navigation Act of 1660, the establishment of Carolina, the capture of New York, the acquisition of Bombay and Tangier, the attempt to create a Dominion in New England, the reorganization of the East India Company, and the founding of the Guinea Company. With the establishment of this Company to engage in the fur trade of Hudson Bay, the interests of the two parties were united – that of the adventurers for profit and that of the government for the development of trade, which in mercantilist terms was seen as an expedient of strategic expansion to check the French in North America. And along with this, England had opportunities for Arctic discovery and scientific inquiry."

PRINCE RUPERT HAS BEEN ACCORDED most of the credit for founding the Hudson's Bay Company. In fact, he directly subscribed to less than 3 percent (£270) of its founding capital, and although he certainly ranked as the Company's chief sponsor, his co-adventurers were a distinguished and potent coalition of dukes, earls, baronets and knights of the realm, joined by some of the most influential of the whiggish merchant princes then beginning to dominate the City of London's blossoming financial district.

---

*The original charter, under glass and kept at a constant temperature, is now stored in the HBC's Toronto boardroom. For its full text, see Appendix One.

The original shareholders were promoters and imperialists in the grand style. "Profit and power ought jointly to be considered," mused Sir Josiah Child, the exalted Governor of the East India Company, to his bustling City cohorts. The post-Restoration investment climate could not have been more welcoming. The HBC took shape just as more and more members of the landed gentry turned their attention to investments abroad and much of Whitehall's hierarchy of courtiers devoted their energies to lobbying for royal charters that could be exploited by floating joint-stock companies. These new corporate innovations were designed to spread the risk through absorption of the suddenly available venture capital. The first exchange, dedicated to dealing solely in the marketing of joint-stock investments, had opened in Amsterdam during the 1602 rush to raise the six million guilders required by the Dutch East India Company, whose grandiose new charter encompassed half the earth's surface: the trade and navigation east of the Cape of Good Hope and west of the Strait of Magellan.*

The Bank of Sweden was about to be established but England did not officially follow suit for another twenty

---

*The exchange got off to a roaring start with traders gathering on the New Bridge, in front of the future site of the Central Station. The market received a boost when shares were issued for the Dutch *West* India Company, which may have been the only stock market issue ever floated to admit openly that its business was piracy. Within a surprisingly short time of its opening, the Amsterdam Exchange adopted most of the fast-money techniques that continue to characterize its modern counterparts: put-and-call options, short and long purchases, fractional share deals and so on. Joseph de la Vega, who wrote history's first market tip sheet, complained that the stock market was "a touchstone for the intelligent and a tombstone for the audacious."

years.* It was during the Restoration that state debtors and private financial creditors began to recognize some common concerns, so that not only Prince Rupert but also Charles II and his brother James, Duke of York, became focal points for City investment decisions in both the public and purely commercial spheres.

In its royal genesis, the HBC was an instrument of foreign trade policy – one side of the imperial coin, the East India Company being the other. The hope was to outmanoeuvre the French, busy exploiting the empire of the St Lawrence, by squeezing them between British-backed fur-trading ventures moving north from the Duke of York's fiefdom on the Hudson River and south from Hudson Bay. The intent was also to command the market in fur, a luxury prized in the Baltic in Russia, then such a strategic source of naval supplies. The confidence with which the original Adventurers risked their means was based on the assurances of royal support they received through their fellow shareholders Lords Arlington and Ashley, then members of the influential Cabal that maintained Charles II in power. No fewer than six of the original HBC investors sat on the King's Privy Council. They, and Prince Rupert's own personal access to royal attention, made it very clear that the HBC could depend on the monarch's support. Quite apart from his territorial ambitions overseas, Charles was more than a little anxious to create additional revenues for himself beyond the reach of Parliament. He had

---

*The Bank of England's formation in 1694 followed the loan of £1.2 million to King William III by a group of City merchants in return for a bank note monopoly and the right to accept deposits. They began to finance governments through bond issues, thus creating a permanent national debt that grew to £800 million by 1815.

already contrived to extract a duty of 4.5 percent from the reluctant plantation owners of the West Indies and no doubt regarded the favourable prospects of the Hudson's Bay Company as one eventual source to finance his extravagances.

Risks were minimized by keeping the initial capitalization low, £10,500 compared with £100,000 for the lavish Royal African Company. The dozen-and-a-half original investors all knew one another through common interests. Most of them had shared investments before, mainly in spearheading the Carolina colony or Barbados plantations, or in providing capital for the Royal African, the Levant and Royal Fisheries companies. Nearly all of them had been staunch Royalists during the Civil War, and eight were founding members of the recently chartered Royal Society of London for Improving Natural Knowledge.

Stuart expansionists all, with a healthy entrepreneurial greed, they shared the vision that pelts taken from the new continent's beavers – animals they had never actually seen and could hardly describe – would make them rich while at the same time advancing the cause of English economic influence.*

THE ORIGINAL ADVENTURERS appointed seven Committeemen, who gathered once a week to consider the Company's slowly expanding affairs either at Rupert's lodgings in Spring Gardens or in the Chamber of the King's Wardrobe, a sort of bursar's office by the Whitehall Palace gates. The domestic operation of the royal household was being managed by Sir George Carteret, who took an increas-

---

*For a description of the original Adventurers, which was the well-earned contemporary name for shareholders, see Appendix Two.

ingly active role in the HBC's policy formation and became Deputy Governor in 1674.*

"Absolutism, pomp, formality and a sense of personal responsibility for retainers – all characteristics of feudalism – marked the rule of the Hudson's Bay Company from the beginning," Agnes C. Laut wrote in *The Adventurers of England*. "They were not merely merchants and traders; they were courtiers and princes as well."

Rupert was no titular governor; his contributions went far beyond the exchange of court gossip, which was the second most popular indoor sport of his day. He interceded again and again with Charles II on the Company's behalf, procuring, for example, an exemption from having to pay duty on trade goods sent out to Hudson Bay.

Early board minutes record gifts of "beaver stockings for the King," "silver tankards, hogsheads of claret" and "cat skin counterpanes for his bed" to friends of the Company. All the Adventurers had to take oaths of corporate fidelity,† and careful provisions were made for possible injuries to the officers and servants being sent into Hudson Bay. The loss of a toe by frostbite was assessed at £4, while more serious (or less frequent) injuries were to be settled on the more enduring basis of a yearly £30. This set the tone of parsimonious paternalism that was to pervade the HBC's regulations from the beginning. Any officer who died in the Company's service was granted a "funeral by torch-light to St. Paul's – Company and crew marching in

---

*The Company's various London meeting places are listed in Appendix Three.

†The first oath of fidelity and secrecy reads as follows: "I do swear to be true and faithful to the Company of Adventurers; the secrets of the said Company I will not disclose, nor trade to the limits of the Company's charter, so help me God."

procession. Cost not to exceed £20."

FOUR WEEKS AFTER THE HBC was awarded its formal charter, the frigate *Prince Rupert* and the pink *Wivenhoe* cast away from Ratcliffe Wharf below the Tower, bound for Hudson Bay, under orders to establish a permanent trading post on the Nelson River.

Prince Rupert and the newly incorporated Committeemen tendered a boisterous farewell banquet to the voyage's leaders: Zachariah Gillam, formerly of the *Nonsuch* and now skipper of the *Prince Rupert*, which also carried Groseilliers; Robert Newland, commander of the *Wivenhoe*, with Radisson aboard; and their newly chosen overseas Governor, a cashiered Quaker named Charles Bayley.*

The Royal treasure hunt was now on in earnest, but the choice of Bayley – the only Governor of an overseas English protectorate ever to be installed in his position straight out of jail – was peculiar. Not much is known of Charles Bayley's early life except that he first saw the light in the London parish of St Paul's Covent Garden during the 1630s and that he had some vague connection with the Stuarts, probably as a childhood playmate of the future Charles II. His French mother was lady-in-waiting to the future king's own French mother, Henrietta Maria, daughter of Henry IV of France, and presumably there was some

---

*The title "Governor" properly applied only to the head of the entire Company, but it was used indiscriminately during most of the 1700s and 1800s to describe officers in charge of major posts and the early supervisors of the whole Hudson Bay area – thus "Governor of Rupert's Land." The title ended with William Tomison, who held the newly created position of "Chief Inland" from 1778 until his retirement in 1803. The York Factory command was made subordinate to the "Chief Inland" in 1786.

backstairs royal blood in the infant. Enticed or kidnapped aboard a ship bound for America while still in his teens, Bayley was forced to endure fourteen years' hardship as a bond servant in Virginia, where he came under the sway of the Quaker missionary Elizabeth Harris.*

Bayley returned to England at the time of the Restoration and immediately went to Rome as part of a hare-brained mission led by an over-zealous Quaker named John Perrot to convert the Pope to their faith. The duo was apprehended and confined to a madhouse, where Bayley fasted in protest for twenty days and began to grow his beard. Eventually, they were thrown out of Italy, but Bayley continued to proselytize his wild faith as he walked barefoot across France. He was frequently arrested and finally jailed when he returned to England for refusing to take the oath of allegiance. His eccentric actions forced the more temperate Quakers to excommunicate him. From various dungeons he wrote letters to his boyhood friend Charles II, warning the king of dangers to his throne and cautioning the monarch that unless he avoided "rioting and excess, chambering and wantonness" he would be "threatened with a share in the whirlwind of the Lord" that was coming to the nation. The royal response was unsubtle and swift – Bayley was transferred from ordinary jails to the Tower of London, where he languished from

---

*Founded by the London preacher George Fox, the Quakers (also known as the Society of Friends) began as a militant sect protesting against established church conventions, preferring the guidance of "inner light" and individual God-given inspiration over scriptural authority. Fox was arrested eight times. Instead of quietly teaching his creed, he and his disciples would attend regular churches to heckle resident reverends during their sermons. Because they believed that each human being could contact God directly and that no one man was therefore any more important than any other, the early Quakers had little respect for earthly authority and suffered much persecution.

1663 to 1669. He was never accused of any specific crime or even examined. The legal problem, presumably, was that it was difficult to charge him with sedition or treason because he was advocating a course of action intended to *keep* the king on his throne. Bayley maintained his correspondence for years, penning direct missives from "the King of Heaven" to "the King of England," and was described by contemporaries in the Tower as "an old Quaker with a long beard" on the edge of madness.

Then a highly unexpected turn of events transformed the discredited zealot into a respected overseas administrator. No evidence exists to document this transmogrification. (According to one whimsical theory, he was a good choice for Hudson Bay because, having spent most of his adult life in prison, he was unlikely to be homesick.) The king released Bayley from the Tower on condition that he "betook himself to the navigation of Hudson Bay and the places lately discovered and to be discovered in those parts," and that he was assured of "conditions and allowances … agreeable to reason and with the nature of his employment." Almost certainly, the go-between was his jailer Sir John Robinson, then both Lieutenant (Chief Administrator and keeper of the crown jewels) of the Tower and Deputy Governor of the HBC. Whatever the process, a very changed Bayley sailed to Hudson Bay in 1669, commander of the first expedition under Company colours. The party landed at the estuary of the Nelson River and nailed the King's Arms to a tree, claiming the territory. Bayley had time for little more than formalities before an autumn gale drove the *Wivenhoe* back into deep water. Her captain decided to winter 720 miles away across the bay at Charles Fort (soon to be renamed Rupert House) where the *Prince Rupert* with Radisson and Gillam aboard was already safely tucked in for the winter.

The new Governor confirmed the treaties Gillam and Groseilliers had negotiated with local Indians the previous season, and the little colony settled into peaceful hibernation. Scurvy was kept to a minimum with generous daily quaffs of spruce brew, though the captain of the *Wivenhoe* and his mate died of influenza. The Indians who came to barter for steel knives and iron axes brought not only furs but fresh deer meat, wild fowl, sturgeon, whitefish and trout. Life took on decidedly civilized overtones as the sailors baked venison pie and pickled the fall geese in brine. The pigs and chickens brought out from England were slaughtered over the winter. In spring two small boats were launched to range down the coast, with Bayley and Radisson trading beaver skins at the mouth of the Moose River.

Over the next nine years, with only one brief interruption, Bayley conducted the business of the fledgling Company with imagination and sound judgment, establishing its presence at the estuaries of the major rivers flowing into James Bay and Hudson Bay (the Albany, Moose, Severn, Eastmain and Nelson) and founding a depot on Charlton Island to supply the James Bay outposts. He staked out the matrix of the Company's "factory" system, which meant that trade would be carried on from coastal forts instead of from aboard ship, allowing the Company to maintain constant contact with its customers. Bayley won the confidence of the Indians by fair trading and even favourably impressed the Jesuit missionary Charles Albanel and the explorer Louis Jolliet, sent north by the authorities in New France to stake a claim over Hudson Bay for the French crown. Despite his background as a religious fanatic, Bayley seemed to have acted as a decidedly calming influence – except on Radisson and Groseilliers, who never trusted him. The feeling was mutual.

The two *coureurs de bois* who pioneered the Hudson Bay route now felt isolated and unappreciated in the service of the HBC. Their every suggestion that its trade be expanded to the interior met with suspicious whispers that they were really determined to desert and entrust their newly won knowledge to the French.

That was precisely what happened. Influenced by the stern invocations of the visiting Jesuit, Father Albanel, offers of four hundred *Louis-d'or* and the restoration of their former estates, plus the promise that their skills and knowledge would be more profitably employed in the service of France, they switched sides in 1674. Radisson, in his autobiographical *Voyages*, claimed that he had been faithful to the Company and had quit only for reasons that "tended to the ruin of the beaver trade and that on all occasions we were look'd upon as useless persons that deserved neither reward nor encouragement."

Five years later, Bayley's term came to an abrupt end when he was recalled to London and accused of unspecified irregularities, mainly on the basis of charges from disgruntled subordinates. Before he could clear his name, he suddenly died on January 6, 1680. Two nights later, Charles Bayley was buried at Company expense (exceeding the official limit, at £31 0s. 9d.) in St Paul's Covent Garden, his body borne through the gloom of London's streets by torchbearers from the crew of the ship that had brought him home. At the cold graveside, Prince Rupert and the Committeemen genuinely grieved the passing of the mad Quaker who had found salvation as the first Governor of Rupert's Land.

FURTHER VOYAGES YIELDED growing returns, and the Dutch merchants who controlled much of the European fur trade quickly accepted the HBC as their major source of supply. Huguenot hatmakers came to value the rich Hudson Bay beavers over the fur from New France or Albany on the upper Hudson River. London began to challenge Amsterdam, Paris and Vienna as the pre-eminent European fur market. The nascent HBC was rapidly developing into a tidy little operation, its management (mainly Prince Rupert and Sir James Hayes) determined to see it survive and gradually weaned away from royal prerogatives to unsentimental business methods. Separate ledgerkeeping for profit and capital accounts was instituted, and the joint stock holdings of the original Adventurers were sweetened by calls for temporary loans (an early form of preferred stock) to finance individual voyages, paid back out of the proceeds. Any cash surpluses were reinvested in expanding the arc of posts around Hudson Bay. Most of the annual "courts" were held at Rupert's lodgings in Spring Gardens. Many important decisions were taken at these early policy sessions: instead of using coloured beads, silk ribbons and tinkling trinkets, the trade with the native peoples would be based on utilitarian goods such as knives, axes, muskets, flannel and wool, copper kettles and so on; ships would be leased rather than owned; the charter would be deposited for safekeeping in Rupert's apartments at Windsor Castle and "an iron chest with a great lock" ordered to prevent it from falling into competitors' hands; the sale of furs would be split into two auctions "by candle" at Garraway's Coffee House.

Moved to the site in 1670 by Thomas Garraway, the coffee house (at No. 3 Exchange Alley, off Cornhill near the Royal Exchange) was celebrated for its fine cherry brandy, pale ale, punch and tobacco. According to the raffish merchant and novelist Daniel Defoe, who frequented it, Garraway's was the place where all the most influential citizens gathered, including Sir Josiah Child, the swash-buckling godparent of the East India Company. Here, in the spring of 1651, took place a momentous event in British history: the first tasting of a new beverage brewed from shredded, dried leaves imported by the East India Company – a soothing drink known as "tea." It was an immediate success, and Garraway's resultant popularity made the tavern a good choice for the fur sales. Bidding was "by candle," in which one of two procedures was used to determine the buyer. A one-inch candle was lit, an upset price of seven shillings was called, and bids were made on separate lots of furs; the highest bidder at the point when the candle guttered out got the goods. Alternatively, a pin was stuck into the tallow and the last bidder before it fell out was declared the purchaser.

The first HBC sale on January 24, 1672 turned out to be a noisy assembly of merchants and gallants led by Prince Rupert and his cousin the Lord High Admiral, the Duke of York. The Restoration poet John Dryden was a sceptical onlooker, later sourly musing:

> Friend, once 'twas Fame that led thee forth,
> To brave the tropic heat: the frozen North.
> Later 'twas gold. Then beauty was the spur,
> But now our gallants venture but for fur.

Not satisfied with their existing charter, Rupert and his fellow Adventurers applied to Charles II on December 11, 1673 for a patent to extend their monopoly over "Buss Island." It was granted two years later, and the quirky document eventually came into the possession of the Earl of Arlington, who willed it to the Duke of Grafton, who in turn presented it to the Northamptonshire Record Society. That sheet of parchment is all that remains of the dubious venture, since Buss Island did not, in fact, exist. Marked on charts of the Atlantic Ocean for three centuries (slightly east and south of Iceland), it had been "discovered" by the crew of the *Emmanuel*, one of the vessels attached to Sir Martin Frobisher's third expedition. (The *Emmanuel* was a buss – a stout, three-masted Dutch fishing boat of sixty tons burden; hence the name.) Henry Hudson searched for the elusive outcrop on his way to discover the Hudson River in 1609, and Captain Zachariah Gillam claimed to have sighted it during his passage to Hudson Bay aboard the *Nonsuch* fifty-nine years later.

Thomas Shepard, the mate of the *Nonsuch*, was actually hired to lead an expedition to Buss but was dismissed for "ill behaviour" before he could depart. Ownership of the mysterious island was carried as an asset on the Company's books well into the 1800s, and critics continued to believe that succeeding governors kept its exact location secret to perpetuate their monopoly. In 1791, Captain Charles Duncan, a progressive navigator on loan to the HBC from the Admiralty, had the nerve and good sense to report after a long voyage trying to trace the mysterious place: "I strove as much as the winds would permit me to keep in the supposed latitude of the *supposed* Buss Island, but it is my firm opinion that no such Island is now above water if ever it was."

PRINCE RUPERT'S SUCCESS IN ATTAINING the supplementary charter for Buss Island was the last royal favour granted him. After 1675 he retired more and more into seclusion in his Windsor Castle apartments. He was still Vice-Admiral of England and used his good offices to authorize the flying of the King's Jack on the HBC supply ships but was being frequently overruled on substantial issues by, of all people, Samuel Pepys, then Secretary of the Navy. Because too many high-born Royal Navy officers knew very little of their craft, Pepys had recommended that every candidate for lieutenant be eligible only after he had served three years at sea, at least one of them as a midshipman. Rupert objected that such service as a midshipman was "beneath the quality of a gentleman," but his uncharacteristically reactionary view did not prevail. Besides, as the historian Thomas Macaulay dryly noted, "There were gentlemen and there were seamen in the navy of Charles the Second. But the seamen were not gentlemen; and the gentlemen were not seamen."

By the autumn of 1682, Rupert's health began to give

way, his old war wounds reasserting themselves. The Cavalier cause for which the Bohemian warrior had fought had been triumphant for more than two decades, but its animating purposes were all but forgotten, its leaders all but dishonoured. No more church bells rang to warn of Rupert's approach, as the wrinkled, rheumy-eyed prince hobbled around the Berkshire countryside accompanied only by a black dog loping at his heels and a majestic hawk on his wrist.

In mid-November Rupert returned to his town house in Spring Gardens and collapsed while out for an evening of theatre. His condition was diagnosed as pleurisy with a high fever. On Saturday, November 25 the HBC Committee met to re-elect Rupert as Governor but he did not have the strength to attend.

On November 29, 1682 Rupert died – eighteen days short of his sixty-third birthday – refusing to be bled and expiring fully in command of himself.*

The funeral was staged at Westminster Abbey a week later, with the court ordered to observe full mourning – three weeks in purple and three weeks in black. Two companies of Foot Guards, followed by the prince's watermen, footmen, huntsmen, grooms, gentlemen servants, pages, physicians, lawyers and chaplains, led the procession. Then

---

*An autopsy revealed the presence of "bones" in Rupert's brain and heart, presumably the calcification of a blood clot and of a mitral valve ring. Rupert's will left most of his possessions (valued at £10,415) divided equally between his first mistress, Peg Hughes, and the nine-year-old Ruperta. His daughter married Brig.-Gen. Emanuel Scrope Howe, later ambassador to the court of Hanover, thus joining the Bromley family, which is still extant. Dudley, Rupert's son by Francesca Bard, inherited one of his residences but was killed at the age of twenty by a Turkish scimitar at the siege of Buda in 1686. Rupert's most prized possession, his mother's pearl necklace, was sold by his executor, Lord Craven, to Nell Gwyn for £4,520.

came his secretaries, pursuivants, heralds and so on up the social ladder – to the barons, bishops, earls, dukes and the Marquess of Halifax, Lord Privy Seal. The coffin was borne by stalwart Yeomen of the Guard from Windsor Castle, and behind them, after another bevy of grieving nobles, with head bowed slow-marched the Chief Mourner – William, Earl of Craven, the loyal retainer from the days of exile – paying his final homage to the last of the Winter Queen's sons.

The body was laid to rest in Henry VII's chapel, but no monument survives to mark Rupert's tomb. Only a bittersweet epitaph identifies the final resting place of the Hudson's Bay Company's founder and first Governor: "A soldier's life is a life of honour," it reads, "but a dog would not lead it."

A DOZEN YEARS AFTER THE GRANTING of its charter, the Company was generating a yearly profit of 200 percent on invested capital and was only two years away from declaring its first hefty dividend. The main problem was finding a worthy successor to Prince Rupert.

It was a sign of how closely the enterprise stayed tied to the politics of the Stuart court that, instead of reaching into the City where a rapidly emerging mercantile class could have provided a dynamic alternative, the Committeemen decided to approach James, Duke of York, brother of the king and his most likely successor. The decision was not automatic and took six meetings to confirm but finally, in January 1683, Deputy Governor Sir James Hayes and Sir Christopher Wren, the architect who served as a member of the Committee between 1679 and 1683, were instructed to attend on His Royal Highness and petition that the second man in the kingdom take the Company under his patronage and protection. The duke accepted the position, but when Hayes returned to Whitehall with a batch of instructions and commissions to be initialled, James imperiously waved him away, declaring that although he had also been appointed Governor of the Royal African Company and of the Royal Fisheries Company, he never, but *never*, signed any documents.

While the Company found itself temporarily on the winning side in the struggle for the English Crown, the Duke of York proved to be as ineffective and short-lived a Governor as he was later king of England. His lack of enthusiasm for the HBC stemmed in part from his desire to stay on good terms with Louis XIV of France and the conflict of interest he felt from the competing beaver preserves he owned in the upper parts of the Hudson River Valley. He had sent ships of war to capture the territory from the Dutch and renamed New Amsterdam, the capital of the little colony New York after himself.

The Duke of York's contemptuous neglect of the Company of Adventurers undoubtedly was rooted in his personality. The second son of Charles I, James was a stiff and stubborn bigot with popping eyes and a tongue too large for his mouth, so that he could hardly drink a glass of wine or water without slobbering all over himself, gulping the liquid down as if he were eating it. Incapable of a graceful gesture, he had little sense of humour and was so obsessed with the sanctity of the monarchy and the doctrine of Divine Right that even when he was alone with his brother Charles, he would spring respectfully to attention whenever affairs of state were being discussed. His fierce loyalty to the Church of Rome was equalled only by his personal paranoia. His fear of enemies, even before he succeeded in making them, was so intense that a French envoy reported James had been busy fortifying the great naval base at Portsmouth on the *landward* side.

James's sex life was as untidy and overpopulated as that of his brother, but not nearly so pleasant. He had two wives, at least twenty children and a series of mistresses who must have been chosen by his priests, as Charles once sniffed, "by way of penance." Catherine Sedley, one of the deadliest blossoms in his bouquet of thistles, was a lean, ugly sadist who was herself puzzled by the violence of the future king's passion. "It cannot be my beauty," she mused, "for I have none; and it cannot be my wit, for he has not enough to know that I have any."

The only good thing about the Duke of York's tenure as Governor of the Hudson's Bay Company was its brevity – only two years, from January 1683 to February 1685. After that date he held on to his stock but resigned to become king of England. The only other mention of James II in Company minutes occurs on October 31, 1688, when Sir Edward Dering, then Deputy Governor, paid the king his HBC dividend of 150 guineas in gold. Five days later, his royal mandate shattered by his inability to seek consensus (much less find it), James fled England, dropping the Great Seal into the Thames on his way to exile.

THE SOUR TASTE left behind by the Duke of York's flaccid stewardship and the strain in relations between France and England made the Committeemen seek the very best-connected candidate for the HBC governorship. There was only one choice. At a dinner on April 1, 1685, Sir James Hayes approached the Right Honourable John, Lord Churchill (later Duke of Marlborough) to assume the post, and the very next day he was sworn into office. Then thirty-five years old, Churchill was about to be appointed a major-general in the army that would defeat the insurgents led by the bastard son of Charles II, the tragic Duke of Monmouth. Churchill was busy consolidating his position in the front ranks of Restoration military commanders and backstage political manipulators. The second son of an impoverished Stuart administrator named Sir Winston Churchill, he originally found a place at court as a page to the Duke of York and was eventually commissioned an ensign in the King's Own Company of Footguards. An imposing youngster with blue eyes and a clear, ruddy complexion, he quickly became embroiled in the court's sexual intrigues, fighting at least two duels over various transferable ladies, and even shared a mistress – the delicious Barbara Villiers, Lady Castlemaine – with Charles II. (Once, when the two young lovers were at play and the king unexpectedly entered the anteroom to the bedchamber, Churchill demonstrated his grasp of appropriate tactics by diving through the open window to the courtyard below. The lady in question was so grateful for his instant, if slightly retroactive, discretion that she gave him £4,500; this sum, lent out at high rates, became the foundation of Churchill's fortune.)

Shortly afterwards he met Sarah Jennings, a maid of honour in Charles II's court and one of its few members who deserved the title. A handsome woman with an indomitable will, she fell in love with Churchill when she was a pert fifteen and married him three years later. The two were inseparable, mutually reinforcing each other's ambitions, and remained wildly in love even though they had very different temperaments. John was determinedly cool and always collected; Sarah was the opposite, full of spirit with temper to match. In a flash of anger at her husband, she once cut off her straw-blonde hair, knowing it was an object of the Duke's admiration. When Marlborough saw her in the shorn state, he betrayed no emotion, pretending not to have noticed the rape of the locks. Ashamed of herself, Sarah never alluded to her rash act. After the Duke's death, when she was searching through a strong-box containing his most prized personal possessions, she found her fall of hair where it had been treasured in silent homage for more than thirty years.

John Churchill rose ever higher in the royal service, eventually attaining a bewildering array of titles and honours, including Duke of Marlborough, Marquess of Blandford, Earl of Marlborough, Baron Churchill (of Sandridge), Lord Churchill (of Eyemouth in Scotland), Prince of the Holy Roman Empire and Prince of Mindelheim. His stunning success in ten major military campaigns raised England to the forefront of the world's nation-states. It broke the domination of Louis XIV's France over Europe and opened the gate to two centuries of successful British imperialism. Yet his epic military victories at Blenheim (1704), Ramillies (1706), Oudenarde (1708) and Malplaquet (1709) were only the most visible manifestations of his career, overshadowing his behind-the-scenes diplomatic authority, which for a long while (certainly during the early tentative reign of William III and Mary) made him virtually the uncrowned king of England. A brilliant political strategist and supreme military tactician, Marlborough viewed the world in stark primary colours, refusing to recognize pastel tones of any kind and, like most other self-made men, came to worship his creator. Because he was not only a duke but also a prince of the tiny principality of Mindelheim (in Swabia, west of Munich), he insisted that he be addressed as "Your Highness" and treated as an equal on his travels among the kings, princes and margraves of Europe.

Armed with the booty of war, he built himself appropriately magnificent dwellings – Marlborough House, designed by Sir Christopher Wren, in London and Blenheim Palace, designed by Sir John Vanbrugh, in the country, a baroque structure of outrageous proportions that enclosed seven acres of floor space and prompted even house-proud Sarah to complain that it was a "wild and unmerciful" dwelling.

According to his splendid descendant nine generations

removed, Sir Winston Churchill,* the Duke was "a greater do-er than he was a man," but there is little doubt that during his seven years as the HBC's Governor, Marlborough rescued the Company from the neglect of his predecessor and placed it on a solid political footing. If Rupert was the HBC's princely founder, the Duke of Marlborough was its noble preserver, assuring the fledgling enterprise of his protection at a time when he was rapidly broadening his civilian and military power base. He applied his influence to have a hundred marines detailed to protect the HBC supply ships on their transatlantic voyages and arranged for several Royal Navy ships to help defend the Company's northern domain. A grateful Company presented him with a gold plate worth a hundred guineas and named a mighty northern river in his honour.

Probably the most significant achievement during Marlborough's important stewardship was the backhand confirmation of the Company's charter by Parliament. The Skinners Company, the Company of Feltmakers in London and competing American fur merchants all had good reasons to complain about the Company's tendency to monopolistic practices, but the sum of their demands was abolition of the HBC monopoly itself because it was based on an antique royal charter that had never received Parliament's approbation. To head off these and other dissenters, the Committeemen petitioned Westminster for an act confirming their charter. It was passed in 1690 with token opposition, but it was to be valid for only seven years. When the arguments were rekindled in 1697, the London fur merchants renewed their complaints. Uncertain it would carry the day, the Company did not even try to revive the

---

*After he retired from politics in 1955, Sir Winston accepted an honorary post from only one commercial enterprise, although many offers were tendered. He became Grand Seigneur of the Hudson's Bay Company and remained so until his death.

act and lay low though everyone concerned tacitly assumed that the charter would remain in force.

One of the unanswered charges that emerged out of the 1690 hearings was that the Company's Committeemen had been guilty of "stock-jobbing" by paying out inordinately large dividends and then unloading their shares. It was true. The Company paid no dividends in the fourteen years after the granting of its charter, but in 1688 – even though French disruptions of the trade on Hudson Bay had caused a cumulative loss of £118,014 over the preceding six years – a fat 50 percent payout was distributed to its tight circle of eight dominant shareholders, including the Duke of Marlborough.

This was followed by another 25 percent declaration and, in 1690, by the largest bonus in the Company's history: a 74 percent dividend, together with a stock bonus of 200 percent in the form of a convertible dividend scrip. Vague explanations were floated that this would bring the HBC's capitalization more into line with the Committeemen's estimates of what the stock was really worth, yet such a forecast of the Company's potential earnings was so far removed from the facts (in the next five years, further losses of £97,500 would be recorded) that a less benign explanation for the extraordinary bonanza seems more likely. British historian K.G. Davies noted that within the next two years, six of the eight Committeemen who voted themselves the bloated dividends had resigned from the Company and sold their stock. "On this evidence," he concluded, "sharp practice cannot be ruled out; nor can opportunism." Watering of the stock (which raised the Company's capitalization from £10,500 to £31,500) increased the value of Marlborough's shares by 400 percent. During the next two years, the HBC quotations at Jonathan's informal stock exchange doubled in value, presumably because investors thought they might be due for another 150 percent dividend. Instead, there followed twenty-eight years of no dividend payments at all.

This was mainly the result of the havoc the French wrought on the fur trade in Hudson Bay, partly due to the economic recession and the currency crisis that cut into an already oversupplied fur market. One reason the HBC endured the drought was that no one was certain precisely how a royally chartered joint-stock company could be wound up. Yet such a drastic course must have been tempting because only through liquidation could the HBC's debts – up to a crippling £30,000 by 1698 – have been eliminated.

The exception was the dividend presented to the royal successor of the unhappy, exiled James II. On September 16, 1690, six of the Company's Committeemen, led by Deputy Governor Sir Edward Dering, called on the new king, William III, at Kensington Palace and presented him with three hundred gold guineas.*

Marlborough resigned as Governor in 1692, having fallen into temporary disfavour (he was actually imprisoned in the Tower for six weeks) and become embroiled in political problems that required his full attention. Political power was passing from the regal palaces to the grand country mansions of the Whig aristocracy, and the source of the pivotal commercial decisions was moving from royal favouritism to the London financial houses. As always, the HBC adapted itself to current trends and appointed as its next Governor a banker and fiscal manipulator named Sir Stephen Evans, who would be Governor for two terms stretching over sixteen years. He was the first and the most peculiar of the succession of City men who were to guide the Hudson's Bay Company during the next two centuries.

---

*The HBC shares originally granted to James II were deemed to be the property of the British royal house. Dividend payments were made to the monarchy until 1764 and the sovereign was officially listed as an HBC proprietor until 1824.

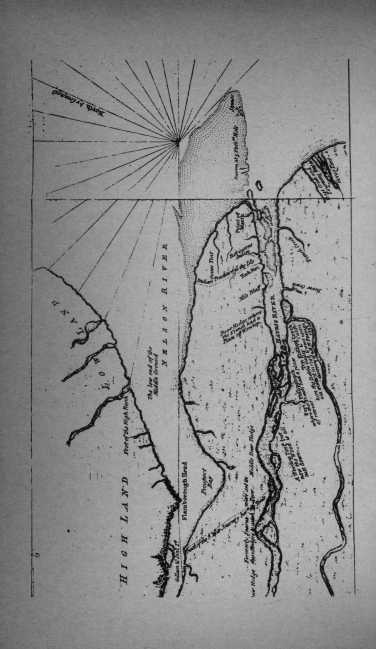

CHAPTER 6

Battling for the Bay

*Forced marches through waist-deep snow, the
hollow boom of cannon fire and the terror of
guerrilla attacks on the inadequately armed forts
became commonplace on the once dormant bay.*

DURING THE HARD–SCRABBLE DECADE before Sir Stephen Evans assumed the helm of the London-based Committee and for the five years that followed, the trading
posts on Hudson Bay unexpectedly joined the mainstream
of world history. They became royal pawns in the escalating hostilities between France and England that led to an
official declaration of war on May 17, 1689. Even though
the writ of European monarchs carried little sanction on
the gravelly shores of the bay, the traders who manned the
wilderness forts found themselves caught up in operatic
clashes not of their own making.

After 1682 the European tug-of-war shifted overseas,
as French flotillas and overland raiding parties from Montreal attacked and pillaged the HBC's fur factories. Because
the HBC traders were far more interested in staying alive to
collect their pay than in sacrificing their lives to defend
storehouses full of pungent pelts, they accepted defeat
with more relief than shame. Except for the sea battles of

1696 and 1697, they seldom bothered to call for help from the Royal Navy. Individual sieges by land were fierce enough to inflict serious casualties on both sides. Some of the posts changed hands half a dozen times.

Yet neither France nor England could determine precisely how much money and manpower the sub-Arctic war was worth. Even the most ambitious fur lords of New France were torn between trying to advance their cause in Hudson Bay and expanding their commercial interests in the warm and infinitely more welcoming climate of the Illinois country south of Lake Superior and beyond. Apart from these considerations – and the serious problems posed by trying to mount marine engagements in a body of water littered with navigational hazards – there was one other reason that prevented either side from pushing to ultimate victory. While most of the battles for Hudson Bay were being fought, the price of beaver pelts on European markets wilted to new lows, mainly because of over-production from New York and other colonies.

The superior warriors from Quebec won most of the bay battles, but failed to follow their brilliant tactical successes with enduring strategic consolidation; the English company limited its concern to survival, but not at any cost. The HBC fought back only hard enough to keep at least one post in its possession at all times (either Albany or York) and concentrated on lobbying royal courtiers and influencing peddlers in the back rooms of St James's and Versailles. Such bland quiescence tallied precisely with the glut in the fur market; in those circumstances, more profit was to be made in controlling distribution of the furs than in harvesting them. What, after all, was the point of victory if it yielded only an increase in the backlog of unsaleable pelts? Better to guard capital and wait out the storm.

Still, forced marches through waist-deep snow, the hollow boom of cannon fire and the terror of guerrilla attacks on the inadequately armed forts became commonplace on the once dormant bay. "All in all, the men in London who guided the Company's affairs before 1763," noted Grace Lee Nute, the Minnesota historian, "never knew what news their captains would bring next from the bay, nor what their servants, staggering into London after months or years in the hands of French conquerors, would report concerning ownership of Bay forts."

In charge of these forts between 1683 and 1686 was Henry Sergeant, an irascible and high-handed Englishman whose small claim to immortality was that he brought the first white women to Hudson Bay: his wife, her companion (a gentlewoman named Mrs Maurice) and their maid.* The overseas Governor, crossly referred to in HBC minutes as "Sergeant and the whole parcel of women appertaining to him," also employed three manservants. His private quarters at Albany Fort had a four-poster bed complete with heavy curtains and a valance. Sergeant's lackadaisical surrender of his home fort to the French after not quite one day's perfunctory fighting prompted the Company to sue him for cowardice and £20,000. The case was never heard, but the charges rang true.

WITH RADISSON PLEDGED to the service of New France, the London Committeemen were aware that the immunity to competition of their northern monopoly was bound to be short-lived. The first agent of their discomfiture was

---

*After Sergeant and his women were recalled, the HBC prohibited any wives from going out to the bay. In April 1684, when Elinor Verner, the wife of an experienced HBC trader placed in charge of Fort Rupert, applied for permission to join her husband, it was denied. Never known for acting hastily, the HBC did not appoint its first woman manager of a northern post for another three centuries: in October 1983, a Cree named Donna Carrière was placed in charge of the Company's store at Weagamow Lake in Northwestern Ontario.

an unusually talented financier from Amiens named Charles Aubert de La Chesnaye, who arrived from France in 1655 as the agent of a group of Rouen hatters and furriers.

A stern and pious merchant, La Chesnaye lived so modestly that the curtains in his home were patched together from old tablecloths and he spent most of his working life wearing the same pair of red flannel trousers. Married three times, he sired eighteen children and remained the outstanding leader of the early New France business community until his death in 1702. Like so many members of France's third estate, he was dissatisfied with his bourgeois status and gave himself a title after acquiring several seigneuries to gain the prestige due a landowner. Montreal's first important venture capitalist, the leathery old trader controlled a significant economic empire as well as holding mortgages on many of the growing community's houses.*

La Chesnaye first met Radisson during a visit to Paris in 1679. That get-together triggered the eventual formation of La Compagnie du Nord as New France's thorny challenge to the HBC. Radisson agreed to lead an expedition to Hudson Bay in return for a quarter of the profits. By 1682, La Chesnaye had organized a flotilla of two small fishing ships and twenty-seven men, carrying Radisson and Groseilliers with orders to establish the Compagnie du Nord's first permanent station at the mouth of the Hayes River.

Radisson had camped at the nearby Nelson River with Charles Bayley a decade earlier and was aware that the

---

*In his last will he asked forgiveness for any wrongs, great and small, he might have committed in his business dealings and requested that he be buried in the paupers' cemetery at Hôtel-Dieu – presumably so that he could appear before his Maker as a simple man of God. To be on the safe side, he followed the custom of arranging for the posthumous celebration of daily mass, in perpetuity, to guarantee the calm repose of his capitalistic but cautious soul.

upper reaches of the Hayes were connected to the wider Nelson, but that because the smaller stream was easier to navigate, most natives preferred to switch to it on the final leg of their journey down to the bay. The adjacent estuaries of these two important rivers, whose sources lie hundreds of miles upstream in prime fur country, would be the site of the bay's major battles, and York Factory, the post that sprouted there, quickly became the area's main settlement. York's initial colonization resembled the speeded-up antics of the silent films' Keystone Kops; its location was moved ten times as its procession of occupants behaved with something considerably less than the cool bravado normally associated with conquerors of a new land.

Edward H. Borins in his thesis *La Compagnie du Nord, 1682–1700* makes a telling point about the whole era. "The *Compagnie du Nord*'s fatal error proved to be its decision to compete with the English by sea. Had the company concentrated its efforts on its posts in James Bay and contented itself with small but regular profits, it might well have survived," he concludes. "But the *Compagnie du Nord*'s directors, who seemed inclined to take gambles, chose to invest all their capital in the expeditions of the early 1690s, which failed. Therefore, the Canadians, who were so well adapted to the rigours of the fur trade, lost to the English, who were far superior in naval skills, which proved to be the decisive factor in the exploitation of the Hudson Bay trade."

The sequence of events began with Radisson's arrival on August 21, 1682, in the two fishing smacks whose crews included his nephew, Groseilliers's son Jean-Baptiste Chouart. Three days earlier another expedition, inbound from Boston aboard the sturdy *Bachelor's Delight*, had put in upstream on the Nelson. Its crew of fourteen, skippered by Benjamin Gillam, son of the original commander of the *Nonsuch*, had settled in for the winter unaware of the French visitors camped on the nearby Hayes. Although they were described as "all bachelors and very resolute fellows" and carried a "charter" from the governor of Massachusetts, the Bostonians were clearly inspired by the revenue-hungry Zachariah Gillam, back in the Company's employ as captain of the supply ship *Prince Rupert* – even then heading for the Nelson from London, carrying John Bridgar, appointed York's first Governor.

Radisson went up country to contact families of Cree with furs to trade while Groseilliers stayed behind to erect a small fort on the south shore of the Hayes. Eight days upriver, Radisson found an Indian encampment and concluded an informal treaty that he later claimed gave New France exclusive trading rights in the area. The day he arrived back at the bay, he heard cannon fire, which upon investigation turned out to be a burying party of the Bostonians paying final tribute to one of their companions who had died on September 12. Radisson paddled over to the Nelson with a few men to investigate. His outrage at finding a band of competing traders was larded with a generous helping of bluff. He told the youthful Gillam that he not only held a commission from the king of France to build a great post and forbid any aliens from trading, but that fifty French marines were encamped on the next river to enforce his royal mission. An uneasy pact was negotiated, beguiling Gillam into Radisson's power.

As the woodrunner and his companions were leaving the little camp, congratulating themselves on the successful ruse, they spotted a large ship under full sail entering the Nelson River. She was the *Prince Rupert* out of London, carrying the official HBC party. To stop them from proceeding farther upriver – where they would be seen by the Bostonians, who would quickly realize that the English had a lot more firepower than the French – Radisson lit a large bonfire and piled it high with smoke-producing grass, hoping to persuade the lookouts aboard the *Prince Rupert* that the tiny clearing was really an Indian encampment. The trick worked. The *Prince Rupert* dropped anchor.

The following morning the dinghies were lowered and a landing party left the *Prince Rupert* to investigate. Radisson posted his men in the bush and positioned himself boldly on shore, a true Caesar of the wilderness deigning to greet the puzzled intruders. Informing the luckless Bridgar that the land had already been claimed for the king of France, he professed to have been in residence for a year, in command of three hundred troops dedicated to enforcing occupation of the area by his most Christian Majesty, Louis XIV.

There followed an impasse that could not be readily resolved since the season was too far advanced for the HBC servants to exercise any option but to winter ashore. All but nine crew members disembarked and began to build winter shelter. Then an act of God intervened: a violent swirl of ice caused the *Prince Rupert* to drag anchor, drift out to sea and sink with all aboard, among them old Zachariah Gillam. The HBC men were now at Radisson's mercy for their future and food supplies.

The uneasy winter truce was broken in February when Radisson and his confrères easily captured the Bostonians' ramshackle stockade; shortly afterward, Bridgar and his men were similarly overrun. Their winter abode was burned (but its trade goods fastidiously saved) as the victorious Frenchmen made ready to build a permanent post and to export their furs. Most of the prisoners were eventually dispatched to Company posts at the Bottom of the Bay aboard a leaky vessel hammered together from the remains of Radisson's two fishing smacks.

Leaving their young relative Jean-Baptiste Chouart in charge, Radisson and Groseilliers boarded *Bachelor's Delight*, the only seaworthy ship that remained of the assembled craft. They loaded the two thousand pelts traded during the winter and sailed off in triumph for Quebec. Once again, the authorities of New France acted against their own interests, confiscating the ship and charging the two preening woodsmen the standard 25 percent duty exacted on local fur catches. That was too much for Médard Chouart, Sieur Des Groseilliers. At sixty-five, he was worn out and frustrated by the succession of short-sighted Quebec intendants. He retired in disgust to his modest seigneury at Trois Rivières, where he died peacefully in 1696.

It was also too much for Radisson. As soon as he learned that the tax collectors rather than he and his brother-in-law were to receive the quarter-share of profits from the hard-won furs, he began to plot reconciliation with his one-time English employers. After a quick reconnoitre in France, Radisson realized the authorities there were much more anxious to appease the king of England than reward their baywise emissary's exploits. Lord Preston, the adroit diplomat then British ambassador to the Court of Versailles, was instructed by Sir James Hayes of the HBC to seek out the renegade trader "who, it is believed, could be brought over again to our service if he were so entreated by your Lordship." Preston was told that Radisson was holding court on the third floor of a house in the Faubourg St-Antoine and sent his aide, a Captain Godey, to negotiate. Godey described Radisson as being "apparelled more like a savage than a Christian. His black hair, just touched with grey, hung in a wild profusion about his bare neck and shoulders. He showed a swart complexion, seamed and pitted by frost and exposure in a rigorous climate. A huge scar, wrought by the tomahawk of a drunken Indian, disfigured his left cheek. His whole costume was surmounted by a wide collar of marten's skin; his feet were adorned by buckskin moccasins. In his leather belt was sheathed a long knife."

Since he could not get any pledges of favourable French action, Radisson was easily seduced by the English overtures, confiding to his journal: "I yielded to these solicitations and am determined to go to England forever, and so strongly bind myself to his Majesty's service ... that no other cause could ever detach me from it." He was welcomed back to London by most of the HBC Committeemen, who swallowed their scepticism after he revealed that his nephew was still in Port Nelson guarding a magnificent hoard of skins awaiting shipment. Rewarded with a silver tankard, £200 in Company stock and the grand if slightly hollow title of Superintendent and Chief Director of Trade at Port Nelson, Radisson sailed again for the bay, this time aboard the aptly named *Happy Return*. His arrival under English colours understandably confused his patient nephew, who by then had garnered a valuable booty of twenty thousand pelts and was now being asked to turn them over to the hated HBC – from under whose corporate snout most of them had been snatched in the first place. No record of the two men's conversation exists, but at the end of it, both the furs and young Jean-Baptiste were taken over by the Hudson's Bay Company.

That season alone, more than seven hundred Cree in three hundred canoes arrived to barter for 300 guns, 10,000 knives and hatchets, 247 hogsheads of tobacco and 15 gross of pipes, 390 blankets and a cornucopia of household items that were becoming regular features of the interchange. Radisson repeated his lucrative visits to the bay for three more years, but since the French government had put a price on his head, he maintained an uncharacteristically unheralded presence there and eventually retired to London. By the close of the seventeenth century, he was sixty-four years old and being only vaguely credited for his exploits on the Company's behalf. Penny-pinching Committeemen with short memories cut his pension, and it took Radisson five years of tedious legal procedures to win it back. The one-time Caesar of the wilderness was reduced to begging the Company for a job as its London warehouse-keeper. Being refused, he had to make do with a pension of £12 10s. per quarter. Pierre-Esprit Radisson died in 1710, his zest for life long since extinguished, his grave unmarked. The only subsequent entry in the minute books of the Company he established was the payment of a paltry £6 for his funeral expenses.

THE HBC POSTS ON THE BAY were becoming far too prosperous for the French to ignore. They were returning an annual £20,000 and diverting a growing proportion of the trade that had originally gone to Montreal. La Compagnie du Nord had little trouble persuading Brisay de Denonville, the governor of New France, to mount a military expedition overland to capture the forts of the English intruders. By March 1686, the little army had been assembled in Montreal: seventy Canadian irregulars, a few native guides, thirty French soldiers and their leader, the Chevalier de Troyes, a Parisian company commander who had arrived in Quebec only eight months before. The troop started out on sleds, dragging thirty-five canoes that they used as soon as spring breakup allowed them to paddle – up the Ottawa River to Lake Temiskaming and down the Abitibi and Moose rivers to James Bay. The eight-hundred-mile journey remains an epic of bush travel and was one of North America's earliest and most successful commando assaults. Because no large expedition had ever travelled this route north overland, no portages had yet been cut. With the canoes and loads of supplies the men had to struggle between various lakes and rivers, stumbling over fallen trees, slippery rocks and tangled underbrush. Eighty-two days out of Montreal, they neared the first of the HBC's installations, Moose Factory, tucked behind its square palisade, eighteen feet high and protected by bastions at each corner. The little fort's defences were impressive, but they were designed to repel attacks from the sea. Since no visitors, friendly or otherwise, could get through Hudson Strait until late summer, few lookouts had been posted and the seven-pound bastion-cannons had been left unloaded. The local Governor, John Bridgar, had sailed for Rupert House the previous day with most of his officers, leaving behind a garrison of sixteen leaderless men. Their main protection was the three-storey redoubt inside the fort, armed with three cannon.

The French attack was launched by two of the Le Moyne brothers, Pierre d'Iberville and Jacques de Sainte-Hélène. Squad leaders under de Troyes, they tippytoed inside Moose Fort while the HBC men were asleep and roped the cannon together so that even if the Bay men managed to stir themselves enough to fire the weapons, the recoil would only bring down the palisades. The dawn attack that followed lasted a scant two hours. The most dramatic moment in the brief scrap was the solo stand of the twenty-four-year-old Pierre Le Moyne d'Iberville, who had been leading the way inside the redoubt when the gate was shut behind him; he had to hold off the entire garrison, sword in one hand and musket in the other, while his companions forced the gateway open again. Shouting the war whoop of the Iroquois, the one hundred Frenchmen quickly overwhelmed the stunned HBC traders, who surrendered in the name of arithmetic and expediency.

De Troyes decided to follow up his easy triumph with an assault on Rupert House, seventy-five miles up the east coast of James Bay. Leaving forty men to guard the captured fort, he set off with the others in his war canoes and soon sighted not only the fort but also the supply ship *Craven*, which had brought Bridgar and his officers from Moose. The main body of Montreal troops attacked the fort and took it handily – a forgotten ladder was still conveniently propped against the side of the redoubt. Up they swarmed to drop lighted grenades down the chimney on the sleeping Englishmen.

D'Iberville was assigned capture of the *Craven*. He silently boarded the ship, shot the one sailor dozing at anchor watch, then stamped his feet on the deck, giving the customary signal to wake crews at times of emergency. As the first three sleepy heads appeared through the companionway, each was greeted with the blunt end of a musket; the rest of the crew meekly surrendered. The captured Bay men were escorted back to Moose while d'Iberville took charge of the *Craven* for an assault on the more heavily armed HBC fortress at the mouth of the Albany River. The main problem was finding it, because the site, a short distance up the river, was not visible from its sea side. The fort's occupants resolved that quandary for their would-be invaders by blithely firing their routine sunset gun just as the attackers were about to sail off in frustration.

Albany was the best protected of the bay forts, but de Troyes and d'Iberville had brought along the heavy siege guns from Rupert House. They mounted them on a patch of frozen gravel outside the palisade and patiently lobbed 140 shots into the fort. As the attacking troops shouted *Vive le Roi!*, an echo of their war cry could be faintly heard – so faintly, in fact, that d'Iberville realized it was emanating from the fort's cellar where the cowardly defenders were huddled in refuge instead of firing back. None of the HBC regulars had dared mount the barricades to lower the Company flag. The cannonade stopped only when the bravest Englishman present made an unexpected appearance. Through the gate the resident chaplain hove into sight, holding aloft a maid's white apron tied to his walking stick.

Henry Sergeant agreed to rendezvous with de Troyes, choosing the middle of the Albany River as a neutral venue. Two small boats set out, one from each river bank. Having lost his fort, Sergeant seemed concerned mainly with the etiquette of the occasion. A bottle of vintage claret tucked under his arm, Sergeant proposed that the two leaders drink a toast to their respective sovereigns. De Troyes's more mundane concern was to prevent the English Governor from noticing how famished and exhausted his men were after their three successive sieges, and how easily they might have been overrun. The only concessions the Englishman won were that they could keep their personal possessions and that they would be shipped to Charlton Island to await the next Company supply ship.

Leaving forty men under d'Iberville to consolidate his gains, de Troyes and most of the other victors marched back to Quebec, where they were welcomed by Brisay de Denonville – though in his report to Versailles, the Governor hedged his bets by stating that the HBC posts had been attacked without his direct orders. The French king was only too delighted with the results of the expedition, but to placate James II of England, then still an uneasy ally, he agreed to sign a treaty of neutrality that guaranteed the *status quo* on Hudson Bay. On the bay itself D'Iberville fretted away the winter, longing for action. Finally he too returned to Quebec and later went to France where he obtained a fast new frigate, the *Soleil d'Afrique*, and a commission to bring out the captured furs.

Not yet thirty, he was appointed commander-in-chief of Hudson Bay. D'Iberville was soon anchored off Charlton Island, loading up the *Soleil d'Afrique* with the accumulated pelts. He set off in a small sloop to gather the furs from Albany and had collected that load too, but just as he was about to leave, he unexpectedly found himself in the shadow of two incoming English warships, the imposing eighteen-gun *Churchill* and the smaller frigate *Yonge*.

The vessels, crewed by eighty-five men, had been sent out by the Company to recapture Albany, and they carried aboard a new Governor, Captain John Marsh, plus the first and only Admiral in the HBC's service. He was William Bond, a veteran bay mariner who had been given the grandiose title to underscore his authority. France and England were not yet officially at war so the two majestic ships peacefully continued sailing up the river.

D'Iberville quickly anchored below the fort. He had only sixteen men under his command but an ingenious mind with which to lead them. He ordered a war party out in canoes to cut loose the river's channel markers. The HBC ships promptly ran aground. By the time they were sufficiently lightened to be floated off, the French had consolidated their land defences. The newcomers parked on an island a short distance from the main fort. Since they hadn't had an opportunity to see inside, the HBC men had no idea they outnumbered the defenders more than four to one. D'Iberville maintained the illusion of superiority by assigning snipers to prey on the British camp. He flatly refused to allow the hungry arrivals the right to hunt for fresh game, thus encouraging the spread of scurvy. Governor Marsh was one of the first victims. Admiral Bond and his mate slipped away on a partridge hunt but were taken captive, as was a search party sent after them, plus a delegation of seventeen men later dispatched to plead for Bond's release. D'Iberville finally administered the *coup de grâce* by dragging a couple of cannon up a bluff overlooking the Englishmen's island. Using extra powder to produce loud reports, he pumped enough rounds into the camp to force its surrender, then sailed home in triumph, his fleet loaded down with prisoners and a well-deserved bounty of fur.

By this time William of Orange was ruler of England and the simmering hostilities with France boiled over into open war. At the urging of the Duke of Marlborough, the English king listed French actions in James and Hudson bays as a major *casus belli*. With d'Iberville vowing to put a permanent end to the English presence, the site of the northern war moved, as if by unspoken agreement, towards the most valuable prize of all: the English traders' bayside headquarters at York Factory. In 1690, d'Iberville arrived off Five Fathom Hole with three small ships and dreams of repeating his triumphs of James Bay, but he found the Factory guarded by a thirty-six-gun man-of-war borrowed from the Royal Navy. Too heavily outgunned to risk a head-on clash, he instead skipped down the bay and quickly captured Fort Severn and its rich store of pelts.

Two years later, the English finally retaliated. Because most of the French fleet had been defeated at La Hogue, London strategists convinced themselves that their rivals could spare no ships to defend Hudson Bay and defiantly dispatched three Company frigates and a fire ship – eighty-two guns in all, with 213 marines and supplies for two years. The war party was led by James Knight, a promoted shipwright wise in the ways of the bay and determined to protect the Company's interests. His first assignment was to recapture Fort Albany, where he had served as Chief Factor a decade earlier.

After wintering on the east coast of James Bay, Knight arrived at Albany late in the spring of 1693; he landed his men and marched towards what he assumed to be an abandoned fort. His troops were met by salvoes of heavy, if irregular, gunfire. On June 23, the guns fell silent. Knight advanced into the fort, discovering to his chagrin that it was occupied by a lone demented French blacksmith chained inside the blockhouse cell. Prolonged interrogation of the unhinged smith revealed that the fort had, in fact, been defended by a cadre of five starving survivors who had magnified their defensive efforts by loading and firing their dead comrades' guns to frighten the English into leaving instead of laying a long siege. Exhausted and discouraged by the odds they were facing, the remaining Frenchmen decided to escape and, on the night of June 22, had wormed their way through their attackers' ranks to start the long trek to Quebec. Knight's triumph was thus muted, though he did have as a consolation prize thirty thousand beaver skins from the Albany warehouse.

By 1694 d'Iberville was back at York Factory aboard one of his two modest warships, facing the thirty-two cannon and fourteen brass swivel-guns of the HBC's most important post. York Factory was at the time being defended by a ghost army called the Independent Company of Foot, commanded by Philip Parsons, its Deputy Governor. Not a single professional soldier had been recruited, and the grandly named I.C.F. consisted of little more than fur traders desultorily trained in small arms drill. The slapdash army's first encounter with the wily d'Iberville proved a predictable disaster. Removing the guns from his ships to the shore, d'Iberville mounted them in such a way that their trajectories reached behind the Factory's artillery, which was permanently pointed out to sea. Then he lobbed in a few experimental shots. By the early evening of October 14, he was ready to order a full-scale bombardment, but decided to send an emissary into the factory first to discuss surrender terms. Much to his surprise, they were accepted with only one proviso: that all hands be allowed a good night's sleep, uninterrupted by the bark of the siege guns. The cannon stayed silent overnight and, following a leisurely breakfast, the fifty-three defenders ignominiously surrendered. D'Iberville renamed the site Fort Bourbon and left for France at the end of the summer with a valuable load of pelts. Ten months later, during his absence, an English sortie by three Royal Navy frigates under Captain William Allen easily recaptured the fort. After a full decade of fighting and winning, the French once again lacked any toehold on the bay.

THE SEASON AFTER THAT, the Hudson Bay war grew serious. In the greatest Arctic sea battle in North American history, the two sides clashed in a drama that deter-

mined ownership of York Factory for the next sixteen years. The engagement should by rights have consolidated d'Iberville's reputation for courage and innovation, but since the battle-prize was only a fur trading post on the margin of civilization, his remarkable exploits were almost ignored.

In the summer of 1697, the king of France dispatched the most formidable fleet ever sent to Hudson Bay. Under the command of d'Iberville aboard the forty-four-gun *Pélican*, the ships were stuck for three weeks among the floes blocking Hudson Strait. When the flagship broke loose, she laid a southwesterly course for the Nelson River, and by September 3, d'Iberville dropped anchor at Five Fathom Hole. The following morning at 9:30, just after he had sent a shallop ashore with twenty-five men to reconnoitre the British-held fortress, he spied the silhouettes of three peaked sails on the horizon. Certain that this was the balance of his fleet, d'Iberville raised anchor and sailed out to meet his mates, yardarms aflutter with signal flags. No response. The trio of newcomers was almost alongside his gunwales when he realized that this was an enemy fleet: two armed freighters – the *Dering* and the *Hudson's Bay* – flying the flag of the Company of Adventurers and a proud man-o'-war, the Royal Navy frigate *Hampshire*. Among them, the English ships boasted 118 guns and full complements of sailors and marines, while the *Pélican* was sadly short-handed: some of her best men were ashore, forty prostrate sailors lay in the sick bay with scurvy, and twenty-seven of her most able sea-hands had been transferred to another of the French ships during a stopover in Newfoundland.

Caught between the English-held fort on land and English cannon facing him at sea, d'Iberville had two choices, surrender or fight – and for him that was no choice at all. He ordered the stoppers torn off his guns, sent his battery-men below, had ropes stretched across the slippery decks to provide handholds and aimed his prow at the enemy. As he swept by the *Hampshire*, Captain John Fletcher, its commanding officer, let go a broadside that left most of the *Pélican*'s rigging in tatters. At the same time, the two HBC ships poured a stream of grapeshot and musket fire into the Frenchman's unprotected stern.

The battle raged for four hours. The blood of the wounded French sailors bubbled down the clinkerboards through the scuppers into the sea. The ship's superstructure was reduced to a bizarre accumulation of shattered wood; a lucky shot from the *Dering* had blown off the *Pélican*'s prow so that she appeared dead in the water.

In a brief respite, when the two tacking flagships were close enough for the commanding officers to see one another, Fletcher called across from the *Hampshire* demanding d'Iberville's surrender. The Frenchman made an appropriate gesture of refusal, and the English captain paid tribute to his opponent's courage by ordering a steward to bring him a bottle of vintage wine. He proposed a toast across the gap between the two vessels, raising his glass in an exaggerated salute. D'Iberville reciprocated. The ships were so close and the two hulls had so many holes in them that the opposing gun crews could see into each other's smoky quarters. Minutes later, d'Iberville came up on Fletcher's windward quarter and let go with one great broadside, the storm of fire pouring into the English hull, puncturing her right at the waterline. Within three ship's lengths, the *Hampshire* foundered, having struck a shoal, and eventually sank with all hands.

It was barely noon and the desperate splashings of drowning seamen still echoed in the freshening autumn wind as d'Iberville manoeuvred his crippled ship to direct the force of his guns against the *Hudson's Bay*. The Company ship let go one volley and surrendered. During a squall, the *Dering* fled for shelter in the Nelson River. As the *Pélican*'s crew began boarding the vanquished *Hud-*

son's Bay, a sudden storm came in off the open water, the shrieking wind melding with the screams of the wounded as the rough heaving of the ships battered their bleeding limbs against bulkheads and splintered decks. The *Hudson's Bay* was lucky enough to be driven almost ashore before she sank, so that those aboard could wade to land, but the *Pélican* dragged useless anchors along the bay-bottom silt in the teeth of the hurricane-strength onshore winds. Finally, her rudder broken, she nosed her prow into a sandbar six miles from the nearest bluff. Her lifeboats had been shot away; rescue canoes from shore were swamped as soon as they were launched. The survivors were forced to swim ashore, towing the wounded on a makeshift raft of broken spars. Eighteen more men drowned, and the others stumbled on shore to find the inhospitable land swathed in snow, with nothing but a bonfire and sips of seaweed tea to comfort them.

The belated French ships arrived within a few days but could not land their troops because of York Factory's cannon. D'Iberville and his tiny band of survivors crept up close to the palisade. They made as much noise as they could, drawing the fire of the English long enough to allow the French ships to land troops and guns. Finding himself in the chronic condition of HBC factors of the day – surrounded by d'Iberville's gunners – Henry Baley, then in charge of York Factory, took the simplest way out: he decided to surrender. Granted only their personal belongings, the HBC men marched out of their fortified sanctuary the following afternoon, drums beating a fast step and a Company flag flapping in the breeze. They retreated with dignity if not a little apprehension into the wilderness of the surrounding forest to face the hazards of the Hudson Bay winter.

The French victory was complete. With frost already in the air, d'Iberville made for home. Sailing out of Hudson Bay for the last time, he was bound for further triumphs in Louisiana and the West Indies before expiring of malarial fever at forty-seven in Havana. His posthumous reputation, which should have ranked him as a minor Nelson or Wellington, was diluted by the fact that the scene of his victories was so far removed from Versailles. A soldier of fortune on his own account as well as his king's, he won France's highest decoration, the Cross of Saint Louis, but was never granted the opportunity to practise his genius on the battlefields of Europe.

York Factory remained under French rule until the Treaty of Utrecht unctuously returned it to the HBC in 1713. Except for the occasional skirmish and commando raids,* the royal charter was never again challenged by a foreign power. It was somehow typical of both the Company's unwarlike character and its enduring diplomatic shrewdness that even though the English lost every important battle, when all the fighting and all the negotiating were done, the Hudson's Bay Company reigned supreme over the territory of its choice, and returned to the happy drudgery of the fur trade.

---

*In the summer of 1709, a force of a hundred Montreal traders and Mohawk Indians attacked Albany Fort. Warned by a visiting hunter, HBC Governor John Fullartine repulsed the assault, killing sixteen attackers and saving the Company's only remaining foothold. In 1782, the French briefly captured Prince of Wales Fort and York Factory.

CHAPTER 7

THE CENTURY OF THE LAKES

Sir Bibye Lake believed that if circumspection in the conduct of the Hudson's Bay Company's affairs was desirable, silence was even better.

THE INDIVIDUAL MOST DIRECTLY RESPONSIBLE for translating the beaver catch into an impressive cash flow was Sir Bibye Lake, a nimble City financier whose family achieved effective control in 1697, and ran the Hudson's Bay Company as a private fiefdom for most of a century. Except for two brief gaps totalling eight years, Lake family oligarchs were either Governor or Deputy Governor of the Company continuously for eighty-seven years. In a remarkable feat of corporate endurance, Sir Bibye himself guided the HBC's fortunes for an unmatched span of thirty-one years.

The Lake family's record in salvaging the HCB's fortunes was all the more remarkable because of the Company's depleted circumstances when they first acquired its stock. Their timely intercession fitted in well with the Hudson's Bay Company's uncanny good luck in attracting precisely the right style of management appropriate for its crisis of the moment.

It was under the stewardship of Sir Bibye Lake that profit, not mock heroics, became the HBC's motivating force. Financial discretion, backed by solid London capital, repeatedly triumphed over valour. Thus was perfected the creative somnambulism that would be the Company's hallmark.

THAT THE DISPOSITION OF THE WILDERNESS around Hudson Bay could become the specific subject of two articles in the Treaty of Utrecht, which in 1713 ended the thirteen-year war of the Spanish Succession, was more the result of the persistence of the Company's petitioners than of its importance as real estate in the conduct of Britain's *realpolitik*. Even in this context, the day-to-day bustle of the City fur markets and London dockside seemed only tenuously connected with the glamour of the sealed royal parchments of 1670 and the glory of the courtier-statesmen who had originally formed the Company of Adventurers.

In the short term, the war had been bad for business. At this low point in its history, the Company could not afford to pay its tradesmen, found it had to dip into the vaults of its bankers to settle wartime excise bills and was reduced to the desperate expedient of borrowing to pay interest on existing debt. Anthony Beale, the Governor of its only surviving fort, Albany, was owed £600 in back pay. Although £100 was borrowed to buy off Pierre Radisson, the Company's irrepressible co-founder, his pension was almost constantly in arrears and the HBC could not or would not raise the extra £40 he was demanding to damp down his public innuendos about the Company's looming insolvency.

According to historian E.E. Rich, the HBC's survival at the turn of the century depended on "the connivance of a-bankrupt Governor." He was Sir Stephen Evans, a goldsmith and Member of Parliament whose judgment at the helm seemed equally dubious in life as in his pitiful, unnecessary death. As a long-time HBC banker, he did manage to cover some of its cash shortfalls (at reasonable profit to himself) and originally underwrote its business of importing Russian hemp from Peter the Great for the Royal Navy ropeyard, although he was soon squeezed out by a ring of naval contractors.

A strangely erratic speculator, Evans was the younger brother of one of Marlborough's generals. He lacked dash and verve and could not keep his mind on any one business for very long. In 1694 he had been dropped from the Customs Board of the House of Commons for poor attendance. As HBC Governor, he paid so little attention to its affairs that he attended only three of the monthly Committee meetings during 1702 and 1703; Thomas Lake, the Deputy Governor, was the real day-to-day manager of the Company. Frequently the aging Sir Christopher Wren – his newly completed dome of St Paul's the shining glory of the City – would fill in when both Evans and Lake were absent.

Sir Stephen, who presided over the Company's affairs for all but four years between 1692 and 1712, was not above using the HBC's good offices for his own purposes. He floated a questionable insurance fund for setting up apprentices in trade and helping to finance their marriages. This eccentric scheme was somewhat less than honest and cost the Company £900, which Lake tried to recover from Evans in City court. Meanwhile Sir Stephen had gone bankrupt from one of his other and even more questionable ventures, which involved a scheme floated at Lloyd's Coffee House to insure merchants against the outbreak of foreign wars. By January 1712, Lake and the other Committeemen won the claim against their quixotic Governor before the Guildhall Commissioners, but they could recover only £11 before the star-crossed Sir Stephen tricked his creditors by committing suicide.

Even this irrevocable act did nothing to improve Evans's reputation for inept decision making. Posthumous examination of his jumble of holdings revealed that the whole thing might have been prompted by a ghastly mistake: he still had £3,574 in HBC Governor's stock stashed away in a forgotten hoard. One theory was that the meticulous Lakes, father Thomas and son Bibye, had become so exasperated with their doddering chief that, to kick him out of the Governor's chair, they conspired to allow him to believe himself bankrupt, not realizing the desperate act of which he was capable.

What kept the Company alive at this point was the Lakes' stubborn lobbying for return of the HBC lands from the French. It clearly required subsidizing the ministry of Robert Harley, Earl of Oxford, whose Secretary of State, Lord Bolingbroke, leader of the British negotiations at Utrecht, archly complained: "There is nothing more persistent in the world than these claims of the Hudson's Bay Company. We are desirous greatly to see all these smug ancient gentlemen satisfied."

When the Treaty of Utrecht was finally signed, the French resigned themselves not only to "cession" of Newfoundland, but also to the full restoration of the Hudson Bay territories.* This was particularly significant to the HBC Committeemen, because their failure in 1690 to obtain parliamentary confirmation of their charter for longer than seven years had left their monopoly claims hanging by the unravelling thread of a royal prerogative granted nearly half a century before. All now depended upon building up squatters' rights on the shores of Hudson Bay. The treaty not only inaugurated an unprecedented thirty-one years

---

*The tenth clause of the Treaty of Utrecht provided that: "The said most Christian King shall restore to the Kingdom and Queen of Great Britain to be possessed in full right for ever, the bay and streights rivers and places situate in the said by and streights, and which belong there-unto no tracts of land or of sea being excepted, which are at present possessed by the subjects of France ..."

of peace between France and England, but it also marked incontrovertible international recognition of the HBC's "title" – the claim to exclusive use of its huge overseas territories.

This might logically have triggered the HBC to undertake some exploration activity, but instead, Bibye Lake and his fellow financiers limited their objectives to remaining solvent and easing back out of public view. Relaxed in their tranquil possession of power, the HBC Committeemen were well content to float along on a policy characterized by E.E. Rich as "unobtrusive sanity."

Throughout the crisis years of the War of the Spanish Succession, the price of HBC shares had responded to the bitter circumstances, with quotes on the new London Stock Exchange dropping to 50 percent of par value. After 1700, in their customary cavalier style, the HBC Committeemen simply stopped having the official price quotations published. By then the stock was rarely traded. Thomas and Bibye Lake held the controlling fistful, while many of the rest of the shares were retained, magpie-style, through fiscal splendour and adversity alike, and passed on as dusty family heirlooms to parishes, deacons, widows and eldest sons. In each of two typical years (1709 and 1711), only one transaction was recorded in the HBC stock transfer book. The Company's General Courts, as the annual conclaves of stockholders continued to be called, were desultory formalities. At the 1707 meeting, only seven shareholders presented themselves, all of them members of the retiring Committee. They promptly re-elected one another plus their two absent colleagues and adjourned the meeting.

Many of the shareholders were not only apathetic, they were dead. The ledgers show that, of forty-nine holders of stock in 1713, seventeen were deceased. The holdings purchased in 1674 by chemist-philosopher Robert Boyle still stood in his name, for example, though he had died in 1691. The trustees, in most cases the Governor or

Secretary acting for the estate, sleepily controlled nearly half the Company's nominal capital – an enviable state of affairs in any company.

The long drought in dividend payments was symptomatic of the change in the Company's character. It had, quite simply, gone into City limbo. Instead of continuing as a fairly popular – and fairly risky – venture-stock on the London Exchange, the HBC had evolved through the cunning of the Lake family into the closed proprietorship it was to remain until Lord Selkirk's takeover in 1809. Adam Smith, the leading economic prophet of the day, accurately described it as "very nearly to the nature of a private copartnery."

WHEN THE BRITISH FUR TRADE is set in its early eighteenth-century perspective, it shows why the HBC, having lost its original court-connected sponsorship, exercised so little domestic political influence. In part it was the result of the reluctance of HBC governors to budget any significant sums for parliamentary bribes. Kings and lords continued to be subsidized, but not the Commons. Generally, it was far better to lie low and not attract interest, only collect it. The governors had the example before them of the East India Company, an overly visible organization which learned to its cost that if politicians could not be bought, they most certainly had to be rented.

At the heart of the matter was a continuing battle between the Court and the City. To retain its parliamentary charter, the East India Company had become so involved in "subsidizing" Parliament and the Crown that a clamour arose from those not exposed to its largess that they too should share the bounty. When the East India Company drew the line, the House of Commons set up a commission of inquiry into East India Company bribery. Presenting their findings in 1695, the parliamentarians reported that the East India Company had been doling out £90,000 a year, £10,000 of which had been going annually into the Royal Household.

The East India Company was allowed to save some face when it generously agreed to lend the bulk of its capital to the Bank of England. But this was not enough, and shrewder heads reasoned that the East India Company could do with a little competition. In 1698 the New East India Company was chartered alongside the old, but "not without heavy bribery of ministers." The new company's terms were almost the same as those of the old, except more evangelical – ships were required to carry a chaplain, and provision had to be made for the maintenance of local ministers and schoolmasters. Directors were required to hold £1,000 of stock, and members of the New East India Company traded co-operatively as individuals, not as a company. The overburdened companies were merged in 1708 in exchange for the transfer of their capital to the National Debt through the Bank of England, which at the same time was given the monopoly of joint-stock banking.

Inspired by the East India experience and by the insolvency of the Royal African Company, the HBC soldiered gingerly onward from year to year, earnestly avoiding public gaze. Still another reason for its retreat into the calm backwaters of superannuated investments was that, essential as the fur business was to the New World, it accounted for an insignificant portion of Britain's overall trade. Although there were no firm statistics (since with the advent of bonded warehouses in London, where silks and furs were held for re-export, no figures on total trade could be made available), the true import of skins, hides and furs from all sources accounted for less than .5 percent of the total value of Britain's incoming trade between 1700 and 1750. Although much has been made of the Company's monopoly, only half of the skins sold at London auction houses originated in the Company lands. Because of its superior capitalization the HBC could ride any market at will.

The most significant competition came out of Boston, New York and the colonies of Maryland and Virginia, famous for the quality of their deerskin. Not all fur went into hats and luxury garments; lower-grade skins were shaved and made into footwear. At first, the superior quality of the Hudson Bay furs had placed them in a class apart (and many still went directly to Moscow or Leipzig), but that distinction soon lost its edge as the immigrant Huguenot hatters learned ways to make beaver-wool from almost any grade and variety of skin. Glue could be added even to rabbit to make a passable imitation; however, such plebeian headgear had an unfortunate propensity to droop and disintegrate in the rain.

Despite its negligible size, the fur trade slotted neatly into England's mercantilist policies which were designed to perpetuate a self-contained empire, aggressively maintained on four vital pillars: England's own growing manufacturing might; the sugar and molasses trade of the West Indies; the degrading but lucrative slave and gold traffic with African chiefs; and the products of the New World's forests, farms and oceans.

It was to preserve this precariously balanced parallelogram that there was a movement in the 1760s by City sugar traders to bargain away Canada so that control of Guadeloupe could be retained instead. Because the French-held islands in the West Indies had progressed much faster than their English-held counterparts, the trading equations had been thrown out of balance and pamphleteers on both sides of the Atlantic began to debate which of the two colonies – a lucrative 688-square-mile island or an apparently empty northern wilderness would make the more lasting contribution to British interests.

The case for Guadeloupe was based partly on the notion

that if the farmers, trappers and fishermen of the New World were deprived of their West Indian markets, they might turn to manufacturing – and cut into the monopoly of the mother country. One pamphlet compared Canada, "which produces nothing but a few hats," with Guadeloupe, rich in "that article of luxury, sugar, the consumption of which is daily increasing both in America and Europe." Another unattributed argument cited in favour of retaining Canada was that "a northern colony is preferable to a southern, being healthier and more suited to the development of a white race."

ONE REASON CANADA WAS NOT UNCEREMONIOUSLY DUMPED in the 1760s was that, half a century before, Sir Bibye Lake had begun the process that was to build the Hudson's Bay Company's toehold into the depot of a continental trading system. Lake could hold his own against the sugar barons, but English politicians came to see the Company as the only countervailing force to claims of the continent's western territories by the troublemakers and land dealers in the Thirteen Colonies. The Committeemen suffered from few illusions that this state of affairs would bear long-term diplomatic consequences, but there is little question that, without their Governor's financial cunning, the HBC would not have survived.

Sir Bibye had been inaugurated into the Hudson's Bay orbit by his father, Thomas Lake, a well-connected London barrister-financier who began buying the Company's stock on May 13, 1697 and rapidly became its largest shareholder. Named Deputy Governor in 1710, Thomas Lake brought his only son Bibye into the Company with a grant of £1,000 in stock. He had sponsored his election to the HBC Committee in 1708 and sent him to Holland to represent the Company in the early stages of the Utrecht peace negotiations, for which the twenty-six-year-old barrister was given a gratuity of £50. Two years later, the young man replaced his father as Deputy Governor and on November 21, 1712 succeeded the ill-starred Sir Stephen Evans as Governor. It was no plum: no dividends had been paid since 1691; the parliamentary confirmation of the Company's charter was still hanging; unsold furs were piled high in its London warehouses; and its activities in the New World were confined to the holding operation at Albany.

In 1711, on the death of his father, young Lake succeeded as heir to the baronetcy that Charles II had granted his loyalist great-uncle. Lake's royal connections were striking. His uncle Warwick Lake, M.P. for Middlesex, had been a supporter of the Glorious Revolution, and a family cousin, Dr John Lake, later Bishop of Chichester and reputedly a good Anglican, had served as tutor to the Duke of York's young daughters, the future queens Mary and Anne. Like his father, Bibye Lake had been trained for the Bar in London's Middle Temple, but his interest was quickly caught by the allure of overseas trade. He eventually became a major shareholder in both the East India Company and the up-again, down-again Royal African Company of which he was subsequently named Sub-Governor. He inherited tracts of virgin land in Acadia and Maine granted to his grandfather, Thomas Lake of Boston. Not only did his successful intervention during the Utrecht negotiations help restore the HBC's North American possessions, but prices on the London fur market also picked up, and in 1718 Sir Bibye summoned the Company's thirty-five surviving shareholders to declare a 10 percent dividend – the first return on their capital for twenty-eight years. (From an original capitalization of £10,500 not all of which had been taken up – the Company was by then recording delectable annual profits of more than £6,000 on yearly turnovers of £30,000.)

Sir Bibye Lake believed that if circumspection in the

conduct of the Hudson's Bay Company affairs was desirable, silence was even better. His insistence that every decision aggrandize the Company's profits while absolute secrecy was imposed would characterize the rule of every governor who succeeded him. This obsession with concealment was such that even the most mundane comments, such as the record of tides through Hudson Strait, the weather observations by the Company's factors, the location of HBC outposts and details of prevailing trade methods with the Indians were kept locked within corporate archives. Letters written home by the servants on Hudson Bay were censored, and the captains of Company ships were ordered to subject all passengers to the indignity of having their personal luggage searched before returning up the Thames. The maritime commanders' own logs and charts were whisked off to the vaults in Fenchurch Street before anyone but the Committeemen could read them, even when they detailed important geographic discoveries. "What little exploration was carried out by Company servants rarely became public knowledge," wrote Glyndwr Williams, the noted HBC historian. "Printed maps of the Bay remained as crudely inaccurate as they had been a century before."

Lake knew the legal value of the HBC's royal charter, which had escaped parliamentary scrutiny in 1697. Members of the HBC's august Committee were warned that under no circumstances were they to discuss the contents of that hallowed document with outsiders. Company employees engaged in the fur trade itself were searched for contraband pelts on leaving or entering their posts. Each employee had to swear formally to maintain secrecy about "all matters pertaining to the Company" – an oath that was enforced by withholding a portion of their wages until retirement.

The HBC's financial dealings were similarly obscured. Stock transfers were handled privately between existing investors. In the most comprehensive guide to the City's main financiers, published in 1740, Sir Bibye Lake is listed only as a director of the Royal African Company, though he was spending nearly all his time on HBC affairs.

Sir Bibye's extravagant stipulations and precautions flowed from the natural reticence imposed on the proprietors of any lucrative monopoly; foreign rivals and domestic interlopers were perceived as potential poachers, even when their interest remained cursory. By the softest, surest pussyfooting, the HBC was able to adroitly circumvent the avalanche of criticism that eventually helped drive the Royal African and South Sea companies out of business. Unlike its overseas rivals, the Company neither requested nor received any government subventions, so that even if it failed to live up to the extravagant mandate of its charter, at least its operations were not a burden on the national treasury.

Sir Bibye was brilliant in his choreography of the HBC's relations with London furriers and skinners, who bought largely for re-export. His manipulations may have provided welcome fodder to the HBC's critics, but it was during Lake's tenure that the Company was transformed from a dubious enterprise dependent for survival on each season's fur sales to a gilt-edged investment company with a proper portfolio and substantial backing in the City. Silence was indeed golden.

No one gained more from this metamorphosis than Sir Bibye himself. Minute books of the time record a series of almost annual "gratuities" voted to him in recognition of the HBC's new and happier fiscal state. He was not averse to using the Company's cash reserves to finance his outside ventures, borrowing from the HBC treasury against anticipated dividends. These loans amounted to as much as £20,000 each, and in 1738 some of the more independent Committeemen secured a Chancery Injunction to prevent him from selling £12,222 in stock he was holding at the time. (He transferred it to his chosen nominees anyway.)

Sir Bibye identified himself so strongly with the Company that he had considerable trouble differentiating between his corporate and his personal interests. When in doubt, he opted for the latter. In April 1718 he borrowed £17,000 from the Company at 3 percent per annum – which it in turn was forced to raise at 5 percent. He was constantly manipulating his HBC stock, selling in May and repurchasing in July, so that he would receive maximum dividends without tying up his capital. Sir Bibye had also borrowed from the Company the £11,000 he paid for his country retreat in Derbyshire, a debt that had not yet been repaid at the time of his death.

Although he was canny enough to steer the Company through the bullish speculation that climaxed with the bursting of the South Sea Bubble in 1720, he came very close to endangering its capital structure with a flamboyant scheme that would have grossly multiplied his own fortune by watering HBC stock. The basic idea (approved by the Company's Committee on August 30, 1720) was sound enough. The capitalization of £10,500 had been raised only once – to £31,500, in 1684 – so that the Company's book value had not caught up to the expanded assets. To remedy this imbalance, Sir Bibye proposed a daring manoeuvre that would have benefited the Company's existing shareholders (himself chief among them) far more than its treasury. He proposed trebling the existing capital base of 315 shares at £100 each to 945 shares (£94,500), with each existing shareholder given, free of charge, 3 new shares for each £100 held, for a total share value of £378,000 – a 1,200 percent dilution on top of the split. Three more shares were to be optioned to each of the fortunate proprietors on the basis of a 10 percent down payment. It was little wonder that the ecstatic shareholders gave the Governor a lavish gratuity of five hundred gold guineas. But the unrealistic anticipation of South Sea profits deflated the British financial markets – when the bubble popped, share values in the absurdly capitalized South Sea Company dropped from £1,000 to £100. Lake's scheme brought £3,150 in cash into the HBC, largely from existing shareholders, so Sir Bibye eventually withdrew the second part of the bargain. Each proprietor was thus credited with £30 for each £10 paid in, the exception being the stock held by George I. The King was thenceforward paid dividends on a holding of £2,970, so that the royal dividends at that point amounted to as much as the monarchy's original investment half a century before. By the end of the complicated shuffle, the HBC's capitalization totalled £103,950, which raised it closer to the value of its assets, although only £3,150 in new cash had actually been injected into its treasury.

Sir Bibye was to spend twenty-three years after the South Sea episode as the HBC's Governor. His smooth helmsmanship left a permanent imprint on the manner of the Company's approach to its several constituencies. Whether they were bartering with the Cree on Hudson Bay or blandishing the Bank of England for the season's working capital, Company officers handled each situation with a mixture of sobriety and shrewdness that exasperated their detractors and pleased their shareholders. The generous dividend flow, which had begun to gush so freely in Sir Bibye's time, was not disrupted again until forty years after his death, when French warships again captured the bay.

Lake's influence on the HBC was so overwhelming that it outlasted his governorship by nearly half a century.*

---

* His longevity was rivalled but not surpassed by Lord Strathcona, the veteran fur trader who rose to the governorship in 1889 at the advanced age of sixty-nine. He held onto that office until he died twenty-five years later in 1914. John Henry Pelly, a former

Seven years after he passed away in 1743, his son Atwell was named Governor and served for the next decade, commuting to London from his estate of Edmonton in Middlesex. Atwell's younger brother, Bibye, served a grand total of thirty-nine years (1743–1782) as a Company Committeeman, the last dozen of those years as Governor. Sir Atwell's eldest son, James Winter Lake (who continued to live at the Edmonton estate), was a member of the Committee for forty-five years, serving as Deputy Governor and, from 1799 until his death in 1807, as Governor. (During James Lake's time as Deputy Governor, the Company established a trading post on the North Saskatchewan River to compete with the North West Company's Fort Augustus and named it Fort Edmonton in honour of the Lake family estate. The tiny settlement grew to be the capital of the province of Alberta.)

The extended domination of the Lake family – and particularly the tenure of Sir Bibye himself – was marked by consolidation, efficiency and prosperity, but also by a narrowness of outlook that prevented exploration inland from Hudson Bay or northward in search for a passage to the Orient. The real paradox of Sir Bibye's remarkable career was how, without venturing farther from London than his country estate, he was able to instil in the HBC Factors, an ocean away, his stubbornly maintained ethic. In this he was aided by the constancy of the seasonal and commercial cycles into which life on Hudson Bay was divided and the unchanging nature of the quest for fur.

East India Company trading captain, was forty-five when he took over in 1822, to become an essential partner with Sir George Simpson in exploiting the amalgamation with the North West Company. He rose to become Governor of the Bank of England and led the HBC through most of its thirty years of greatest influence.

III ANCHORING OF EMPIRE

CHAPTER 8

ASLEEP BY THE FROZEN SEA

"The Company have for eighty years slept at the edge of a frozen sea; they have shewn no curiosity to penetrate farther themselves, and have exerted all their art and power to crush that spirit in others."

— *Joseph Robson*

IT OWNED THE WORLD'S most valuable land monopoly – a third of the still-to-be-explored northern part of the American continent. Yet during most of the eighteenth century, the Company was hived into a handful of economically marginal and physically unprepossessing outposts around Hudson Bay, squeezed between the boreal forest and an inhospitable sea.

Sir Bibye Lake and his fellow proprietors, preoccupied with smoothing the fluctuations in London's money and fur markets, hinted at invincibility in the field and omnipotence at home, but the Company's true position could more accurately be gauged by its sparse representation on the bay itself – at one point fewer than thirty shivering souls. Between 1693 and 1714, the French almost succeeded in elbowing the Company away from the bay altogether, with only Albany Fort's garrison of twenty-seven defenders doggedly flying its banner. The diminutive scale of the forces that tussled over control of the huge territory was dramatically illustrated in 1714, when James Knight, the veteran HBC administrator, was sent from London to reclaim York Factory from its French occupiers. Bearing a royal mandate which rested on the grandiose terms of the Treaty of Utrecht, he found a quaint cluster of rickety shacks manned by a wretched crew of just nine French defenders, including a chaplain, a surgeon and an apprentice. In a vivid dispatch to his principals in London, Knight complained that York's facilities were "nothing but a confused heap of old rotten houses without form or strength very not sufficient to secure your goods from the weather, not fit for men to live in without being exposed to the frigid winter. My own place I have to live in this winter is not half so good as our cowhouse was in the Bottom of the Bay, and I have never been able to see my hand in it since I have been there without a candle. It is so black and dark, cold and wet withal, nothing to make it better but heaping up earth about it to make it warm."

Except for the very occasional foray, the Company's disposition was to sit quietly on the periphery of the bay, routinely manning its trading posts.

The dynamics of the fur trade had grown static, if not altogether comatose. Hardly anything interrupted its monotonous rhythm, unless it was some outrage of the interlopers from Montreal or a diplomatic spat in Leipzig. The financial reporting and management methods put in place by Sir Bibye Lake functioned as if the perpetual Governor had perfected a perpetual money machine. As long as the Company's profits were reflected in respectable dividends and the Indians continued to fetch the furs, there was judged to be no particular need to expand the Company's activities, no purpose in initiating grand new policies on a search for the North West Passage, inland exploration or very much else.

HUDSON BAY IS AN INLAND SEA nearly as large as the Mediterranean; its shoreline meanders for 7,600 miles, a distance only 300 miles shorter than the earth's diameter at the equator, but during the eighteenth century, the HBC governors dispatched no more than two hundred men at a time to exploit their immense holdings. John Oldmixon, in his 1708 study *The British Empire in America*, admitted that he should have led off his book with a description of the Hudson's Bay Company's territories, but explained, "There being no Towns nor Plantations in this Country, but two or three poor Forts to defend the Factories, we thought we were at Liberty to place it where we pleas'd, and were loath to let our History open with the Description of so miserable a Wilderness." Except for Albany Fort and the reoccupied York Factory (1714), the physical presence of the Company for more than fifty years was limited to trading-depots at Moose Factory, Rupert House and Churchill (Prince of Wales's Fort), with out-stations at Eastmain and, later, Henley House and Severn.

It was by a quirk of geography and navigational limitations (and the influence of Radisson and Groseilliers) that this initial British occupation of Canada came through its north-central back door, a territory that nearly three centuries later would still be struggling unsuccessfully for economic viability. "The search for the North West Passage," noted University of Winnipeg geographer Dr Tim Ball, "coupled with the practice of latitude sailing and efforts to avoid the North Atlantic Drift, resulted in early explorers to Canada arriving via the Davis and Hudson straits into Hudson Bay, so that the earliest trading-posts were established on its shores."

Except for its relative proximity to Britain and the fact that the estuaries of several large river systems emptied into it, inviting the movement of goods to and from the continent's interior, Hudson Bay was hardly a comfortable choice.

The November 1754 issue of *The Gentleman's Magazine* carried the sensible suggestion that "the countries bordering on Hudson Bay might serve as an English Siberia, where we might hold our convicts, instead of hanging them by thousands at home, or transporting them to corrupt the natives of our colonies." Then it righteously added: "Convicts should always be sent to a country barren, and in a manner uninhabited, because there they cannot corrupt by their bad example; are secure from their former temptations; and must be industrious – and consequently have the best chance of reforming, and growing good." The Public Records office of Northern Ireland in Belfast contains documents that outline a similar proposal, suggesting that the Irish government take over Hudson Bay and turn it into a huge penal settlement, administered by one simple rule-of-thumb: the worse the criminal, the farther north he should be sent "with the most enormous and confirmed offenders handed over to the Eskimos as slaves."

The HBC posts were not prisons. They were more reminiscent of lunar colonies. During their tours of duty (three, or more usually five years), the Bay men had to be utterly self-reliant. Except for the brief annual visit of a solitary Company supply ship (weather, ice and French raiders permitting), the tiny posts were on their own. Pride in being thrust into such self-reliance seemed to have its therapeutic aspects because many loyal Company men signed up for term upon term. One servant named John Paterson stayed at Churchill for seventeen years without requesting a visit home – a measure of his family life in Britain, perhaps, or of the defiant euphoria of sheer survival.

The daily and seasonal cycle of events at the HBC's outposts was meticulously recorded by the resident Factor in each post's journal, laboriously lettered with goose-quill pen and thawed ink, either in his own hand or, at the larger posts, dictated to his "writer." Entries in these journals, dispatched to London once a year on the returning supply ships, consisted of weather information and trade figures, along with deferential descriptions of the duties performed by each "officer" and "servant." The reports were similar in style to ships' logs – brief and impersonal, justifying rather than explaining, documenting their authors' adherence to standing instructions, scrupulously avoiding innovation.* These laboriously maintained volumes were coffined in "packets"– wooden boxes 1 ½ feet by 2 feet by 4 feet – into which mail was collected from each post. Year after year, generation after generation, these packets were shipped across the North Atlantic with the season's fur catch. Each was perused by the Committeemen before they issued the next season's instructions. Then regardless of the content and quality of the dispatches, the books were solemnly interred in the Company's confidential vaults,

---

*Although local Factors exercised great power over everyday events, they had almost no policy functions, even to decide who should run their posts. Each Factor was left to make his own day-to-day decisions like the captain of a ship at sea. In 1742, when the factors at Moose and Albany protested that the appointment of captains of supply ships to positions on the posts' governing councils was an infringement of their independence, they were rebuked and told to devote their limited talents to fostering the fur trade and leave the London Committee to settle policy matters.

where they would remain, inaccessible, for the next two centuries.*

Each Wednesday noon, the Governor, Deputy Governor and half a dozen Committeemen would gather at Hudson's Bay House in the heart of London's financial district and spend the afternoon issuing their various decrees.

Because the Company's strictly observed policy was neither to allow public access to its factors' journals nor to welcome any visitors to the bay's shores, the only firsthand description published and circulated about the HBC's activities in the first half of the eighteenth century was that of an early corporate renegade: Joseph Robson's *An Account of Six Years Residence in Hudson's Bay*. Robson had first entered the Company's service as a stonemason in 1733 for a three-year term and had returned overseas in 1744 as the Surveyor and Supervisor of Buildings. After completing the first authentic charts of the lower fifty miles of the Nelson River and mapping York Factory, he was transferred northward to Churchill and ordered to carry out similar surveys. There he came up against Robert Pilgrim, the resident Factor. A rheumatic former ship's steward who seemed to be bitterly at odds with everyone he met, Pilgrim traded unfairly with the Indians, neglected the maintenance of his post's buildings and was particularly incensed at Robson's direct and often angry criticism of his methods. Just before Robson returned to England,

---

*Again and again, exasperated factors urged the Committeemen to take the trouble to read their journals, feeling that the nature of the questions that kept flowing from London clearly indicated that their dispatches had not been adequately studied. The Committeemen sometimes acted more like schoolmasters than governors, not so much concerned with the contents of the bayside journals as with their form. "Your general letter is not wrote in paragraphs which you must not fail to observe for the future, answering distinctly each paragraph of our letter," they admonished James Isham, when he was in charge of York Factory.

his dealings had deteriorated to near-mutiny, and Pilgrim whined to the London Committee that Robson and two of his companions had "declared themselves Your Honours' Enemies." In his book published five years later, Robson severely criticized the HBC's slipshod trading practices and its haphazard construction methods at Prince of Wales's Fort. He alleged that penetration up the rivers into the continent was easy, that corn and other vegetables could be cultivated as far north as York Factory and that local mining and fishing enterprises as well as permanent colonies could be established on Hudson Bay. It was the mean-spirited blockade of innovation at any level, he claimed, that had hindered such possibilities. "The Company have for eighty years slept at the edge of a frozen sea," he wrote in what became a rallying cry for the growing legion of the HBC's self-appointed critics. "They have shewn no curiosity to penetrate farther themselves, and have exerted all their art and power to crush that spirit in others."

HIS ACCUSATIONS WERE TRUE ENOUGH, but Robson was so anxious to discredit the Company that he minimized the difficulties of expanding the operations on the bay. Chief among the problems was the region's dismal climate.

Few places on earth experience such extreme weather fluctuations. Because it is out of reach of moderating ocean currents, Hudson Bay is more frigid than the iceberg-packed Arctic Ocean or the North Pole itself. Temperatures of -82°F have been recorded – colder than most polar lows. For nine months of the year, the sun hugs the horizon; the fierce winds snarl across the beaches and eskers, and on overcast days drifting snow creates a disorienting white void that obliterates all points of reference. "Rich as the trade to these parts have been or may be," wrote John Oldmixon, "the way of living is such that we can not reckon any man happy whose lot is cast upon this Bay …

for that country is so prodigiously cold that nature is never impregnated by the sun; or, rather, her barren womb produces nothing for the subsistence of man."

Oldmixon's distressing description was not based on his own observations but on the verdict of those familiar with the bay's climatic tantrums.* Their reports were hardly encouraging. Captain Christopher Middleton, one of the company's most experienced sea captains and a dogged bay explorer, wintered at Churchill in 1741–42 and kept a detailed weather log. On October 11, Middleton proposed a birthday salute to George II. He noted in his journal later the same evening that "the wine with which the officers drank the aforesaid healths, and which was good port wine, froze in the glass as soon as poured out of the bottle."† By the end of the month, the snow was twelve feet deep and the men had to use axes to hack ice off the *inside* walls of the Factor's house. William Wales, the London astronomer who visited the same post twenty-seven winters later, left behind a graphic description: "The head of my bed-place, for want of knowing better, went against one of the outside walls of the house; and notwithstanding they were of stone, near three feet thick, and lined with inch boards, supported at least three inches from the walls, my bedding was frozen to the boards every morning; and before the end of February, these boards

---

*The first hundred years of the Company's occupation of the bay is known to meteorologists as the Little Ice Age. Samuel Champlain found "bearing" ice on the shores of Lake Superior in June 1608, while a lake in Scotland was reported frozen over in August 1675.

†The apparent anomaly of wine which *pours* from the bottle but *freezes* immediately in the glass can be explained by the fact that wine which is corked is held under pressure and can be kept below its freezing-point without solidification (i.e., supercooled). When the cork is removed and the pressure released, the liquid forms an icy slush as it is poured into the glass.

were covered with ice almost half as thick as themselves. Towards the latter end of January, when the cold was so very intense, I carried a half-pint of brandy, perfectly fluid, into the open air, and in less than two minutes it was as thick as treacle; in about five it had a very strong ice on the top; and I verily believe that in an hour's time it would have been nearly solid."

Factors' journal entries for the period reflect not merely bleak temperature levels but the awesome furies of a Hudson Bay winter: "Insufferable cold. Almost froze my arm in bed"; "Very troublesome to write, ink freezing on my pen"; "Frozen feet and no wonder, as the thermometer for the last three nights was -36, -42 and -38"; "Men cannot see a hundred yards to windward – neither can one get out of our gates for snow"; "Some quicksilver that had been put out some time ago for trying the cold was observed to be frozen while the thermometer was only 36 below zero, which proves the weather to have been six degrees colder than per thermometer"; "Rain froze as it fell – if we have one hour fine weather, we have ten bad for it"; "Hail the size of a Musket Ball"; "Twenty-one years in this country and never see or hear so dismal a night…"

Samuel Hearne, the good-natured northern explorer who regularly wintered at Prince of Wales's, described in detail the fort's spring snowfall in a letter to Humphrey Marten, then in charge of York Factory: "The winter in general has been the mildest I ever knew at Churchill and till the first of March the least snow that has been remembered, at which time a violent snow came on the NNW and lasted four days without intermission. The snows were higher than the house – consequently, all the windows of the upper as well as the lower storey were entirely blocked up … The depth of drift in the yard is about twenty-two feet."

The brief summers brought little respite. Temperatures could rise as high as 80°F, but the numbing agony of the winter's cold was replaced by intolerable plagues of "mosketos" and "sand flyes."* Writing in *Hudson's Bay, or Every-Day Life in the Wilds of North America*, Robert Ballantyne complained how "day and night, the painful, tender little pimples on our necks and behind our ears were constantly being retouched by these villainous flies. It was useless killing thousands of them; millions supplied their place. The only thing, in fact, that can protect one during the night (*nothing* can during the day) is a net of gauze hung over the bed, and as this is looked upon by the young men as somewhat effeminate, it was seldom resorted to."

While he was at Churchill, James Knight gave way to near-hysteria in his August 11, 1717 journal entry describing the hellish insects: "Here is now such swarms of a small sand flyes that wee can hardly see the sun through them and where they light is just as if a spark of fire fell and raises a little bump which smarts and burns so that we cannot forbear rubbing of them as causes such scabbs that our hands and faces is nothing but scabbs. They fly into our ears nose eyes mouth and down our throats as we be most sorely plagued with them … Certainly these be the flyes that was sent as plagues to the Egyptians as caused a darkness over the land and brought such blotches and boils as broke out over them into sores."

Knight, who dominated the HBC's overseas history during the first two decades of the eighteenth century, also penned the classic definition of another of the region's peculiarities, permafrost, when he noted that "the sum-

---

*The black flies of Hudson Bay can be vicious, leaving their victims with a toxin that produces an influenza-like sickness. The number of mosquitoes defies description. A mathematician who accompanied the Curran-Caulkins expedition of 1912 estimated there were fifteen million mosquitoes per cubic yard of free air on the east coast of James Bay.

mer never thaws above the depth of what the following winter freezes." Permafrost in the Hudson Bay area inhibits efficient drainage so that little plant life can flourish. Rain and snow are permanently trapped in shallow lakes and ponds; the east wind snaps the earth's outcrops into a brown cement, turning the landscape into a bleak tableau of muskeg and rock.

The dramatic natural event of the year, then and now, is breakup, when spring runoffs and warming currents combine to soften and fragment coastal ice, forcing the polar bears ashore, where the huge carnivores den and whelp their pups before returning to the floes in the fall. The spring sun once again warms the soul and the rivers draining the Canadian Shield's winter accumulations become torrents as they rampage towards the bay. On May 7, 1715, when the Hayes River thawed inland before its mouth was clear of ice, Knight, then York Factory's Governor, was sitting down to dinner when a flash flood forced him and his entire garrison "to leave the factory and betake our selves to the woods and gett on trees ... the water rising above nine foot upon the land and continued up for six days, wee looking every minute when the factory would be tore to pieces. The ice lay heap'd and crowded at least twenty foot higher than the factory ..."

Knight shifted York Factory's buildings to higher but still temporary ground. When a similar catastrophe overtook the post on May 7, 1788, causing "almost universal destruction," Joseph Colen, then resident at York, took advantage of the flood to choose for the Factory a more enduring site. Observing that "water is as true a level as can be found," he splashed about in his canoe until he located the highest dry promontory where new, more protected permanent buildings could eventually be constructed.

Nature's malevolence in the bay lowlands was the private, if universal, nightmare of those who had invested their lives in the Company's service. But it was the sailors in the HBC's employ who spread the region's reputation as an "evil vortex" at the edge of the known world. In addition to the usual hazards and privations faced by mariners of the day, they encountered conditions that often turned their six-month voyages into endurance tests. One hazard unique to the bay was that shore ice, broken up by winter gales into huge floes, would pile up, sheet upon sheet, and coagulate into solid rafts up to thirty feet thick. These could hole a sailing ship on contact. Icebergs, drifting down from Davis Strait, shut off the Atlantic entrance and exit of the bay for all but three months of the year. The bergs, no respecters of calendar dates, could be deadly even during the navigation season.

These dangers were at least visible, but the sailors, dependent on rudimentary navigational aids in unmarked waters, also found themselves travelling so close to the north magnetic pole that their compass needles tended to dip downward and lose directional stability. Even when veterans of many passages learned to compensate for this disorienting phenomenon, magnetic storms and the large iron-ore bodies on the floor of Hudson Bay sapped compasses of navigational value. Existing charts of the bay looked like children's drawings, so that ships' captains had to rely on a combination of intuition and prayer. They posted crowsnest look-outs trained to spot changes in water colour that might warn of submerged dangers.* To these

---

*The government of Canada did not install navigation lights, beacons and buoys in Hudson Bay until 1914. Then, because of wartime security, all aids were extinguished the following year – and not relit until 1932. As recently as 1965, only the principal harbours had been surveyed; two years earlier, aerial reconnaissance between the Belcher Islands and Hudson Bay's

uncomfortable problems were added an unusually high incidence of cloudiness that prevented celestial sightings and (except for the long, curving and hilly bight in the south-eastern part of the bay) flat coastlines that provided no easily identifiable reference points. The warmer winds rising from the water meeting the cold land in fall and early winter produced impenetrable fog banks, as did the warm, moist offshore winds in spring and early summer. These pleasant offshore breezes could be deadly, carrying many a canoeist out into Hudson Bay beyond rescue. Early harbours were marked only by barely distinguishable cairns and the pine flagpoles of each HBC post. Another questionable aid to navigation was the firing of cannon, both from shore and ship's decks, to help locate the forts. The original beacons guiding ships seeking Moose Factory were tall trees stripped of their branches, with the local Cree occasionally assigned to raise a flag when they sighted an incoming ship.*

Despite these hazards, the number of accidents was surprisingly small. During more than three hundred years of dispatching its fleet into the bay, the Company lost only

eastern shore had revealed numerous islets and above-water rocks, unreported in more than three centuries of navigation. These included a rock pinnacle sweeping 120 feet up from the sea-bed to the surface, just north of Grey Goose Island, which sank the M/V *North Star* in 1961.

*The last prominent beacon, the seventy-five-foot foremast of the sunken schooner *Fort Severn*, was put in place by the Company in 1953. A similar navigational aid (a ninety-six-foot mast) had been erected on North Bluff near the mouth of the Moose River, but it blew down during a 1922 gale. The beacon at Marsh Point, which splits the mouths of the Nelson and Hayes rivers, is still in place.

thirteen ships.* The fact that nearly half of these sank in the twentieth century is a reflection of the modern arrogance of confronting nature. In the past the practice during storms had been to grapple the ships onto ice, on the theory that, as when fighting an opponent much stronger, the advantage of greater strength can be negated by hanging on.

Like the rest of the HBC trade, shipping settled into its own predictable annual cycle. Two or three square-riggers would ghost out of Gravesend in May, tack northward along Britain's eastern shore and, after loading up with fresh water and recruits in the Orkneys, bear away across the Atlantic. The voyage took about twelve weeks. Its landfalls were uncertain. Churchill had fair holding ground and Moose offered reasonable refuge below the Factory, but at all other ports of call the silted mudflats deposited by river outflows kept seaborne visitors at a distance. At York Factory, vessels anchored seven miles out at "Five Fathom Hole" and at Albany, an awkward fifteen miles from the post. Smaller, shore-based sloops unloaded the

---

*Ship	Location	Date of Sinking
Prince Rupert I	Port Nelson	Oct. 21, 1682
Owner's Love	Hudson Strait	Sept. 3, 1697
Mary I	Weston Island	Aug. 27, 1724
Hudson's Bay IV	Cape Resolution	July 3, 1736
Esquimaux	Hudson Bay	Oct. 20, 1836
Prince Arthur	Mansel Island	Aug. 13, 1864
Cam Owen	Churchill	Aug. 30, 1886
Lady Head	Gasket Shoal	Sept. 26, 1903
Stork	Charlton Island	Oct. 10, 1908
Sorine	Charlton Island	Sept. 3, 1910
Bayeskimo	Ungava Bay	July 23, 1925
Fort York	Fort Severn	Sept. 28, 1930
Nascopie	Cape Dorset	July 21, 1947

trade goods and ferried out the season's fur catch.

Because of distances and climate, the posts were almost as separate from one another as from England. It took the Bay men most of a century to organize an informal system of exchanging winter packets of mail between settlements. With no emergency assistance available from either side of the Atlantic, each post had to calculate the limits of its survival, and little was left to chance. Every incoming item was carefully logged and stored, to be produced at the appropriate occasion. Turnaround time was at a premium, as fussy clerks pored over lengthy rosters listing nails, muskets, sealing wax, beads, axe heads and all the sundry items required for trade and survival during another twelve months' isolation. The ships' captains, proud men who tended to patronize their shore-bound colleagues, did little to disguise their impatience to be away from that bleak wilderness. Every hour counted; the days grew shorter as the nippy dawns of September signalled the urgency of their departure.

Their return to England was a forced dash through an ice-ridden Hudson Strait, past Resolution Island into the angry Atlantic. It would be late October before they could butt their way around the Kentish coast and tie up at their assigned slips on the welcoming Thames.

This drawn-out schedule meant that the reports addressed to the HBC's Committeemen were as much as fifteen months out of date. "It was on the basis of intelligence thus hopelessly stale that they made their decisions," noted historian Richard Glover. "If in doubt about some point of policy, they put a question to the Governor of one of their forts, twelve months must pass before they could send instructions based on his reply, and their decision could not begin to be carried into effect till the situation it was intended to meet had had ample time in which to alter."

LIFE ON THE BAY, once the season's supply ships had weighed anchor and set off, flying for home, settled into dreary routine. Endurance was the prime virtue. Like the inhabitants of a closed Darwinian archipelago, the Bay traders assumed local coloration, appearing, according to York Factor James Isham, "more like beasts than men, with the hairy cloathing we wear."

Winter dress consisted of a combination of pelts that must have made the Hudsonians resemble a surrealistic mutation of every fur-bearing animal within trapping range. The outer garment was of mooseskin, with cuffs and a cape of beaver, marten or fox. The breeches were cut from deerskin and lined with flannel over three layers of cut-up blankets. Shoes consisted of a shaped piece of tough leather wrapped around the instep and fastened securely. This whole ensemble, which made movement ponderous, was in fact the standard winter *indoor* uniform. It was merely underwear for the outdoors.

Winter wood- and food-gathering excursions required the addition of yet more protection, though limbs and faces often froze. According to astronomer William Wales, venturing outdoors entailed adding "a beaver skin which comes down so as to cover their neck and shoulders, and also a neck cloth or cravat made of a white fox's skin, or, which is much more complete, the tails of two of these animals sewed together at the stump ends. Beside these they have shoes of soft tanned mooseskin and a pair of snow shoes about four feet or four and a half feet long."

Cleanliness was a forgotten divertissement. Isham describes in his York journal that fur traders commonly had "a beard as long as Captain Teach's,* and a face as

---

*The beard in question was that of a firebrand pirate named Edward Teach, also known as Blackbeard. "Teach allowed his beard to grow untrimmed," notes Hugh F. Rankin in *The Golden Age of Piracy*. "It was long and rose on his face

black as any chimney sweeper's." Soap was a rare luxury, seldom indulged, and so if the Bay men rarely saw the colour of their own skin, it was probably merciful.

Their dwelling places, defiantly called "forts," were makeshift huts of fir or pine logs laid one upon the other, crudely caulked and enclosed by palisades. Because urgency for shelter did not permit the wood to season before construction, the timbers shrank and cracked open the caulked seams. "In summer," Joseph Robson wrote, "the water beats between the logs, keeping the timber continually damp; and in the winter the white frost gets through, which being thawed by the heat of the stoves, has the same effect, so that with the water above and the damp below, the timber both of the foundation and super-structure rots so fast that in twenty-five or thirty years the whole fort must be rebuilt with fresh timber."

Added to the discomfort of draughts knifing through the widening chinks between the logs was the smoke belching from the none-too-sophisticated brick stoves.* As soon as the night fires were banked, chimneys would be closed with iron gates to retain whatever heat had been coaxed

---

almost to the level of his eye… Before an impending engagement, he exaggerated an already frightful appearance by tucking slow-burning matches under his hat, wreathing his face in wispy curls of smoke, as if he were the Devil himself, fresh from Hell's outer reaches." The much-married Captain Teach (one contemporary claimed that of the pirate's fourteen wives, "a dozen might still be living") was shot dead in North Carolina in November 1718.

* An essential winter-related mission was felling trees for the wood-burning stoves, with the lumber crews forced to move ever further inland to find enough fuel. A "stout" winter's supply at Prince of Wales's Fort was calculated to be "two large piles each forty-three yards round" and Joseph Isbister estimated that providing firewood for the fort took at least nine months of the year. Coal was eventually brought in, as ship's ballast.

from the hard-won fuel. The daylight hours were no more cheerful; windows were boarded up for the winter with three-inch shutters. Iron shot was heated red-hot in the stoves and hung around the room, but nothing really helped.

Occupants were frequently laid up, unable to work because their joints were too seized up to flex. Aching with arthritis and chilblains, they found their only cheer was that of the bottle, but even this was often frustrated by the temperature. Because of their low alcohol content, wine and beer quickly froze solid and turned insipid when thawed over a stove. One inspired solution put into effect at Prince of Wales's Fort in 1741 was to bury the kegs in an eight-foot-deep pit, cover them with fresh horse dung and hope they would stay unfrozen. They did.

The only accommodation with a touch of refinement was the Factor's or Governor's House, particularly at Prince of Wales's Fort, where the quarters were spacious enough for entertaining the post's officers on Wednesday and Saturday evenings. There was also opportunity to do a little fancy trapping. Moses Norton, the Factor, boasts in his November 1, 1759 journal entry of how he entertained himself by catching three foxes in the fort's yard by dangling bait on fish-hooks out of his bedroom window. Norton, a notorious womanizer, had a more comforting time of it than any of his compatriots. It was whispered that he maintained a harem of at least five Indian wives.

The fort itself was an anomaly in the fur trade. Built six miles from the site first occupied by James Knight in 1717, with four angular bastions mounting forty cannon, Prince of Wales's Fort had been commissioned by Sir Bibye Lake in 1732 and took forty years to complete.* It

---

*Building went on intermittently until 1771. J.B. Tyrrell, the Canadian explorer, toured the ruin in 1892, recording this description: "It is 310 feet long on the north and south sides, and 317

was intended to become the most secure fortress in North America, a formidable star-shaped pile of dressed masonry more than three hundred feet square, with walls up to forty feet thick. No written justification for its construction survives, but Lake, who did not expend Company funds freely, had at least three purposes in mind: that the fort could serve as a major provisioning point for exploitation of northern mineral resources; that it would become a profitable fur-trading centre, due to its location bordering the lands of the Cree, Chipewyan and Eskimos; and, most importantly, that it would act as the strategic centre for the HBC's defence of its trade and territories. Not one of these objectives was realized. Arthur S. Morton, an astute historian of the Canadian West, has speculated that "the plan must have had to do with the ships taking refuge in the commodious harbour under the shelter of the fortifications. In that case their crews would go to manning the fort … In case of meeting the enemy in overpowering numbers, they could find safety in the Churchill River, the crews man the fort, and present an impregnable front to the foe."

Even this strategy seems questionable. Because it was on the wrong river – the Nelson drained a much larger hinterland – fur returns at Prince of Wales's never exceeded half the take at York Factory. Gathering in only about ten

---

feet long on the east and west sides, measured from corner to corner on the bastions. The walls are from 37 to 42 feet thick, and 16 feet 9 inches high to the top of the parapet, which is 5 feet high and 6 feet 3 inches wide. On the outside the wall was faced with dressed stone, except towards the river, while on the inside undressed stone was used. The interior wall is a rubble of boulders held together by a poor mortar. In the parapet are forty embrasures and forty guns; from six to twenty-four pounders are lying on the wall near them, now partly hidden by low willows, currant and gooseberry bushes."

thousand made-beaver per season, the garrison was reduced to fewer than forty men – a ridiculous one-to-one ratio with the number of the fort's artillery pieces. The fort was supposed to be an answer to France's Louisbourg, but even if it were reinforced with an extra hundred men off the Company's ships, it could still not have held off an attack of any size or intensity.

TRYING TO DIVINE THE DAILY LIVES of the men who endured on the bay during the eighteenth century, the dispassionate observer finds it difficult to escape the conclusion that their main preoccupation was eating and drinking. Factors, anxious to fill the pages of their journals, often described menus at their posts, detailing the remarkable quantity, if not variety, of the food consumed. James Knight at York Factory records that during three days of feasting at Christmas in 1715, he allocated to each mess hall of four men a helping of four geese, a large slice of beef, four hares, seven pounds of fresh pork, two pounds of drippings, a pound of butter, three and a half pounds of fruit preserves, four pounds of flour and a hogshead of strong beer. Records at Moose Factory show that on one Christmas Day in the early 1700s, each four-man mess had been doled out enough victuals to make the York Factory rations look like a snack. The bill of fare read: five geese, twelve partridge, sixty fish, eight pounds of mutton, three pounds of suet, two pints of rice, twenty pounds of flour, two pounds of bacon, eight pints of oatmeal, four pounds of biscuit bread, two pounds of cheese, two pounds of raisins, a pound and a half of butter and one piece of salt beef. This was special fare, but the daily rations were only slightly more modest. Andrew Graham, who spent most of his life on Hudson Bay, complained that "the major part of the people can not use all their allowance but are forced to give it to the natives."

PLANS of YORK and PRINCE of WALES's FORTS

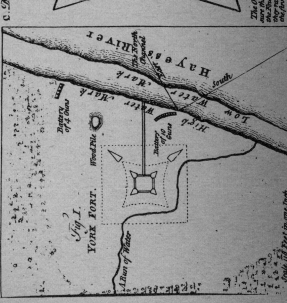

Since food was one of the few human appetites that could safely and prodigiously be satisfied within the confines of their circumstances, the catering at such feasts seems only slightly incongruous with the otherwise desolate lives of the HBC outlanders. Provisioning was partly from the holds of the annual supply ships, with beef, pork, cheese, flour, oatmeal, peas, malt, vinegar, raisins, butter and spices being the main staples, though cases of sherry, port and other civilizing potables were provided for the Factor's tables. The goods did not always arrive intact. This was particularly true of the salted beef and pork, which were often maggoty or just plain putrid. "In opening the cask of hogs' cheeks," complained Anthony Beale at Prince of Wales's Fort, "we find the whole cask to be infected. I had some of them dressed at my table but it was so bad it could not be eat. Therefore ... must be obliged to give it to starved Indians."

The imports were supplemented by "country provisions." Most of the Committeemen never did comprehend that even if northern England and the bay were astride similar latitudes, it was impossible for their expatriates to reproduce English vegetable and flower gardens – even if, as one London-based financial knight noted in his fanciful description of the primordial soil around York Factory: "Such rich mould has laine fallow, it may be from the Creation."

The growing season (sixty days at best) was desperately short and the only crop regularly supported by the thin layer of soil that surrounded the HBC posts was wild dandelion.* The weed was used for a bitter but vitamin-rich

---

*There is circumstantial evidence that the Bay men grew so fond of their dandelion brew that when they began to journey southward, they took the sticky yellow pompon with them – as a crop.

salad, was occasionally fermented into wine and proved to be a useful anti-scorbutic. The season was too frosty for grain crops, but local gardeners could cultivate potatoes up to the size of hens' eggs as well as limited pickings of radishes, turnips and lettuce. The greatest problem was maintaining cattle for milk and horses as draught animals. There was little hay to provide winter fodder, and the beasts could not forage for themselves. Moses Norton, the oddly playful Factor at Prince of Wales's Fort, tried taming caribou to pull sleds, but they refused to be domesticated.*

The most important indigenous source of food was the seasonal bird hunts. Wild geese and partridge, ducks and curlew were taken in the spring and autumn, while the willow ptarmigan (an Arctic grouse) was caught in huge nets baited with the gravel the birds' gizzards need to aid digestion. (The net was stretched over a heap of gravel and held in place by a stake that could be jerked away at the appropriate moment.) Isham refers to catching seventy or eighty birds at one haul. The explorer Thomas Button and his crew shot 21,600 during his one season on the bay, and the eighteenth-century account of Nicolas Jérémie claims that during the winter of 1709–10, the eighty men then stationed at York Factory (temporarily renamed Fort Bourbon) consumed 90,000 ptarmigan and 25,000 hares.

Local fish, mainly Arctic char (referred to as "salmon"),

---

*In 1767, Norton sent a pair of live moose to London as a gift to the HBC Committeemen. One died in transit, but the other became a burden on the Company's coffers. A board minute nervously notes that she cost £9 10s. 11d. in feed from October 1767 to February 1768, when the problem was solved by presenting the beast to George III. The King promptly passed the buck, shipping the hairy expatriate upriver to the Royal enclosures at Richmond Park.

were cured in a very peculiar way, as an official Company guidebook documents:

> Take whole salmons split them up ye back (not through ye belly) and take ye bone clear out, wash and clean them thoroughly, then double them together, and lay them to drein in ye shade, a whole day, then at night begin to salt them. Put a little bay [leaf], and a common salt at ye bottom of ye tub, after which open ye salmon and lay them in with ye skin downward, then sprinkle it with ye same salt, and lay them one upon ye other, ye skin still downward, and continue sprinkling with salts between each fish, till ye tub is full. Let them lye so for ten days, to be kept in a cool place, then provide casks, and put ye fish therein, in ye same manner laying them open with ye skin downwards, without anymore salt, and head them up being well pressed down then take ye pickle out of ye tubs, and put it into ye cask's at ye bung hole, keeping them every day fill'd up for ten days. Then stop them up close.

For variety, caribou and moose meat could be traded from the Indians. Many of the caribou were slaughtered while crossing rivers. Indian women and children would gather on both shores, shrieking, hollering and throwing stones so that the confused animals would be forced to remain in deep water, unable to flee or defend themselves. The commotion set up by the women and children was no benign baying at the moon; this was a fierce and primitive pageant that chilled the marrow of any HBC man who heard it. Into this madness would paddle the Indian hunters with spears and sticks sharpened in bonfires. They were soon consumed by the lust of the moment, killing the hapless caribou as much for pleasure as for sustenance, oblivious of anything but the ecstasy of their slaughter. Here was an assertion of their superiority, a feeling they could not achieve from the passive acts of trapping or fishing. The Cree tried to strike the beasts in their unprotected kidneys, driving their spears straight in, then twisting upward, massacring their prey in an orgy of murderous pleasure.

Deer tongues were a particular delicacy. Food was such a priority that its trade sometimes took precedence over fur. During the largest single month's business recorded at Prince of Wales's Fort (November 1774), the Indians brought in only six hundred made-beaver, but they also traded 9,651 pounds of deer flesh, eight hundred deer tongues, twenty-four hares and one great shaggy muskox.

The Bay men, particularly recruits from the Orkneys' rocky shores, were offered daily fare much superior to any nourishment they might have expected to get at home. No wheat was grown on the islands off northern Scotland; few farmers could afford to slaughter domestic animals, and the sheep fed mostly on seaweed, which made the mutton practically unpalatable. In this and other ways life on Hudson Bay, although hellish at times, was fairly bearable by comparison with life in eighteenth-century Britain. Orkney roofs of thatch produced draughty homes not much better than their bay counterparts. Much of London's housing stock had been renewed in brick following the Great Fire of 1666, but those Bay men from the British capital left behind a city that offered few comforts. The Industrial Revolution was still in its nascency, with most of English society divided into patrician, property-owning families and a labouring class that drifted aimlessly from job to job, with all but the particularly skilled alternating between casual farm work, odd jobs and petty pilfering. A posting on the bay could be a godsend for some. The middle class, which would eventually contribute most HBC recruits, was as yet only a small group.

Despite the relative abundance of nourishment at the bay, almost constant dissatisfaction was expressed by the

Company's servants. Apart from the monotony and the natural tendency of isolated men to take out their frustrations on the only corporate scapegoat available, part of this trouble stemmed from the salting method used to preserve food between hunting and fishing seasons. In the fall of 1757 when the Prince of Wales's messes had been served greasy, salted-down Arctic char every Monday and Friday for months, Ferdinand Jacobs, the fort's Governor, found the men, one dinner hour, "flinging it in one another's faces, and turning up their noses at it." Five years earlier, under Joseph Isbister, one of Jacobs's predecessors, partridge had been the object of a similar disturbance. "In my absence," he wrote in his journal, "some of the corrupted ones stird up most of our men to throw away all their partridges ... when Mr. Walker and I came into the Factory, we was surprised to see the partridges strowed about in the dirt and gravel. I toke one of them up in my hand, smelt it and found it as sweet as when it was killed." Isbister, like a boarding school headmaster faced by naughty boys, accused his men of "behaving in a mutinous manner" and threatened "to whip and cane them all." One dissatisfied diner, James Flat, was in fact flogged for his partridge protest, and the gastronomic uprising was quickly quashed.

Another reason for the men's crankiness may have been the difference they could observe between their own rations and the delicacies reserved for the Factor's table. Andrew Graham, who served in various capacities on the bay from 1767 to 1791, observed that the Chief Factor's table "is always handsomely supplied with provisions, very seldom having less than three dishes; and on particular occasions, fourteen or sixteen.... The officers have wines and French brandy plentifully allowed them; and the men London porter, and British spirit (raw gin) served out at the discretion of the Chief."

One advantage of the bay diet was that it contained enough fresh meat and vegetables to discourage scurvy, the scourge of explorers, mariners and other adventurers in the pre-refrigeration age. (The Royal Navy did not start issuing lemon juice on a daily basis until 1793.) A common local panacea, called wishakapucka (Labrador tea), was claimed to cure everything from "giddiness in the head" to "fainting fitts," not to mention "gangrenes, contusions and excorations." More serious medical complaints included "country distemper" (a form of fever combined with catarrh) and syphilis. The factors argued that venereal disease was endemic among the Indians, and their journals frequently complain about repentant sinners coming down with "the Clap" or being "in a salivation for the venereal disorder." Apart from that particular curse, the occasional accident and frequent cases of frostbite, the Bay men enjoyed remarkably good health. In his characteristically exuberant style, Samuel Hearne caught this mood in a letter to York's Factor, Humphrey Marten: "Myself and people are as usual all in good health, but that is no wonder since the pureness of the air and the wholesomeness of the diet makes it the healthiest part in the known world and what is very extraordinary at this place some of us think we never grow any older."

The daily cycle of assigned work was devoted mainly to self-preservation, but garrisons had every Sunday and half of each Saturday free, and holidays were celebrated at the slightest excuse. Besides Christmas, New Year's Day and Easter, there were St George's Day (April 23), Guy Fawkes Day (November 5), royal birthdays, accession dates and May 2 – "Bay Day" – the anniversary of the Company's Charter. Card and dice games were popular and, in the summers, football games of a sort were played using inflated whale bladders.

Religion was an afterthought.* The London Committee, buttonholed by the Society for the Promotion of Christian Knowledge, piously required that all its servants worship on Sunday mornings at divine service conducted by resident Factors – unless, of course, the heathen should choose the Sabbath to arrive with a particularly appealing canoe-load of pelts.

Such evangelical diversions did little to relieve the men's frustrations. They were trapped in an inhospitable climate, at the edge of an unknown universe. The monotony of the seasons – there were two, a long winter and a short spring – and their own aimless activity produced lethal doses of cabin fever for which there was only one cure: alcohol. The Company quickly realized that liquor was a greater enemy than the climate to its trade on the bay, but no matter how many prohibitions it proclaimed and no matter how often it paid off informers to halt the smuggling of brandy casks on outgoing ships, the booze flowed steadily across the Atlantic. Exceptional was the Company servant who failed to organize surreptitious caches of several gallons or so of brandy for his private stock.

---

*There were few resident chaplains on the bay during the British occupation. One early exception was the Reverend Thomas Anderson, who helped draw up the surrender terms – in Latin – of York Factory to the French in 1693. Sundays at most bay posts were made even more leisurely by the erratic pattern of local religious services held at the discretion of the Factor in charge. Samuel Hearne, a deist and follower of Voltaire, contented himself with reading only a sermon and did not demand that his Prince of Wales's garrison pray in unison.

Much later, when Bishop J.N. Provencher, as Apostolic Vicar of Hudson Bay, wanted to take up residence at York Factory, the Company refused his request with the curt comment that the conflict among opposing beliefs would be harmful to the spiritual and material welfare of the Indians.

As early as 1682, the HBC had shipped 440 gallons of brandy to its posts, mainly for use as part of the trading ceremony with the Indians. Each subsequent liquid cargo was accompanied by long written instructions such as this 1692 notice sent to George Geyer, then Governor at York Factory: "Whereas we have sent you a very large quantity of new french brandy, which we procured with great difficulty, our desire is that what you shall not have emediate use for it in the Factory to trade either with the Natives or our Servants." Anthony Beale, an HBC apprentice who rose to be Governor of Albany, received an even sterner admonition on June 10, 1713: "… Trade as little brandy as possible to the Indians, we being informed it has destroyed several of them."

But by the middle of the eighteenth century, the French traders operating out of Montreal had introduced enough brandy and rum into the native economy that little fur could be traded with the abstinence requested by the HBC's absentee landlords. As suited their style of pragmatic entrepreneurship, the London Committeemen accepted the fact that liquor was a necessary part of their operations and became canny about its use and manufacture. Since brandy from France was expensive and scarce because of the frequent conflicts between Versailles and the British throne, the HBC governors abandoned the French product and introduced a mixture they christened English Brandy. This was cheap (almost raw) London gin to which were added drops of any of several tinctures (usually iodine) to duplicate the rich auburn colour of the real brandy. "We have sent in the medicine chest a bottle of tincture to colour the English Brandy," explained an official communication dated May 2, 1735, from Hudson's Bay House in London to Thomas Maclish, then Governor at Albany. "When there shall be occasion, four or five drops thereof are sufficient to colour a pint and so in proportion for a larger quantity."

This raw recipe worked, but the iodine was soon replaced with molasses that not only coloured the rotgut but gave the potent brew a touch of sweetness.

With kegs of "brandy" freely available for the Indian trade, the Company instituted regular rations (one quart each Wednesday and Saturday) for its own personnel. According to account books at Prince of Wales's Fort, by 1721 the *official* average per capita staff consumption amounted to seven and a half gallons per year, but because there were several teetotallers, it was probably closer to ten gallons – not counting the active illicit trade.

There was no great consistency in the Company's policy. Despite the London Committee's sanctimonious protestations against the evils of alcohol, servants who performed beyond the call of duty were rewarded by local trading post commanders with extra rations. Thomas Smith, a stonemason at Prince of Wales's Fort, for example, was granted an extra ten gallons of brandy a year in return for risking his life blowing up rocks for the Fort's walls – an activity that the local Factor's journal laconically noted resulted in regular wounds to "the head, legs and hands that were not mortall."

The Factors complained in their journals to London about "the sots" they had been assigned and urged the Committeemen to recruit fresh-faced country lads "not debauched by the voluptuousness of London." The effects of so much drink – by 1766, York Factory alone was storing 2,474 gallons of "brandy"– were occasionally bizarre, such as this incident detailed in the York Fort journal about the would-be suicide of a "servant" named James Robertson: "… This evening James Robertson, whose hand was cut off ye 3d. of this instant, made an open confession. He went out of ye Factory with a full resolution to lay violent hands on himself. He had saved half pint of brandy for six days before to drink in the cold air, so as to make himself elevated … he likewise carried a piece of rope, but after he had drank the brandy, he throw'd the rope away … so went to ye steel trap with a design to make away with himself … But after he had been fast in the trap for almost two hours by his own confession without attempting to get out of the said trap and by that time the fumes of the brandy having evaporated and come a little to his sences he got himself out of ye trap."

The demand for liquor grew so fast that by the end of the eighteenth century the Company shipped to its post at Churchill a dismantled still, capable of turning molasses into a hundred gallons of "cordials." But for undetermined reasons, the machinery was never installed and was returned to England the following year. A highly successful brewing operation was by then flourishing at every HBC outpost, with the Company supplying most of the required malt. The recipe for spruce beer, a valuable antiscorbutic, was literally explosive because gunpowder was used to accelerate the aging process.

> To brew this beer, the kettle being near full of water, cram the kettle with small pine; from one experiment you will judge the quantity of pine that will bear a proportion to your water. Let the tops of the pine be boiled in the water until the pine turns yellow, and the bark peels, or the sprigs strip off readily on being pulled; then take off your kettle, and the pine out of the water, and to about two gallons of liquor put a quarter of a pint of molasses. Hang your kettle on, giving the liquor off, put it into a cask in which you have before put cold water, the quantity of about two gallons. Then take a gun with a small quantity of powder, and no wad; fire into the bunghole. It will set the liquor a working; in about twenty-four hours stop the cask down, and the liquor will be ready to drink.

One dramatic instance of the corruption of discipline by alcohol occurred on Christmas Day 1735, when the newly rebuilt post at Moose was ravaged by fire. The blaze had been set in the cookhouse and quickly spread through the wooden palisades. According to resident Factor Richard Staunton, "drunkenness and debochery" caused the misfortune: "Vice and ignorance predominated to a monsterous degree of wickedness both amongst the English and Indians." He reported that the Indians had brought their women into the post and thereby gained influence over the English and themselves learned "much villainy."

Moose Factory was one of the Company's earliest settlements, dating back to its choice in 1673 as the principal factory at the Bottom of the Bay. It quickly evolved into the equivalent of a provincial capital, becoming the transportation hub for the chain of southern outposts and the magnet for Indians from the mesh of rivers that empty into James Bay. After being destroyed by the French under the Chevalier de Troyes, it was rebuilt in 1730, but Moose was never a happy post. It became the most "corrupted" of all the HBC factories. The guzzling of brandy remained the biggest problem. "Many of the accidents at Moose were alcohol-related," concluded Frits Pannekoek in his study, "Corruption at Moose," published in *The Beaver* magazine. "One man consumed so much 'bumbo'– that fur-trade mixture of rum, water, sugar and nutmeg – that he fell off the sloop and promptly drowned. With some regret and much haste, his mates lost no time in auctioning off the contents of his chest. The chief factors were always afraid that the men on watch, who were too often drunk, would, spitefully or accidentally, set fire to the buildings. The courage to commit suicide could also be found in the bottle. 'Brandy-death' was common, and known in Rupert's Land as a Northwester's Death."

In order to reform the social disorder at Moose, the London Committeemen dispatched a tough disciplinarian named James Duffield, whose disruption of the local pattern of co-existence with the Indians drove the community to anarchy. He personally patrolled the post's grounds from sunrise past sunset, armed with a brace of pistols and a stout cane for self-defence, strenuously enforcing his myriad regulations – which the militant Company servants interpreted as a loss of their previous liberties.

In that dreadful winter of 1741, Duffield devised an intriguing method for preventing any of the malcontents from setting fire to his post. Each evening before his uneasy slumber, he would lash the most likely troublemaker to the stove so that he would be among the first victims of any conflagration. To prevent late-night drunken brawls with local Indian women, he had the doors to the men's cabins removed. When a particularly outspoken mutineer with the unlikely name of Porto Bello swore to hang himself unless Duffield relaxed his disciplinary measures, the Factor calmly provided him with a rope, and when that produced a meek complaint that it really wasn't long enough, the Factor handed him a longer one.

Curiously, Duffield blamed most of the troubles at Moose on the dominance of the Masons, the secretive organization that had influenced the HBC's founding father, Prince Rupert, and many of the crowned heads of Europe. Duffield's journal contains the bitter complaint that he felt he had been "dropp'd down amongst a nest of free and accepted Masons, without being initiated by ye bretheren, but as an intruder on their laws, by virtue of ye Compys authority: and therefore at all events I was to be hoodwink'd and kept from discovering their secret measures … such a scandalous society."

The unhappy Duffield was recalled to London in 1744, but the disciplinary problems at Moose and many of the other bay forts continued. "For the most part," notes historian Glyndwr Williams, the Factors "ruled by a series of compromises. Conventions and practices developed in the Bay outside the range of knowledge and approval of the distant London Committee. This is not to say that life at the posts was a squalid orgy, with drunken servants forcing Indian women into prostitution, and robbing the Company at every turn. The Company could not have survived if this were so, but it is no more of a caricature than the assumption that the garrisons lived by the letter of the Company's annual instructions. What had evolved was a local and distinctive lifestyle, based on a combination of trading considerations, sexual needs and the requirements of a harsh physical environment."

This trade-off – the acceptance of Company edicts in principle and their evasion in practice – resulted in a devil's brew of distrust and tension between its servants and officers. On one occasion, the Chief Factor at York went to Churchill to have a key made because he could not trust his own armourer. Punishments, which took the form of fines and canings, occasionally acquired some odd twists, as when Henry Pollexfen, Factor at Moose in 1757, resented being asked for a new work assignment by one of his crew. "I desired him not to be saucy nor to give me any ill language, and I gave him a little blow on the head," Pollexfen noted in his journal. In return, the Factor was himself knocked to the ground. He promptly placed the unruly servant in irons until he could be sent back to England.

The main reason why this potentially explosive set of human relationships functioned surprisingly well was the kind of men the HBC hired. Because England spent most of the eighteenth century at war, military service was difficult to avoid and career choices were limited. Unlike some of the other far-flung trading companies, which tended to pick as their officers cultured English gentlemen whose education as generalists hardly fitted them for life in the wilderness, the HBC depended for most of its recruits on the unexcitable Orkneymen. Dour they might be, but the Orkneymen's own sea-borne history had implanted character traits well fitted for survival under stress. Canny moderation, self-control, resourcefulness and rivalry without animosity characterized their approach to life.

It was not an easy route to great fortune, but service with the HBC was sometimes the only hope for the fourth son of a farmer or fisherman. Chief Factors in the eighteenth century were paid £100 to £300, though they could usually make as much again by private trapping; sloop captains received £40, and each rank was paid on a descending scale, with apprenticed clerks earning about £15 a year. Skilled tradesmen could make up to £36 per annum, but an ordinary labourer started at £6 a year, with annual increments of 40 shillings a year to a maximum of £14.

In London unskilled workers earned 10 shillings a week but, unlike the HBC employees, received no free board and lodging. Henry Kelsey, who first penetrated the Canadian prairies and remained in the Company's employ for thirty-eight years, including a term as Governor of Albany, earned a lifetime total of less than £2,500 and two suits of clothes. The main fiscal advantage of service on the bay was that the men hoarded most of their earnings – none more assiduously than Anthony Henday, who saved £113 of the £120 he was paid during twelve years of service.*

The Company could be heartless. Few of its Factors contributed more to its economic well-being than Andrew Graham, whose several volumes of observations of nature were classic works. He served on the bay from 1749 to

---

*Inexplicably, the Company did not pay its employees if, in the line of duty, they were held prisoner by French or other raiders. This was one reason why Edward Umfreville, one of the most articulate of the HBC's servants, decided to switch loyalties to the North West Company. Captured by the French at York Factory on August 24, 1782, his wages promptly ceased. He left the Company on February 27, 1783, after he was returned to England from France.

1775, holding in turn all the major posts including the governorships of York Factory and Churchill. During all that time he asked the London Committeemen for only one personal favour: that he be allowed, at his own expense, to send his daughter (by his Indian mistress) to England for her education. "I will with pleasure give my security for her maintenance," he pleaded. "I have settled one thousand pounds upon her, and if you choose it shall be lodged in your hands. You are many, if not all of you, fathers; let then what would be the feelings of your own paternal hearts on such an occasion plead in my behalf, and let not humanity and Christianity be forgot. Let me then have cause to bless your goodness."

The reply was short and not sweet: "In regard to your request respecting sending from Hudsons Bay the infant child you mention, it being of such tender age we must decline such permission until a farther opportunity, as we think its safety much to be apprehended by the voyage for want of the care that may be necessary to a female child."

Graham took his child to England later and, probably more than that of any other Factor, his loyalty remained unbending. It was he who had attempted to stem the private trading in furs that was undermining the Company's bayside profits. His detailed descriptions of how the illicit trade was carried out (3,136 skins from one post alone) helped reduce the traffic, though it never ceased to be a problem. This black market came very close to being institutionalized into an elaborate system of bribes for the supply ships' crews. Servants caught attempting to enrich themselves privately were liable to be lashed, though many Factors engaged in the same shadowy commerce with impunity. James Knight, for example, while he was in charge of York factory, sold his own furs at the Company's auctions, and the rcord books for 1718 show Mrs Knight at a London address being credited with £52 2s. 9d.

Like other aspects of life on the bay, private trading illustrated the distance between theory and reality. This was most apparent in the difference between the London Committeemen's optimistic perception of how their overseas possessions could be defended and the flimsy military capabilities of those on the ground. The Company's precise tactics were clouded in ambivalence, both among the armchair strategists in London and the men in the trenches abroad, but there definitely was a military dimension to its occupation of Hudson Bay. The adventurers had landed as unarmed conquerors, brandishing their Royal Charter, and the carrying of the flag of trade into any new territory was seldom far removed from the profession of arms.

The Company's wilderness settlements were eventually modelled on contemporary defensive architecture, much like those erected at the other side of the world by the East India Company. They were situated inside a quadrangle of wooden bastions mounting various gauges of cannon, joined by palisades of upright logs, sometimes with iron points. The main buildings were meant to be unassailable redoubts with parapets pierced by embrasures for fixed eight-pounders, but were more often flimsily protected shacks. The area required for a clear field of fire inside the stockades inevitably grew crowded with outbuildings, workshops and piles of winter firewood that any attacking force could easily set aflame, destroying the entire "fort." The outer bastions were used as storehouses for pelts rather than as serious defence points. Prince of Wales's, the only fort worthy of the name, was considerably weakened against possible siege because the twenty-four-foot-wide moat was just a shallow ditch and had initially been built with a *fixed* bridge. This would-be moat was a source of constant annoyance because its banks kept crumbling, structurally weakening the fort's palisades.

Depending on the prevailing circumstances and the militancy of the local Factor, the Company's servants were expected to take part in regular musket drills, to practise firing the heavy guns and to repel whatever invaders might happen by. The journals of the period deal less with the military aspects of such operations than with minute enquiries into the extent of the Company's liability should any servants or officers be killed or injured in its defence. "It should be remembered," notes Michael Payne, social historian of Prince of Wales's Fort, "that the men garrisoning the fort had signed on with the company as tailors, masons, blacksmiths and labourers and not as soldiers. Their desire to court death or dismemberment in the defence of their employer's property was probably slight. The Company, recognizing this fact, offered cash benefits for those wounded in defence of its forts, and money for the estates of those killed. A sum of £30 was to be paid to any man who lost an arm or a leg in the defence of a company fort, and for those who died an equal sum of money would be paid to their beneficiaries. Other injuries would be compensated for as the Committee saw fit. All cases of injuries were at the 'Charge of the Company'."

THE BEST OF THE BAY MEN DISPLAYED an esprit de corps comparable to that of the Royal Navy. The wilderness was their ocean, their outposts the ships. Such an analogy was deliberately fostered. Like the Hudson's Bay Company, the Royal Navy reaches back to the dawn of British world span, each providing an essential impetus to the affairs of empire. Like the Royal Navy, the HBC evolved from royalist mercenary beginnings to play out its role of innocent pomp while undertaking grave circumstance.* "The service assumed an anthropomorphic character," commented

---

*It was an obscure Sultan of Morocco during the 1880s who took the true measure of Britain's senior service when, after a tour of the Royal Navy's latest battleship, he was asked what had impressed him the most – the powerful turret guns, the

the Welsh bard James Morris in a description of naval traditions published in the magazine *Encounter*, "hard-drinking but always alert, eccentric but superbly professional, breezy, naughty, posh, kindly, Nelsonically ready to disobey an order in a good cause, or blow any number of deserving foreigners out of the water. To Britons and to foreigners alike, in the meridian years of Empire the Royal Navy *was* Britain, and the truest national anthem was not *God Save the Queen*, but *Rule Britannia*."

Seniority, sobriety and the ability to keep neat journals brought command in the service of the Company. Instead of elaborate sets of King's Regulations and the threat of court martial, it was often the Factor's fists that ruled. Social stratification was strengthened by the strict rule that all "commissioned gentlemen" had to be addressed as "Mr" by both subordinates and superiors. The arrival and departure of a post's commanding officer demanded cannon salutes. Even if the setting was bush-primitive and the facilities were threadbare, every attempt was made to duplicate in the North American bush the grand protocol and mannered grandeur of the Royal Navy.

This depended on a rank structure with the subtlest of shadings. The choice of thwarts in a canoe, entitlement to a segregated campfire, even the location of pews at the occasional Sunday worship all signalled one's position in the hierarchy.* "Gentlemen had to be just that, socially as

---

massive engines, the torpedo boats carried aboard or perhaps the electric light throughout. "The captain's face," was his reply.

*A list of 105 Rules and Regulations, issued in 1887, defines privileges and duties so precisely that even the amount of pepper allocated to each rank is listed. Commissioned officers were allowed twice as much as clerks, who in turn could use twice as much as postmasters. The most noticeable dietary difference was in tea rations, with officers getting ten times as much as interpreters.

FORT PRINCE OF WALES 1734

well as administratively superior to the servants whose labour they commanded," concluded Philip Goldring in a study of the HBC's labour practices. "Everybody found reason to be grateful for superiority over someone else." HBC Governor Sir George Simpson articulated this attitude most directly in a scathing comment on staff members who were promoted beyond their capabilities – men who "came into the Country as labouring men, but either through favour or cunning got advanced to the rank of Clerks and thereby became useless."

Designations of rank varied with the evolving sophistication of the fur trade, but the eventual structure consisted of nine gradations:

Labourers. Sometimes called "middlemen," they performed the basic physical drudgery – shovelling snow, portaging boats, cutting firewood, loading and unloading ships.

Apprentices. Frequently the country sons of HBC traders, they were paid lower wages than labourers but enjoyed better prospects of promotion. They acted as understudies and assistants to other ranks.

Craftsmen or *Tradesmen*. They were the cattlekeepers, carpenters, blacksmiths, coopers, boatbuilders, fishermen, store porters, net-menders, tinsmiths and cooks.

Guides and *Interpreters*. Tenured time-servers who knew native languages and dialects, they performed minor but invaluable interlocutory functions in the fur trade. One indication of how minute were the gradations between the HBC ranks was the 103rd Resolution of the HBC Council, adopted in 1824: "In order to draw a line of distinction between Guides, Interpreters and the Gentlemen in the service, no Guide or Interpreter, whether at the Factory Depot, or inland, be permitted to Mess with commissioned Gentlemen or Clerks in charge of Posts."

Postmasters. Usually promoted labourers, they had little to do with the mail but occupied the only ambiguous stratum between servants and officers, as they were frequently placed in charge of small outposts.

Apprentice Clerks. Dewy-cheeked lads in their mid-teens who came to Hudson Bay fresh from English schools, they were equally eager to probe the secrets of the fur trade and the mysteries of young Indian women. Their apprenticeships lasted five years, their virginity much less.

Clerks. The lowest of the officer (non-servant) class, they were placed in charge of smaller units and were the cadre out of which future leaders were recruited. Their pay was three times that of apprentice clerks.

Chief Traders. Thirteen to twenty years as a clerk with what the Company judged to be the appropriate skills and attitudes could bring promotion to the level of Chief Trader and responsibility for the actual fur bartering.

Chief Factors. Only Chief Traders were eligible to become Chief Factors. The title seemed to be freely interchangeable with "Factor" or "Governor" during most of the eighteenth century, although there was only one *real* Governor, who ran the Company and resided in London.

Men's dress reflected their rank and occasionally became absurd. In 1783, when the Company's posts were being raided by the French, a directive was drafted to outfit all servants in regimental uniforms.* The order (which was

---

*Such parish bluff survived into the 1940s, when the Company was still differentiating the ranks of its employees in Northern services by forcing them to wear peaked caps decorated with enamelled badges and various configurations of gold braid. The once-rigid rank structure is still to be found in the graveyards, now tucked behind respectful but incongruous white picket fences at the posts. Crude time-worn crosses, mottled with lichen and twisted to crazy angles by the heaving permafrost, mark the servants' graves. The officers repose in calm dignity and posthumous glory beneath granite or even marble head-

never carried out) cited three reasons for the battle dress:

"1. To excite emulation and ambition as well as proper confidence in our men.

"2. It would give the Indians an idea of our determined resolution of defending ourselves to the utmost, and thereby securing them strongly in our interest.

"3. By a spirited unexpected uniform appearance, it might give the enemy an opinion of our having received succors and tend to dishearten them or strike them with a sudden panick, as we read of numerous instances from similar causes."

Much of the HBC's routine and ritual was modelled on Royal Navy custom. The Company's own flags flew on ships and stores.* The paramilitary atmosphere was emphasized by naming even the least prepossessing moose pasture outposts "forts." The martial air of the daily routine was unrelenting. The so-called forts (few of which were ever successfully defended against attack) were built on the typical imperial plan found in Cape Colony, India, Hong Kong and Australia: officers' quarters in the centre of the courtyard with a bachelors' hall and the men's huts banked against the outer palisades. A powder magazine was tucked safely away on the periphery, and armed bastions faced each other diagonally across the enclosure. Like the Navy,

---

stones on which have been carefully carved not just their names and dates but the highest rank they achieved in the service of the Company.

* By a special warrant dated July 21, 1682, Prince Rupert, Vice-Admiral of England (who also happened to be Governor of the HBC at the time), granted the Company the right to use the Red Ensign ("King's Jack") at its forts and on its ships entering Hudson Strait. No other private concern enjoyed the same privilege. The Governor's standard, consisting of the Company coat of arms on a field of white, has been in use at least since 1779.

the Company recognized spontaneous valour or oncoming senility with its own medals* and counted elapsed time on its own calendar.†Its motto, *Pro Pelle Cutem*, was a less straightforward choice. A whimsical derivation of the vengeful biblical "an eye for an eye" sentiment, it meant, roughly, "a skin for its equivalent." The original saying was probably intended to convey the risks incurred by the early adventurers, as in "we risk our skins to get your pelts" and meant "a skin for a pelt." A more earthy application to the fur trade was "we skin you as you try to skin us," or, during the days when liquor became the effective medium of exchange, "a skin for a skinful."

The naval atmosphere of the northern posts was reinforced by the fact that changes in shift, meals and bedtimes were signalled by the sounding of ships' bells. In both services, the bell was a symbol of a disciplined and punctual workforce. "The day was arranged rather like watches on a ship," according to historian Glyndwr Williams. "Many of the officers went into the Company as the equivalent of midshipmen, spent thirty years or more on the bay, with rigid discipline and long periods of isolation, rose up through the ranks to the equivalent of post captains or rear-admirals, then went on the half-pay list. The key characteristic was continuity."

As in the Royal Navy, discipline depended on maintenance of as much distance between officers and men as physical circumstances would allow. This was achieved

---

*Nine special medals have been struck, including a silver George III medal that the HBC awarded to Indians who brought the most trade to Company posts. Long-service medals were issued until 1965.

†To place things in their proper perspective, the HBC calendar dates back to the birth of the Company in 1670 instead of to the nativity of Jesus of Nazareth; 1985, for instance, is still referred to in correspondence with Northern stores as "Outfit 315."

through the provision of distinct quarters and different messing arrangements; officers were served by stewards at separate tables while servants drew their rations from large communal pots. Anyone late for a meal had to absent himself politely and go hungry; as in a naval wardroom, no strident discussion was allowed in the messes.

Cultivating the pride of privilege and the cap-doffing subservience required to maintain such rigid social equations in a rough land was not always easy, especially because most of the Company's Chief Factors and Traders (unlike most Royal Navy officers, who seemed to be bred for their billets) could not claim particularly impressive class credentials. Even though fur trade society was highly structured, status differentiations reflected rank rather than family tree, school tie or even military title. Much later, when Jonas Oxley, who had served as a lieutenant in the British army, objected to serving under a Company officer named Joseph Greill who had been only a sergeant – and in a regiment of German mercenaries at that – Sir George Simpson, the then Governor, wrote him a curt reply: "Sir, your impertinent and ridiculous note of this evening shall be treated with the sovereign contempt it merits. Your honor and rank in his majesty's service are quite immaterial to me & all I require of you is to do your duty faithfully as a Clerk in the service of the Honourable Company."

NOT A SINGLE EMPLOYEE during the eighteenth century asked to remain on Hudson Bay following his retirement from the service. The early HBC men thought of themselves as sailors ashore on a sea coast rather than as settlers, however temporary, on the edge of an exciting new land.

Light years removed from the sherry-tippling gentility of their overlords, they were nevertheless subject to strict control by the London-based Committeemen. In the hierarchical society of eighteenth-century England, such an impotent existence was accepted as part of the given social order, rousing little if any resentment. The traders were too preoccupied with staying alive.

The struggle was not so much against distant authority as against rugged geography and a merciless climate – a contest with the elements that yielded few victories, only the postponement of defeats.

CHAPTER 9

THE SALTY ORCADIANS

"They pulled the wilderness round them like a cloak, and wore its beauty like a crest."
— *Bernard De Voto*

BECAUSE HISTORY DEMANDS DOCUMENTATION, most Hudson's Bay Company chroniclers have concentrated on two mines of information: the official corporate minutes that hint at the austere manipulations among London-based Committeemen and the self-justifying daily journals kept by Chief Factors and explorers in the field.

But most of the Company's servants – the men who actually staffed the posts – fit into neither of these categories. They kept no records, got on with their jobs and left behind only a scattered legacy of their own memories as having been part of a grand enterprise. Yet they did most of the real work, and it was their loyalty to the Company they served and their canny attitude towards the Indians with whom they traded that allowed the HBC to rule its distant domain and barter in good faith with the native harvesters of fur.

During the 1700s, more than three-quarters of these unknown soldiers were recruited from the Orkneys, a cluster of sixty-five bleak islands off Scotland's north coast.

If the combination of determination and oatmeal* produced the ideal Scot, the Orkneyman was a product of sandstone and spindrift. The Orcadians' penchant for uncomplaining servitude plus the fact that they were used to labouring at home under conditions as rigorous as those on Hudson Bay made them ideal for manning the distant swampy ramparts of the HBC's early empire. They were cheaper to hire than Englishmen and more tractable than the Irish; and they had yet to share the aspiration for self-determination that infected the tight-lipped Highlanders.

Many original HBC servants had been recruited from the bands of scavenging urchins who roamed the Thames docks. But John Nixon, the HBC's second overseas Governor (1679–83), complained about "our London born childring" pestering him, and asked for country lads instead. The Company did recruit a few youthful strays from charity schools to serve seven-year terms of indenture, but the naval press gangs stalking the London docklands deprived the HBC of its pick of the best available manpower.

In their annual ritual, the HBC supply ships would slip anchor, edge out of Gravesend at the mouth of the Thames, then heeling over in a freshening breeze, race northward along England's east coast, past Newcastle and Aberdeen, across to Stromness. The Orkney Islands' tiny harbour town was the last stopping point for fresh water† and

---

*Dr Samuel Johnson defined oats as "food for men in Scotland, and horses in England."

†The water was drawn from Login's Well, near the granite quays of the settlement. The well was sealed in 1931, but its life-giving water had sustained HBC ships for most of two hundred years. Its water had also slaked the thirst of the crews of Captain Cook's *Resolution* and *Discovery* during their homeward voyage of 1780 and of the outward-bound voyagers aboard *Erebus* and *Terror* before they were led into the doomed search for the North West Passage by Sir John Franklin in 1845.

provisions before crossing the North Atlantic by the great circle route.* Since the ships were there anyway and because the Company was always short of capable and willing servants, local Orkney lads were enlisted after 1702. Their prowess was so impressive that Stromness quickly became the HBC's main recruiting ground. Of the 530 employees on the Company's overseas payroll in 1799, 416 were Orcadians. Stromness had a population of 1,400 at the time, with many a rich shopkeeper but only half as many young men as women; most of the able-bodied males had departed for Hudson Bay.

Orkneymen enlisted in the Company's service at £6 a year, with increases running up to a maximum of £4. After 1779, they were offered a £2 bonus for inland service and a scheme of modest premiums based on their posts' fur returns. Because they were granted "all-found" (free food and bed) and had no place or need to spend money at the bay, they could look forward to returning to their native hearths and local lasses with enough savings to purchase fishing boats or small holdings. Many brought home new blood as well. By the end of the 1770s, so many of these hardy expatriates had fallen in love with Indian women that a small college was founded at St Margaret's Hope in South Ronaldsay to school their offspring.

Recruits from the northern isles were not all Orkney-men. In 1806, a recently arrived HBC servant named John Fubbister arrived at the post of Alexander Henry, a North West Company fur trader at Pembina, and begged for

---

*This was true to their concept of latitude sailing and the desire to avoid direct confrontation with the Gulf Stream/North Atlantic Drift. The general route to North America from the Orkney Islands was to the Isle of Sheep and the southern tip of Greenland, bringing ships into Davis Strait and then on through Hudson Strait.

help. Henry recalled the encounter in vivid detail: "I was surprised at the fellow's demand. I told him to sit down and warm himself. I returned to my own room, where I had not been long before he sent one of my people, requesting the favor of speaking with me. Accordingly I stepped down to him, and was much surprised to find him extended on the hearth, uttering dreadful lamentations; he stretched out his hands toward me, and in piteous tones begged to me be kind to a poor, helpless, abandoned wretch, who was not of the sex I had supposed, but an unfortunate Orkney girl, pregnant, and actually in childbirth. In saying this she opened her jacket, and displayed a pair of beautiful, round, white breasts; she further informed me of the circumstances that had brought her into this state. The man who had debauched her in the Orkneys ... was wintering at Grandes Fourches [an outpost on the Red River]. In about an hour she was safely delivered of a fine boy, and that same day she was conveyed home in my cariole, where she soon recovered."

The only postscript to this odd incident was the terse entry in the journal of a Company trader named John Kipling, who noted that one of his fellow HBC men "turned out to be a woman, and was delivered of a fine boy in Mr. Henry's house. The child was born before they could get her breeches off." (John Fubbister was really Isabel Gunn. The father of her baby boy, was identified as an Orcadian named John Scarth, an experienced HBC veteran who returned home in 1812. Isabel stayed at Albany until 1809, working as a nurse and washerwoman.)

Some of the more sanctimonious London Committee-men were not amused. Shortly afterward, David Geddes, the resident recruiting agent at Stromness, received a stinging complaint about the quality of recent Orkney recruits: "Of late, many men have been sent out, who on their arrival were found totally unfit for the Service. The Board will not consider themselves bound by any agreement you make, unless the men engaged by you are *stout, able, and active.*"

Most of the human traffic between the Orkneys and the bay was more mundane, with local HBC representatives screening applicants and giving them rudimentary medicals. Notices of incoming ships and Company hiring requirements were posted on church doors in the islands' various parishes, so that local boys attending divine service knew when, where and how to apply. The annual arrivals and departures of the ships quickly developed into the highlight of the sombre Stromness social calendar.

Visiting captains gathered local supporters, playing up parental feelings as they invited the families of departing youngsters to dine aboard in their private cabins. Wardrooms were used as public reception areas, and nightly dances transformed docksides into a carnival. When it was time to leave, the Company flag, with its red cross and four sleepy beavers, was run up the harbour tower. The low hills protecting Stromness reverberated as the island's thirty-two-pounder fired farewell salutes to the departing ships, borne by the racing ebb tide past Hoy Sound into the grey Atlantic. The enduring final glimpse of his home ground for many a young Orkneyman was the crowd of burghers gathered on the point of Ness, waving handkerchiefs and cheering in a thin and fading chorus as the ships raised sail and set course for the New World.

Signing on to serve five years at a time in the flourishing ring of outposts on Hudson Bay – Rupert, Moose, Severn, Albany, Prince of Wales's Fort and York Factory – the youngsters were quick to adapt to the climate and cramped circumstances. "The Orcadian was the perpetual migrant," Richard Glover has written of the islanders of that era. "Women went into domestic service in Edinburgh, Newcastle, and London. Men found outlets in the Iceland or Greenland fisheries and also turned to the Hudson's Bay Company, for even the wilderness of North America offered them a higher standard of living and a better chance of saving money than a labouring life at home."

Most of those who stayed became slaves to subsistence farms, tilled with near-prehistoric implements, fertilized by seaweed and yielding crops that hardly fed their cultivators. While a few fertile farms raised cattle and sheep, the main cash crop was kelp, burned for its iodine. One minor source of income was the breeding of a particularly ugly and brutish kind of coarse-haired pig; its bristles, twisted into ropes, were used by the islanders to pluck birds' eggs from cliffside nests in spring. Farmhouses were meticulously constructed from flagstone chinked with peat since there was little money to buy the lime for mortar that might have made insulation more adequate and rooms drier. The beasts of the field were allowed inside during winter to add their body warmth to the household.

Apart from such domestic discomforts, the Orcadians had to suffer through winters bound to reaffirm an only slightly facetious island saying – that its sons moved to Hudson Bay to get warm. Less than eight degrees south of the Arctic Circle, the Orkneys straddle the 59th parallel, sharing the latitude of some of Hudson Bay's more northern posts. At the stormy apex where the Atlantic crashes into the Norwegian Sea, then sweeps down to meld with the North Sea, the Orkneys are swept by prevailing winds that blow so fiercely few trees ever take root. The islands' rocky eastern shores are whipped by avalanching water as the tides of the North Atlantic slam into the ebb and flow of the North Sea, reaching the Orkneys with equal strength from opposite directions.* Temporarily calm anchorages

---

*According to H. Lamb's *Climate, History and the Modern World*, "A bizarre occurrence – serious for the individuals concerned – presumably resulting from the great southward spread of the polar water and ice was the arrival about the Orkney Islands a number of times between 1690 and 1728, and once in the river Don near Aberdeen, of an Eskimo in his kayak."

can suddenly be filled or emptied by cascades of water that flow in and out at sixteen knots or more. The seas are so turbulent that salt crystals are permanently suspended in the atmosphere, their refraction splitting the sun's rays into an intensified glow. That particular quality of light and a topography both gentle and jagged give the islands an aura of unyielding beauty.

The characteristics that made the island lads so sought after as HBC labourers were their natural frugality, adaptability and inbred obedience to authority which made them docile without being servile. If not particularly imaginative or enterprising, they were possessed of a strong sense of self-sufficiency. Authenticity mattered to them more than originality, and they felt instinctively mistrustful of self-aggrandizement or virtuosity. Shy to express emotion, they would conceal minor crimes such as theft – even as its victims – feeling it was sinful to be the instrument of another's suffering.

Because of its remoteness, the great movements of history bypassed Orkney, but the islands presented such a peril to navigation that a steady supply of shipwrecked sailors marrying local girls kept the culture from becoming too inbred. The islanders' linguistic ability and a parish school system that encouraged Orcadians to master the rudiments of reading, writing and arithmetic produced recruits with skills particularly suited to the dogged ledger-keeping of the fur trade.

The austere and highly structured life at the little log outposts on Hudson Bay required their inhabitants to practise a system of working relationships based on the mutually acceptable interplay of discipline and deference between Company officers and servants. Unlike the independent-minded Highlanders or the orphaned exiles from London (where tension between social classes was beginning to foster egalitarian demands), the Orcadians did not feel uncomfortable "knowing their place" – providing, of course, that the bounds of obligation and service were well respected and annual salaries were credited on time. One example of how structured the fur trade society had become was the nightly encampments of the first HBC brigades travelling inland; they were divided into three campfires, one for the Indians, another for Company servants and the third and grandest for the accompanying HBC officer or Chief Factor.

Another quality highly appreciated by early bayside governors was the Orcadian affinity for the sea. Patient fisherfolk, splendid boatmen and wise sailors, they knew how to read the wind, estimate a tide or ride out a storm. Latter-day Vikings, they manned the sloops that connected the HBC's early posts and headed north to hunt for whales and Eskimo customers. Paradoxically, it was the islanders' spreading reputation as able seamen that eventually deprived the HBC of their services. British admirals, hard pressed by Napoleon's navies, needed more and more Orkneymen to man the lower decks. Seafarers they might be, but warriors they were not. To escape the rounding up of involuntary candidates for the press gangs, able-bodied Orkneymen hid themselves in glens on the moorland, inside hollowed-out peat stacks, in secret compartments under the floorboards of their houses or in age-old cliff-caves invisible from the sea, where their anti-English slogans still adorn the walls.

Within the Hudson's Bay Company, opinion of the Orcadians' effectiveness was at times sharply divided. Samuel Hearne, the explorer who led a group of them inland to establish Cumberland House, noted in his journal that "the Orkneymen are the quietest servants and the best adapted for this country that can be procured. Yet they are the slyest set of men under the sun and their universal propensity to smuggling, and clandestine dealings of every kind, added to their clannish attachment to each other, puts it out of the power of any one Englishman to detect them." Sir George Simpson, the greatest of the overseas governors, disparaged the Orcadians for their "slow, inanimate habits," and one officer, William Walker, priggishly requested that he be recalled "if any person from the Orkney Isles should be placed over me." The London Committeemen accused the Orkney servants of cowardice during the HBC's battles with the French, and Colin Robertson, who was to command the Company's Athabasca district, condemned them as being fit only to serve at bayside posts.

Some of this criticism was justified. The penny-pinching Orkney expatriates took much greater pride in returning home with a nest egg than in exploring the new continent or trying to extract the last pelt from visiting Cree. Yet Philip Turnor, the first of the Company's bona fide surveyors, noted in his 1779 journal that the very Orcadians condemned by Hearne were "a set of the best men I ever saw together, as they are obliging, hardy, good canoe men." Ten years later, Edward Umfreville, the HBC officer who had switched to the North West Company and had competed against the Orcadian labourers along the Saskatchewan rivers, wrote that "they are a close, prudent, quiet people, strictly faithful to their employers, and sordidly avaricious. When these people are scattered about the country in small parties among the Indians, the general tenor of their behaviour is conducted with so much propriety, as not only to make themselves esteemed by the natives, and to procure their protection, but they also employ their time in endeavouring to enrich themselves."

More specific praise came from Sir John Franklin, who commanded a crew of Orcadians during his first northern trek: "It is not easy for any but an eyewitness to form an adequate idea of the exertions of the Orkney boatmen. The necessity they are under of frequently jumping into the water to lift the boats over the rocks compel them the whole day to remain in wet clothes, at a season when the temperature is far below the freezing point. The immense loads they carry over the portages is not more a matter of surprise than the alacrity with which they perform these various duties."

Whether they lauded or damned them, at least some of the HBC officers did not bother to identify their Orcadian servants by name, relegating them to the role of a collective presence, like domestic staff in a noble house. The main exceptions were the very few islanders who stayed with the Company long enough to crack the officers' ranks. The first of this select group was Joseph Isbister, son of a Stromness merchant, who became Chief Factor at Albany and Governor at Prince of Wales's Fort. Even more successful was William Tomison from South Ronaldsay, who joined the HBC in 1760 as a labourer and stayed on for the next fifty-one years, rising to be the Company's first "Chief Inland." *The New Orkney Book*, a collection of essays by some of the islands' most notable sons, states with pride that "From the western Arctic to Red River, and from Red River to Ungava, Orcadians of the eighteenth and nineteenth centuries made paths, hewed clearings, built portages, erected buildings, and planted gardens in the wilderness that was Rupert's Land."* In the enduring phrase of the American historical essayist, Bernard De Voto, they constituted a legion of brave and hardy men who "pulled the wilderness round them like a cloak, and wore its beauty like a crest."

The flood of Orkneymen into the HBC continued well into the twentieth century, but soon after the Battle of Waterloo their proportion diminished. The North Ameri-

---

*Only a few Orcadian place names survive in modern Canada – Orkney and Kirkwall in Ontario, Binscarth and Westray in Manitoba, Birsay and Orkney in Saskatchewan and Scapa in Alberta. There is a Stromness Bay on Victoria Island in the western Arctic.

can offspring of Orcadians and native women took some of their places; Canadian voyageurs recruited from Montreal occupied others. To bypass the press gangs, the Company sought staff in other countries during times of prolonged British conflict – in Ireland during the Napoleonic Wars and in Norway at the time of the Crimean War. But when the Earl of Selkirk required sturdy pioneers to establish his colony at Red River, his vanguard of seventy was recruited at Stromness.

As Sir George Simpson, himself a West Highlander, took over more and more of the Company's affairs, the recruiting emphasis changed, and the supply ships that called at Stromness in 1860 picked up as many new servants from the Highlands, the Hebrides and the Shetlands as from the Orkneys. In 1891, the HBC captains stopped calling at the storm-battered islands altogether.

CHAPTER 10

A SAVAGE COMMERCE

*"European records made a big thing of how
impressed the Indians were with their trade goods;
Indian oral tradition tells the reverse – how
impressed the Europeans were with the furs that
the Indians didn't value particularly highly."*
— *Professor Jennifer Brown*

THE INDIANS, WHO ALONG WITH THE ORCADIANS were
the proletariat of the fur trade, seldom troubled the
consciences or inhabited the journals of the HBC. With
some exceptions, Company factors and factotums treated
their presence as an amorphous, slightly out-of-focus
collective reality not far removed from the backdrop of
local vegetation and animal life: an offstage Greek chorus
supplying an endless abundance of furs.

They are the ghosts of Canadian history.

Canada's Indian nations were not conquered like the
American Sioux or massacred like the Andean Incas, yet
their lives were torn apart by the arrival of the white
man; they became (like the Welsh, in the telling phrase
of the late Gwyn Thomas) "a people deeply wounded
in their minds."

The Indians' loss of a continent and its rich resources
has yet to be adequately documented. "The picture of the

Indian as a human being presented by writers of Canadian history is confusing, contradictory and incomplete," concluded Nova Scotia historian James W. St. G. Walker, after studying the literature. Unlike their voluble white counterparts, who seemed to spend more time scribbling entries in their ledgers and journals than swapping furs, the Indians made much history but wrote very little. They lived within a hallowed oral tradition, masterfully employing the spoken word. Their chiefs were capable of magnificent oratory; individual bands would stage four-day-long miracle plays from memory; and family heads could recite ritual prayers by the hour without the omission of a single syllable. But because they had no written record – only tribal memories and sustaining myths – they were dismissed as having no past. Even the few conscientious white chroniclers who tried to understand their vanishing culture were almost invariably fooled, because most Indians, considering it more important to give a pleasing answer than an informative one, told the white man precisely what they thought he wanted to hear.

Since he was so different, the "red man" was regarded by his white contemporaries as inferior, treacherous, barbaric and fickle. A "pagan," he did not subscribe to Christian ideals, refused to observe the European sabbath, allowed his women to go naked and tortured his prisoners – all traits considered decidedly un-English and therefore "savage" and beyond the pale. (Ironically, many so-called civilized Englishmen referred to Scottish Highlanders as "savages" well into the eighteenth century.) There was not even a hint of hesitation about the manifest destiny of European civilization spreading across the continent. The only good Indian, in their thinking, was the stout chap willing to go along with that inevitable tidal wave of empire. Commercial pacification on such a massive scale required its clearly defined heroes and antagonists. The French claimed the former by preserving the memory of mutilated Jesuit martyrs, while the English created the latter by subscribing to the veracity of lurid descriptions of Indian survival habits such as this report about hard times at York Factory in the early 1700s: "When at the point of starvation, the father and mother kill their children and eat them, and then the stronger of the two eats the other. I have seen a man who had eaten his wife and their six children, and he said his heart had not failed him until he came to eat the last child, as he loved him more than the others, and when he was opening the head to eat the brains, he was touched by the natural affection of a father for his children, and had not strength to break the bones to suck the marrow."

The basic pattern of the Hudson Bay trade was one of mutual exploitation, yet there were few places on earth where commerce came to terms with an indigenous population under less violent circumstances. The exchange of peltry for trade goods resulted in a balanced reciprocity of purpose: two radically different cultures and totally dissimilar economies finding common ground in order to attain their diverse objectives. The ledgers of the Company may provide the figures and totals, but they reveal very little about the transactions' social implications.

One whimsical example of how profoundly the two cultures differed enlivens a memoir by American painter George Catlin, who observed the behaviour of a group of Indians he guided through Paris in the early 1840s. The natives were not particularly overawed by large buildings nor wildly impressed by the carriages and litters; they managed to suppress any sign of enthusiasm for white women and retained their dignity even when pawed over by various impertinent royal personages assembled to inspect them – but they were utterly flabbergasted by the way Parisian women treated their dogs. The visitors were unable to understand the affection showered on the pooches when they had seen orphanages filled with unwanted children.

They could not comprehend the horror on a saleswoman's face when they tried to buy the main course for a traditional dog feast. One of the Indian visitors carefully produced a table of Parisian dog-walking habits that ironically presaged later anthropological reports on North American Indians:

Women leading one little dog	432
Women leading two little dogs	71
Women leading three little dogs	5
Women with big dogs following (no string)	80
Women carrying little dogs	20
Women with little dogs in carriages	31

The French visit was followed by a tour of England by a dozen Chipewyan from the HBC territories in 1848. All but three died of pneumonia and English cooking.

TOO OFTEN THE FOLK MEMORY of the Indian-HBC trading relationship is reduced to the nature of a simple swap: furs for trinkets. That may have been temporarily true during initial European contact, but as the interchange between societies grew in frequency and intensity, it evolved its own complicated cultural repertoire.

The tribes saw themselves not as fur suppliers to the HBC or as trappers for gain but as part of an interlocked, animate universe in which every animal was treated as a relative of man. Hunting was very much a spiritual experience. They communicated in dreams with the sacred "keepers of the game" who told them where to hunt and sought permission to kill from the animals themselves. They knew that they would be granted the bounty of pelts only if they proved worthy of it. When the invading Europeans demanded that the Indians slaughter the creatures of the woods merely for profit, they could not know how very much they were asking.

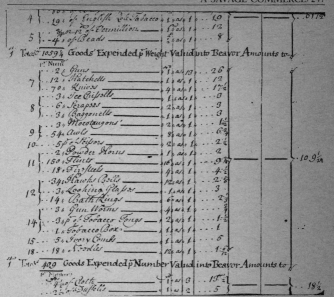

The main reason the fur trade operated as smoothly as it did was that, without really being aware of it, the HBC factors tapped into an existing Indian economic network dating back as much as five thousand years. It extended from Hudson Bay across the prairies, inland from the Pacific, from the St Lawrence to the Great Lakes, and eventually right across the continent. The greatest of these networks, formed by tribal alliances and the natural water routes connecting them, was the Mandan trading empire. This shrewd tribe of Plains Indians once spread its influence from the Missouri River to the Spanish settlements of early Mexico, as far east as Lake of the Woods and north into present-day Saskatchewan and Alberta. The Mandan tribes lived in semi-permanent, domed earth-lodge villages and evolved such sophisticated business patterns that they organized annual fairs featuring chanting dancers offering special bargains. One incentive to traders completing the trek across the plains to the Mandan villages was the attitude towards the women of the tribe. (HBC servant Richard White typified this attitude when he observed that the Indians were "a sensible people, and agreed their women should be made use of …")

The Mandan had a well-deserved reputation as canny traders with their nomadic neighbours, often exacting markups of 100 percent or more. The Crow sold horses to the Mandan at double the price they had paid the Shoshoni for them, and the Mandan in turn at least doubled the price to the Cree. These trading links were jealously guarded against efforts of white intruders to short-circuit them.* The network that terminated at Hudson Bay had the scantiest population yet the richest fur supplies, stretching all the way back to the Athapaskan region in the west as well as along the waterways south and east of the bay. From the first tentative trades in the 1600s until 1763, the Cree along with the Assiniboine and Chipewyan exercised a virtual monopoly on trade with York Factory and most of the other Hudson and James Bay posts. It wasn't until the HBC permeated the interior that nearly every other tribe in the American Northwest became their trading partners, such as the Ojibway, the various Athapaskan tribes, members of the Blackfoot confederacy, the Chinook, Haida and Nootka of the Pacific coast, and the Carrier and Chilcotin of inland British Columbia. Early HBC journals are filled with admonitions from "savages" advising against any ventures to the interior because of great danger from hostile tribes. In reality, this was the Cree way of maintaining a comfortable monopoly; they were especially anx-

---

*The fur merchants of New France were the beneficiaries of a similar sequence of alliances, at first with the Huron and later with the Iroquois, threatening those tribes trading at the bay with punitive raids by their resentful neighbours.

ious that no enemies of the Mandan be supplied with guns.*

Until the Company circumvented the Cree by setting up its own inland operations, these and other native middlemen exacted high tribute for their services. Guns received in trade at York Factory for fourteen beaver pelts were peddled to the Blackfoot for fifty. The northern Chipewyan paid nine furs for the hatchets that had cost the Cree three made-beaver. Michael Asch, a University of Alberta anthropologist, contends that these middlemen had genuine economic power and that their image as the fur trade's unwilling victims is false: "I have never seen a finer sense of profit than in a trading Indian. He knew exactly the effort that went into getting a gun from York Factory, had a highly developed idea of what the traffic would bear and was aware not only of the utility of what he bought but also of the social status that would accrue, and he built that into his price."

The Swampy Cree who dominated the trade out of Hudson Bay were a powerful coalition of nomadic bands, encompassing in their Algonkian language grouping the caribou-hunting Woodland Cree of northern Saskatchewan and the buffalo-hunting Plains Cree of the Qu'Appelle River region. All had successfully adopted ways of life that blended with their varied environments. The bands who chose to live permanently around the HBC posts became known as the "Home Guard" Indians, as contrasted with the "Upland" Indians who would gather for the annual trading sessions. Jennifer Brown, the University of Winnipeg historian who has examined the records, makes a strong argument for the mutuality of these transactions:

---

*The Mandan were almost wiped out by a smallpox epidemic that came up the Missouri by steamboat, and by U.S. cavalry raids. By 1837 there were only a hundred survivors of what had once been North America's richest economic culture.

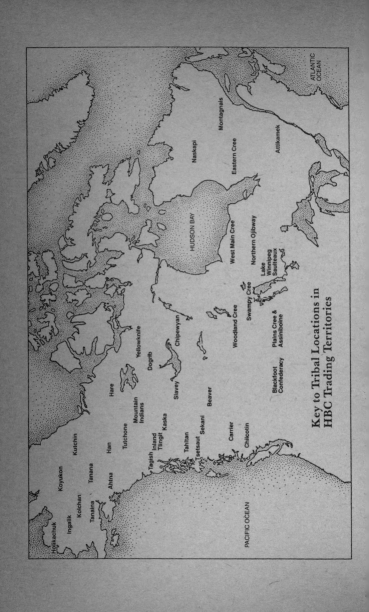

**Key to Tribal Locations in
HBC Trading Territories**

ATLANTIC
OCEAN

Montagnais

Naskapi

Attikamek

Eastern Cree

HUDSON BAY

West Main Cree

Northern Ojibway

Lake
Winnipeg
Saulteaux

Swampy Cree

Woodland Cree

Plains Cree &
Assiniboine

Chipewyan

Yellowknife

Dogrib

Blackfoot
Confederacy

Slavey

Hare

Beaver

Mountain
Indians

Sekani

Tutchone

Carrier

Kaska

Chilcotin

Inland
Tlingit

Tahltan

Tsetsaut

Tagish

Han

Kutchin

Koyukon

Ahtna

Tanana

Tanaina

Kolchan

Ingalik

Holikachuk

PACIFIC OCEAN

"The Indians saw themselves as partners, not as the exploited victims of the fur trade. The European records made a big thing of how impressed the Indians were with their trade goods; Indian oral tradition tells the reverse – how impressed the Europeans were with the furs that the Indians didn't value particularly highly. So there was a sort of mutual exploitation going on, based on a lack of knowledge about how each side perceived the value of the goods it was trading."

Some Indian academics take a more severe view of the relationship. "The Indian people inadvertently became dependent on European goods for their own survival," states Blair Stonechild, a Cree who heads the department of Indian Studies at the Saskatchewan Indian Federated College in Regina. "Some goods such as knives and kettles made life easier, but soon items such as traps and rifles became necessary to ensure the economic and political welfare of Indian groups and so-called 'traditional enemies' among Indians developed. One example of this phenomenon was the Cree-Déné animosity, some of which arose out of trade-based conflicts in the mid-1700s. Indians identified bows and arrows with hunting, not human carnage, but the arrival of the rifle brought a marked increase in human violence."

Stonechild and others point out that even if the actual trading pattern was not unjust, the economic base of the Indian survival mode was undermined through the massive slaughter of fur-bearing animals and, later, through depletion of the buffalo for pemmican supplies. Dr Oliver Brass, a fellow faculty member of Stonechild's who has four degrees, is from Peepeekisis, one of the File Hills reserves in Saskatchewan. He rarely shops at The Bay, insisting that the Company was a corrupting and co-opting influence. Brass claims that Indians in the United States have been able to remain far more distinctive and independent because they had to wage an armed struggle to survive.

The difference in the way Indians were treated in the evolving countries that would later become the United States of America and Canada is a recurring theme in native history. Stan Cuthand, a Saskatoon-based professor of Indian studies whose father, Jose, starred in Buffalo Bill's Wild West Show, contends that the fate of Canadian natives has been the more humiliating. "In Canada, the Indians were not directly shot at, but they were degraded and had no choice about the way they were treated. It was a case of *cultural* genocide, and the Hudson's Bay Company was certainly part of that process."

However one views such strong interpretations, there was a very real contrast in the ways indigenous people were treated. This was especially true of the territory under HBC control, where strict Company rules and regulations prevented the spawning of a vigilante mentality, whereas settlement of the American West amounted to military conquest of Indian lands. "On the other hand," Stonechild points out, "one should note that Indian treaties and sovereignty received earlier recognition in the United States because of the conflict nature of Indian/white relations and early resort to the judicial system for clarification of Indian rights. In Canada, because of the omnipotence of the Indian Act, questions of aboriginal rights and status of treaties were never fully addressed."

The invasion of white trappers in the United States – the notorious "mountain men" – and colonists anxious to grab Indian acreage guaranteed violent confrontation.* "Mili-

---

* The worst examples of cruelty probably occurred in the New England states, where "sniping redskins to watch them spin" became a popular frontier pastime. Canadians have no reason to feel smug on this account. The once-populous Beothuk Indians, a gentle and peaceful people who originally inhabited Newfoundland, were similarly slaughtered, being hunted by local trappers and fishermen for sport. Between 1613 and 1829 they

tary action was personal and vital, not imposed in drilled ranks and chalked white pantaloons for some remote dynastic or territorial ambition of a monarch,'' wrote Barbara Tuchman in her wise *Practising History*. ''Conquest of the plains took fifty years of incessant warfare. Eventually, when the Civil War released armed men to the frontier, the struggle was won by the fort, the repeating rifle, starvation, treachery, the railroad, the reservation policy and, ultimately, the extermination of the buffalo which had provided the Plains Indian with food, shelter, and clothing. The last battle was fought in 1890 – less than one hundred years ago.''

ONE REASON THE SWAMPY CREE and most other North American Indians were so eager to swap beaver was that the white man's goods transported them instantly from the Stone Age into the Iron Age. That quantum leap had immeasurable social consequences, but at the level of conducting their daily lives, it meant that meals could be cooked in copper pans over fires instead of in birch bark cauldrons containing red-hot rocks, and that fish could be caught on strong metal hooks instead of threaded carved beaver teeth or bird bones. Describing the impact of one such item, the axe, on his people, Chief Dan George, the Canadian activist and actor, once explained: ''Imagine its impact on a people whose main implement was still a sharpened stone. Five strokes of an axe and a sapling is down; one day, and a stockade is built – the Iron Age

---

were wiped out, and not a single white ''hunter'' was ever punished or charged with any crime. A trapper named Noel Boss boasted of having killed ninety-nine Beothuks, but only wounded his hundredth victim – a young girl called Shanawdithit who survived briefly to become ''the last of the Beothuks'' in 1829.

attached to a wooden handle! ... The Industrial Revolution came across the ocean under canvas, and the Indian wanted a part of it for good reason. So he became a fur trader, a year-long job that began in winter with the laying of the traps ... You came down to the forts in the early summer and you wanted the whole bazaar – guns, blankets, axes – even the trinkets and love beads for the long winter nights."

The transfer of technology was not all one-sided. Indian families provided the white man with the means of moving inland by introducing him to snowshoes, birch bark canoes, moccasins and toboggans. They taught the early trader how to harvest wild rice, make clothes from deer or caribou hides and how to put up pemmican, a mixture of dried meat, fat and berries that, pounded and packed into ninety-pound bags, became the staple food of the inland fur trade.

Although they were dealing with a foreign culture, the Cree were surprisingly canny shoppers. Not only did they successfully play off the French against the English and vice versa but they refused to trade items they considered unnecessary, such as dolls, raisins and metal shields; faulty guns were returned, as was tobacco that had been damaged in flooded warehouses.

The act of bartering goods for furs evolved a culture of its own, distinct from the two societies involved and yet very much an expression of their particular and respective priorities and values. The Company was generally fair in its dealings, but that attitude had little to do with decency or altruism and everything to do with preserving the natives as a cheap and convenient labour force. The relationship was somewhat akin to that of a modern-day agricultural implements dealer living in an isolated rural community, his livelihood very much dependent on the health of the crops of his customers who in turn can achieve price efficiency only by unrestricted use of the dealer's technology – even if the dealer has to lend them machinery in bad times.

Carol Judd, an Ottawa historian who has examined the HBC's personnel policies, takes a realistic view of the Company's motives in dealing with the Cree of Hudson Bay. "The Company exchanged as many furs for as few or as inexpensive trade goods as it possibly could," she wrote. "At the same time, it perceived itself as humane, fair, even generous: feeding starving natives, healing their sick, providing employment, educating their children. It also introduced schemes for conserving fur-bearing animals and, whenever monopoly conditions prevailed, it stopped selling liquor to the Indians. Beneath the humanistic veneer, the Company did all of these things because they were essential to its own long term economic and political interest ... To the Company the only good Indian was tending his trapline – starving and sick Indians could not trap furs."

Each side approached the transaction from a different premise. The English and Scottish traders operated in the European tradition that endowed the accumulation of material objects with social approbation and viewed the gaining of profits as the ultimate goal, but most Indian people admired the sharing, not the ownership, of goods. Despite their roles as middlemen among their own peoples, they had no framework within which to calculate fur prices that fluctuated as a result of the balance between European supply and demand. They therefore tacitly elected to regard the fur trade's equivalent of price – the standards of trade per made-beaver – as an immutable measure. In Professor Abraham Rotstein's telling analogy, it "was equivalent to the way we think of three feet adding up to one yard. If they believed, for example, that three beaver skins were worth one axe head, then that was that."

Rotstein, who mapped the price levels of HBC goods, discovered that the official rates of exchange for thirty-one of the fifty-five major trading goods were not altered for more than a century (and the others were changed only slightly) no matter how much the price of the trade goods purchased from English manufacturers went up or down or how quotations on the London fur market fluctuated. In 1785, for example, beaver skins sold on the London market for twenty shillings a pound; in 1790, for thirteen shillings; in 1793 for ten shillings.

The ritual of the trading process itself was rooted in the ancient formalities of tribal councils – the ceremonial format for renewing the peace alliances that governed Indian life. (Modern stereotyped terms such as "burying the hatchet," "smoking the peace-pipe" and "an Indian giver" came into the language from these ceremonies.) The ritual began every June or July, even before the Indians arrived at any fort, their canoes assembling upstream just out of sight to plan a grand entrance; only then would the flotilla sweep noisily around the bend of the river. The boats of the trading captains led the way, flying a Union Jack or a small flag of St George. The outriders chanted and fired their fowling pieces in an exuberant salute to the process about to begin. Having waited a long winter and spring for this day, the trading post men would spring into action, raise the Company flag and respond with a volley or two from their own saluting guns.

After the Indian party had landed, cleared a site, pitched its tepees and lit campfires, the Trading Captains* and their lieutenants would come calling on the Governor or Chief

---

*William Asikinack (Blackbird) of the Saskatchewan Indian Federated College points out that this term was not an internal designation by Indian tribes. As far as they were concerned, each individual could do his or her own bargaining. When people wanted to trade collectively, the person who had the ability to negotiate and to get the best possible "price" for fur was chosen by the group. In the original language of the Ojibway, the only name this person would have was "leader" and this would be only for the specific notion of trade at any given time.

Factor. Because most tribes recognized no hereditary command structures, these Captains were chosen for each voyage on the basis of their familiarity with canoe routes and knowledge of the white man. Since they taxed their followers a beaver skin per canoe, the Captains attempted to recruit large flotillas, which would also elevate their prestige in the eyes of the HBC.

The initial encounter in the fur exchange was an elaborate greeting procedure that was part of Indian religious ritual: the smoking of the peace-pipe. The Captain and the Chief Factor would puff, pause and pass the pipe, then puff again – saying nothing. The buzz of deerflies and mosquitoes and the spank of the Company flag in the summer wind were the only sounds heard for most of an hour. The peace-pipe used in these preliminaries was carved of a special stone mined in northern Minnesota. Its four-foot stem was decorated with bear claws and eagle talons, its bowl filled with tamped-down Brazil tobacco leavened with dried local herbs. HBC trader Edward Umfreville, who was a frequent witness, described the ceremony which began with the Factor, "who takes the pipe in both hands, and with much gravity rises from his chair, and points the end of the stem to the East, or sunrise, then to the Zenith, afterwards to the West, and then perpendicularly down to the Nadir. After this he takes three or four hearty whiffs, and having done so, presents it to the Indian leader, from whom it is carried round to the whole party ... When it is entirely smoked out, the Factor takes it again, and having twirled it three or four times over his head, lays it deliberately on the table; which being done, all the Indians return him thanks by a kind of sighing out of the word 'Ho!' "

Then the talk would slowly begin. In a *sotto voce* chant, his eyes fixed on the ground, the Trading Captain would describe how many canoes and how much fur he had brought with him and what had happened upcountry since his last visit. Then he would tentatively enquire, as a throwaway line, how the white man was feeling and what kind of goods he might like to trade. That was the signal for the Chief Factor to bid his visitors a generous welcome, explaining in great detail why he loved the Indians and how he would always be kind to them. It was all part of a liturgical foreplay leading to a dénouement both sides knew would eventually be based on mutual, if unexpressed, self-interest.

At some point in the proceedings, the Trading Captain would be outfitted (at the HBC's expense) in a uniform befitting his station: a red or blue cloth coat lined with baize, decorated with stripes of broad and narrow orris lace, with regimental cuffs and collar. He would wear a matching waistcoat and breeches; a white open shirt with sleeves narrowed at the wrists with lace; yarn stockings, one blue, the other red, tied below the knees with worsted garters; a hat, bedecked with three colourfully dyed ostrich feathers, a sash around its crown with the ends hanging down each side to his shoulders and a small silk handkerchief tucked into the hatband's knot. For his part, the Chief Factor would bedeck himself in equally elaborate plumage. His suit of black or dark blue might be set off by a white silk shirt, velvet frock coat and a long cloak made of Royal Stewart or some other appropriate tartan, lined with scarlet or blue coating. Such cloaks had soft Genoa velvet collars fastened across by mosaic-ornamented gold clasps and chains.

Once this elaborate costuming was accomplished, everyone could relax and nibble on bread and prunes. Then the visitors were presented with gifts, usually including a two-gallon barrel of liquor and a fathom or two of tobacco, which came in long, twine-like rolls.* Having accepted

---

* Although tobacco had been cultivated by North American Indians since prehistoric times, they much preferred the white man's milder mixture and soon stopped growing their own. Only the

these and other offerings, they marched back to their camp in predetermined formation. The parade was led by an HBC servant carrying the Ensign, while another beat time on a snare drum; Company men followed bearing the gifts, and behind them came the Chief Factor and the Trading Captain, conversing as they walked – men of the world exchanging prospects and pleasantries under the noonday sun. Then followed the Indian lieutenants and sundry camp followers. Once back inside their compound of tepees, the Indians turned the long night into a gaudy extravaganza of singing, dancing and arm-wrestling – the jubilant release of pressures from the winter in the bush. The bonfires were reflected in increasingly glassy stares as the liquor took hold and the fights started in earnest, old scores being settled and new ones started, with many a bitten-off nose or ear to show for it.

Under the sober morning sun, the ceremonies resumed with yet another round of peace-pipe, bread and prunes. Then the Trading Captain would proudly launch his oration:

> You told me last year to bring many Indians to trade, which I promised to do; you see I have not lied; here are a great many young men come with me; use them kindly, I say; let them trade good goods, I say! We lived hard last winter and hungry, the powder being short measure and bad – being short measure and bad, I say! Tell your servants to fill the measure, and not to put their thumbs within the brim; take pity on us, take pity on us, I say! We paddle a long way to see you; we love the English. Let us trade good black tobacco,

---

Blackfoot people continued to raise small plots of ceremonial tobacco until 1940. The Company at first imported Bermuda tobacco but in 1684 switched to a substance known as Brazil tobacco, which actually came from Trinidad and from the valleys of the Amazon. The use of tobacco had highly symbolic overtones. If passed from band to band without being smoked, it could be the sign for war.

moist and hard twisted; let us see it before it is opened. Take pity on us; take pity on us, I say! The guns are bad, let us trade light guns, small in the hand, and well shaped, with locks that will not freeze in the winter, and red gun cases. Let the young men have more than measure of tobacco; cheap kettles, thick and high. Give us good measure of cloth; let us see the old measure; do you mind me? The young men love you, by coming so far to see you; take pity, take pity, I say; and give them good goods; they like to dress and be fine. Do you understand me?

The Chief Factor would respond by proclaiming the deep affection of the great men of England for the Indians, detailing the trouble and danger with which they had sent the big ship yearly full of goods to supply their wants. He exhorted the Indians not to be lazy but to trap more beaver, haranguing them about the smallness of the measures offered by the traders from Montreal, emphasizing the largess of the Company's larder. As he talked, the assembly approached the post's trading window, a hole in the wall of the storehouse that served the very important psychological purpose of separating the two parties in the transaction. Only the Trading Captain was allowed inside, so that he could inspect the procedure and assess the measure as each member of his canoe flotilla presented his furs and was given the requested goods in return.

Hatchets and ice chisels (for trapping beaver), knives, files, flints, kettles, cloth, beads and tobacco were the standard items, with each Indian trading the equivalent of about a hundred made-beaver a season. They were little inclined to hoard or "put away for a rainy day," so that as the resident HBC factors accurately observed, giving the visitors more goods in exchange for their furs would only have resulted in fewer furs being brought in. This was no impulse buying: the choosing of barter items could take up to five days. It was an awkward, slow and suspicion-laden process, especially when compared with the haphazard

free-for-all bush exchanges of the *voyageurs* from Quebec, who often used liquor at the time of the actual barters (instead of before) to mellow their customers.

In the last two decades of the eighteenth century, a new trade item rapidly gained popularity. This was the famous Hudson's Bay "point" blanket, so named because its size and trading value was marked right in the weave with small black stripes – three points, or stripes, equalling three made-beaver, and so on. Manufactured by Thomas Empson of Witney, in Oxfordshire, of quality wool pounded with wooden mallets to prevent shrinking, the blankets made valuable winter clothing. They were often cut into leggings and hooded coats, their snowy colour enabling hunters to stalk their winter prey without being seen. (The colourful stripes were added later.)

The most sought-after item in the white man's inventory was the gun, but the easy assumption that it quickly replaced the bow and arrow ignores the many disadvantages of the flintlock muskets traded by the HBC for most of the first two centuries. The awkward muzzle-loader required more than a dozen motions to prime and fire. Its barrel would occasionally blow up, killing or maiming the owner; wet powder or a misplaced gunflint would render the weapon useless; unlike individually marked arrows, musket-balls did not identify the owners of felled game; and, worst of all, the noise of one shot might scare away nearby animals.* For these and other reasons, the gun did not become a prime hunting weapon among the Indians until the introduction of the repeating rifle in the 1860s.

---

*The early guns were so ponderous to use that a German writer in 1640 boasted that his prince's musketeers, in a battle lasting six hours, had fired their pieces five times. The accuracy of the weapon was so poor that according to one contemporary estimate a soldier was obliged to fire away his own weight in lead for every enemy killed.

Instead, its earliest importance was as a symbol of authority and as an instrument of war. Braves on the warpath improved their aim by holding their fire until they quite literally saw the whites of their enemies' eyes and learned to reload faster by carrying extra balls in their mouths and spitting them down the gun barrels. The weapons were lovingly protected with coatings of wolf grease and became objects of such reverence that they were thought to have extrasensory qualities. Guns were shot into the air to drive off thunder and lightning; a meeting attended by warriors with empty guns was a sure sign of trust and friendship. The gun became "the great persuader," used by the Cree to raid south and west over the Prairies, down the Mackenzie to its delta and up the Peace River into the Rocky Mountains. The Chipewyan used the weapons to oppress the Athapaskan tribes, the Dogrib, the Slavey and the Yellowknives.

The most persistent legend about the gun trade – which every Indian swears is true and every HBC man swears is not – claims that the early flintlocks were bartered for a pile of pelts equal to the length of the barrel. According to the elaboration of this tale, the Company kept introducing longer and longer gun barrels to take in more furs. The length of the barrel was indeed increased from the original thirty-seven inches to forty-four inches and later to sixty-six inches, but the reason stated was that the length gave the slow-burning powder more time to ignite, raising muzzle velocity. (Indian hunters sometimes sawed off the gun barrels because the long weapons were hard to handle in the bush.) The very idea of trading guns for piles of furs, thus bypassing carefully preset measures of trade, is dismissed by students of the HBC as "unhistorical rubbish" and the physical dimensions of such an exchange would seem to support their scepticism. To make up the five-and-a-half-foot pile of furs reaching to the top of the longest gun barrel would have required at least four hundred beaver skins. No Trading Captain was uninformed enough to agree to such an exchange when the going rate was the equivalent of about a dozen made-beaver per gun.*

Another contentious fur trade issue was the way the Company covered its overhead, the fluctuating cost of maintaining its ships and forts plus the expenses of the gifts and other facilities granted visiting Indians. Because both sides in the exchange had agreed not to vary the accepted standards, the HBC traders introduced a concept called "overplus" to take up the fiscal slack. "The official standard did remain unchanged for long periods," according to Professor Glyndwr Williams, "but there was another, local, more flexible standard of trade, and it was the difference between the two standards which was the overplus."

Arthur Ray, who has made the most complete study of the Company's trading records, has estimated that between 1725 and 1735 traders at York Factory advanced their standards 50 percent above the official rates. Between 1735 and 1755, when the French expanded into the York Factory hinterland, the markup level at the post declined to 33 percent. Following the French withdrawal, an advance of 50 percent was again exacted until the Nor'Westers ended the company's monopoly in the 1780s. At the same time, the HBC traders were often guilty of placing a heavy

---

*The only modern HBC man to experiment with duplicating the exchange, to quash the myth once and for all, was Hugh Ross, post manager at Temagami in Northern Ontario. It took 170 skins to reach the muzzle of a sixty-dollar rifle, "and at that point the damn things kept slipping all over the place, so I couldn't make a pile more than halfway up the gun," he reported. Yet, as late as 1976, at the hearings of the Mackenzie Valley Pipeline Inquiry, Henry Simba, a resident of Kakisa Lake, testified: "You bought a gun with skins, piled to the height of the gun, even before you received it ... I saw two people buy guns like that, trapping all winter long. They just piled all their cache for the whole winter and got the gun."

thumb on the scales when weighing gunpowder or shot, cutting shorter lengths of tobacco and deliberately mismeasuring bolts of broadcloth and duffle material – and later, diluting brandy with water. Why the Indians complained only mildly about these departures from the accepted trading standards remains a mystery.

On the other side of the ledger from the questionable practice of charging overplus, the Company gave its preferred customers considerable credit and looked after their subsistence needs during periods of hardship and starvation. In 1748, for example, a hundred Cree were fed through a long harsh winter at Fort Albany and nearly as many again at Moose Factory. Hunters who had suffered a poor season were often advanced equipment and supplies until they could resume their trapping. This private form of social welfare was certainly helpful, but it also placed the Indians under severe restraint and obligation. Yet that obligation was mutual. The debt load did give them a certain measure of power over the traders: the hunter who starved to death was the worst credit risk – so the HBC became committed to his welfare.

The gist of the credit relationship was plainly articulated more than two and a half centuries later, after the pattern had been well established. One HBC district manager, James Ray, defended his doling out of several tens of thousands of dollars in credit, advances and outright gifts by noting: "The natives are our asset … we must keep them alive for future profits, even though we carry them at a loss till such time shall come."

Mutual exploitation was paralleled by mutual dependence. As the trade developed, the Indians lost their selfsufficiency, involuntarily revolutionizing their way of life so that trade goods became necessities instead of novelties. At the same time, the traders began to realize just how indebted they had become to their customers. Merchant adventurers they might be, but they were heavily outnumbered and totally dependent for their survival on maintaining the good will of their Indian hosts.

Surveying the end-effects of the fur trade, University of Toronto political economist Mel Watkins observed: "If you look at the range of contacts between white and native peoples, the least of the evils was the fur trade. Compared to any other contacts, it was relatively benign. Of course, who came out of it better is unambiguous – the HBC moved on to other things, while the Indian was reduced to a lumpen condition."

Only one voice among the loyal Company men of the early fur trade was raised to suggest that Indian contact with the HBC had been a mixed blessing. Samuel Hearne, the HBC explorer and blithe spirit who survived the Barrens in the late eighteenth century, wrote in his diary of that time on the bay: "I must confess that such conduct [encouragement of the fur trade] is by no means for the real benefit of the poor Indians – it being well known that those who have the least intercourse with the Factories are by far the happiest."

THE MOST CONTROVERSIAL ASPECT of the Indian-white relationship had little to do with business, yet it touched the most sensitive nerve of the isolated society that grew up around the fur trade. Because liaisons between Indian women and HBC traders were officially considered a menace to the security of the Company forts, London perfunctorily decreed they never should and never would take place. The men of the HBC may have been loyal but they were not monastic, and no head office directive was more widely or happily ignored.

Quite apart from the sensual pleasures involved, HBC men who teamed up with daughters of prominent Indian families gained a concentrated course in wilderness survival. Growing up in the relatively urban environment of

C.W. JEFFERYS

the British Isles provided no training in snaring rabbits with willow twigs, readying raw furs for market or chewing tough moosehide into pliable moccasins. More important, these liaisons allowed the traders entry into Indian society; the women acted as interpreters and mentors, true partners in a relationship which, when it worked, went far beyond sexual congress. On the most elementary level, it provided the HBC men with cheap scalp insurance. Through a simple ceremony *à la façon du pays* – an indigenous marriage rite sanctioned by Indian custom – they took "country wives," acquiring personal security and the inestimably beneficial support system of the country wife's family. For their part, the women won access to the relative comforts of living year-round at or near the HBC forts; they gained social prominence and, usually, some form of special consideration for their relatives at the Company stores.

The Indian leaders perceived most of these live-in arrangements as advantageous, because their society operated along strong kinship lines and such semi-permanent partnerships extended family allegiances into the white man's valuable networks. This was, of course, not universally true, but it did happen often enough. Trading Captains calling at Company posts sometimes paid local factors the honour of offering their daughters in country marriages to forge blood-brotherhoods. At another level, living within the intimacy of these wilderness pairings was an ideal way to pass the long postings. The most effective traders were often the veterans of such tacit marriages. "About the only way you could learn the grunts and twists that go with most Indian talk is from a sleeping dictionary," inelegantly concluded an American free trader named Andrew Garcia, who spent his life on the bush frontier.*

---

*According to Walter O'Meara's *Daughters of the Country*, two of Garcia's buddies settled in very direct fashion a feud

Although the HBC did not officially sanction marriage between its employees and Indian women until the nineteenth century, Sir George Simpson, its outspoken Governor, set down the Company's blunt policy when he wrote to the London Committee from Fort Wedderburn in the Mackenzie River District on May 15, 1821: "Connubial alliances are the best security we can have of the good will of the natives. I have therefore recommended the Gentlemen to form connections with the principal Families immediately on their arrival, which is no difficult matter, as the offer of their Wives and Daughters is the first token of their friendship and hospitality."

Individual tribes, bands and families had their own sexual rules and customs, but most girls were fairly uninhibited before their weddings, suffering from few of the premarital constraints that characterized the upright young ladies of eighteenth-century England and Scotland. After marriage, the Indian girls became the "property" of their husbands, who could lend them out, or sell them or beat them if they were found to have played false. The restraints of marriage could be severe, but divorce was often as unceremonious as pushing the rejected wife outdoors and telling her not to come back. A wife could leave an intolerable husband just as unceremoniously. Some of the more curious native rites were not shared with the white

---

over an Indian girl they both loved. The partners, known only as Fink and Carpenter, had been in the habit of demonstrating their trust in each other by filling a cup full of whisky and taking turns shooting it off each other's heads. To settle the love match, therefore, they decided to prove their good will by repeating their familiar performance. Fink won the coin toss for the first shot. "Hold your noodle steady, Carpenter," the gunman commanded, "and don't spill the whisky." A trigger squeeze later, Carpenter was stone dead with a bullet hole in his forehead. "Aw, shucks, Carpenter," Fink reproached his late partner, "you spilled the whisky ..."

men, though the Nor'Wester Alexander Henry the Younger once witnessed a Mandan orgy he described with vicarious gusto: "About midnight we were awakened by some extraordinary noise in the village. On going to the outer porch door I saw about 25 persons of both sexes, entirely naked, going about the village singing and dancing. At times they withdrew in couples, but soon rejoined their companions in the dance and song. During this short separation from the rest they appeared to be very closely engaged, and not withstanding the night was dark I could perceive them occupied in enjoying each other with as little ceremony as if it had been only the common calls of nature."

While Indian women were at the mercy of an *ad hoc* social structure devised primarily to meet the needs and desires of European males, Sylvia Van Kirk, in her important study of women in fur-trade society, *Many Tender Ties*, maintains that they played an active part in the promotion of its material and cultural changes. "Generally, the women agreed to being offered to the white men and should they be refused, they could become very indignant at this insult." In the longer term, suggests Van Kirk, "… the norm for sexual relationships in fur trade society was not casual, promiscuous encounters but the development of marital unions which gave rise to distinct family units … The marriage of a fur trader and an Indian woman was not just a 'private' affair; the bond thus created helped to advance trade relations with a new tribe, placing the Indian wife in the role of cultural liaison between the traders and her kin. In Indian societies, the division of labour was such that the women had an essential economic role to play. This role, although somewhat modified, was carried over into the fur trade where the work of native women constituted an important contribution to the functioning of the trade."

The relationship, once again, was a case of mutual

exploitation – but the odds were uneven. Their terms of service ended, most HBC men would vanish on the September supply ships, leaving their country wives no choice but to rejoin their tribes in a state of widowhood and await another husband. This traders' habit of what was called "turning off" – discarding their mates to suit their HBC contracts – was the worst aspect of the interchange. One Hudson Bay country wife named Mademoiselle Censols was reputed to have gone through eight "husbands." There were many long and happy unions, but George Nelson, an observant Nor'Wester, quoted the bitter lament of an Indian who hoped to pass off his second wife to a white man because he considered her to have been debauched by past associations with them: "They take women, not for wives – but use them as Sluts – to satisfy the animal lust, and when they are satiated, they cast them off, and another one takes her for the same purpose – and by and by casts her off again, and so she will go on until she becomes an old woman, soiled by everyone who chuses to use her. She is foolish – she has no understanding, no sense, no shame."

Country marriages were the preferred life-style, but prostitution also flourished around the bay, as did various forms of venereal disease. The Chipewyan were known to take their women hundreds of miles to indenture their bodies to the traders' demands. Ferdinand Jacobs, when he took over from James Isham at York Factory in 1761, complained that "the worst Brothel House in London is not so common a stew as the mens house in this Factory." Alexander Henry the Younger, who found more than one Indian chief's daughter in his bed, documented one of the many swaps of women for horses: "On the 12th, one of my men gave a mare that cost him … currency equal to £16 13s. 4d. for one single touch at a Slave [Slavey tribe] girl."

A limited slave trade in Indian women did take place,

mostly in the form of white men buying female war captives from friendly tribes. Henry's journal records instances of Indians "who have disposed of their women to HBCo.'s people in barter for bear meat," and he cites the case of a spirited young mare being traded for "a young wife about eight years of age." (The highest bids seem to have been for sterile women who did not burden their mates with unwanted children.) Describing the pattern during the early operations of the Hudson's Bay Company, when the traffic in women was lucrative enough to attract tribes from the distant western plains, American historian Walter O'Meara wrote that "female captives taken in slave raids by the Blackfoot were sold to the Cree or Assiniboin, who in turn disposed of them on the Bay. During the long journey from the Saskatchewan River to York Fort, the women were passed around the camp at night. On arrival at York they were traded, along with beaver pelts and buffalo robes, to the factors of 'the Honourable Company.' Those for whom there was no sale were said to have been destroyed."

The Hudson's Bay Company journals and archives are silent on these sexual transactions. Officially, there was no intercourse between Company men and Indian women.

Liberated from Presbyterian mothers who would not allow them even to play cards on Sundays and stern fathers who equated sensuality with sinfulness, the young HBC clerks suddenly found themselves surrounded by attractive tawny-skinned women willing and proud to express their uninhibited sexuality. Love-making on the frontier did not always carry much emotional baggage, being routinely offered and casually accepted. The women were there, every day and every night, within sight and sound of the forts, an overpowering presence, causing yearnings that erupted into mad dark evenings of ecstasy and pain. By guttering candlelight in a trader's wood-gathering camp and by firelight among the country family members, the rough or sweet enchantments of intimate moments became a phenomenon that pervaded HBC life through the centuries.

MORE CREDIT FOR THE RELATIVELY BENIGN treatment meted out to the Indian peoples by the Company must go to the HBC men on the spot than to their English overlords. Again and again, local factors urged London to adopt more enlightened policies. The most eloquent appeal came from William Auld, an Edinburgh surgeon who had become Chief Factor at Churchill. He wrote to the London Committee: "Your servants of every rank, your Chief Factors and Traders alike with myself are utterly disqualified for wringing from the bloody sweat of these poor creatures any more advantages worth a moment's consideration and we recoil with horror at the thought of these *advantages* being rejected at the judgement seat of Heaven where your Honours as well as ourselves must deliver in the accounts of our government. There, distinctions of colour cease and it will avail but little if we transgress the rights of our coppered Indians to satiate rapacious Tradesmen of a fairer hue. ..."

IV MARCH OF EMPIRE

CHAPTER 11

PATHFINDERS

*The HBC traders felt uneasy away from the tang
of salt water, suspecting they might starve once
removed from the protection of their forts – fears
that were compounded by tall tales of upcountry
famine and cannibalism earnestly recounted by
visiting Cree.*

AND SO THE COMPANY MEN PERCHED on the desolate
perimeter of Hudson Bay, sitting out the first half of the
eighteenth century. The slowly revolving cycle of the
fur trade – the spring and autumn goose hunts, winter
ptarmigan and rabbit shoots, freeze-up and breakup, the
summer curse of the mosquitoes, the annual arrival and
departure of the supply ships – these and other minor
interruptions only rarely disturbed what was otherwise a
dreary survival mode, fostering from one generation to
the next not only a fixed sense of place but a rigid state of
mind.

It was a mood of inertia so pervasive that the HBC
residents found themselves in a society under a siege of
their own making. The Bay men kept their thoughts focused
homeward, as if the unexplored regions behind and beyond
the bay were occupied by the land-equivalents of the
allegorical creatures in the "Here Be Dragons" admonitions of early sea charts. A 1782 map of North America,
published in London by Thomas Conder, depicted all

the land west of Hudson Bay as a blank, with the notation: "These parts intirely unknown."

To remain rooted in their primitive sanctuaries, where
they could preserve the tenuous umbilical link to their
mother civilization, was an obsession. Almost without
exception, the few hardy souls who made flash trips
inland instinctively rushed back home with the determination of spawned-out Atlantic salmon spurting down
to the sea.

Then, as the vigorous entrepreneur-traders from Montreal began to divert fur and intercept Indians bound for
the HBC posts, the Company men realized they had to
venture inland for sheer commercial survival. They began
to range into the mysterious hinterland, coming to terms
with its gargantuan dimensions and settling posts at its
river junctures. They started to penetrate the straggling
black spruce curtain of the Canadian Shield, becoming
adept woodsmen and swift canoe travellers, gradually
mastering their new environment.

This was no sudden metamorphosis. During the seven
decades between the signings of the Treaty of Utrecht in
1713 and the Peace of Paris in 1783, the fur trade and the
Hudson's Bay Company itself were transformed. For the
first time since its founding, the HBC began to take full
measure of the empire granted by Charles II's casual
charter. Such a dramatically expanded landscape called
not just for new skills and fresh assumptions but for a
different breed of men.

When the HBC first ventured overseas, the North American continent was still presumed to be bisected by the
mythical Strait of Anian, connecting the Pacific with a
western outlet of Hudson Bay somewhere near Roes
Welcome. The main reason for this speculation was that
Luke Foxe, the British navigator, had reported upon
returning from Hudson Bay in 1632 that the wide range
of local tides pointed to the existence of an ocean passage

nearby. Cartographers from Juan de la Cosa, in 1500, to Jonathan Carver, in 1778, depicted Anian on their maps. Navigators vainly sought to find and control the secret passage to break the Spanish hold on Pacific-Orient trade.

Apart from a dash to the mouth of the Churchill River from York Factory by two HBC captains, John Abraham and Michael Grimington, in 1686,* only the journey of the boy explorer Henry Kelsey four years later into buffalo country disrupted the bay-bound isolation. The HBC traders felt uneasy away from the tang of salt water, suspecting they might starve once removed from the protection of their forts – fears that were compounded by tall tales of upcountry famine and cannibalism earnestly recounted by visiting Cree. (The Indians were understandably loath to have their delicate trading relationships with farther-flung tribes thrown out of balance by foreign penetration.) As late as 1749, James Isham, the Governor of York Factory and a seventeen-year Company veteran, testified before a British parliamentary committee that inland posts were not practicable because the rivers were too full of shoals for trans-shipping supplies, no corn could be grown to maintain permanent settlements – and even if these difficulties were overcome, nothing would be accomplished beyond diverting the fur trade away from existing HBC posts.

The Company's Committeemen were all too ready to be convinced. They were caught up in the belief that the fur trade could remain profitable only so long as the wilderness south and west of Hudson Bay was kept inviolate. Any disruptions – particularly the influx of

---

*The following year, Abraham left the employ of the HBC and, along with another ex-Captain named John Outlaw, attempted to claim the river for private trade. They were caught in the ice of Hudson Strait, rescued by a Company supply ship, taken to York Factory and summarily returned to England.

large-scale trade through a North West Passage – would menace their monopoly. The London governors treated reports and rumours of goods-laden French free-traders moving westward from Montreal as a harmless and temporary aberration, certain that the fiscal instability of these freelance operations would inevitably cause their collapse. They took great pains to perpetuate the isolation of their posts; in 1725, for example, when a trader named John Butler wanted to send his son "up into the Country with the Northern Indians in order to learn the Language," they disapproved the idea: "We do hereby order you not to suffer him or any other Person to be absent from his Duty on such pretence …"

The fact that the Committeemen were proved wrong on every one of their assumptions was due not so much to their lack of foresight as to what Professor Richard Glover described as "the fog of war – the way in which a commander must grope for knowledge of his opponent, fight for the very information without which he cannot fight, and at times put all to the touch without the knowledge that makes the difference between success and failure. Few commanders in the field have been as handicapped by this fog of war as the Hudson's Bay Company in the long struggle for the fur trade with their competitors from Montreal …" One solution might have been to appoint a resident overseas Governor with full executive authority to make decisions according to local conditions. No individual was entrusted with such powers, however, from the tenure of Charles Bayley in the 1670s, and his two immediate successors, to the creation in 1810 of the HBC's Northern Department under its own authority, headed by William Auld.

The Company continued to operate precisely as a landed Scots estate, whereby his lordship entrusted all the details of trade and management to his hard-headed "factor" but kept the profit strictly to himself. It was no internal change of attitude but external pressure that finally lifted this siege mentality. Determined to break the French hold on North America, the English government, encouraged by commercial rivals jealous of the HBC monopoly, pushed the Company into taking up those conditions of its original charter dealing with sea and land exploration. When the HBC's neglect of its obligations was brought up during the 1749 parliamentary hearings, the Company was forced, in self-defence, to remind the MPs of the wanderings of its apprentice Henry Kelsey, more than half a century earlier.

KELSEY IS EITHER BILLED as "The Discoverer of the Canadian Prairies" or dismissed by historians such as Lawrence Burpee, who concluded that his narrative was "too unsubstantial to afford any safe ground for historical conclusions."

Kelsey would later in his career become one of the HBC's senior overseas governors, spending nearly forty years in faithful, prosaic anticlimax to his 1690 mission. He was sent, not on a voyage of exploration, but "to call, encourage and invite the remoter Indians" to bring their furs eastward to the bay. North America's first travelling salesman, he carried a packet of trade samples such as twenty pounds of Brazil tobacco, glass beads, hatchets and kettles. Heading southwest from York Factory, he reached a sheltered bend in the Saskatchewan River below what is now The Pas, Manitoba, and after a successful wintering continued westward into the Assiniboine country, reaching the buffalo-rich Touchwood Hills southeast of present-day Saskatoon. Kelsey was gone for two years, but apart from his attempts to make trade treaties and to mediate between warring tribes, not much evidence of his exploits survives beyond a journal, much of it in amateurish doggerel, written to while away the hours spent hunched in a canoe.*

> Because I was alone & no friend could find
> And once y^t in my travels I was left behind
> Which struck fear & terror into me
> But still I was resolved this same Country for to see …

> Gott on ye borders of ye stone Indian Country
> I took possession on ye tenth Instant July
> And for my masters I speaking for y^m all
> This neck of land I deerings point did call …

> This wood is poplo ridges with small ponds of water
> There is beavour in abundance but no Otter …

Kelsey did accompany Indians on a bison hunt, was the first Bay man to view the Prairies and arrived back at York Factory at the head of a "good fleet of Indians."

Yet, judging by the lack of follow-up, his journey might never have happened. "What, if anything, the Company made of Kelsey's journey is totally obscure," commented Glyndwr Williams. "It failed to use, publish or even preserve the notes of his findings. No evidence of his wanderings appears on contemporary maps; the episode was an isolated and soon-forgotten feat in an era when Company servants were reluctant to move away from the bayside posts."

A SIGNIFICANT BUT MYSTERIOUS FIGURE in the long roster of errants who risked themselves on the land's illusory mercies, James Knight spent four eventful decades

---

*The original was not found until 1926, when it turned up among the papers of Major Arthur F. Dobbs, a descendant of Arthur Dobbs, the Irish anti-HBC lobbyist.

in the Company's service. Originally apprenticed as a shipwright at Deptford, he joined the HBC in 1676 and was sent to the bay as a staff carpenter. The energetic Knight proved himself so capable that only six years later he was named Chief Factor at Albany. But after his return to England he was accused of private trading in furs and summarily dismissed. His exile proved temporary. During the last quarter of the seventeenth century, when the French held most of Hudson Bay and the Company was organizing an attack flotilla to recapture Albany, Knight (described at that point in the HBC minute book as "… of London, Merchant") was rehired to lead the expedition. He had waited a month before accepting – a deliberate delay that would bring him a £500 bonus if he succeeded*– and sailed off in June 1692 with a four-ship convoy and 213 men, the most formidable expedition the Company ever sent into the bay. Knight's troop quickly recaptured the almost-abandoned Albany; he stayed on as its Governor until 1697, when he returned to England, wealthy enough to acquire £400 in HBC stock.

That purchase, plus Knight's practical experience, was recognized in 1711 when he became one of the very few overseas Bay men to be honoured with a seat on the London Committee.† Duly promoted in Company minutes to "… of London, Gentleman," he acted as Sir

---

*The crusty Knight drove a hard bargain. By stalling negotiations, he won the promise not only of the monetary bonus but also a share in the profits of any new trade in furs, "sea horse teeth" (walrus ivory or narwhal tusks), minerals, oil and bones that his efforts might stimulate, plus a free beaver coverlet for his bed and the right to keep any presents that the vanquished French might choose to give him.

†Only two others shared this distinction during the eighteenth century: John Fullartine (on the Committee 1711–14), who

Bibye Lake's adviser during the Utrecht negotiations and, once the Treaty had been signed, in 1713, was charged with returning to the bay to accept the surrender of York Factory from the French commander Nicolas Jérémie.

Knight was by then well past seventy years old, but his imperious nature had not mellowed. He not only forbade the members of his garrison to drink, use profanity or have contact with the Indian women but actually tried to *enforce* such restrictions. His elaborate plans for re-invigorating the fur trade were set back when Captain Joseph Davis returned to England without unloading his 1715 supply ship, the *Hudson's Bay III*. He had scudded back and forth along the coast for three weeks, trying to find an entrance to the Hayes River, and at one point his ship had actually been spotted from shore as she was anchored in the mouth of the river. The ship would probably have reached York Factory on the flood tide if her misguided captain had simply allowed her to drift gently towards shore instead of setting sail for his return voyage. Knight was beside himself, furiously scratching in his journal that "none but a Sott or a Madman would have done it!"

With no replenishment of its badly depleted stores, York Factory faced a bleak winter. Fourteen bushels of turnips were forked out of the gardens, and none of the resident sheep or goats survived through to spring breakup. As word spread that the English were back in charge, the up-country Indians returned to trade. Many arrived without their bows and arrows, in the certain expectation they could barter their furs for powder and new guns. When told there were no goods available, they refused to leave. Although worried that their families might starve if they

---

had served twice as Governor of Albany, and George Spurrells (1756–65), who had commanded thirty-five successful supply voyages into Hudson Bay.

did not return home, they feared the three-month journey even more – they could not face a winter unarmed, either travelling or at the post's gates. By mid-August, there were more than a thousand angry, starving Indians camped along a hundred miles of riverbank up from York. The HBC men dared not venture outdoors to hunt or even to collect firewood, and Knight ordered that no meals be cooked in case the smell of food incited violence. Several Indians prostrated themselves in a death vigil in front of the fort's entrance, and a band that had already massacred several of the garrison's Frenchmen in 1712 was rumoured to be preparing another attack. Knight blustered and bluffed his way through the predicament, promising that new supplies from England were due at any moment – but he was simultaneously rushing to complete a high wooden inner palisade so he would have some semblance of defence if no ship arrived. The structure was finished on August 31, 1716, and three days later a most welcome cannon salute was heard out at sea.

Next morning, the lifting fog revealed an HBC supply ship at anchor near Five Fathom Hole, complete with a new, sharper-eyed captain. The HBC men pretended nonchalance, but the Indians whooped it up, yelling and dancing on the shore long into the night, their animated silhouettes reflected against the bonfires and torches beside the cold black water.

HAVING RESOLVED HIS MOST PRESSING PROBLEM, Knight turned to the more complicated challenge posed by the Montreal free traders. He had been at Utrecht while Sir Bibye Lake lobbied against allowing the French to hunt, or even travel, within the Company's land limits, but now that he was on the spot, Knight realized that the diplomatic punctiliousness that had seemed paramount

in Utrecht was hardly applicable here. With a trading post built only seven days' paddling up the Albany River, the French and their Huron and Algonquin allies were hemming in the HBC posts with increasingly effective competition, siphoning off the flow of prime furs to Hudson Bay.

Since Knight had not enough men or arms to force a confrontation with the French, he decided to try out-flanking "the woodrunners" by seeking new fur-trading grounds to the north, out of reach of their Montreal-based routes.

West beyond the Churchill River was the land of the Chipewyan. This tribe tended to shy away from contact with the HBC posts because they as yet lacked the firearms with which they were periodically ambushed by the gun-toting Cree. To negotiate peace between the two tribes and to measure the potential fur yield of the Chipewyan territories, Knight dispatched a small peace mission into the wild country northwest of York Factory. The expedition was led by William Stuart, a Company servant only semi-literate in English but fluently articulate in Cree. He left no journals of his year-long absence, but his voyage pushed into brief prominence one of the most remarkable personalities of the early Canadian fur trade: Thanadelthur, the Slave Woman.

There is no description of her appearance, though Chipewyan history stresses her youth and attractiveness. More to the point, she was self-possessed, shrewd and plucky, one of the very few Indian women to stamp her individuality on native history. Originally a member of a clan of Chipewyan known as the Slaves,* as a teenager

---

*The Slaves occupied the western half of Great Slave Lake's shores and, except for their feud with the Nahanni, had a reputation of being peaceable and inoffensive, protected by their prowess in witchcraft. They caught woodland caribou by

she had been captured by the Cree in the spring of 1713, had escaped and eventually stumbled into a goose-hunter's tent at Ten Shilling Creek near York Factory. Knight was impressed with her intelligence, and when she declared herself anxious to help him make peace with her people to provide them access to the Company's valuable trade goods, Knight entrusted her to Stuart as his interpreter. He gave Thanadelthur samples of HBC trade goods and instructed her to tell her people of his promise to build a fort closer to them, at the mouth of the Churchill River, the following summer.

The Stuart expedition, which initially included 150 Cree, headed north and probably reached Great Slave Lake. But they were too large a group to be sustained by the land and within a few months they drifted apart, breaking into smaller squads, hunting along the way. The mission's failure seemed certain when the main party came across the bodies of nine Chipewyan massacred by their former companions. Fearing revenge, the remaining Cree wanted to flee, but Thanadelthur assumed command and persuaded them to wait ten days until she went to her people to negotiate a peace. She tracked the Chipewyan to their camp and, as Stuart reported, "made herself hoarse with her perpetual talking." She persuaded her brothers to forget past grievances and make peace with the Cree in order to gain access to the white men's goods. With theatrical precision, she duly reappeared on the tenth day, silhouetted on the horizon backlit by the dawn, with two Chipewyan emissaries by her side. When Stuart welcomed them into his tent, she gave a hand signal and a hundred northern young men materialized out of the morning mist at the edge of the clearing.

---

running them down on snowshoes or snaring them with the help of dogs in the spring, and fished with lines made of twisted willow bark and hooks fashioned from ptarmigan claws.

Thanadelthur mounted a high rock platform and encouraged her brothers to approach more closely. As Chipewyan legend has it, "when she beheld her people coming, she sang with joy."

According to the less lyrical Stuart, she "made them all stand in fear of her as she scolded at some and pushing of others ... and forced them to ye peace. Indeed, she was a divellish spirit and I believe if there were but fifty of her Country Men of the same carriage and resolution, they would drive all the [Southern] Indians out of their country ..."

Stuart and his new allies marched back into York Factory on May 7, 1716. Thanadelthur spent the summer and fall instructing her fellow Chipewyan how to cure furs for trade purposes, and when one elder suggested that less-than-prime pelts be surreptitiously bartered to the HBC, she "ketcht him by the nose, pushed him backwards and called him a fool." On one occasion her temper flared at her benefactor, James Knight, when he caught her giving away a kettle he had presented to her. She flew into a rage, claiming the kettle had been stolen, and warned the greybeard Governor that if he ever set foot north of the Churchill River, she would order her people to kill him. "She did rise in such a passion as I never did see the like before," Knight marvelled in his journal, adding: "So I cuffed her ears for her." The next morning, Thanadelthur came to him begging forgiveness, slyly assuring Knight that he was like a father to her and diplomatically reiterating that all Indians everywhere would always love him.

Shortly after these diversions and her marriage to a Chipewyan Lothario, Thanadelthur taught herself fluent English and began to spin into Knight's attentive ear alluring tales of rich mineral deposits. Like all Bay men since Prince Rupert, he had long dreamed of such an El Dorado and had even brought with him "Cruseables,

melting potts, borax &c., for the Trial of Minerals"
from England to York Factory. Thanadelthur's promise
to lead Knight to the mineral showings went unfulfilled
because she took ill and died on February 5, 1717.

Distressed but only temporarily deterred from his great
purpose, the doughty old Governor established a permanent post at the mouth of the Churchill River, fulfilling his
pledge to the Chipewyan and hoping to tempt them into
trade. Churchill was meant to provide a harbour for the
Company's whaling fleet and, most important of all, to be
the northern jumping-off point for Knight's intended quest
for the legendary mines of the Copper Indians. Certainly
its blasted environs offered few attractions, prompting
Knight to confide to his journal: "York Fort is badd but this
is tenn times worse!"

Thanadelthur had described to Knight a broad strait
in her country through which great tides ebbed and flowed,
suggesting the existence of the ever-elusive North West
Passage. But the HBC veteran was much more enthralled
by her tales of "Yellow mettle" and "black pitch"
– possible references to Klondike gold and the Athabasca
tar sands. Her disjointed narrative had been peppered with
vague tales of a lost tribe of bearded white giants gathering
bags of pure gold and mining mountains of copper somewhere beyond the northern horizon. Joseph Robson
reported that the gossip among HBC posts at the time was
that "Governor Knight knew the way to the place as
well as to his bedside." One group of visiting Chipewyan
drew him a rough map of the Copper Indians' country,*
sketching a specific route to the Coppermine, fourteen
river-crossings to the north and west of Churchill. They

---

*The Copper Indians were really the Yellowknives, a tribe
  with characteristics similar to the Chipewyan; they lived farther
  north in the vicinity of Great Bear Lake and the Coppermine
  River.

assured him that just beyond these copper hills lay the Great Western Sea and that inhabitants there had spotted strange vessels, which Knight took to be Japanese or Tartar ships at the western end of the North West Passage.

Hardly able to contain his excitement, the credulous veteran hurried back to England in the fall of 1718 to obtain the Committee's backing for a major voyage of discovery. While Knight had earned the respect of the HBC's governors and was a particular favourite of Sir Bibye Lake, he was returning to England at an awkward time. The war-weary nation had enjoyed less than five years' peace since 1688, and trade prospects were only slowly recovering. Yet, reluctantly persuaded by their elder colleague's faith in the existence of distant lucre, the London Committeemen granted Knight their blessing and the funds to outfit two vessels, the hundred-ton frigate *Albany* and the forty-ton sloop *Discovery*, with a twenty-seven-man crew between them, plus two captains and ten "landsmen passengers." Knight was directed to explore the west coast of Hudson Bay north of the sixty-fourth parallel and plant the Company flag on the mineral treasures assumed to exist en route, the search for the Strait of Anian being very much a secondary goal. Knight was granted a one-eighth interest in his own discoveries, given enough brick to build a portable shelter and supplied with great iron-bound chests in which to stow the expected hoards of gold and copper.

The HBC Committeemen's instructions contained a highly unusual codicil: Knight's captains were expressly forbidden to land at any Company post on Hudson Bay or even to trade south of latitude 64° north where commercial contact had already been made. This was presumably put in to avoid exacerbating the quarrel between Knight and his York Factory Deputy and successor, Henry Kelsey, the one-time boy explorer. After arriving in London, Knight lost no time in filing a complaint

with the Committee, accusing Kelsey of conniving with
the Indians in the theft of Company goods. His charges
were not taken very seriously, and Kelsey was confirmed
as Governor of York, but there was strong mutual distrust
between the two. The younger and intensely ambitious
Kelsey thought he had made history with his wilderness
trek into the interior but complained he had not been
sufficiently recognized by the HBC hierarchy; the old
Governor, who had held every honour within the Company's grant, felt on the other hand that he had yet to
make any history or earn much of a fortune.

Neither man would attain his goal. Knight was to die
in frigid isolation on one of Hudson Bay's bleakest out-
croppings; Kelsey would be recalled to England under
a cloud of unsubstantiated suspicion and vanish from the
Company's books with no official mention of his thirty-
eight-year loyal service, of his magnificent journey inland
or his important role in reinvigorating the HBC trade after
1714.*

More puzzling still was the uncharacteristically
desultory way in which the Committeemen dealt with
their former colleague's tragic disappearance. Although
the outcome of the Knight expedition ranked second only
to the Franklin tragedy in the number of men lost, no
one seemed particularly concerned about their fate.
Without ever resolving the reason for their disappearance,
on September 29, 1722 the Company wrote off their two
ships and crews in its books as "being castaway to the
northward in Hudson Bay … " Joseph Stephens and

---

*Kelsey's subsequent application for return to Hudson Bay was
refused. The only other reference to Henry Kelsey in the
HBC archives is a petition of his widow, Elizabeth, pleading
for funds "to buy her son, John Kelsey, clothes, she being
wholly incapable to do it herself." The Company awarded
her six guineas.

Samuel Hearne stumbled on the physical remains of the expedition forty-eight years later, on Marble Island, but that discovery did little to clear up the mystery of Knight's voyage.

ON JUNE 4, 1719, SIR BIBYE LAKE and his Committeemen rattled down the bumpy road to Gravesend in a convoy of carriages to bid farewell to James Knight and the two HBC ships, manned by their forty treasure-seekers. They tipped the men for drinks, bought fresh vegetables for the officers and wished the proud octogenarian "Godspeed."

On June 19, Henry Kelsey left York Factory to sail north in the hoy *Prosperous*. Accompanied by the Churchill-based *Success*, he set sail to explore the coastline north of Marble Island, which would be Knight's landfall later that summer. The two groups knew nothing of each other's itinerary, though Kelsey was probably prospecting for the same copper mines. His voyage also had a darker purpose: trading two Indian slaves for two Eskimos he hoped to train as interpreters. The Company later claimed before the 1749 British parliamentary committee that Kelsey had been under orders to search for the North West Passage, but according to Professor Glyndwr Williams this was his "least concern." Knight's movements are not known because no record survived his death, some time between the summer of 1719 and the summer of 1721.

The fact that it took the HBC nearly half a century to locate the expedition's remains and document its tragic demise defies explanation. Between 1719 and 1721, Kelsey and his emissaries sailed north three times, but except for the casual complaint of one HBC captain ("Mr. Handcock tells me the Goldfinders winter'd where we had been last Summer and had traded with those Indians and spoiled our trade"), there is no record of any effort to find the missing explorers. In the summer of 1721, Eskimos offered Kelsey objects clearly belonging to the Knight expedition, but instead of waiting out the winds to land at Marble Island, he returned by mid-August. Later evidence indicated that some of Knight's men were still alive at the time.

The following summer, Kelsey ordered John Scroggs to cover the same territory for trade leads – but issued no instructions to watch for survivors. Scroggs was an indifferent navigator and, after fumbling about at the entrance to Chesterfield Inlet, sailed south and set a boat ashore on Marble Island at a spot where the spar from a ship's foremast had been found floating on his outward voyage. His shore party retrieved from local Eskimos parts of a cabin lining, a medicine chest and ice-poles, all belongings of Knight's crews. Without trying further to find the ships or any survivors, Scroggs hurried back to Churchill and reported that all of Knight's men had been massacred by the "Eskemoes, which I am heartily sorry for their hard fortune."

In the packet of instructions from London to York Factory that arrived in the summer of 1721, Kelsey was told by the Committeemen not to winter north of Churchill ("at the hazard of your life") but there was no mention of Knight, despite the fact that by then he and his men had spent two whole years in the same locale. The following summer the sloop *Whalebone* sailed north to trade with the Eskimos, still lacking instructions to seek Knight. According to the authoritative compilation in Alan Cooke's and Clive Holland's *Exploration of Northern Canada*, between 1720 and 1764 twenty-three HBC vessels as well as six discovery ships from England operated in northwestern Hudson Bay – and at least eight of their crews went ashore at Marble Island. While collecting driftwood, seamen sent ashore from the *California*, on August 13, 1747, even found "a piece of oak about two feet in length with such trunnel holes as are made in ship's sides," and the vessel's log noted that the object in all probability had come from one of Knight's ships.

The HBC trading sloop *Churchill* logged landings on Marble Island twice in the 1750s *after* the *California*'s discovery, but no attempt was made to confirm the Knight find. As W. Gillies Ross and William Barr, two Canadian geographers who studied Knight's disappearance, have pointed out: "The total length of coastline on Marble Island is approximately thirty-two miles. Two groups of men walking in opposite directions around the shore could have circled the island easily in a day ... Assuming that the men were honest, sober, of normal vision, and unhindered by fog, it seems inconceivable that they could have missed the Knight relics, which were numerous, large and prominent." It was not until July 20, 1767 – forty-eight years after Knight vanished – that some HBC sailors off the *Success* spotted the expedition's remains, including "eight chaldrons (288 bushels) of good burning coal" and three large anchors. Two weeks later, Samuel Hearne, then mate of the *Churchill*, arrived on Marble Island and found the ruins of a stone house, an anvil and some muskets. These items were sent to London without a hint that they might have belonged to Knight. Two years later Hearne returned to Marble Island, located the wreckage of the *Albany* and *Discovery* five fathoms deep in a cove on Marble's stony southeast shore and, by interrogating local Eskimos, finally reconstructed the expedition's last days.

The natives confirmed to Hearne that Knight had been driven ashore by a storm and had built a house. By the second winter illness had reduced the survivors to only five men. The last two had expired in abject misery: "Many days after the rest, [they] frequently went to the tip of an adjacent rock, and earnestly looked to the South and East, as if in expectation of some vessels coming to their relief. After continuing there a considerable time together, and nothing appearing, they sat down close together and wept bitterly. At length, one of the two died, and the other's strength was so far exhausted that he fell down and died also, in attempting to dig a grave for his companion.''*

This may indeed have been the tragic finale of the Knight expedition, but the sequence of events leading up to such a miserable ending makes little sense. Marble Island is within easy sight of the mainland. Rankin Inlet is less than ten miles away.†Knight's men were reported by their Eskimo observers to be at work lengthening one of their longboats in their first season on Marble Island. Why would they sit out two summers in ever-declining numbers within sight of shore? They were about four days' sail from Churchill, the post that Knight himself had founded. Scrogg's report that they were murdered by the Eskimos hardly seems credible – the bodies were eventually found scrupulously buried; logically, a sudden massacre would have left the survivors too demoralized for large-scale interment duties. Besides, it is unlikely that the Eskimos were devious enough to invent a sympathetic chronicle of the expedition's decline if they had been the murderers. It seems equally baffling that Knight, whose compulsion to record the minutiae of all his activities fills many a journal now in the HBC archives, would not have left a record of his experiences or tried to send a written message out with the Eskimos who occasionally supplied the dying men with whale blubber and seal flesh. One explanation might be Knight's

---

*Glover makes a strong case that the sad duo saw the sails of Henry Kelsey's hoy *Prosperous* and were forced to watch her bear away and disappear over the horizon.

†The gap is so easily traversed that during the 1760s whalers would call at Marble Island and set fires to attract Eskimos in kayaks from the mainland to trade venison for European artifacts.

inherent fear of the Ice People, which he described in his journal at the time he was building the post at Churchill: "Them natives to the Norward are more savage and brutelike than these and will drink blood and eat raw flesh and fish and loves it as well as some does Strong Drink." That fright was physically expressed in the way Knight planned his Marble Island survival house – a brick bunker designed for defence and positioned so that it would be difficult to approach it undetected across a nearly featureless terrain.

Reconstructing the fate of the Knight expedition, it is impossible not to conclude that the HBC really did not want the old explorer to succeed. A note in a pamphlet published in 1743 by Captain Christopher Middleton, the veteran Hudson Bay skipper, maintained that "the Company were against him [Knight] going, but he was *opiniatre*, they durst not disoblige him, lest he should apply elsewhere." In his book about the HBC, Joseph Robson noted that when word of Knight's disappearance reached England, "some of the Company Committeemen said upon this occasion that they did not value the loss of the ship and the sloop as long as they were rid of those troublesome men."

Knight's disappearance endures as one of the Arctic's mysteries and an unexplained exception in the HBC's usually precise dealings with its senior Factors.

Marble Island remains a haunted place. It was used as a Company whaling post until 1772, but nine voyages in more than eight years yielded only five whales. Fourteen more seamen perished when two American whalers (the *Orray Taft* and the *Ansel Gibbs*) were wrecked off its desolate south shore in 1873. The aura of dread abides. Marble Island is seldom visited, but those few modern-day Inuit who go there crawl up its ghostly beaches on knees and elbows, obeying the legend that some terrible event will strike the person who walks ashore. No one knows whether they are assuaging the unquiet spirits of their ancestors or paying tribute to the futile endurance of Knight and his doomed crew.

THE NEXT IMPETUS TO ARCTIC EXPLORATION came from an unexpected quarter. Peter the Great, the six-and-a-half-foot tyrant who ruled Russia for thirty-six years, enjoyed the plebeian pastime of quaffing mugs of beer in the taverns of St Petersburg. There, from visiting shipwrights and sailors, he learned about others' efforts to plot a water route across the roof of the world. At the time, he was rebuilding the Russian navy, having launched fifty-two ships-of-the-line as well as hundreds of galleys and other craft so rapidly that he had had to recruit foreign officers to command them. One was a Dane named Vitus Jonassen Bering, a native of the Jutland port of Horsens, who had first gone to sea in the early 1700s aboard the supply ships of the Dutch East India Company. Invited to become a sub-lieutenant in Russia's fledgling fleet, he changed his name to Ivan Ivanovich, fought with distinction in the Baltic, Black and White seas and rose rapidly in rank to Captain (Second Class). Temporarily denied advancement, he resigned to study exploration on an estate at Vyborg, on the Gulf of Finland.

Invited back by Peter the Great in 1724, he became a Captain (First Class) and was ordered to head a secret expedition into terra incognita eastward beyond the Asian continent. His main assignment was to probe what is now the Alaskan coast to see if he could pinpoint the western outlet of the so-called Strait of Anian. Bering's four-year trudge from St Petersburg six thousand miles eastward to the harsh Kamchatka Peninsula was a logistical nightmare, eventually involving one hundred men, two dozen boats and a thousand horses. The expedition set sail in July 1728. Bering reached latitude 67° north and discovered St Lawrence Island, now a part of Alaska, and the Diomede Islands, but missed the mainland of America by a few miles. On his return to St Petersburg in 1730 he wrote a report of which a copy fell into the hands of a French geographer, Jean-Baptiste Du Halde. Bering believed that he had found a new ocean route from the Baltic to Japan and, blaming himself for having been overly cautious in turning back so soon, recommended to the Russian Admiralty that he be sent out again to explore the new-found coast to establish the separation of the continents.* It took three years to draw up orders, and when Bering got them they included detailed instructions to Christianize the natives of Siberia, build a chain of lighthouses on Russia's Pacific coast and establish a postal system as he went along in order to mail reports of his expedition back to St Petersburg. It was the most ambitious, most expensive and most foolhardy Arctic foray ever mounted. As time went on and as more and more bureaucrats and specialists added their pennyworth to the planning, the logistics became a nightmare. An odd assortment of expectations and abilities, this Bering party eventually numbered nearly three thousand men. It included two landscape painters, three bakers, seven priests, a dozen doctors, fourteen bodyguards, four thousand horses, an awkward convoy of fifteen-foot telescopes mounted on wheels, plus a library of several hundred volumes.

The motley caravan took half a wretched decade to cross the northern steppes and tundra, their horses gradually becoming supper instead of motive power. Thousands of Siberian exiles were conscripted to drag bargeloads of useless supplies against the angry currents of

---

*Captain Semen Dezhnev had sailed between the two continents in 1648 but the report of his journey was not found until 1736, eight years after the start of Bering's first voyage to the same area.

ice-cold tributary rivers. Bering eventually reached salt water and set sail from Petropavlosk in June 1741. By now Bering was a harried and exhausted man of sixty. He was captain of the *St Peter*, with Aleksei Chirikov commanding the companion vessel, the *St Paul*. The ships soon became separated, never to meet again. Chirikov reached the American shore by July. Anchoring near Sitka, he sent out two boats to find safe harbour. The boats were seized and their crews massacred by the natives. He then cruised aimlessly along the shores for about a month and turned for home. On July 16 Bering had sighted the North American coast near Kayak Island on the Gulf of Alaska. Only a few weeks later, with his crew weakened by scurvy and exhaustion, Bering's voyage of discovery ended ignominiously when the *St Peter* went aground on an isolated rocky promontory of Bering Island. It provided so little building material that shallow pits had to be dug into the sand as temporary shelters. By the end of November, the survivors found their will to endure at such low ebb that Arctic foxes began swarming into their dugouts, gnawing on the dead and attacking the dying. The sand pits had to be reinforced with frozen corpses and carcasses of clubbed foxes. Bering himself died on the morning of December 19, the sand from his shelter trickling into his nostrils, expiring as much from the sorrow of failure as from frost and hunger.

The only positive commercial legacy of this inglorious expedition was that its few bedraggled survivors (who had fashioned a boat from the wreckage, loaded it with furs and eventually reached Petropavlosk in the summer of 1742) received such good prices for their haul that many of them returned to initiate a lively commerce in blue fox and sea otter. This trade culminated in the establishment of the Russian-American Company, which would eventually give the HBC stiff competition on Canada's West Coast. English captains, sailing to Russia's European ports in the hemp trade, brought word to London about that country's accelerating tempo of northern exploration, and the information prompted the Committeemen to reconsider their own expansion plans on Hudson Bay.

THE CHIEF ELEMENT IN THE MIX of slowly fermenting forces that would eventually drive the Bay men inland was the remarkable advance westward of the nimble traders from Montreal. While the French and English had been grappling for control of Hudson Bay, the colonists who had settled the shores of the St Lawrence almost succeeded in encircling Hudson Bay by land. Daniel Greysolon, Sieur Dulhut, a dashing leader of the early *coureurs de bois*, had been licensed as early as the 1670s to push past Lake Superior in the search for lucrative furs and the Great Western Sea. He built a rough-hewn stockade on the northeast side of Lake Nipigon (to intercept the Assiniboine and Cree trappers on their way to Albany) and by 1688 had penetrated with his partners as far west as Rainy Lake, only two hundred miles east of where Winnipeg now stands. The Treaty of Utrecht formally prohibited France from contending ownership of the land around the bay, but the Quebec traders redoubled their overland efforts. By 1728, the Compagnie du Nord appointed Pierre Gaultier de Varennes, Sieur de La Vérendrye, commander of *les postes du nord*. Born in Trois-Rivières, son of the district's governor, he was schooled in France and had fought in Europe with the armies of France at Malplaquet against Marlborough (and was left for dead on that blood-soaked ground with eight sabre cuts in his body). Drawn by the magnet of discovering the alluring "sea of the west," he sailed back across the Atlantic. During the 1730s and early 1740s he and his four sons established seven trading forts, planting the first semi-permanent white settlements in Western Canada. Harassed by his angry financial backers (who wanted him to make money, not discoveries), distracted by colonial governors uncertain of their own authority and by his own irresolution in the face of daunting odds, La Vérendrye was never able to realize his potential as an explorer but did lay down the matrix of Montreal's future inland trade across the routes to Hudson Bay. "He was," wrote Lawrence Burpee in the *Canadian Geographical Journal*, "in a real sense the discoverer of Western Canada; first to descend the Winnipeg River, first to see Lake Winnipeg, first to cross the great plains to the Missouri."

The more important immediate effect of La Vérendrye's enterprise was to slash the HBC's fur harvest drastically. York Factory, for example, which then accounted for half the Company's take, slipped from shipping 52,000 made-beaver in 1731 to only 37,000 the following year, as La Vérendrye and his sons probed as far west as the Black Hills of South Dakota.

The HBC met its burgeoning competition from the Montreal pedlars by reducing prices on some of its most popular trade goods. This list shows the difference in prices by made-beaver equivalents:

	Pedlar price	HBC price
Guns	20	14
Ice chisel	4	1
Knife	2	4
Ball	10	1 lb.
Powder	¼ lb.	1 lb.
Cloth	1½ yds. per 10 M-B	1 yd. per 3 M-B
Blanket	10	7
Tobacco	¼ lb.	¾ lb.

The Indians took happy advantage of the escalating rivalry, playing off one set of European traders against the other and becoming participants in the contest themselves, with the Cree and Assiniboine benefiting most as middlemen. The French were willing to trade on the Indians' home ground, eliminating their need to pack, paddle and portage for weeks to Hudson Bay and back. Added to this was the Montreal traders' generosity with French brandy, which was becoming the fur trade's most desirable staple. The English equivalent was much inferior, though in tobacco the advantage was the other way. Company-dispensed Brazil brand was much preferred to the French product, which was said to taste like sawdust.

The French frequently became victims of the tribal feuds they helped generate, while the English concentrated on promoting commerce. On an individual level, the French traders played dangerous games by carrying off young Indian women against their will, forcing them to share their beds, while the English and Scots were usually careful to secure bedmates according to the formalities of Indian society – by purchase or the consent of fathers, husbands and, often, the women themselves. Even if the ravished Indian girls might be pardoned for missing the subtle difference, it was often sufficient to allow HBC traders to pass through Indian territory unmolested, while the *coureurs de bois* were getting into brawls and stumbling into ambushes. For example, in 1758 Fort Bourbon, near the northwest side of Lake Winnipeg, was plundered by the Indians, while Joseph Smith of the HBC, bound for the country of the Assiniboine, sauntered safely by.

In 1743 the Company decided to experiment with the opening of Henley House, its first post away from Hudson Bay, at the junction of the Albany and Kenogami rivers. The tiny settlement was put in place by Orkneyman Joseph Isbister, then Chief Factor at Albany, when he heard that the French had established their own trading post 120 miles upstream from his home fort. London approved his move but insisted that the little outpost's main function should be defensive rather than commercial.

The fiercely independent Isbister ran Albany (and Henley, where William Lamb was nominally in charge) like military garrisons, using a cat-o'-nine-tails to impose his edicts against strong drink. He rigidly policed Company regulations against the harbouring of Indian women at HBC posts, but since he allowed one exception (himself), his moral authority was hardly convincing. When William Lamb would not allow Indian males access to his post's provisions, Woudbee, the Captain of the Albany Home Guard Indians, was so enraged that in December 1754, accompanied by his sons Snuff-the-Blanket and Sheanapp, he plundered the post and massacred its occupants. The three were apprehended and jailed in separate cells at Albany. Before interrogating the prisoners, Isbister first went outdoors and fired two shots into the sky. Then he told each of the captives that the other two had confessed and been executed and that there was no further point denying the crime. The ensuing confessions were authentic – but so was the provocation. Lamb had appropriated against their will two Indian women for the winter, one of them Woudbee's daughter, the other one of his son's wives. When the Woudbee men arrived at the post, Lamb had haughtily dismissed their protests and refused to welcome them, insisting they camp outside the stockade. The massacre ensued. The three Indians were hanged on June 21, 1755.*

Henley House was not resettled until 1759, when within a few weeks a raiding party once again massacred its master, George Clark, and his assistant. This time the

---

*Isbister was reprimanded by London not so much for the executions as for his unwillingness to re-establish the Henley post. He was recalled the following year for his own safety and in 1760 emigrated to Quebec City, where he lived on the rue des Remparts. He died eleven years later of "decay and wore-out lungs."

apparent motive was carrying off the trade goods, though HBC men then believed the attack was actually staged by French traders led by Louis Ménard from Nipigon. Henley House was reopened in 1763, following the end of the Seven Years' War. It never became an important post, but the violence of its brief history helped delay the HBC's move inland.

CHAPTER 12

THE DOBBS INTERVENTION

"When the Sky falls, a great number of Larks may be catched…"

— *Captain John Merry*

WHAT FINALLY HELPED TURN THE TIDE upriver was a drawn-out campaign against the Hudson's Bay Company staged by a persistent Irishman named Arthur Dobbs. The avowed purpose of Dobbs's intervention was to force the Company into an active search for the North West Passage, but this worthy undertaking was mixed with selfish commercial impulses. Even though the eventual effect of the Dobbs initiative was to force the Company into the outward exploration that helped save its charter, loyal HBCers two centuries later still dismiss him with the vitriol due a brigand.

From two only tenuously connected facts – that the North West Passage had not been found and that the HBC owned most of the land around its eastern egress – Dobbs concluded that either the Company had kept the existence of the waterway secret for its own commercial reasons or that it had not been discovered because the Adventurers were not adventurous enough. He seized on British expansionist sentiments and built his anti-HBC stand into a national crusade of no mean impact. As noted by his biographer, Desmond Clarke, Dobbs "viewed the Hudson's Bay Company, like many others, as a fat, wealthy monopoly sated with profits, and sleeping in inglorious ease while the French increased their power and influence in Northern Canada ... Dobbs was in every sense a carrier and exponent of the imperial energies that intended to make the Pacific a British instead of a Spanish lake."

Most historians stress the romantic aspect of Dobbs – a visionary trying to resurrect the tradition of the Elizabethan buccaneers who blended religion, patriotism and profit into a pageant of exploration – or they picture him as a busybody, a schemer dedicated to transferring the HBC monopoly to his own control. Whatever his motive, Dobbs's campaign was based on what at the time appeared to be scientific observations. The basis for his conviction that the North West Passage did indeed exist was his study of the height and direction of the flood-tides on Hudson Bay's western shores. Geographers of the time thought that those tides, if they were indeed flowing directly from the Pacific, would understandably be at much higher levels than if they were merely the distant eddy from an Atlantic surge, their source a thousand miles to the east. When the British navigator Luke Foxe had been bumbling around Hudson Bay in the summer of 1631, he reported a flood-tide of eighteen feet at latitude 64°10' north. The leap in logic seemed simple enough: by following that tide to its source, any explorer would inevitably be drawn into the North West Passage. One other observation supported the belief that Hudson Bay was a strait instead of an inlet: black whales were often seen off its western shores but had never been sighted passing into the bay from the North Atlantic.

Enticing as Dobbs's various arguments may have sounded, they were derived from a selective reading of sometimes questionable sources. The high tide in Roes Welcome, for example, is caused by water rushing past

White Island, funnelled through Frozen and Fisher straits, neither of which had been discovered when Dobbs was formalizing his plans. The whales came not from the Pacific but from Baffin Bay through Hudson Strait during spring breakup. Dobbs drafted an elaborate seventy-page abstract outlining his theories, but he made his real impact through the access he gained to British politicians.

The son of the high sheriff of County Antrim in the north of Ireland, Dobbs multiplied his family wealth by marrying the heiress Anne Osburn and sat in the Irish House of Commons from 1721 to 1730. Tutored in part by a very young Jonathan Swift, then serving as a village parson, Dobbs won appointment to the post of Surveyor-General of Ireland, expanding his interest in science and meteorology. Doggedly ambitious, he became friendly with Lord Conway, a cousin of Sir Robert Walpole, the British prime minister. Seeking to widen his influence, Dobbs crossed in 1730 to London where he was introduced to many of the City's leading functionaries. Bursting with brilliant if sometimes oddball schemes, he wrote essays on free trade and on the Aurora borealis and penned a plan to attack Quebec that was successfully carried out twenty-five years later. He also began to advocate a resumption of the search for a North West Passage. Colonel Martin Bladen, a Lord Commissioner of the Board of Trade and Plantations, passed him on to Sir Charles Wager, First Lord of the Admiralty, who in turn persuaded Samuel Jones, the HBC's Deputy Governor, to grant him an audience. Jones expressed no interest and refused to let Dobbs examine the Company's charter. (Colonel Bladen later got a copy for him.) Dobbs then tried to persuade the South Sea Company to send whalers from Davis Strait into the bay with instructions to find the Passage, but there were no takers. Dobbs finally confronted Sir Bibye Lake and pointed out that the Charter specifically charged the Company with furthering the search. Lake, whose contempt for meddlers in the HBC's corporate realm was matched only by his passion for silent diplomacy, treated the voluble Irishman as a noisy pest.

Dobbs had meanwhile made contact with Captain Christopher Middleton, one of the HBC's most experienced supply ship veterans, who agreed to share his knowledge of Hudson Bay. The Irishman also enlisted the active support of a few City financiers, who recognized that his efforts might help them make a dent in Lake's cosy fur monopoly. To this mercantilist appeal Dobbs added a dollop of anti-Spanish sentiment as a sop to Britain's more nationalistic politicians and seasoned the brew with pious references to evangelizing "the savages"– not forgetting a nod towards finding new outlets for English woollens.

It is easy to sympathize with Dobbs's frustration. His efforts, if fully exploited, would have benefited no group more than the HBC's shareholders, yet the Company's governors refused to take him seriously. Lake did order Richard Norton at Churchill to have a whaling sloop seek an opening up the bay's west coast near Roes Welcome, but the voyage lasted only six weeks, did not reach within two hundred miles of the Welcome and came back with only three barrels of blubber and twenty pounds of walrus ivory. That this was really a commercial voyage and not a journey of discovery was betrayed by the fact that the sloop-master and crew were signed on for 10 percent of its trade profits. Lake promptly reported the fruitless trip to Dobbs and excused the Company from further exploration ventures.

Realizing that the Company had been trifling with him, Dobbs brought Captain Middleton into the fight and during the next dozen years maintained the most concentrated attack ever mounted on the HBC. It was his linking of the search for a North West Passage with his attack against the HBC monopoly that garnered the support of

City barons and Westminster backbenchers. When Dobbs petitioned the Royal Navy to mount a full-scale expedition in search of the Passage, the Admiralty's Sir Charles Wager demurred for financial reasons, though he agreed with Dobbs that "the Hudson's Bay Company do not desire to have any body interfere with them in the fur trade in those parts; they seem to be content with what they have, and make, I believe, considerable profit by it."

Middleton, who became a tragic victim of the Dobbs intervention, had served aboard privateers before joining the HBC as second mate of the *Hannah*, later becoming her captain. His observations of magnetic variations in the bay were published in the *Philosophical Transactions of the Royal Society*, which elected him a member. A thoroughly competent navigator of impeccable integrity, Middleton was caught up voluntarily in Dobbs's manoeuvrings because he believed in the existence of the Passage and felt ideally equipped to find it. His appeals to be appointed the commanding officer of a voyage of discovery into the bay reached the ear of George II, who casually approved the idea. Middleton was allocated a converted bomb-vessel, the *Furnace*, and an ex-collier, the *Discovery*, but had to rely on press gangs to recruit most of his crew. Their participation in the gallant venture was ensured only by posting armed guards at the gangways before the ships' departure. Middleton complained later that "no ship was ever pester'd with such a set of rogues, most of them having deserved hanging before they entered with me." Although this was the first Royal Navy expedition to leave England in search of the North West Passage, it aroused so little interest that the only newspaper report about its departure, in the *Daily Post* of June 3, 1741, managed to scramble the facts by reporting: FURNACE AND *DISCOVERY* BOUND TO RUSSIA TO FIND OUT A NORTH WEST PASSAGE TO INDIA.

Middleton realized that any worthwhile exploration

would require wintering on Hudson Bay, and that meant obtaining the Company's support when his ships put in at Prince of Wales's Fort, the stone fortress near the mouth of the Churchill River on which HBC masons had been labouring for a decade. Pressured by the Royal Navy, the HBC sent a niggardly note to its local Factor advising that Middleton should be sheltered, but only if "by inevitable necessity [he was] brought into real distress and danger of his life or loss of his ship." But when Wager, at the Admiralty, heard about the HBC's attitude, he attacked it for conduct "very unbecoming for a Company which subsists by his Majesty's favour, having only an old charter which no doubt they made several breaches in." Lake relented by amending the instructions to grant Middleton "the best assistance" in the Company's power.

The two ships arrived within hailing distance of Prince of Wales's Fort on August 8, 1741, and Robert Pilgrim, the resident Factor, promptly fired a volley across the ships' bows. The baffled vessel commanders could only respond by raising white surrender flags. This incident – Company cannon firing at Royal Navy ships with impunity – appropriately summed up the intensity of the HBC's proprietary impulse. That impulse would not be diluted during the more than three centuries of the Company's occupation of Hudson Bay.

MIDDLETON NEGOTIATED PERMISSION to house his crew in the remains of the old factory founded by James Knight at Churchill, six miles upstream from Prince of Wales's Fort. Two weeks later, Pilgrim was replaced by James Isham, a talented naturalist who shared Middleton's appetite for scientific investigation. The two reached a sensible compromise: the Royal Navy crew would not trade in furs, and the HBC residents would help provision

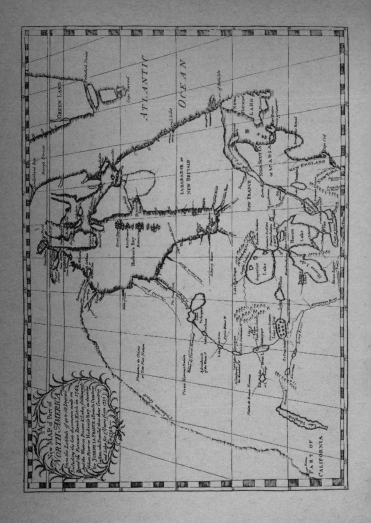

ATLANTIC OCEAN

GREEN LAND

Cape Farewel

Frobishers Streights

Cumberland Bay

Baffins Streights

LABRADER or NEW BRITAIN

NEW FRANCE

NEWFOUND LAND

C. Britain

NOVA SCOTIA or ACADIA

NEW ENGLAND

Hudsons Bay

Superior Lake

Huron Lake

PART OF CALIFORNIA

A New MAP of Part of NORTH AMERICA
From the Latitude of 40 to 68 Degrees
Including the late Discoveries made on
Board the Furnace Bomb Ketch in 1746 and 1747,
And the Western Rivers & Lakes falling into Nelson
River in Hudsons Bay as described
By JOSEPH LA FRANCE a French Canadese
Indian, who Travelled thro those Countries
and Lakes for 3 Years from 1739 to 1742

them through the winter. It was an arrangement that would eventually create problems for both men.

Middleton moved into the relative comfort of the fort to join Isham in taking astral observations. The two groups shared the chilly misery of a Hudson Bay winter in a semblance of camaraderie, fuelled magnificently by the Royal Navy's generous liquor rations. Bountiful quantities of grog were issued to mark every "holiday," many of them self-proclaimed. The Christmas revelries staged by Middleton lasted a full fourteen days, with the men being given "strong beer and brandy every day all the time." The little post had temporarily become a pub. Isham's tailor froze to death in a drunken stupor, and three of his troop had to be arrested for their own protection when in the afterglow of a night's brandy-swilling they grandly declared they were going "to sleep by the river." The ships' surgeons were kept busy amputating frozen toes and fingers, and vainly trying to hold back the scurvy that eventually claimed the lives of eleven sailors.

The two commanders genuinely liked each other, but Isham's patient hospitality was stretched to the limit when Middleton recruited five of his best men into the Navy. They parted gladly on the last day of June 1742, and despite a crew so incapacitated by illness that only five men were fit enough to climb aloft and reef sails, Middleton struck out for the Arctic. He probed and named Wager Inlet and sailed to the sandy terminus of Roes Welcome, being so disappointed it wasn't the Passage that he named it Repulse Bay.

On the way back, the two ships carried out a perfunctory probe of the bay's menacing and shallow western shore; they stayed three leagues out to sea, thus missing the entrance to Chesterfield Inlet. With this one exception, Middleton's charts were later proved to be remarkably accurate. He had sailed farther north in the bay than any white man before him and had brought his ships home safely, even though on the return voyage only two men were well enough to handle the wheel. Yet Middleton was immediately challenged by Dobbs for not pursuing his exploration and accused of having been bribed by the HBC.

Dobbs had changed tack. Instead of concentrating on opening up the Passage, he was now determined to break the HBC's trade Charter so that inland settlements could be put in place before the next phase of exploration began. At the same time, members of Middleton's crew, including his former mate John Rankin, began sabotaging their captain, claiming that he had indeed been paid by the HBC to falsify his report. Middleton's 150-page reply to these and other accusations, filed with the Admiralty, clearly vindicated him, but he was never again given an important command. Only seven years after his historic voyage, Middleton (now forgotten by Dobbs) was retired on a paltry pension of four shillings a day. He died in 1770, according to a report in the 1784 edition of the *Monthly Review*, "in the utmost penury and distress, having long before been drove to the necessity of parting with Sir Godfrey Copley's Gold Medal, which had been presented to him by the Royal Society in 1742, for his account of Hudson Bay. His children, four daughters, brought up in ease and elegance by the product of his labours in the early part of his life, all died before him, some of them, at least, in a more wretched situation than himself..."

Dobbs's obsession suffered a setback with Walpole's fall from power in 1742, but he was no longer isolated, having consolidated his contacts in the City by becoming an active partner in a scheme to purchase a large tract of North Carolina wilderness. He set about publishing what became his best-known book, which tried to make up for its dubious literary distinction by the length of its title: *An Account of the countries adjoining to Hudson's Bay, containing a description of their lakes and rivers, the nature of the soil and climates, their methods of commerce &c shewing the benefit to be made by settling colonies and opening a trade in these parts; whereby the French will be deprived in a great measure of their traffic in furs, and the communication between Canada and the Mississippi be cut off: with an abstract of Captain Middleton's Journal and observations upon his behaviour during his voyage and since his return, the whole intended to shew the great probability of a North-west Passage, so long desired; and which (if discovered) would be of the highest advantage to these kingdoms.*

The volume was a somewhat disjointed attack on "the darling monopoly" and "avarice" of the HBC, "who, to deter others from trading or making settlements, conceal all the advantage to be made in that country … " Even if Dobbs used exaggeration as his main literary device, the core of his sermon was perfectly accurate – that if the Company did not drastically alter its tactics, the French would occupy the new continent's central plains. The message struck a sympathetic chord in liberal-minded Englishmen who loathed both monopolies and the French. The first book published about the HBC, it revealed the extravagant terms of the original Charter but grossly overestimated the Company's annual profit at 2,000 per cent. Its most valuable historical contribution was the description of the extraordinary exploits of a "French Canadese Indian" named Joseph La France.

The son of a French trader and an Ojibway mother, La France had been a rambunctious renegade existing on the fur trade's illicit fringes. When the authorities in Montreal put a price on his head, La France decided to walk to Hudson Bay and join the English. The journey to York Factory via the Nelson River took him three years, but he emerged from the scrub forests with a crude map and some intriguing observations on the continent's potential wealth. Even if it placed Lake Winnipeg perilously close to California, his was the first map of a water route from Lake Superior to Hudson Bay. La France advised the HBC to move inland and lower its standard of trade, but no one except Dobbs took him seriously.

In the spring of 1745, a £20,000 prize for discovery of the North West Passage was offered by Parliament. News of the reward revived Dobbs's spirits. He organized the North West Committee, which handily raised £7,200 to equip a new expedition into Hudson Bay from City merchants anxious to form their own North American trading company. Its ships, the *Dobbs* and the *California*, were commanded by William Moor and Francis Smith, who shared a common background as mates on HBC supply ships but little else. The two men quarrelled continually, agreeing only to winter at York Factory before launching their explorations. James Isham, who had extended a hand of friendship under similar circumstances to Captain Middleton, had been moved south to York and, having been reprimanded for being too co-operative the first time, resolved not to sweeten his welcome. This created awkwardness because the ships' captains held commissions from the Admiralty empowering them to act as privateers and, as such, they had the right to call for aid from British subjects overseas. Isham was not impressed. He greeted the arrivals at York Factory not only with cannon shot but by removing the buoys leading to the anchorage at Five Fathom Hole so that one of the ships ran aground in the mud.

The crews settled in for the winter at Ten Shilling Creek in log-tents provided by Isham, but the captains continued feuding. They could not even decide how to divide the Indians' partridge hunt between them and asked Isham to adjudicate. Smith and Moor paced their ramshackle abodes dreaming up new quarrels and during one two-month period exchanged not a single word. Deranged by cabin fever, Smith finally abandoned the shelter, abandoned Moor, abandoned his wife, Kitty, and sought asylum at the Factory. When the vessels left the following spring, Isham did not, as was customary at the time, consign the seafarers to the protection of the Almighty.

After a half-hearted exploration of Chesterfield Inlet, the ships' longboats ventured up Wager Inlet, which led them to a dead-end stream at Brown Lake. The *California*'s subsequent return across the Atlantic was so stormy that only Smith was well enough to take the helm and he had to commandeer a Royal Navy crew in the Orkneys to pilot his ship back to the crowded Thames.

Once again, Dobbs applied his self-serving logic to the expedition's inconclusive outcome: the existence of the Passage had not been *disproved* – therefore it must exist. He petitioned the King in Council to grant his North West Committee trading arrangements similar to those of the HBC, in effect demanding precisely the kind of monopoly he had been condemning. At the time, British merchants, especially in the burgeoning ports of Liverpool and Bristol, were engaged in a co-ordinated attack on the perpetuation of London-based trading monopolies, including the overextended Royal African Company, which collapsed in 1750. Eventually, seventeen petitions questioning the HBC's charter reached Parliament from Britain's leading industrial ports, and a special committee was struck to hear the complaints. Headed by Lord Strange, the group listened to a long litany of criticism inspired by Dobbs and his entourage, including that of Joseph Robson, the unhappy Prince of Wales's Fort stonemason, and John Hayter, a former house carpenter at Albany, who insisted that wheat could be cultivated inland if only the Company had the nerve to move there.

The HBC's Governor, Thomas Knapp, did not deign to appear but sent the special committee a stack of documents, including a suddenly resurrected description of Henry Kelsey's epic journey and the log of every ship that had ever stuck its bow north of Churchill. James Isham, the dependable old trouper, crossed the Atlantic to testify on the Company's behalf, providing a calm rationale for its status-quo policies. Finally, the HBC's solicitor went so far as to pledge a careful move towards cautious expansion.

After hearing twenty-two witnesses, Lord Strange ruled that there was no case for annulling the HBC Charter or interfering with the Company's trade position – in other words, no case for doing anything. The parliamentarians realized that even if Dobbs's mythical passage did exist, it would not be commercially navigable, and that in view of the climate and geography of Hudson Bay, the Company's understandable accent on survival could not be condemned. The verdict seems to have hinged on the dispassionate conviction that since the northern fur trade had to be supported by a chain of permanent forts, only a monopoly or the government itself could finance this far-away commerce. The Royal African Company, whose slavery monopoly was successfully challenged at about the same time, had no permanent posts but did have militantly dissatisfied shareholders. By contrast, the HBC's shareholders throughout the Dobbs intervention met only to praise their Committeemen, boasting that "Mr. Dobbs cannot produce any single Adventurer that makes any complaint." In an aphoristic condemnation of Dobbs's fantasies, Deputy Governor John Merry sarcastically scribbled in the margins of the Irishman's pamphlet advocating the harvesting of huge, imaginary quantities of timber on Hudson Bay: "When the Sky falls, a great number of Larks may be catched…"

The main effect of the parliamentary inquiry was to expose the Company to unprecedented publicity. Its shareholder lists, business methods, standards of trade, profit margins (30 percent on an annual outlay of £27,000) and anti-exploration policies had become a matter of public debate. This was aggravated by the publication of Robson's critique in 1752, which put forth his famous accusation that the Company was asleep at the edge of a frozen sea.* As for the disgruntled Dobbs, he retired to his "rural amusements" in Carrickfergus to study the swarming habits of bees and leave the search for the Passage to "some more happy Adventurer." The pugnacious Irishman was named Governor of North Carolina in 1754 and died there eleven years later, still sighing over the elusive Passage to the South Sea.

Exploration continued in desultory fashion until a century later, when the search for survivors of Franklin's expedition triggered the activity that finally sketched in the awesome dimensions of the continent's northern margin. One explorer, Charles Duncan, felt the disappointment of not finding the Passage so keenly that on the way home to England he was stricken by "brain fever" and made so many attempts to jump overboard that he had to be lashed to his bunk. John Bean, a Company sloop captain accompanied by Moses Norton, spent a harsh season searching for the Passage and bitterly concluded: "This fly-away River resembles old Brazil – not to be seen but by some chimerical persons." Norton, who as Governor at Churchill was to send Samuel Hearne on his overland journey, also sailed 130 miles up Chesterfield Inlet into the dead-end flats of Baker Lake, eliminating that possibility as a western outlet of the Hudson Bay. He realized early on that the only way to fix the position of North America's Arctic coast would be by a land route.

Exhausted by Dobbs's assaults, the Company assured its factors: "We have nothing more at heart than the

---

*Historian Glyndwr Williams has documented that Dobbs actually wrote a good part of the Robson critique.

preservation of our factories, the security of our people and encrease of our trade." At the same time, the parliamentary hearings had convinced the Committeemen that if their territory were not explored, the Company's vaunted charter would prove to be no more than a scrap of old parchment. It could no longer protect them: royally chartered companies had clearly become historical anomalies, and Parliament was already demanding that the Company define precisely the extent of its land claims.

It would be another two decades before the HBC seriously began moving inland with the establishment of a permanent post at Cumberland House, but one immediate effect of the public outcry was that the London Committee authorized a journey into the interior by a volunteer from York Factory to "draw down many of the natives to trade." The long trek, undertaken by a former smuggler and HBC net-mender named Anthony Henday, was to be the first officially sanctioned inland journey since the peace mission of William Stuart and Thanadelthur into the land of the Chipewyan and Henry Kelsey's meandering westward probe and back half a century before.

Although the immediate trigger for Henday's historic run may have been the Dobbs affair, it was also a response – twenty-three years after the fact – to the founding by Pierre Gaultier de Varennes, Sieur de La Vérendrye and his sons of trading posts a thousand miles to the southwest at Fort La Reine on the Assiniboine and at Fort Pasquia near The Pas.* Because these "woodrunners" occupied many of the traditional canoe routes along which furs were brought out to Hudson Bay, the Company was anxious to make contacts beyond the range of French

---

*These Canadians were pedlars from Montreal, who carried an assortment of trade goods and made housecalls at Indians' tents.

penetration, where, as the younger Chevalier de La Vérendrye put it, "the Cree of the Mountains, Prairies and Rivers rendezvous every spring to deliberate as to what they shall do – go and trade with the French or with the English."

Like Kelsey before him (and Hearne after him), Henday travelled as supercargo with a group of Indians heading to their home country. After four months kneeling in a canoe and toiling across the rolling parkland, they reached a patch of bald prairie near the present site of Edmonton. Instead of empty wilderness, he encountered French traders busy loading their canoes. "I don't very well like it," he recorded apprehensively in his journal. "Having nothing to satisfy them on what account I am going up the country and very possably they may expect me to be a spy … " His competitors left him alone, mainly because he was accompanied by a large troop led by a Cree named Attickasish who, Henday noted, "has the charge of me." His constant companion was a Cree woman who acted as his food gatherer and cook and was officially listed as his interpreter, though Henday referred to her in the version of his journal not sent to London as "my bed-fellow."

On October 1, 1754, seven stern hunters dressed in bison skins and armed with bone-tipped spears rode into Henday's camp, located southeast of the present-day site of Red Deer, Alberta. They were Bloods from the powerful Blackfoot Confederacy that reigned supreme in the Western Prairie and controlled the approaches to the mysterious foothill country. After much preliminary prying, they escorted Henday to their main camp, a wilderness city of more than two hundred painted tepees pitched in two long rows. The encampment was abuzz with excitement as the white man was led to the great meeting hall, a buffalo-hide lodge that could seat fifty elders. Sweetgrass smoke was wafted about and calumets were lit and served in a hush as the rulers of the plains quizzically examined the stranger who had come from the shore of the inland sea. Boiled buffalo meat was served in baskets of woven grass, and the gift of a dozen buffalo tongues, the tastiest of local delicacies, was formally presented to Henday. But when the visitor began to bargain with the Blackfoot chief to send some of his men back with him to York Factory, Henday was rebuffed first by silence and later with the sensible explanation that the Blackfoot would not leave their horses or abandon the buffalo hunt, that they did not know how to use canoes and that they had heard of many Indians starving on their journeys to Hudson Bay. A chastened Henday, who was a better bush traveller than negotiator, confided to his journal, "Such remarks I thought exceeding true." Though the conversations continued over the next six months, the Blackfoot chief's only concession was to present Henday with two comely young women.

The Henday expedition, which at times was reduced to only eleven Cree, including five women and four children, continued moving west, reaching the site of the present town of Innisfail, Alberta, less than forty miles from the future location of the famous trading post, Rocky Mountain House. The geographical co-ordinates of Henday's westernmost location – 51°50′N, 114°W – placed him within clear view of the Rocky Mountains, but his journal is curiously silent on his reaction to such a dramatic sighting. Like every other explorer of his day, Henday hoped to discover a western ocean, not a massive rock barrier, and when facing the immensity of the Rocky Mountains that stretched like a continent unto themselves, he may have chosen to deny their existence. "The water very salt, smells like Brine," he scribbled in his journal while tramping through the rolling western parkland.

On the return journey, his accompanying flotilla some-

times swelling to sixty canoes, Henday realized that the Cree were too established in their role as fur-trade middlemen to permit interior Indians to undertake the long Hudson Bay journey themselves. The documentation of that elementary proposition, which would eventually prompt the HBC to appreciate some of the complexities of the inter-tribe fur trade, was the most valuable contribution of Henday's long mission. That and his report about the sophistication of the French traders at Fort Pasquia: "The French talk several languages to perfection; they have the advantage of us in every shape, and if they had Brazile tobacco would entirely cut our trade off." Significantly, Henday's own Cree companions twice traded their furs to the French for brandy.

When the salute guns boomed York Factory's welcome on June 23, 1755, Henday had been away for a year and had completed an astonishing journey. James Isham questioned the traveller closely and accepted the burden of Henday's report,* suggesting to London that the HBC dispatch several men inland with roving commissions to bring the Indians out to trade and "root the French out." The Committeemen balked at such heresy, rewarded Henday with a £20 bonus – and promptly went back to sleep.

Henday made several more inland probes but seven years later he left the Company, heartbroken at not being promoted above the rank of net-mender and angry at being abused by supply ship crews for not wanting to buy their bayside luxuries. In the autumn of 1755, even as Henday was sailing out of Hudson Bay, history was on the

---

*Henday's original journal was never found, but four copies survive in the HBC Archives in Winnipeg, though they contain serious inaccuracies and contradictions. Historian Glyndwr Williams has argued convincingly that Henday tried to paint his achievements in "a dishonestly optimistic light."

march, all but obliterating the memory of his great exploit. The Royal Navy was already at sea with the Duke of Newcastle's orders to intercept supplies from France for its American colonies, so that without any formal declaration, the Seven Years' War had begun, threatening the existence of the French fur trade.

The surrender of Quebec in 1759 convinced the London Committeemen that their golden age of monopoly had finally dawned, that the "woodrunners" would somehow vanish and leave all the furs to them. Yet by 1764, the western trading routes were once again crowded with Montreal canoes. The new interlopers were of a much more impressive cut than their French predecessors, who had been limited in their thrust westward by a meddlesome Versailles bureaucracy and the stingy budgets of hard-pressed colonial administrators. Not only had these restraints been lifted, but Montreal was bursting with freshly landed entrepreneurs with access to capital and a thirst for new conquests – feisty Scots quartermasters and adventurous Irish hawkers, as well as shrewd Yankee veterans of the Mississippi fur trade. London had petulantly dropped any attempt to enforce a monopoly in the fur trade, so that suddenly the western territories were open to all comers. The geography of the fur trade was about to undergo a sea change.

CHAPTER 13

Samuel Hearne's Odyssey

This was no North West Passage; it was a rocky suburb of Hell.

SOUTH OF RUPERT'S LAND, THE UNION JACK now snapped and fluttered from hundreds of whitewashed flagstaffs in what was called "Canada." The three remaining barriers to freedom of trade in the Americas were the half-serious claims by Spain (based on the Papal Bull of 1493), by Russia (based on Bering's discoveries along the West Coast) and the HBC monopoly in the north. By 1774, Spanish navigators had charted the Pacific rim up to the Queen Charlotte Islands, while Russian fur traders were pushing southward from Alaska. It was becoming evident that the North West Passage, even if it did exist, was located north of the continent and was very much longer and less accessible than had been hitherto suspected. The elusive Passage now took on a new imperialist dimension: its discoverers and claimants would be able to command the Canadian subcontinent and gain considerable advantage in the contest for sovereignty on North America's Pacific Coast.

Exploration accelerated as the Montreal traders followed the setting sun. Alexander Mackenzie, hardiest of the North West Company's travellers, would soon stand on the shores of the Bella Coola River and, using a pomade of vermilion face-paint and bear grease, leave his proud mark: " ... from Canada, by land, the 22nd of July, 1793."

In London, the HBC perspective was shifting under the influence of Samuel Wegg, who became Deputy Governor in 1774 and Governor six years later, temporarily breaking the Lake family domination. Unlike his predecessors, Wegg welcomed geographers, naturalists and explorers into the Company archives. He served as Treasurer of the Royal Society for thirty-four years and became an indefatigable member of the select Thursday Club, which met at the Mitre Tavern on Fleet Street to discuss the disposition of the Empire over claret and a haunch of venison.* "The achievement of Samuel Wegg was that he helped the Company of his day to distinguish between information which because of its commercial importance was properly confidential and that which was not," wrote Glyndwr Williams. "The charter was no longer attacked – it was simply ignored by the traders who inherited the old French routes west from Montreal and pushed on towards the Pacific." The Montreal-based pedlars kept arguing that the part of Rupert's Land in which they travelled and traded belonged to the French King's domains and was thus not subject to the HBC charter which specifically excluded the lands of "any other Christian Prince."

Two unconnected events prompted the Hudson's Bay Company to take a more active stance in exploring its own hinterland. Alexander Cluny, who described himself as "an old experienced trader" (though he had spent only one short season on the bay), published a detailed pamphlet about North America. Nothing if not ingenious,

---

*Various guest lists included Captain William Bligh (of *Bounty* fame), Benjamin Franklin and Captain James Cook.

Cluny advocated turning Hudson Bay into a metropolis with no fewer than a dozen towns and the setting up of a whale fishery that would employ eight hundred ships and sixteen thousand men. Cluny riveted the attention of the HBC Committeemen when he described large lumps of virgin copper he had allegedly picked up north of the bay. Cluny's mythical find turned suspiciously real when at about the same time Moses Norton, the Governor at Prince of Wales's Fort, then visiting London, plunked down a chunk of rich copper ore on the polished mahogany Committee-room table. Norton reported that the metal had recently been brought out of the north country by two Chipewyan – Matonabbee and Idotliaze – dispatched by him to search the northern rivers five years earlier. The natives reported that the rivers between the copper mines were thick with beaver.

Hardly able to contain their impatience, the London governors ordered Norton to mount an expedition "far to the north, to promote an extension of our trade, as well as for the discovery of a North West Passage [and] Copper Mines .... taking observation for determining the longitude and latitude, and also distances, and the course of rivers and their depths."

In the discussion that followed, the man picked to lead the HBC venture was Samuel Hearne, an enthusiastic young sailor then serving under Norton as mate of the trading brigantine, *Charlotte*.

HEARNE HAD GROWN UP in England's capital, where his father was secretary of the London Bridge Water Works Company. When his mother, Diana, was widowed, the family moved to Beaminster in Dorset. Young Samuel's schooling was sporadic, and he proved equally incapable of mastering the fundamentals of spelling, grammar or mathematics. According to normal practice for ambitious boys of his class, Hearne volunteered for the Royal Navy at the age of twelve. He was taken on as a boy servant to Captain Samuel Hood, then in command of *HMS Bideford*, a frigate on convoy duty in the Bay of Biscay and the Mediterranean. Hearne spent half a dozen years at sea, growing inured to the foul diet, harsh discipline and tensions of the lower deck. He took part in several fire fights with French transports off Cape Finisterre, the capture of two privateers and the bombardment of Le Havre. When the Seven Years' War ended in 1763, Hearne, having no hope of preferment, left the Navy and three years later joined the HBC as mate on the little sloop *Churchill*, then engaged in the northern whaling trade.

In the late summer of 1768, Prince of Wales's Fort received its first distinguished visitor, William Wales, the British astronomer-mathematician sent to Hudson Bay by the Royal Society to observe the transit of Venus across the face of the sun.* His stay presented Hearne with the opportunity to improve his knowledge of surveying and chartmaking, which he had already gleaned while serving with the Royal Navy. The following spring, Hearne, twenty-four and in full vigour, was distressed at being transferred to the Company's hundred-ton whaling brig *Charlotte*, not as her captain but still as mate. He found himself serving under Joseph Stephens, whom he described as "a man of the least merit I ever knew," and promptly appealed to London for a more senior assignment "where

---

*Wales sailed around the world as chief astronomer on Captain James Cook's second expedition and later became mathematical master at Christ's Hospital, where he numbered among his students Charles Lamb, Leigh Hunt and Samuel Taylor Coleridge. Because of the schedules of supply ships, Wales had to spend a full year (September 1768 to September 1769) at Churchill to record a celestial event that lasted only seven hours – most of it invisible because of cloud cover.

there is greater probability of my making some returns, and giving satisfaction to my Employers."

The real reason Hearne's superior, Moses Norton, picked him to lead the trek inland was only partly based on the youthful seaman's proven abilities. The two men despised one another, and the best solution was geographical separation. In his posthumously published journal, Hearne described the Prince of Wales's Governor as "one of the most debauched wretches under the sun, who wished to engross every woman in the country to himself. He kept for his own use five or six of the finest Indian girls, took every means in his power to prevent any European from having intercourse with the women of the country, even owned a box of poison to be administered to anyone who refused him his wife or daughter. He showed more respect to one of his favourite dogs than he ever did to his first officer." Hearne accused Norton of, among other villainies, poisoning two of his women "because he thought them partial to other men more suitable to their ages." His portrait of Norton as living "in open defiance of every law, human and divine" is a little too one-dimensional to be entirely believable, but it is the only source available.

The son of a former overseas governor of the HBC,* young Norton had been educated in England. Back on the bay in the Governor's chair, he provided himself with elegant private apartments, furnished with leather-bound books, paintings, an organ and a parrot. The Company

---

* Moses Norton is described by Hearne as having been of mixed blood, but historian Sylvia Van Kirk has questioned this. She points out that no one else mentions it, that "it would be absolutely incomprehensible in terms of HBC policy that a native-born half-Cree would be given charge of one of their major posts in the mid-eighteenth century" and that later employees who wanted to find work for their mixed blood offspring never mentioned the Norton precedent.

left him in charge of Prince of Wales's Fort for more than a decade, and in only one instance was his behaviour questioned: his London principals warned Norton to conduct his trade "in the best manner, so as not to give the Indians any disgust."

Whatever the truth about Norton's disposition, Hearne was delighted to leave the relative comfort of the fort for the unpredictable wilds.

SAMUEL HEARNE'S THREE JOURNEYS INLAND took him into the brutally beautiful Barren Ground, which sprawls across the top of North America like some discarded purgatory. At its southern edges, in sheltered hollows, gale-blasted evergreens peter out into scatterings of dwarf spruce that take three centuries to grow to the height of a man, like natural bonsai shaped by some horticultural deity.* Northward, the underbrush gives way to a topographical void under featureless skies. A relic of the Pleistocene Epoch, the mainland section of the Barrens rolls on for half a million square miles in a rough upside-down triangle formed by Hudson Bay, the sawtoothed perimeter of the Arctic Ocean and the Mackenzie River system. "Viewed by a summer traveller on the ground," wrote Farley Mowat, "the tundra gives the feeling of limitless space, intensified until one wonders if there can be an end to this terrestrial ocean whose waves are the rolling ridges. Perhaps nowhere else in the world, except far out at sea, does a man feel so exposed. On the northern prairie it is as if the ceiling of the world no longer exists and no walls remain to close one in."

---

*In 1907 naturalist Ernest Thompson Seton visited the Barren Ground and recorded finding a dwarf spruce less than eight feet high, which by its growth rings he estimated was at least three hundred years old.

Two hundred years after Hearne's audacious probes, this land mass had yet to be crossed on foot by more than half a dozen white men. It is an Arctic desert, its annual precipitation averaging eleven inches – less than falls on the outer edges of the Sahara. Because only the top few inches of the ground in the Barrens ever thaws, even this light sprinkling does not drain away but lies in huge muskeg patches and an endless chain of shallow lakes, which when frozen over resemble hammered pewter.

In late spring and early fall, the lake surfaces flicker with the wings of migrating ducks and geese. Even in winter there are sporadic touches of life, with small herds of muskox exploiting their uncanny ability to forage beneath the snow. For brief weeks, summer suffuses the mossy ground mattress with a carpet of miniature bloom and brings the return of the Barrens' most important seasonal inhabitants, the caribou herds. No estimate of the caribou which roamed the north in Hearne's time is possible, but contemporary accounts indicate they were beyond counting. They migrated with the wildfowl, thronging to the Arctic prairie in spring to give birth, marching back to the forest for winter, their numbers darkening the horizon. Once in perfect balance with their two main predators (wolves and human hunters), the caribou in modern times have been indiscriminately slaughtered.* "The natives gave fresh caribou meat to whalers and fur

---

* A bizarre example of this careless butchery occurred in northern Manitoba during the Second World War, when the U.S. Army Air Force was occupying Fort Churchill. There were so many caribou migrating through the area in the 1940s that some years it took several days for them to file by. Many were used by machine-gunners for target practice and their frozen bodies propped up in parallel lines to mark the boundaries of the landing strips in the snow. Pilots took off and landed between this gruesome guard of honour instead of the usual spruce tree markers.

traders, exchanging flesh for firearms," Dr Albert Hochbaum, the well-known Manitoba naturalist-painter, has observed. "The deer supplied energy to run the dog teams, which steadily required more bloody red fuel as their size and numbers were increased to meet the HBC demand for fur. Ammunition became a major trade item as millions of rounds were available to fire the ever-more-efficient breech-loading rifles. Then came the gasoline engine, which consumed time and space – the two most precious commodities to the caribou. No part of the north country remains safe or secret from anyone from anywhere. Now, suddenly, there is an overwhelming incursion of bureaucracies – federal, provincial, territorial, corporate, Canadian and foreign – each in its own way coveting some part of the land that belonged to the caribou."

Historically, the only inhabitants of the southern Barrens were the Chipewyan, named for the Cree term meaning "pointed skins" – a reference to the poncho-style caribou-hide shirts worn by Chipewyan of both sexes, cut with a point or tail at the back and front.

Because they compete for caribou, the Chipewyan have been almost constantly at war with the Eskimos. They blamed their enemies' conjuring for any illness or death among the elders and tried to drive the ice people ever northward, ambushing any hunting parties that followed caribou into the southern Barrens. In 1756 at Knapp Bay north of the Churchill River, the Chipewyan massacred more than forty Eskimos for no other reason than the fact that two of their elders had died of mysterious illnesses the previous season.

The antagonism worked both ways. The last authenticated massacre of Indians by Eskimos took place on the Peel River at Fort McPherson in 1850. A group of Indians were fishing when the northern caribou hunters came in to trade. That night, with no warning and no apparent reason save proximity, the Eskimos attacked and killed all the Indians except one little girl who had hidden in the undergrowth.

This traditional enmity has survived into the twentieth century even though no one seems certain exactly how it started. One explanation is that of Dr Robert McGhee, an archaeologist with the National Museum of Man, who has postulated that "Their mutual hostility can be best understood within the context of Indian hostility against other Indian groups, Inuit against other Inuit – the hostility between most neighbouring groups living in tribal societies. The main cause of trouble seems to have been covetousness of one's neighbour's wife, or of his other possessions. In addition, they shared a shamanistic theory of disease caused by sorcery. Neighbouring groups were generally thought of as adept sorcerers, and often blamed for disease or other misfortunes, which exacerbated hostilities. In specific cases, there was probably also economic competition for hunting grounds, good fishing spots and resources such as native copper."

The important point is that Hearne found these pristine people warring. The edge of the Barrens was no Eden, but very much the same thing was going on between bands and tribes in the rich southland. These struggles were mostly stand-offs; a coup of some kind was much more important than seizing land or bringing home a particularly desirable woman. In their study of human aggression, *The Imperial Man*, Lionel Tiger and Robin Fox have documented that at the primitive level there never was much "war," but many raids and skirmishes: "The actual violence took much less time than the elaborate male rituals of violence, of preparation and celebration. In many cases there was nothing obvious to fight about ... Sometimes 'real' causes could be assumed – disputes over territory, hunting rights, water holes, women, real or imagined insults to tribal honor. But for the most part, enemies were what were traditionally defined as such. No Shoshone needed any 'real' cause for fighting the Sioux: they existed to be fought. A great deal of this fighting was highly ritualized so that the men could get the maximum satisfaction from their sense of danger and exercise of courage, while neither side lost too many lives … The showing of courage and skill and the braving of dangers were more important than the wholesale slaughter of the enemy."

Chipewyan life revolved around hunting. Men became heads of families and chiefs because of their skill in tracking and killing game. They followed the migrating caribou, spearing them in summer and snaring them in enclosures during winter. In rutting time the caribou were lured to their death by decoys, hunters who tied antler stems to their waists and rattled them to reproduce the sound of bulls fighting for a female's favour. When a curious bull appeared, he was shot by an arrow. (The Chipewyan used bone rather than stone arrowheads because bone tips break off and work themselves toward the animal's heart.) A lone hunter, disguised under a caribou skin and a set of antlers, would infiltrate a herd and kill its fattest member. Traditionally every part of every animal was used, with the caribou foetus considered a particular delicacy. Even the skeleton of the caribou was reduced to bonemeal and added to stews for nutritious flavouring.

The Chipewyan dwelt in a universe of animalistic spiritualism, their lives permeated by ritual and superstition. It was wrong, for example, to stretch two nets across a stream because one would be jealous of the other and neither would catch fish. Women would never eat the gristly muzzle of the caribou for fear of growing beards, and young men were afraid that eating bear feet might insult the bear's spirit and slow their own running. It was believed that the dead travelled in stone boats to a beautiful island abounding with game, but that only the good would reach the island; sinners would be capsized and struggle in the water forever.

According to Chipewyan legend, the birth of the world occurred in the cave of a lone Indian woman who rescued a dog-like animal. When she made love with it, the animal was magically transformed into a handsome young man whose sexual ecstasy equalled her own. At daybreak he resumed the dog's form, and "the mother of the world" scarcely remembered or understood the dreams of her night's passion until she gave birth to a superior being who grew so tall his head reached the clouds. With a huge walking stick he marked out the earth's lakes and rivers. Then he killed his dog-father and tore him to bits, and the entrails became fish, the flesh caribou and the skin birds. The tall man told his mother that her future offspring would have the ability to kill as many animals as they required, assuring the abundance of game and orderliness in the world.

Whenever two parties of Chipewyan met in the Barrens they would advance to within a stone's throw and sit on the ground in silence. Elders from each group would then rise and recite the litany of deaths and misfortunes visited on their band since the last encounter. After much wailing and prolonged, cathartic crying, pipes would be passed and gifts exchanged – and only then would real conversation begin. Unlike some of the Cree, the Chipewyan, too proud to become hired hunters and provisioners, never surrendered their independence to the HBC. Instead of loitering around Churchill or Prince of Wales's Fort, they preferred to roam the Barrens, trading with the tribes of the Far West and exacting costly commissions for Company goods.

Because the Chipewyan were so unpredictable – appearing unheralded once a year out of the forbidding Barren Grounds with tales of vast mineral treasures and distant seas – the early HBC traders treated them with attention and curiosity. The Company men were also beguiled by the Chipewyan's sex lives. The HBC journal-writers described at such length and in such detail the Indians' sexual proclivities that one is tempted to conclude that much of their knowledge must have come from firsthand research.

They knew most about the Cree around them on the bay. James Isham, for instance, noted in high dudgeon that at York Factory "maidens are very rare to be found at thirteen or fourteen years of age, and ... none at fifteen." Hearne described how it was common for a Cree to make free with his brother's wife or daughter, and how "many of them cohabit occasionally with their own mothers, and frequently espouse sisters and daughters."

No such sexual transgressions were observed among the Chipewyan. Here was male frontier fantasy at its best, or worst: a tribe that openly treated its women as slaves and concubines. Wives could be jettisoned by the simple expedient of administering a good drubbing and turning them out. In return for supplying game and protection, some of the Chipewyan men maintained harems of up to eight wives. New sex mates were won by barter or physical contest. The first man thrown to the ground in these flash wrestling bouts was the loser. An opponent could most readily be downed by grabbing his hair (and so they kept it cut short) or by twisting his ears, which were often greased. No one seemed to care how the women felt, and there was no recourse or appeal once a woman had been won or lost. "On these occasions," Hearne reported, "their grief and reluctance to follow their new lords has been so great, that the business has often ended in the greatest brutality; for in the struggle I have seen the poor girls stripped quite naked, and carried by main force to their new lodgings." The only relief women enjoyed was during their menstrual cycles when they went to live away from the main tents. It was an essential escape, and Hearne slyly noted: "I have known some sulky dames to leave their husbands for five days at a time, and repeat the farce twice or thrice a month, while the poor men never suspected the deceit."

Chipewyan women had clear brown skin but, according to Hearne, did not meet the white man's standard of beauty: "Ask a northern Indian what is beauty, and he will answer – a broad flat face, small eyes, high cheek bones, three or four lines across each cheek,* a tawny hide and breasts hanging down to the belt."

"Chipewyan women ranked lower than in any other tribe," observed Diamond Jenness in his definitive study of Canadian Indians. "Separated from all boy companions at the age of eight or nine, married at adolescence often to middle-aged men, and always subject to many restrictions, they were the first to perish in seasons of scarcity. In winter they were mere traction animals; unaided, they dragged the heavy toboggans. In summer, they were pack animals, carrying all the household goods, food and hides on their backs." It was nothing out of the ordinary for a Chipewyan woman to be lugging a 140-pound pack in summer and dragging twice as much on a sled in winter.

In the harsh climate of the Barrens, life was so brutish and short that alluring girls turned into cackling crones by the age of thirty. They were obliged to draw sleds, dress skins, cook meat, pitch tents, mend breeches and keep their men satisfied. The sexist attitude of the day was summed up by Matonabbee, the Chipewyan chief, who explained to Hearne: "Women were made for labour; one of them can carry or haul as much as two men can do. They also pitch our tents, make and mend our clothing, keep us warm at night … Though they do everything, [they] are maintained at a trifling expense; for as they

---

*A tattoo acquired by pushing an awl through the skin, withdrawing it and rubbing charcoal into the raw wound.

always cook, the very licking of their fingers in scarce times is sufficient for their subsistence."

TO VENTURE ACROSS THE BARREN GROUNDS in Samuel Hearne's time meant stepping off the edge of the known world. It also meant having to cross the gravelly, spongy sphagnum the latter-day explorer R.A.J. Phillips described as being very like trying to wade through "porridge sown with razor blades."

Hearne himself explained the effect of trudging through this cursed terrain when, halfway through his appalling forty-mile-a-day return journey from the Coppermine, he looked down at the tatters of his lower extremities, shook his head in despair and noted in his journal that he had acquired an advanced case of "foundered feet."

Still, the mood was festive as Hearne set off on his first expedition during a pre-dawn snowflurry on November 6, 1769. Accompanied by two Company servants and a pair of Cree hunters from Prince of Wales's Fort, he left at the same time as a group of Chipewyan led by an Indian known as Captain Chawchinahaw. Only three weeks later, two hundred miles north of the fort, Chawchinahaw and his band abruptly plundered Hearne's food stocks, then decided to turn southwest, mockingly suggesting that Hearne and his companions find their own way home. As the Indians decamped, "making the woods ring with their laughter," Hearne's survival instinct asserted itself. Deprived of provisions and flintlocks, the five survivors set off south, escaping starvation by snaring a few rabbits and gnawing the boiled hide of their jackets. It was a mortifying experience, but Hearne's skills had been sharpened; by the time he stumbled back into his home fort, he had been transformed from an ineffectual camp-follower to a resourceful man-of-the-land.

By February 1770 Hearne was itching to set off again,

and Norton once more chose his companions, this time placing him under the dubious protection of a hired Indian named Conne-e-quese who claimed to have seen the Arctic copper mines. With their usual shrewdness, the northern Indians had come to realize that the white man would reward them for telling him exactly what he wanted to hear; they saw nothing wrong in spinning a few tall tales about rich copper mines in return for free guns and other supplies. The small party, equipped with one moosehide tent, a Hadley quadrant and a few guns and trinkets, struck north towards Baker Lake. The "Keewatin" or north wind blew, and prodigious cold chilled the travellers to their marrow. Pulling air into their lungs became a major undertaking. It was so bitterly cold that Hearne was able to trap several marten by falling on top of them and holding them down for a few minutes until he could feel them stiffen, frozen to death.

By June the spruce had thinned out. They were on the edge of the Barrens, Hearne stumbling along, weighed down by a sixty-pound shoulder sack and his awkward quadrant, his face smeared with goose grease to ward off the swarms of mosquitoes and flies so thick they shadowed the sun. Finding no game to shoot, the party was soon reduced to munching cranberries and chewing scraps of hide and burned bones from long-abandoned fires. Hearne was now at Yathkyed Lake, deeper into the Barrens than any white man before him. Here his group was joined by parties of roaming Chipewyan, who eventually swelled the aggregation to nearly six hundred. The incompetent Conne-e-quese, no longer certain where he was or whether the copper outcrops really existed, decided they would winter with the nomads. Hearne had no choice but to go along. Shortly afterward, his quadrant was destroyed by a gust of wind as he was setting up a sighting. Hearne was at Dubawnt Lake, far from his home fort; his few trade goods were long gone, and his companions were grumbling about how useless he was. His future course was decided for him when several of the Indians stole his personal possessions. Instead of getting angry, Hearne played on Chipewyan psychology by exclaiming that the lighter load would make his journey pleasanter and politely asked for the return of his razors, his awl, a needle and some soap. Taken aback by the unexpected civility, they agreed, and Hearne smugly noted in his diary that even if they returned only one of his razors, "they chose to keep the worst."

The heralding chill of winter was in the air; Hearne was lost and alone. Having deprived him of his possessions, the Indians dropped away. Fearing that he would soon freeze or starve, Hearne permitted himself a rare note of self-pity, complaining to his journal: "I never saw a set of people that possessed so little humanity, or that could view the distress of their fellow creatures with so little feeling and unconcern..."

He had no snowshoes, no tent or warm clothes. He trudged south for three days, falling asleep later and later each night, trying to hold off the moment when his will power would be exhausted and he would collapse into delirium, surrendering himself to the long Arctic slumber from which there is no waking.

Then occurred one of those theatrical entrances that characterize the Hudson's Bay chronicles. On September 20, 1770, just a day before Hearne might have frozen to death, there materialized out of that uninhabited void a tall, dark apparition. It was Matonabbee, the greatest of the Chipewyan chiefs. Samuel Hearne had found his mentor and soulmate. The two men would forge a unique partnership evolving into mutual admiration and even love. Hearne praised Matonabbee for a "scrupulous adherence to truth and honesty that would have done honour to the most enlightened and devout Christian," describing his personality as an admirable mixture of "the vivacity of a Frenchman and the sincerity of an Englishman with the gravity and nobleness of a Turk."

A handsome six-footer with a hawk nose and brooding eyes, Matonabbee was born at Prince of Wales's Fort, the son of a Cree slave-girl and a local Chipewyan hunter. Adopted by Richard Norton (Moses's father), the young Matonabbee learned to speak Cree and some English, as well as teaching himself the workings of the fur trade. He was probably the only Chipewyan of his time who felt at home both on the Barrens and inside the HBC forts. He had been to the Coppermine country, distributing Company trade goods to the distant Copper and Yellow-knife Indians, and was practised at maintaining the uneasy peace between the errant tribes of the Barrens and the sullen western Cree of Athabasca. He was proclaimed "Captain" of the Chipewyan by HBC traders, though that tribe did not recognize any overall leadership function outside the hunt and its dealings with the Company.

And so Matonabbee plucked Hearne from the shores of eternity, provided him with otter robes, directed him to woods where they made snowshoes and sleds, then guided him back to Prince of Wales's Fort. The two men agreed en route to strike out for the Coppermine River together. Only twelve days after his return from this second gruelling journey, Hearne slipped silently out of the Company post. This time he went alone, attaching himself to Matonabbee and his accompanying retinue of up to eight wives and nine children, thus becoming a member of the Indian's extended family. "Probably no Canadian explorer depended so much upon one Indian for the success of his venture," notes historian Maurice Hodgson, who continues, "It is impossible to conceive of the success of Hearne's last expedition without [appreciating] the degree to which Hearne allowed himself to be physically and psychologically captured by the Indians, and more specifically by his attachment to, and affection for, Matonabbee."

At the time, this was a most unusual arrangement. Englishmen simply did not subordinate themselves to natives they were still pleased to call "red savages." Hearne gave himself up to the natural rhythms and diet of the Barrens; he turned over to Matonabbee the success of his mission and his personal safety. His final and successful Coppermine journey, which lasted nineteen months, saw Hearne reduce his travelling party to the minimum – himself – and melding into the nomadic bands of accompanying Indians so effectively that he nearly became one of them.*

One reason Hearne was able to surrender his individuality so completely was that he felt himself more of an observer than a participant, living out most of his emotions in the entries of his journal. That painfully honest chronicle of his epic journey – published twenty-three years later as *A Journey from Hudson's Bay to the Northern Ocean* – turned out to be as important a legacy as the journey itself. The perceptiveness that allowed Hearne to view each new experience without the inhibitions of his time made his diary a classic in the literature of northern discovery. The candid quality of his observations came through in such jottings as this graphic description of native ingenuity: "When I was on my passage from Cumberland House to York Fort, two boys killed a fine buck moose in the water, by forcing a stick up its fundament; for they had neither gun, bow, nor arrows with them."

He was amazed but not shocked when the Indian wife

---

*All that Hearne carried with him into the wilderness, apart from his quadrant, was some tobacco, a few knives, one spare coat, a pair of drawers, a blanket, his gun and ammunition, and "some useful ironwork."

of a Company servant named Isaac Batt, who had recently lost an infant, was forced "to suckle a young Bear," and seemed absolutely mesmerized by the Indian medicine men's cure for constipation: "For some inward complaints, such as, griping in the intestines, difficulty of making water, etc., it is very common to see those jugglers blowing into the anus, or into the parts adjacent, till their eyes are almost starting out of their heads: and this operation is performed indifferently on all, without regard either to age or sex. The accumulation of so large a quantity of wind is at times apt to occasion some extraordinary emotions, which are not easily suppressed by a sick person; and as there is no vent for it but by the channel through which it was conveyed thither, it sometimes occasions an odd scene between the doctor and his patient …"

He happily gorged with his companion on delicacies such as deer entrails, buffalo foetuses, the genitals of unborn caribou and baby beaver torn from their mothers' wombs. He grew especially fond of a Chipewyan version of haggis: caribou meat was first cut into bite-sized pieces and given to small boys to chew. The softened bits were then stirred in with the half-digested contents of the animal's stomach with enough water added so that the whole mess would boil up into a mush, then stuffed into the stomach lining and cured over a smoky fire.*

Such a menu, together with the unrelenting hardship

---

*Hearne drew the line only at eating lice and warble flies, which the Indians happily nibbled after picking them off their garments and out of their hair. Hearne diplomatically explained to Matonabbee that he did not want to become addicted to the taste of the insects because he could not obtain a handy supply once he was back in London. He got so used to eating such delicacies as raw deer brains that, years afterward at fine London restaurants, he would order his trout and salmon "not warm to the bone."

of crossing the Barrens, might have brutalized another man, but it served only to open Hearne's eyes to the logic of that nude landscape. His salvation was that he rarely grew cynical, taking pleasure out of even the most disconcerting experiences. When he first encountered the Copper Indians deep in the northern Barrens, they encircled him and poked his bodily parts. After the most intimate examination they pronounced him to be a perfect human being – except for his skin, which they thought looked like boiled meat, and his blond hair, which they agreed among themselves was the colour and texture of a piss-stained buffalo tail. "As I was the first [white man] whom they had ever seen, and in all probability might be the last," he benignly noted in his journal, "it was curious to see how they flocked around me, and expressed as much desire to examine me from top to toe, as an European Naturalist would a non-descript animal."

It took Matonabbee and Hearne four months to reach the Thelewey-aza-yeth River, where tent poles were cut, meat was dried and birch bark collected for making portage-fording canoes before the plunge northward into wild Slave country. At times they were accompanying an unruly mob of as many as sixty Chipewyan, and even though he displayed the same stoicism as his companions, Hearne retained his British sense of civility and never lost sight of his own objectives. They were a ragged little army following their stomachs, their timing and direction dependent on the migrating caribou. Hearne tagged along, scratching in his journal, lugging a thirty-year-old Elton quadrant, trying to puzzle out exactly where he was. At Clowey Lake, Hearne's party was joined by a foraging band of mysterious Indians who refused to explain why they were heading north.

Hearne loped northward, trying to keep from slipping into one of the many potholes that dot the terrain.

At one point progress was slowed when the thighs and buttocks of one of Matonabbee's wives froze, producing blisters the size of sheep's bladders. The travellers nudged one another, jeering at her for having belted her clothes so high. "I must acknowledge that I was not in the number of those who pitied her," Hearne primly noted in his journal, "as I thought she took too much pains to shew a clean heel and a good leg; her garters being always in sight, which, though by no means considered here as bordering on indecency, is by far too airy to withstand the rigorous cold of a severe winter in a high Northern latitude."

Of more concern to Hearne was another Chipewyan woman who gave birth on the trail: "The instant, however, the poor woman was delivered, which was not until she had suffered all the pains usually felt on those occasions for nearly fifty-two hours, the signal was made for moving when the poor creature took her infant on her back and set out with the rest of the company; and though another person had the humanity to haul the sledge for her (for one day only), she was obliged to carry a considerable load beside her little charge, and was frequently obliged to wade knee-deep in water and wet snow."

Hearne missed little, describing even the ethos of muskox dung: "It is perhaps not generally known, even to the curious, therefore may not be unworthy of observation, that the dung of the muskox, though so large an animal, is not larger, and at the same time so near the shape and colour of that of the Alpine hare, that the difference is not easily distinguished but by the natives, though in general the quantity may lead to a discovery of the animal to which it belongs."

One of Hearne's more alluring observations was of the "Alarm Bird," a boreal owl used by the Copper

Indians to detect approaching strangers.* "When it perceives any people, or beast, it directs its way towards them immediately, and after hovering over them some time, flies round them in circles, or goes ahead in the same direction in which they walk. They repeat their visits frequently; and if they see any other moving objects, fly alternately from one party to the other, hover over them for some time, and make a loud screaming noise, like the crying of a child. In this manner they are said sometimes to follow passengers a whole day."

The expedition had to devote inordinate time to Matonabbee's wives. His roster varied between two and eight, with various unblushing brides dropping out or joining the caravan at unpredictable intervals. Hearne had difficulty distinguishing their separate identities but when the youngest and comeliest of them eloped with a muscular traveller, Matonabbee was disconsolate; he stood howling in the middle of the half-million square miles of Barrens and wanted to call off the expedition and go home. Hearne persuaded him to stay by appealing to the strength of his vow when he undertook the journey. By calming Matonabbee's distress, Hearne successfully drew him into the European value system. Their relationship worked both ways. Still, when it came to the occasional showdown, there was no question that Hearne was considered the outsider. At one point the Chipewyan ambushed a party of Indians, plundered their possessions and gang-raped their women, treating them, according to Hearne, "in so barbarous a manner as to endanger the lives of one or two of them." When the HBC explorer objected, the Chipewyan not only did not stop, "they

---

*Hearne's "Alarm Bird" was probably the short-eared owl, *Asio flammeus*, a common summer inhabitant of the Barren Ground.

made no scruple of telling me in the plainest terms that, if any female relation of mine had been present, she would have been served in the same manner."

The caravan slanted north and west, dropping most of the wives and children at a camp near Kathawachaga Lake ("Congecathawachaga" in Hearne's diary) while preparations went on for the final dash towards the Arctic Ocean. The strangers who had integrated themselves with the main convoy now made for themselves inch-thick wooden shields, carved and painted with primitive spirit-symbols Hearne recognized as having nothing to do with hunting. He gradually realized that the newcomers – Copper Indians from the east – were taking over the direction of the expedition and that their purpose was to massacre Eskimos known to be frequenting the Coppermine River. Matonabbee himself was not particularly anxious to participate in a killing spree, and Hearne, after making several exasperated objections, scribbled defensively in his diary: "I did not *care* if they rendered the name and race of Esquimaux extinct."

The war party sped north, covering eighty miles in four days, and crossed the Coppermine River at Sand-stone Rapids, about forty miles south of Coronation Gulf. Instead of a wide and accommodating passage that could be used by Company ships, Hearne found himself on the bank of a broad, rock-strewn stream with turbulent rapids and no sign of an ebbing tide that might have led to the Arctic Sea. This was the shank of the 1771 summer sea-son, yet on July 3, a raging snowstorm obliterated their tracks. Huddling in the lee of boulders, the warriors shivered in the teeth of the blizzard and dreamed of their prey. Scouts sent ahead found the quarry and reported that an Eskimo hunting camp of five tents had been set up at a cataract of the river which Hearne would later appro-priately christen Bloody Fall. At this news the Chipewyan tensed, then set about painting their faces, tying up their hair, removing their leggings and finally stripping down to their breechcloths. Gliding silently from stone to stone, they crept along the riverbank. Hearne had been told to stay behind, but nervous that he might be killed by one of the escaping Eskimos, he went along, armed with a spear.

Just after midnight on July 17 the massacre began. The Indians slithered right up to the tents and hurled themselves at the sleeping Eskimos. The scene was more reminiscent of an abattoir than of a battle, with the panic-stricken victims rearing out of their cozy tents and being impaled on out-thrust spears. More than twenty men, women and children, their faces still sweet from inter-rupted slumber, were slain within minutes, their death rattles despoiling the Arctic silence. A young Eskimo woman ran desperately towards Hearne, the one man not engaged in the killing. A Chipewyan wheeled and plunged a spear into her side. "She fell down at my feet," Hearne wrote later, "and twisted around my legs, so that it was with difficulty I could disengage myself from her dying grasps. Two Indian men were pursuing this unfortunate victim, and I solicited very hard for her life. The murderers made no reply until they had stuck both their spears through her body and transfixed her to the ground. They then looked at me sternly in the face and began to ridicule me by asking if I desired an Eskimo wife; meanwhile paying not the slightest heed to the shrieks and agony of the poor wretch who was still twining around their spears like an eel. Indeed, after receiving much abuse from them, I was at length obliged to desire only that they would be more expeditious in despatching their victim out of her misery; otherwise I should be obliged, out of pity, to assist in the friendly office of putting an end to a fellow creature who had been so cruelly wounded. On this request being made, one of the Indians hastily drew his spear from the place where it was first lodged, and pierced it through her breast near the heart. The love of life, however, even in this most miserable state, was so predominant that though this might justly be called the most merciful act that could be done for the poor creature, it still seemed to be unwelcome. Though much exhausted by pain and loss of blood, she made several efforts to ward off this friendly blow."

The aftermath was even worse. Hearne mercifully leaves out the details from his journal, remarking only that "the brutish manner in which these savages used the bodies that had been so cruelly bereaved of life was so shocking that it would be indecent to describe it …"

Except for the spearing of an old man "until his whole body was like a cullender" and the murder of one elderly half-blind Eskimo woman who had been fishing nearby by stabbing her in the non-vital parts so she would die slowly, the ghastly encounter was now over. Hearne composed himself, noting somewhat ambivalently: "I am confident that my features must have expressed how sincerely I was affected by this barbarous scene."

The killing had stopped, but the plunder continued. Their blood-lust played out, the Chipewyan destroyed all evidence of the Eskimos' very existence, hurling their tent poles into the river, even though they might well have been useful. Then the satiated victors sat down for a feast of fresh char.

Within the hour the marauders reverted to being explorers, hiking the eight miles from Bloody Fall to the Arctic Ocean. Although some later explorers, including John Richardson and Eric Morse, have questioned whether Hearne actually descended the river or merely viewed its mouth from atop a nearby hill, Denis St-Onge, a veteran of the Geological Survey of Canada who spent a decade combing the same patch of wilderness, has no doubt about what happened. "Hearne was there," he has maintained. "His descriptions of Coronation Gulf are much too accurate for him not to have seen its shore. He was right there, on this silly mudflat at the end of the Coppermine, and if he tasted the water it would have been fresh, because the river flows into a huge delta where the tide is less than one metre."

Hearne had reached the Arctic Sea at the western end of Coronation Gulf. Here was the destination of all his efforts: journey's end, the ocean he had spent so many agonizing months trying to reach. He stood there, transfixed by disappointment in what he saw: a waddle of seals on a nearby floe and a flight of curlew wheeling over the sterile marshland. Nothing else. This was no North West Passage; it was a rocky suburb of Hell. The fabled Coppermine, its mouth blocked by a ridge and impassable shoals, would never accommodate Company ships or anything else.

It was one o'clock on the bright morning of July 18, 1771, and the dream of finding a channel across North America had just ended.

Men would cast themselves into the quest for another one hundred and thirty-five years, but no one would ever equal Hearne's walk.*

Hearne snapped out of his reverie and, being a good Company man, did the only sensible thing: "erected a mark, and took possession of the coast on behalf of the HBC."

---

*The Admiralty, for one, did not recognize the validity of Hearne's exploits. Twenty years later, on April 1, 1791, George Vancouver left Falmouth with instructions to look for a passage through the North American continent. But the great navigator had few illusions. "No small measure of mirth passed among the seamen," he noted in his log, "in consequence of our having sailed from old England on All Fool's Day for the purpose of discovering a North West Passage."

On the way back, three days' march up the Coppermine then east across Burnt Creek past the September Mountains, Hearne was guided by Matonabbee to the copper hills that garnished so many Indian legends.* After a four-hour search they found only one sizeable chunk of loose metal – a four-pound lump the shape of "an Alpine hare couchant." There was much evidence that ore had been taken out of the ground, but with winter coming and the Chipewyan impatient to be back with their women, Hearne had little time for mineralogy.†

The Indians tramped flat out back to their family camp, and for the first time Hearne began to lag behind, his feet punctured by gravel that ate into his flesh, his toenails peeling away. Each step he took left a footprint of blood. Hearne's return journey took nearly another year, partly across a frozen Great Slave, the world's eleventh-largest lake, three hundred miles long and two thousand feet deep. On June 29, 1772, eighteen months and twenty-two days after he had left Prince of Wales's Fort, Hearne found himself only ten miles from the fort. In the hunter's way, he settled in to savour one last camp on the land, planning to make the most of his entrance the following morning. As he sat by the feeble embers of the campfire, he scratched a final triumphant entry into his

---

*According to mythology, the copper mines were discovered by a woman who for several seasons guided the Indians to the richest ore. But when they took sexual liberties with her, she vowed in revenge to stay at the mines and sit on the copper deposits until both she and the deposits sank into the ground. When the Indians came back the following season, she was buried to her waist, and there was much less metal; when they returned a year later, both the woman and the copper were gone.

†John Franklin explored the same site in 1821, and many mineral claims in the area were filed between 1913 and 1968, though at only one spot (Hope Lake) was a shaft ever sunk.

travel journal: "Though my discoveries are not likely to prove of any material advantage to the Nation at large," he wrote, "or indeed to the Hudson's Bay Company, yet I have the pleasure to think that I have fully complied with the orders of my Masters, and that it has put a final end to all disputes concerning a North West Passage through Hudson's Bay."

Hearne's odyssey has rarely if ever been matched. His round trip of about 3,500 miles, the equivalent of the distance as the crow flies from Gibraltar to Moscow, or Quebec City to Juneau, Alaska, was an epic adventure on a grand scale. This intrepid naif had been the first white man to reach the Arctic Ocean by land, discovering en route Great Slave Lake and the Mackenzie River system. He pioneered a new technique of exploration – the propensity to go native.

THE COMPANY RESPONDED to Hearne's magnificent achievement in its customary cavalier style. He was paid a £200 bonus and promptly posted back to his former job as mate of the *Charlotte*, but the fact that he had traversed a region half the size of "European Russia" was not lost on the London governors. He had come to their notice, not merely as a promising neophyte but as a dependable explorer ready to take on other assignments.

His circumstances were improved a year and a half later by the sudden death of the tyrannical Prince of Wales's Governor, Moses Norton. Suffering from an untreated intestinal infection, Norton called his officers and concubines to his private quarters on December 29, 1773, rudely proclaiming the details of his last will, which left all his goods to a wife in England he hardly ever saw, except for the miserly sum of £10 a year to clothe his several Indian women on the bay. As he lay there, alternately cursing his illness and writhing in the painful spasms of its effects, Norton spied a subordinate and one of his younger Indian wives whispering together. "Goddamn you for a bitch!" he bellowed in what turned out to be his valedictory. "If I live, I'll knock your brains out!"

"A few minutes after this elegant apostrophe," Hearne cheerfully reported, "he expired in the greatest agonies that can possibly be conceived."

CHAPTER 14

THE BLOOD FEUD BEGINS

It was an uneven battle fought with all the passion of a Sicilian vendetta. But in the process of trying to outdo one another, the competing fur traders roughed out the contours of upper North America.

SIX MONTHS BEFORE MOSES NORTON'S DEATH, an HBC bookkeeper named Matthew Cocking returned to York Factory after a lengthy journey up country to report with grave concern that the Montrealers were monopolizing the fur trade of the Saskatchewan River area and were poised to cut off the HBC from its main supply of furs. This hardy scribe, who had little idea of how to steer a canoe, had managed to penetrate as far as the Eagle Hills (just south of present-day Battleford), had hunted with the Blackfoot, observed the flow of the fur trade but, unlike his emotional and romantic predecessors, came back to record in his precise copper-plate script the operational details of the inland panorama. "The natives are very dilatory in proceeding," he noted. "Their whole delight is to sit smoking and feasting. Yesterday I received an invitation to no less than ten feasts." He was disturbed by his camping companions. "I get no rest at nights," he complained, "for Drumming, Dancing, &c."

Cocking's accountant's-eye view of the wood buffalo country, his tidy reconstruction of the extent to which the pedlars were controlling the fur trade and his exact descriptions of how this rich fur country could be exploited confirmed the London Committeemen's inclination to act – that, plus the actuarial evidence supporting his contention that the pedlars were drying up the fur traffic to the bay. York Factory's return in 1773 was only eight thousand made-beaver, down from an annual average of thirty thousand made-beaver in the decade before 1766. There had been a running argument within Company circles about inland posts since Anthony Henday's journey. The specific decision to move, taken in May 1773, was based on recommendations from Andrew Graham, the chief factor at York Factory, and first-hand testimony from Isaac Batt, one of the HBC's most experienced inland travellers.

And so, London woke from its slumbers and ordered Cocking and Hearne to establish Cumberland House, the HBC's first permanent western inland settlement.*

At this time "Canada" extended only from the Detroit River east to the Gaspé and as far north of the St Lawrence River as Lac St-Jean. The land to the north and west of the St Lawrence Valley belonged either to the HBC or to nomadic tribes. The HBC had been able to butt heads with the Montreal-based competition in this huge domain by sending its emissaries inland to lure the Indians out to Hudson Bay, where they could still obtain the best

---

*Upon his return, Cocking settled at York Factory. He later succeeded Hearne at Cumberland House and became Master of Severn. He died in York, England in 1799, and the York Factory Council provided that each of his three half-breed daughters be given "gingerbread, nuts, etc., as they have no other means of obtaining these little luxuries, with which the paternal fondness of a Father formerly provided them…"

bargains and the heavyweight goods that the pedlars did not carry.*But after 1770 the freelance traders began to form partnerships, temporary coalitions of interests that allowed them to carry on their business much more aggressively. In the nick of time, just before these annually financed "outfits" were consolidated into the North West Company, the Hudson's Bay Company finally snapped out of its reverie of more than a century and set out to claim Prince Rupert's empire.

During the next half-century, HBC traders would march across the continent, eventually commandeering the vast territory from the Great Lakes to the Pacific. "The Company's success sprang in no small degree from the timely foundation of Cumberland House in 1774," Richard Glover has pointed out. "Had this step not been taken when it was, the Company's chance of surviving and triumphing in its struggle with its rivals would have been much reduced. The margin by which it survived and won was small enough as things were."

---

*The pedlars often catered to individual Indian needs more astutely than did the HBC. Garments called "surcoats" were made in Montreal, for example, and shipped west without sleeves attached; the sleeves were sold separately in three lengths, so that the clothing conformed more closely to customers' sizes. But some of the HBC trade goods had advantages of their own. Because the best pelts for feltmaking were the furs off the Indians' backs, the Company provided woollen blankets made to native specifications – the ubiquitous Bay blankets dyed with bands of black, yellow, scarlet and green still sold today. The French trades provided no equivalent. The HBC also stocked lightweight copper pans and kettles while the competing traders continued to supply massive iron cookware completely unsuitable for long portages. English rum was a cheap product of the West Indian slave colonies, while French brandy (though much superior) had to be tediously aged in casks. Probably the HBC's greatest trading advantage was the quality of its Brazil tobacco.

SAMUEL HEARNE HAD WINTERED at York Factory, preparing for his excursion inland and recruiting a reluctant clutch of Orkneymen to accompany him. They set off in the spring of 1774 as passengers in deep-laden canoes with Indians returning to their hunting grounds, each canoe carrying 180 pounds of Brazil tobacco, pouches of gunpowder, shot and six-gallon kegs of brandy as well as some building supplies. Every advantageous trading site Hearne saw along the way was already occupied by pedlars hawking rum, knives, flint, awls and needles.

About sixty miles west of the modern-day location of The Pas, in the evergreen slough of northwestern Manitoba at Pine Island Lake (now Cumberland Lake in Saskatchewan) Hearne finally found his spot. He decided to clear ground for a permanent post to be called Cumberland House. It was a good choice. Cumberland was strategically situated at convenient river connections to Lake Winnipeg, the Rockies and the Nor'Westers' route towards the Athabasca country, yet it was only 450 miles, about forty days' paddling time, from its supply base at York Factory. (The pedlars were five months' travel away from Montreal.) A low-slung log bunker, thirty-eight by twenty-six feet, with a leaky plank roof and moss as caulking was eventually completed.

Wood-smoke curling from its makeshift chimney, the first full-fledged inland post of the Hudson's Bay Company opened for business. New supplies (including thirty-five gallons of brandy*) arrived from York, but no extra food was brought in and they almost starved the first winter. When one of Hearne's nine fellow residents, Robert Longmoor, went out to hunt game and came back "with both his Big Toes much froze," Hearne had to

---

*This was an insignificant whistle-wetter. Every freight canoe leaving Montreal at this time was capable of carrying (and usually did carry) two hundred gallons of rum.

"open them up" and pack the inner rind of larch-tree roots close to the bone, because this was "generally used among the Natives to prevent mortification."

Faced for the first time with having to winter in the wilderness not with indigenous Indians but among white men who had never before strayed from the shore of the bay, Hearne emerged as a resolute leader. He rotated the members of his little band in twelve-hour shifts, insisting that they never let down their guard. Despite his stern regime, none of the Orkneymen deserted to the pedlars. Some 150 rival traders had set up their bivouacs nearby. The "distant civility" with which the Company directed its servants to treat the Montrealers had been maintained. With spring breakup, Hearne proudly led a fur-burdened flotilla of thirty-two canoes down to York Factory. His mission to Cumberland House had succeeded,* and although he was ambitious to push the HBC farther inland, the 1775 supply ship from London brought him a promotion. At the age of thirty he was given command of his former home base at Prince of Wales's Fort.

DURING HEARNE'S FIRST AUTUMN as Governor, his old friend Matonabbee, by then the acknowledged chief of

---

*The oldest permanent settlement in Saskatchewan, Cumberland House was moved a mile upstream in 1789 and remained an important distribution depot until it was overshadowed by Norway House in northern Manitoba; it finally became a pemmican storehouse for passing brigades. By the mid-1850s Cumberland House had been reduced to just another outpost on the margin of civilization instead of the entry-point to a continental empire. As late as 1905 three steamboats worked out of the settlement, but its importance as a regional distribution centre gradually declined. It remains an HBC post, and local Indians still trap the muskrat marshes that supported Hearne's original little community.

all the northern Indians, arrived leading three hundred Chipewyan with a goodly pile of prime pelts. He knew he had brought out the largest Chipewyan fur haul in a hundred years and was not about to go unrewarded. The ensuing orgy of gift-giving (quite apart from the trade goods owed for the furs) was without precedent in HBC annals, and at least part of Hearne's generosity must have been prompted by his gratitude for his comrade's guidance to the Coppermine and back. After dressing him up as a Captain and completely outfitting his six wives, Hearne also gave Matonabbee "seven lieutenants coats, fifteen common coats, eighteen hats, eighteen shirts, eight guns, 140 pounds weight of gunpowder with shot, ball, and flints in proportion; many hatchets, ice chisels, files, bayonets, knives; and a great quantity of tobacco, cloth, blankets, combs, looking-glasses, stockings, handkerchiefs; besides numberless small articles such as awls, needles, paint and steels."

Not satisfied, Matonabbee started to bargain, brazenly demanding gifts of "twelve pounds of powder, twenty-eight pounds of shot and ball, four pounds of tobacco, more articles of clothing, and several pieces of ironwork, to give to two men who had hauled his tent and other lumber the preceding Winter." Hearne later complained to his journal: "This demand was so very unreasonable, that I made some scruple, or at least hesitated to comply with it, hinting that he was the person who ought to satisfy those men for their services; but I was soon answered, That he did not expect to have been denied such a trifle as that was; and for the future he would carry his goods where he could get his own price for them. On my asking where that was? he replied, in a very insolent tone, To the Canadian Traders."

All told, Matonabbee received goods the equivalent of 1,100 made-beaver – the largest single barter up to that time. That even a friend of the HBC, born at one of its posts and long engaged in its service, would threaten to switch loyalties was a dangerous indication of how vulnerable the Hudson Bay trade had become to the incursion of the pedlars. Freshly returned from Cumberland House, Hearne knew precisely how powerful the competition was.

The next half-decade was the happiest of Hearne's life. His governor's quarters were turned into a miniature zoo. Hearne's menagerie included tame lemmings, imported canaries, horned larks, foxes, eagles, snow buntings,* squirrels and several beavers.† The beavers were so domesticated that "they answered to their names and followed as a dog would do. They were as pleased at being fondled as any animal I ever saw. During the winter they lived on the same food as the women and were remarkably fond of rice and plum pudding."

Hearne's other relaxations included watching Indians fashion flutes from the wing-bones of whooping cranes and reading the astringent essays of Voltaire. For the first time in his adventurous life, Hearne felt secure enough to fall in love. The object of his affections was Mary Norton, the polygamous Governor's young daughter. Sixteen and as innocent as a freshly opened flower, she would, he confided to his journal, "have shone with superior lustre in any other country: for if an engaging person, gentle manners, an easy freedom, an amiable modesty, and an unri-

---

*Hearne noted that the snow buntings were excellent mimics –"When in company with canary birds, quickly learning to imitate their song."

†Hearne wrote: "The beaver were so fond of their company that when the women were absent for any considerable time, the animals displayed great signs of uneasiness and on their return shewed equal marks of pleasure by crawling on their laps, sitting erect like a squirrel and behaving to them like children who see their parents but seldom."

valled delicacy of sentiment, are graces and virtues which render a woman lovely, none ever had greater pretensions to general esteem and regard. . . ." The intrepid explorer settled into a life of peaceful domesticity with this benevolent and humane woman, the offspring of the irascible Moses Norton.

Unfortunately, their idyll was brutally interrupted by the last, and most improbable, attack on Hudson Bay.

The revolution in the Thirteen Colonies, which began while Hearne was still at Cumberland House, had grown into the War of American Independence. For a month in 1779 a combined French and Spanish fleet commanded the English Channel, and an invasion seemed imminent. The major English naval success was in the West Indies; Hearne's former captain, now Rear-Admiral Lord Hood, accepted the surrender of the French flagship, the 110-gun *Ville de Paris*, following a fierce engagement on April 12, 1782 that broke the French line of battle and scattered its twenty-six surviving warships. Three of the vessels – the seventy-five-gun *Sceptre* and two frigates of thirty-six guns each, the *Astrée* and *Engageante* – were ordered to mount an attack on the posts of Hudson Bay.

The ships were well equipped, carrying three hundred marines, two eight-inch mortars, three hundred bombs and four cannon, but why these fast-sailing, copper-bottomed men of war should be detached for half a year at a time when the French might have regained at least some of their influence in the Caribbean Sea remains obscure. "Weighed in any sane strategical balance, the French attack ... was pure nonsense," according to historian Richard Glover. "As such it offers a specially glaring example of that tendency which Mahan so eloquently deplored in French naval policy, a weakness for frittering resources away on commerce destruction, instead of seeking to dispute, to win and to hold, the command of the sea."

The French fleet sailed due north. Its commander, Jean François de Galaup, Conte de La Pérouse, later noted in *La Gazette de France*, that his main concern was not with waging war but with navigation: "I burned with impatience to arrive speedily at Prince of Wales. This was the first place which I proposed to attack; I had not an instant to lose, the rigour of the season obliging all ships to abandon these seas by the first days of September; but my impatience was put to a new proof. On the 3rd of August, sailing with security enough in the Bay of Hudson, I was enveloped in a fog, and immediately surrounded with large islands of ice, which extended beyond our view ... But on the 5th of August the bank of ice, in which I was engaged, opened a little, and I determined to force through it by a press of sail, whatever risque my ships might run. I was happy enough to accomplish it; and on the 8th of August in the evening, I saw the colours of Fort Prince of Wales."

With less than a month of navigable weather left open to him, the French admiral must have looked up at the massive battlements and wondered how he could successfully lay siege to this impressive wilderness apparition. The fort was known to have limestone embrasures up to forty feet thick and forty guns, and by those standards should have been the continent's most impregnable stronghold. La Pérouse's ships approached within a league and a half (about five miles), carefully staying out of artillery range; the French admiral raised English pennants to divert its gunners and lowered his boats to sound the harbour entrance.

Nothing stirred. Instead of displaying evidence of a hectic round of preparations for its defence, the fort appeared to be steeped in stony indolence.

At two o'clock in the morning of August 9, 1782, La Pérouse sent off 150 armed men in six longboats to land just below the fort's battlements and ordered the *Sceptre* to slip within firing range. Still no response from shore. The landing party reported that the fort betrayed no intention of trying to marshal any defences. Instead of the expected onslaught, the silence was deafening. Hardly believing his good fortune or suspecting a ruse, La Pérouse sent an emissary accompanied by a drummer to seek a parley.

The fort's gates were immediately thrown open and a white tablecloth run up its flagpole. The incredulous French conquerors marched in and raised the fleur-de-lys. The "invincible" fortress had fallen without a shot, its only casualties being the post's two horses, which the French promptly shot and made into soup.

La Pérouse and Hearne amicably negotiated the terms of surrender, which was unconditional except that it allowed the English to keep their personal possessions. Hearne's lightning capitulation has puzzled historians, particularly since the map-maker David Thompson, later a junior at the fort, alleged that the men "begged of Mr. Hearne to allow them to mow down the French troops with the heavy guns loaded with grapeshot, which he absolutely refused ..."

In fact, Hearne, who could see at once that the visiting ships had hostile intent, had served long enough in the Royal Navy to realize the havoc the vessels' naval cannon could inflict – particularly since he was in command of a garrison of only thirty-eight men. Each gun required a crew of about ten men, and Hearne was grievously over-gunned and understaffed; further, many of the pieces defending the fort were of museum quality, dating back to the reign of William and Mary. The fort itself had been poorly designed to withstand a siege; its embrasures were ill-built, it had no defensible moat and no internal water supply. La Pérouse accurately pointed out that the Sceptre's seventy-four guns could quickly have firebombed the HBC men into submission. Hearne might well have put up token resistance but waging uneven military encounters was not his forte, and he had no wish to risk the lives of his men in a battle he could not win.

If all Englishmen had lived by Hearne's rules, pragmatism would have become Britain's state religion. As an archetypal Company man, Hearne was more concerned with keeping a proper tally of the pillage than with trying to stop it. His report of the incident includes a meticulous account of the furs and other stock carried off by the French – leaving the observer to wonder who had time to count the goose quills:

7,607	Beaver Skins
187	Doe Deer Skins
3	Elks Skins
9	Black Bear Skins
3	Buffalo Skins
9	Wolf Skins
102	Wolverine Skins
110	Otter Skins
7	Grizzled Foxes
54	Red Foxes
72	Musquashes
329	lb. featherweight of Goose feathers
160	lb. weight Castoreum
221	Buck Deer Skins
9	Fawn Skins
1	Polar Bear Skin
1	Cub Bear Skin
4,100	Marten Skins
2	Wejack [fisher] Skins
207	Cat Skins
120	Arctic Skins
4	Blue Foxes
5	Gray Foxes
30	Jackasses [mink]
17,350	Goose Quills

La Pérouse and his men spiked the cannon, blew up the arches of the magazines in the bastions, and torched anything that would burn. The great fort, which had taken thirty-eight years to build, took half a day to destroy. It would never be occupied again, its battlements a bleak monument to man's presumptions about the invulnerability of citadels. The French admiral was reasonably gracious in victory, distributing powder and shot to a group of Indians who happened to witness the fort's destruction so that they would not starve on the way back to their hunting grounds. The HBC men were herded onto the French ships, and the victorious flotilla weighed anchor to sail to its next objective: the fur-rich storehouses at York Factory. From plans he found at Prince of Wales's Fort, La Pérouse knew that the HBC post was manned by sixty Englishmen armed with twenty-five cannon and a dozen swivel guns. It was supplied with thirty head of cattle and had adequate water sources within its stockades.

With less than three weeks of open navigation remaining on the bay and scurvy sweeping the men on his lower decks, La Pérouse rushed his advantage and landed an attack group of 250 men, plus mortars, cannon and eight days' provisions, at the Nelson River estuary behind York Factory. An HBC turncoat named John Irvine* was bribed to guide them across the isthmus between the Nelson and the Hayes rivers, but the path was so swampy that the Frenchmen wasted three days hacking and sloshing their way to their goal. Having watched the French ships arrive, resident Governor Humphrey Marten hurriedly loaded most of the post's furs aboard the HBC supply vessel *Prince Rupert*, which on a moonless night slipped

---

*Despite the evidence of his treachery, after he was repatriated to England by the French, Irvine was paid his HBC wages in full up to the day of his betrayal. -

away past the French ships and headed straight for England.

At eleven o'clock on the morning of August 25, 1782, the French troops rallied for their assault outside the factory gates. Marten, having acted as the good Company man and saved the bulk of the furs from being captured by the French, now felt there was no reason to risk having his men killed defending an empty warehouse. "Their numbers appeared so formidable," he later noted, "that it was thought prudent to demand a parley." A less charitable reconstruction was offered by Edward Umfreville, then York Factory's second-in-command: "During their approach, a most inviting opportunity offered itself to be revenged on our invaders, by discharging the guns on the ramparts. But a kind of tepid stupefaction seemed to take possession of the Governor at this time of trial, and he peremptorily declared that he would shoot the first man who offered to fire a gun. Accordingly ... he ... held out a white flag with his own hand, which was answered by the French officer showing his pocket hand-kerchief.... the place was most ingloriously given up in about ten minutes, ... to a half-starved, wretched group of Frenchmen, worn out with fatigue and hard labour, in a country they were entire strangers to."

And so York Factory changed hands for the eighth time. With the nip of winter already in the air, La Pérouse's men hurriedly pillaged its stores, burned the timber palisades and scuttled back to their ships. Although the French commander's main fear during the brief York Factory campaign was that the Company men might tempt the Cree with brandy and gunpowder to take arms in their defence, he again carefully saved from the wholesale destruction a cache of powder, shot and firelocks so that Indians who had taken refuge in the nearby woods would not be caught without supplies for the winter. Most of the HBC prisoners, including Hearne, were shifted to the Company's sloop *Severn*, which had been anchored off

York Factory at the time, and La Pérouse even towed the vessel as far as Cape Resolution. When the French cut the little sloop loose for her voyage across the Atlantic, Umfreville noted that La Pérouse's "politeness, humanity and goodness secured him the affection of all the Company's officers; and on parting at the mouth of Hudson's Strait, they felt the same sensation which the dearest friends feel in an interview preceding a long separation." Hearne and the French admiral had become friendly during their brief time together; La Pérouse had read parts of the explorer's journal and was so taken with it that he chivalrously insisted its early publication be the essential precondition of returning it to Hearne.

The London Committeemen seemed only mildly chagrined by the plunder of their main outposts, even though the surrender of their possessions caused the Company a loss estimated at £14,580 and halted the payout of dividends for four years. Hearne and Humphrey Marten were appointed to reoccupy their former posts and, although the HBC governors decided not to rebuild Prince of Wales's Fort, tried to carry on business as usual. But the stench of ignominious defeat was not that easy to dispel. The Chipewyan trade with Prince of Wales's had been disrupted and would never again reach its former levels. The inland HBC traders who once had come out for supplies now found only burned, empty posts. Besides losing prestige and two seasons' fur returns, the remaining Company men were so strapped for goods that they were forced to purchase ammunition from the hated pedlars to survive the winter. Their most faithful Indian allies on the Saskatchewan, who had boasted that the Englishmen were their countrymen, now moved within the trading sphere of the Montreal-based partnerships.

At Prince of Wales's Fort the Home Guard Indians, no longer in contact with their HBC confrères, scattered into the wilderness. Mary Norton, who had led a sheltered life – first pampered by her father and then indulged by her lover Hearne – was frightened by the French conquerors and bolted into the Barren Ground. Distraught and unaccustomed to the harsh demands of nomadic life, she soon starved to death among her Indian relations.

Another victim was the proud Matonabbee. His authority had become so dependent on the English presence, his sense of honour so closely bonded with the HBC and particularly to Hearne himself, that with the fort destroyed and, as he believed, its occupants taken out on the foreign ships to be drowned, there seemed no reason to continue living in shame. His spirit broken, Matonabbee decided that his sad circumstances demanded self-destruction. After he hanged himself, six of Matonabbee's beloved wives and four of their children, bereft of their protector, starved to death during the winter of 1783.

At about this time, the Chipewyan were ravaged by a smallpox epidemic spreading north from the Mississippi region; it claimed a staggering toll among the tribes of the Canadian northwest, including nearly half the Chipewyan. The journal of William Walker, then an HBC officer, paints a pathetic landscape of "Indians lying dead about the Barren Ground like rotten sheep, their tents left standing and the wild beasts devouring them." An even more dramatic description is contained in the journal of David Thompson, who reported that from the Chipewyan, the plague "extended over all the Indians of the forest to its northward extremity, and by the Sieux over the Indians of the Plains and crossed the Rocky Mountains. More men died in proportion than Women and Children, for unable to bear the heat of the fever they rushed into the Rivers and Lakes to cool themselves, and the greater part thus perished. The countries were in a manner depopulated, the Natives allowed that far more than one half had died, and from the number of tents which remained, it appeared that about three-fifths had perished; despair and despondency had to give way to active hunting both for provisions, clothing and all the necessaries of life; for in their sickness, as usual, they had offered almost everything they had to the Good Spirit and to the Bad to preserve their lives, and were in a manner destitute of everything."

By the fall of 1783 Hearne was back on Hudson Bay, greeted by the chilling news of the tragic deaths of the two people he most loved – his gallant comrade, Matonabbee, and the beguiling Mary Norton. Too bereft to express his own feelings for her, he instead entered in his journal a quote from the Restoration poet Edmund Waller, that ends with the line: "Here rests the pleasing friend and faithful wife."

"Reason shrinks from accounting for the decrees of Providence on such occasions as this," he wrote bitterly in his journal, adding a quizzical philosophical note about Matonabbee's having acted so much like a defeated Roman general falling on his own sword: "Poor man! He was a stranger to the lenity of European warriors, but naturally thought the French had taken us all out to sea in deep water and murdered us ... He is the only Northern Indian who, that I ever heard, put an end to his own existence."

The balance of Hearne's service was merely an assignment to be performed, no longer a vocation to be cherished. He erected a wooden hut that had been prefabricated in London ("a brown-paper building," he called it), five miles upstream from the destroyed fort, on the site James Knight had occupied sixty-five years before, and tried somewhat listlessly to reawaken Churchill's prospects. But with the move of the trade inland, the post had become dormant, to be run eventually by a single post-master; its decline into oblivion was halted only during the twentieth century by its revival as a grain port, air hub and terminus of the Hudson Bay Railway.

Devastated by the smallpox epidemic and disillusioned by the HBC's inability to defend Prince of Wales's Fort, the Chipewyan now seldom emerged from the Barrens, preferring to trade at Fort Chipewyan on the Athabasca, a rudimentary post founded by the independent trader Peter Pond near what is now Old Fort Bay.* Downstream was Lake Athabasca, the hub of the mighty Slave, Peace and Mackenzie river systems that drain the virgin beaver country of northern Alberta. Battling their way up the treacherous Peace into the Buffalo Head Hills and eventually to within sight of the awesome Rocky Mountains, the Montreal pedlars opened for trade a huge watery delta that proved to be the continent's richest storehouse of quality furs.

The Treaty of Paris (1783) ended the fighting, but peace did not filter through to the Canadian fur trade. The American Revolution had driven more and more of the eastern traders deep into the Canadian northwest where nothing disturbed their entrepreneurial inclinations. Aided by their mastery of the water routes, the feisty pedlars were now rampaging across the continent in solid control

---

*One of the Canadian frontier's more eccentric characters, Peter Pond spent his early life as a shoemaker, soldier and sailor, drifting into the Mississippi fur trade during the 1770s, having already killed a competitor in a duel. He moved north into previously untapped areas and in 1779 came out of the Chipewyan country with an astounding eighty thousand prime beaver skins. He was later accused of murdering a fellow-trader – the Swiss entrepreneur Jean-Etienne Waddens – and of being involved in yet another white killing and was eventually banished from the woods. He was the first to map the Mackenzie River system and to identify the tar sands of northern Alberta, later found to contain one of the largest reservoirs of oil in the earth's crust. Probably Pond's greatest contribution to the fur trade was that he solved its provisioning problem by developing the pemmican trade.

of the inland fur trade. By 1779, their seasonal, short-term partnerships had been formally amalgamated into the North West Company, dedicated to capturing control of Canada's fur trade from the venerable but vulnerable HBC.

Not so much a financial vehicle as a loose confederation of common interests, the North West Company enjoyed the advantage of being able to make decisions on the spot. Its inland partners and Montreal-based agents met each summer at Grand Portage on the northwest shore of Lake Superior to plan the next season's fur harvesting strategies and ways of outflanking the still-powerful but pompously inflexible Hudson's Bay Company.*

The Company's London-based Committeemen, who had successfully held the reins of their field operations as long as they were confined to the shores of Hudson Bay, found themselves attempting to rule a commercial empire they could no longer control. To keep up with leap-frogging Nor'Westers, the HBC in 1786 appointed William Tomison its first inland Governor, thereby relegating the bay posts to a subordinate trans-shipment function. But as Tomison moved upstream on the North Saskatchewan River (from Manchester House to Buckingham House to Edmonton House), the London-based governors lost track of what was happening and where, certain only that their commercial survival depended on outrunning their new rivals. Initially, whenever the two companies occupied adjacent posts, their traders had been friendly, often exchanging books and joining in football games. But as the supply lines grew longer† and each company's

---

* The Nor'Westers moved their base forty miles north to Fort William, now Thunder Bay, in 1805.

† The distance from the North West Company forts on the Athabasca River to Montreal was three thousand miles, one way.

resources became increasingly strained, they began to wage a war of attrition that would eventually exhaust them both.

The continent-wide confrontation, which quickly became one of the deadliest feuds in commercial history, was seen simply as a duel between the dull but dependable functionaries of the HBC and the dashing but extravagant fortune-seekers of the North West Company. Such oversimplifications did little to explain the significant differences between the two sets of traders, who shared very little except the quest for fur. The location of their home-bases – Montreal/Fort William and London/York Factory – also determined the character and function of their operations.

The HBC continued its century-old trading pattern in and out of Hudson Bay, but with one great difference – most of the furs had to be collected at posts inland rather than being transported to the bay by unpaid Indian paddlers. That meant having to set up, for the first time, a transportation network between the bay and the inland posts. In this, the Nor'Westers had a distinct advantage because they already had easy access to both the technology and the raw material required to make canoes.*

---

*One of the two main types they used was the *canot du maître*, up to forty feet in length, with a capacity of four tons and manned by ten paddlers. At the western end of Lake Superior, the goods were re-embarked into *canots du nord*, smaller vessels with half the carrying capacity but light enough for two men to lift across portages. Birch bark was the only indigenous material strong enough to carry economical loads, yet sufficiently light to be spun away from rock outcrops with a flick of the steersman's wrist. Cedar frames were bent (using heat) into half-circles, and the bark was sewn on with wattape made from spruce roots and then caulked with spruce gum. Two large canes shaped the gunwales and shorter rods of beechwood were formed into paddlers' thwarts.

There were no birch trees on the shores of Hudson Bay. The canoes built by the local Cree, makeshift at best, were not more than eighteen feet long with a carrying capacity of less than 350 pounds. These craft might have been suitable for the HBC trade if the Indians had been willing to become dependable hirelings, and to perform the necessary ferrying function. But such notions of servility were foreign to their nature; the receipt of free goods or payment of wages imposed no clearly recognized obligations. The usual result of assigning either a load of trade goods or a consignment of furs to the Indians' care was that neither was ever seen again. In 1775, Hearne had thought that one way to resolve this dilemma would be to have light timber skiffs built in England for assembly at York Factory, but when the ungainly craft arrived the HBC men refused to board them. By importing the necessary materials from their land-bound posts and teaching themselves the art of canoe-making, the HBC's traders were gradually able to overcome this early crisis, though for bulk freight they eventually settled on York boats, the double-ended, forty-foot-long craft originally designed at Albany in 1746. Descended from sturdy inter-island skiffs, they had a gaff-rigged sail and, being flat-bottomed, could be rolled on logs across portages while fully loaded.

At the time the HBC was facing its first major assault from the North West Company, it suffered not only from a shortage of usable canoes but also from a lack of crews to man them. For one thing, the NWC had a much larger manpower pool from which to draw recruits. Quebec after the conquest was estimated to have a population of about sixty thousand, and it increased rapidly thereafter with the highest birthrate ever recorded. As late as 1799, the HBC still had only 498 men posted in North America.* Space for bringing new employees across the Atlantic was severely limited by the fact that most of the supply ships' holds were crammed with trade goods, not recruits. England was at war for twenty-eight of the forty-seven years between the founding of Cumberland House and the amalgamation of the two companies in 1821. Orkney seamen were liable to press gangs. The wars of 1778–1783 and 1793–1815 had stripped the Orkneys of seamen at such a rate that at one point the HBC was permitted to recruit only locals shorter than five-feet-four – the height restriction of the Royal Navy. The Company's agent in the Orkneys could meet his recruitment quota only by taking on boys twelve to fourteen years old.† Another disruption was that gunsmiths in England had been seconded to the war effort, leaving for the fur hunt mostly badly made muskets that tended to explode and take part of a hand with them.

The obvious alternative – to hire *voyageurs* from Montreal – was not practical because of the complications caused by the short navigation seasons of Hudson Bay and the St Lawrence, and also because the HBC traders did not trust their NWC counterparts, whose short tempers ignited

---

*Of the total, 180 were still employed on the bay. At this time there were 1,276 Nor'Westers engaged in the fur trade, 903 of them west of Grand Portage.

†The combination of youthfulness and short stature prompted the Cree wife of James Spence, an HBC officer at York Factory, to comment as she watched the lilliputians leave a supply ship: "James, have you not always told me that the people in your country are as numerous as the leaves on the trees? How can you speak such a falsehood? Do we not all see plainly that the very last of them is come; if there were any more would these dwarfs have come here?"

more violence and distrust among the various tribes than the HBC was willing to tolerate.

Most of the Nor'Westers were bellicose risk takers unhampered by the discipline of a strict corporate structure. Steeped in the frontier ethic of sacrificing long-term stability for short-term gain, they based much of their commerce on an explosive mixture of rum and violence, indiscriminately exploiting Indian trappers and seducing their women. Edward Umfreville, an HBC officer who defected to the NWC, complained that "The Hudson's Bay traders have ingratiated themselves more into the esteem and confidence of the natives than the Canadians.... The great impudence and bad way of living of the Canadian traders have been an invincible bar to the emolument of their employers."

In practical terms, the carefree behaviour of some of the Montreal traders meant that, fearing possible reprisals, few dared to winter in the same locality twice. This precluded them from establishing stable business patterns. Although the Nor'Westers enjoyed a longer trading season (from April to October) than their bay-bound competitors and travelled through land that abounded with fish and game (in contrast to the "starving country" west of Hudson Bay), these advantages were overshadowed by the length of their supply line. Manufactured goods had to arrive in Montreal from overseas by November of one year so they could be sorted, bagged and baled for the voyage inland the following April. Taken by cart, and later canal, around the Lachine rapids, they were tallied and packed into the big freight canoes. Forty days and thirty-five portages later, they arrived at the tip of Lake Superior for trans-shipment to the smaller "northern" canoes. Only then could the Nor'Westers make for the fur country, still a thousand miles to the west, where they wintered. They then had to double back along the same route, so that a single transaction often took up to twenty-four months to complete.* William McGillivray, one of the North West Company's guiding spirits, complained about the difficulties of having to compete against a company that imported its goods at less than half the expense incurred by the Nor'Westers.

It was an uneven battle fought with all the passion of a Sicilian vendetta. But in the process of trying to outdo one another, the competing fur traders roughed out the contours of upper North America.

AN EARLY CASUALTY OF THE FUR TRADE WARS was Samuel Hearne. Now Governor of a narrowing fiefdom, he hunched in his Churchill hut, feeling far removed from the action and, though not yet forty, a full generation behind the youngsters taking over the fur trade. There was almost no Home Guard left around Churchill to stimulate local commerce; only a few Chipewyan still made the seven-month round trip to the bay; the whale fishery to the north bore lean results; and the bored Orkneymen in Hearne's service indulged in illegal private trading. Once the Company's showpiece, the post had become a dingy liability. Not surprisingly, the fretful London Committeemen blamed Hearne for the slack. Stung by their criticism and still grieving for his soulmates, Matonabbee and Mary Norton, who had defined his life, Hearne requested home leave. On August 16, 1787, he sailed out of Hudson Bay for the last time.

The valour of his Coppermine journey had scarcely prepared Hearne for the vanities of London society. The

---

*Another handicap was that the colony of Lower Canada had to collect taxes for local improvements; levies on fur exports provided an obvious and ready revenue amounting to about £20,000 a year. No penalties of that kind were exacted on the barren shore of Hudson Bay.

only surviving portrait of Hearne painted after his return to England depicts him as a pasty-faced and slightly wall-eyed dandy, done up in a lace blouse and blond wig. Yet in the field, fellow fur traders remembered him as a handsome and robust wilderness man with a ruddy complexion, who stayed in condition by racing against moose.

He chose to reside in modest quarters in Red Lion Square, spending most of the time preparing his journal for publication. He drew £600 from his savings with the Company, was reported to have joined the Bucks Club* and expended considerable energy defending himself from the harsh harassment of Alexander Dalrymple, who had published a pamphlet entitled *Memoir of a Map of the Lands about the North Pole* in which he questioned Hearne's accuracy as a surveyor.

The former chief cartographer of the East India Company and the future hydrographer of the British Admiralty, Dalrymple may have been history's busiest armchair geographer. Having drafted charts of a vast, mythical Pacific continent named the Great South Land, he was furious with Captain Cook when that doughty navigator not only could not locate it but proved it did not exist. The disinherited seventh son of a Scottish baronet, Dalrymple was an energetic manipulator who advocated exploitation of a land-bound "North West Passage" *through* America instead of around it. This scheme called for a grand amalgamation between the Hudson's Bay Company and the East India Company, then holding a

---

*The Order of the Bucks, a spurious offshoot of the Freemasons, was primarily a drinking club that met at various London pubs, its adherents exchanging bawdy tales and smashing glasses in the fireplaces. The only membership rule seems to have been that no Buck could wear the same waistcoat to more than one Bacchanal.

monopoly on trade to both China and India. It proposed combining their assets and spheres of influence to eliminate the Russian middlemen who were beginning to reap extraordinary profits from the American-Asian fur trade. Dalrymple visualized the furs being collected at a Pacific port located an "expedient distance from Hudson Bay," for trans-shipment to China. Conjuring up his improbable dreams behind the Ionic façade of East India House on London's Leadenhall Street, the cartographer pored over Hearne's charts and journals, borrowed from Samuel Wegg, the HBC Governor, and decided to make a few alterations.

Dalrymple still hoped to discover an easy passage from Hudson Bay to the West Coast and hated to admit that Hearne's observations shattered that possibility. If he could nudge Hearne's route map a few degrees southward, he reasoned, there was always a chance that a channel still existed to the north. The first part of his wish came true when he correctly calculated that Hearne had committed errors in his observations at the mouth of the Coppermine River. By recording his position as 71°55′N and 120°30′W (instead of 67°48′N and 115°47′W), Hearne had placed himself to be more than two hundred miles farther north than he actually was.

The error was excusable. Hearne had been reduced to making many observations by dead reckoning. His only instrument, an Elton quadrant that had been lying around York Factory for thirty years, was smashed on his way back to Hudson Bay. The Hearne observations were corrected half a century later by an 1821 expedition led by John Franklin across part of the same territory. Equipped with every advantage then known to science, Franklin returned to a hero's welcome and a knighthood.* In vivid

---

*Joseph Burr Tyrrell, the pioneering Canadian surveyor who traversed similar ground in 1893, wrote: "It has been my good

contrast, Hearne lived out his days working on his journal, noting that it was not meant "for those who are critics of geography" but for readers who might be "gratified by having the face of a country brought to their view." His health and his money gave out before the book was published.

Having spent so much of his life outside the money economy, Hearne tended to lend what modest funds he had with more generosity than discretion. The eighteenth century's equivalent of Lawrence of Arabia, Hearne had dared the impossible and succeeded, but in the process he assimilated the survival techniques of a civilization so foreign to his own that he found it impossible to thrive within the urban sophistication of England. It was only with the help of his old friend, the astronomer William Wales, that he was able to negotiate a good contract with the publishers of *Cook's Third Voyage*. His £200 advance for *Journey to the Northern Ocean* was relatively generous – certainly so when compared with the £10 Jane Austen was paid for some of her early novels. But only a month after he signed the publishing contract and a full three years before his book was actually printed, Hearne died of dropsy, a condition usually associated with cirrhosis of the liver.

Neither the man nor his book enjoyed more than a brief posthumous following. Hearne's austere style of northern travel was sniffed at by the traditionalists who still subscribed to more formal schools of discovery, even if their bravura approach was about to lead a whole

fortune to travel over parts of the same country through which Hearne had journeyed 123 years before me, and into which no white man had ventured in the intervening time. The conditions which I found were just as he describes ..." In the mid-1950s, the Geological Survey of Canada still carried notations on maps of the terrain crossed by Hearne warning: "relief data incomplete" and "highest elevation unknown."

generation of valiant men seeking the North West Passage to their deaths. Hearne's picaresque approach to life and his disregard for timetables and drawing room niceties made him something of an outcast even among his peers. It was the final irony of Hearne's magnificent but muted career that the chief disciple of his gentle, naturalistic approach to exploration would be Dr John Rae, a nineteenth-century HBC Chief Factor whose main claim to fame would be his discovery of the doomed Arctic expedition of Sir John Franklin, who was the most flamboyant exponent of the old-school-tie approach to exploration.

"Hearne was a contradictory mixture of indecision and persistency, and his weakness seemed always on the verge of overwhelming his strengths – but … he had a habit of coming out on top," concluded Gordon Speck, his biographer. Had Samuel Hearne's exploits been sponsored by a less circumspect agency than the Hudson's Bay Company, his magnificent Coppermine journey would have made him an international folk hero.

Instead, his only monument is the elegantly hand-chiselled grafitto – Sl. HEARNE JULY ye 2 1767 – he himself carved into the smoothly curving granite on tidewater at Sloops Cove, within sight of the long-abandoned palisades guarding Prince of Wales's Fort. The fortress's restored splendour haunts Hudson Bay to this day – silent and foreboding, its blocks of stone square and solid as if cut by the very hand of rectitude.

CHAPTER 15

THE ARCTIC FOX

John Rae, the tough HBC surgeon, never let up expanding his reports of cannibalism among the Franklin expedition's survivors. This went directly against the strictly held tenet of the Royal Geographical Society that English gentlemen do not devour one another.

THE BAY TRADERS WHO DARED TO CHALLENGE the northern wilderness of the American continent left precious little evidence of their gallant lives and tumultuous times. The climate's harsh cycles quickly devastated their ramshackle forts – flimsy, frost-heaved log shacks with jerry-rigged stockades – leaving sparse testimony to their passing. The trails they blazed and the unspeakable physical and psychological hardships they endured were recorded only in quill-pen reports to the Company's distant proprietors.

Across the ocean, apart from the occasional devoted Governor and his immediate entourage, most of the HBC Committeemen were choleric financiers with an appetite for fat dividends or titled nabobs with superannuated reputations. The HBC's early pictorial records consist almost entirely of canvases and engravings featuring such balance-sheet watchers. Framed in their gilt, these portly grandees peer beyond imagined northern horizons, their

ample jowls projecting the tranquil authority appropriate to their high station. Except for the official portraits of Prince Rupert, James II and the Duke of Marlborough, the HBC's trio of earliest eminences, they appear self-protectively couched in their brilliant plumage. The best of them have the grace to betray a touch of awkwardness, as if trapped by circumstance into a more formidable historic function than was their intent.

In Canada itself, the early artists concentrated on portraying the trappers and traders of the Lower St Lawrence, so that most Canadian canvases are populated by recent emigrants from Brittany, Normandy and the shores of Biscay. Men with woods-keen eyes and untrustworthy moustaches, they appear convinced that their trade routes, stretching into the mysterious continent's North and West, would yield gold or rare spices, not merely pungent furs.

One painting in this long gallery of merchant-adventurers stands out: Stephen Pearce's 1858 portrait of John Rae, M.D., LL.D., F.R.S., F.R.G.S., M.R.I., M.R.C.I., Chief Factor of the Hudson's Bay Company.* Rae's glance-over-shoulder pose seems neither hesitant nor overconfident. The artist has caught him in unaccustomed repose, fully in charge of his worth and his world. The broad back beneath the glossy finery, the handsome alertness of eye and clear, impatient flare of nostril – the composite is that of a Rhodes thirsty for empire.

---

*Stephen Pearce (1819–1904) was a London portrait and equestrian painter, whose best-known canvas was the *Arctic Council, Planning a Search for Sir John Franklin*. Pictured at an 1851 meeting (which did not take place) of the Council (which never existed) are ten of the Admiralty's most prestigious officers involved in the search for their missing colleague. The painting was exhibited widely and used as a prop to stir up public support for the Franklin search parties.

A wilderness physician, ardent naturalist and professional iconoclast, John Rae (1813–1893) was the HBC's most accomplished and most controversial northern explorer. He led four Arctic expeditions and mastered the Eskimo techniques of living off a savage land whose inhabitants had to scavenge for every morsel of food to fuel their bodies against the cold. In the course of his various journeys, he walked an incredible 23,000 miles. Unlike the earlier explorers of Samuel Hearne's vintage, who entered the primaeval wilderness as supercargo on Indian voyages, Rae was an exuberant solo adventurer of almost boyish enthusiasm. Yet his journeys were scientifically planned and parsimoniously executed. He reported, for example, that his search for the lost Franklin expedition had cost precisely £2 15s. per mile. A loyal Company man, Rae did everything on a typical barebones HBC budget. His 1847 journey of 1,200 miles, which connected John Ross's survey of "Boothia" with William Parry's explorations of Fury and Hecla Strait, cost less than £1,400, including Rae's salary. The Parry expedition, by contrast, cost the British taxpayer a lavish £120,000.

Alone among the land explorers of his day, Rae moved fastidiously from divination to observation, from experiment to experience, from vague hunch to logical conclusion. He was the paragon of *professional* Arctic explorers, mapping more than 1,700 miles of the continent's unknown upper crust where compass needles whirled in magnetic confusion. "John Rae," wrote the Manitoba-born Icelandic-American anthropologist Vilhjalmur Stefansson, "first combined the scientific point of view with leadership, imagination and physical prowess to a degree such as we recognize to have been needed by the Mayo brothers in surgery and the Wright brothers in aviation."

Rae's Arctic voyages moved the Company's trade frontier out of the thinning beaver swamps of the south into the Arctic watershed. His meticulous delineation of the eastern portion of the North West Passage came closest to fulfilling the original impulse that had led so many explorers to batter their vessels and themselves against the brute force of the wind and ice.

The supreme irony of John Rae's expeditions was that, though the great sea voyages northward of the protocol-encrusted admirals claimed all the glory, many of their routes had first been mapped by this remarkable Orkney-man. Shooting the roaring rivers and tacking north in twenty-foot dinghies, he trekked the void of that crucial *terra incognita* between King William Island and the Boothia Peninsula. His find of the tide-scoured strait that bears his name unlocked the seaway that would allow determined ships to enter the high latitudes and cross the top of the world. Rae resolved many of the remaining geographical blanks on North America's Arctic maps; what followed was mainly confirmation of detail, plus the symbolic race to reach the North Pole.

Despite this record, Rae's reputation soon lapsed into obscurity. His name is perpetuated mainly in the charts of untended corners of Canada's Arctic. As well as Rae Strait, there is a Rae Isthmus at the base of the Melville Peninsula, a Rae River (its mouth at Coronation Gulf) and a Fort Rae at the northern end of Great Slave Lake.

Such lack of recognition may have been partly due to his reputation as a renegade among explorers of his day. Rae's heretical notion was that northern travellers should harness the Arctic environment to their advantage instead of struggling against it. Rather than lugging ungainly tents, he sheltered in simple snowhouses he built at day's end – and many of his days were twenty hours long. He wore the slitted whale-bone snowgoggles of the Eskimo, used snowshoes and backpacks in place of heavily laden sleds and poked irreverent fun at "the gallant knights" who dabbled in the bravura of Arctic travel, lavishly victualled by the Admiralty for picnicking on the drift ice. Utterly unsnobbish, he cared passionately about the safety of his native companions, who readily volunteered to join his voyages. (The only loss of life in Rae's several expeditions was in 1841 at Bloody Fall, when Albert, an Eskimo interpreter, drowned because of the mistake of a steersman.)

Sir George Simpson, the Company's great nineteenth-century Governor, shared Rae's cantankerous contempt for gentlemen explorers, as witnessed in his trenchant comments about the 1821 Franklin expedition, then in the field. "Lt. Franklin, the officer who commands the party, has not the physical power required," sniffed Simpson. "He must have three meals per diem. Tea is indispensable, and with the utmost exertion he cannot walk above eight miles in one day, so that it does not follow if those gentlemen are unsuccessful that the difficulties are insurmountable."

This turned out to be a prophetic comment, because the last survivors of Franklin's doomed expedition eventually starved to death only three hundred miles west of spots where Rae had successfully wintered twice without incident. He came out of that wild land not only with his hide intact but with his men hauling more provisions than they had originally carried out with them from York Factory. On another expedition, Rae provided food for twenty-two of the twenty-seven months of his journey on the spot, half of it with his own rifle. Fresh meat was all-important. "A party situated as mine was, but with a commanding officer who could not shoot," he later commented, "would in all probability have either perished or have been unable to perform any lengthened spring journey."

John Rae pugnaciously subscribed to the unwritten first commandment of the northern aborigines which held that the measure of a true leader was that he must outperform his followers. This was in marked contrast to the operational code of the Royal Navy, based on pyramidal delegation that had officers detailing boatswains to order seamen to do the actual work. On "official" British expeditions, commanders required their accompanying native guides to procure local game; on Rae's journeys, it was he who hunted for his helpers, and his men seldom missed a meal. The most consistent characteristic of Rae's northern probes was the speed at which he travelled, loping relentlessly like a great Arctic fox across the frozen land. During the winter of 1851–52, he went on a forced march of 1,300 miles within the Arctic Circle, averaging 25 miles a day. He once raced by snowshoe the 100 miles over the Hudson Bay lowlands swamp, from Moose Factory to Fort Albany, in one twenty-four-hour span. At the age of forty-five when he was temporarily living in Hamilton, Ontario, Rae decided to visit Toronto for supper, snowshoed the 48 miles in seven hours flat and dined out the same evening without any particular sign of fatigue.

Despite his virile triumphs (and, more likely, because of them) Rae was disparaged by some contemporaries as indiscreet, mercenary and arrogant. Such charges were based mainly on his 1854 trip into the North, during which he met the Eskimos who sold him artifacts abandoned by members of the Franklin expedition, providing first word of their disappearance and the horrendous truth of their final days: that they had indulged in ghastly acts of cannibalism to keep themselves alive a bit longer. The shocking news of the find mesmerized the civilized world but caused unexpected abuse to be heaped on Rae. He was accused of not following up Eskimo tales to double-check their authenticity and of rushing back to London to claim the £10,000 reward for having discovered the fate of the Franklin voyagers.

The tough HBC surgeon never let up expanding his

reports of cannibalism among the Franklin expedition's survivors. This went directly against the strictly held tenet of the Royal Geographical Society that English gentlemen do not devour one another. In 1913, when Vilhjalmur Stefansson praised Rae before the Royal Geographical Society in London, a distinct chill greeted his remarks, even though the good doctor had by then been dead twenty years. "Rae," Stefansson later recalled, "was apparently considered in certain quarters as not having been quite in the high tradition of the gentleman explorer." Stefansson, an avid disciple of Rae's approach to Arctic survival, loved to quote the remark that an officer of the Royal Geographical Society had made to Sir Ernest Shackleton, the polar explorer. "Of course anybody can succeed," the armchair geographer had explained, "*if* he is willing to go native." After Rae uncovered the Franklin tragedy and recommended to Admiralty poohbahs that future expeditions seeking the North West Passage should adopt, as best they could, the Eskimos' method of travel, lifestyle and clothing, it was suggested: "The prime objective of foxhunting is not the killing of the fox, but the observance of good form during the pursuit and at the kill. The objective of polar explorations is to explore properly and not to evade the hazards of the game through the vulgar subterfuge of going native." The prevailing attitude was that those wretched Franklin survivors stumbling across frozen drifts and rock had been commendably correct in hauling along their swank silver tea services and crystal decanters of port, and that they might have been allowed to expire magnificently as true imperial gentlemen had it not been for the unspeakable evidence of "that dreadful Dr. Rae." He had tampered with the Victorian dream; by denying Franklin his essential heroic mystery he deprived the British of a martyr.

Rae also made enemies effortlessly. He maintained a

running feud with Rear-Admiral Sir Francis Beaufort, Hydrographer of the Royal Navy, who credited Rae's discoveries to British naval officers, particularly Sir Richard Collinson. "The (Royal Navy) Hydrographer," Rae wrote, "seemed astounded at my audacity or my 'antagonism,' as he was afterwards pleased to call it, in venturing his right coolly to hand over about 700 miles of Arctic coast surveyed by the Hudson's Bay Company's expeditions to a naval officer who visited the place a year later and made a survey far less minute."

When Rae threatened to go public with his charges against Beaufort, the Royal Navy hydrographers beat an ungracious retreat. But it was the Admiralty that ultimately stood in the way of Rae's being recommended for the knighthood his epic treks so clearly deserved.*

John Rae left no monuments except tumbled Arctic cairns. His legacy is the compendium of letters to the Company's Committee in London, detailing his commonsense approach to Arctic exploration and discussing the close-to-the-ground techniques Hudson's Bay Company men had adopted and adapted in the fur-trapping areas to the south. What allowed Rae his moment of greatness was that he never hesitated to push his luck, to take the calculated risk – plus the fact that his period of exploration coincided with renewed interest in discovery of the North West Passage.

---

* Rae's only published book, *Narrative of an Expedition to the Shores of the Arctic Sea in 1846 and 1847*, was completed shortly after his return to London in 1847 but not issued until 1850 because the publisher submitted the manuscript to the Admiralty for clearance – "so that any interest there may have been in the subject has passed away," Rae complained. "The narrative had also been so remodelled that I did not know my own bantling when it reached me about three years after I left England."

RAE OWED HIS REMARKABLE ABILITY TO COPE with northern hardships directly to his Orkney origins. He was born on September 30, 1813, the fourth in a family of nine, at the Hall of Clestrain near Stromness in the Orkney Islands. His father was Factor of the estate of Sir William Honyman. As a boy Rae grew up to the boom of the signal guns as their detonations echoed over the harbour, announcing the HBC supply ships. Young "Jock" Rae spent most of his boyhood like an apprentice Viking, stretching his sinews on the nearby granite cliffs, messing about in a twenty-foot dinghy, stalking grouse and deer with the family blunderbuss. "By the time I was fifteen," he later recalled, "I had become so seasoned as to care little about cold or wet, had acquired a fair knowledge of boating, was a moderately good climber among rocks, and not a bad walker for my age, sometimes carrying a pretty heavy load of game or fish ... on my back. All of these acquirements, often thought useless, were of great service to me in after life."

He left home at sixteen to attend the medical school in Edinburgh, graduated four years later and immediately signed up as ship's surgeon on the HBC supply packet *Prince of Wales*, bound for Moose Factory. There he made such a favourable impression on Chief Factor John George Mactavish that a letter was promptly forwarded to George Simpson, entreating the Governor to hire the young Orcadian as a permanent HBC employee. The ever-parsimonious Simpson replied that he would be pleased to do so and offered Rae a five-year contract at £100 per annum, "feeling satisfied, from the report I had of your character, and from what I know of your family, that you would do honour to my recommendation ... in the double capacity of Clerk and surgeon." Rae politely declined the clerkship but signed on as post physician for twenty-four months. The two years stretched to a decade, during which Rae tended the sick in lower James Bay, learned to trap and practised shooting game. Rae took hunting seriously, "acquiring some knowledge of the pecularities of the game I was in pursuit of."*

With hindsight, Rae realized something obvious, though a novelty for his time: that native skills could best deal with the problems of surviving in the wilderness. He befriended local Indians, went along on their hunting expeditions and compiled a Swampy Cree vocabulary. In August 1843, when Simpson was in Moose Factory for the Southern Department of Rupert's Land annual meeting, Rae received permission to leave on a brief furlough to visit friends in the south. It took him seventy days of canoeing and walking to reach Kingston, in Canada West; he then proceeded to Lachine, near Montreal, for another conference with Simpson. The Governor must have been impressed, because he proposed that Rae take charge of the Company's Rupert River District. The promotion was superseded when Simpson, who had been looking for the appropriate Company man to send "to delineate the Northern Shores from the Straits of the Fury and Hecla," picked Rae. "An idea has entered my head," the old voyageur wrote on May 11, 1844, "that you are one of the fittest men in the country to conduct an Expedition for the purpose of completing the Survey of the Northern Coast. As regards the management of the people and endurance of toil, either in walking, boating or starving,

---

*He became such an expert in animal habits that he later published a learned paper on the birds and mammals of Hudson Bay and the Arctic Coast. He contributed thirty articles to such publications as the *Anthropological Institute Journal* and *Nature* on such topics as the flow of sixty-one icebergs in Hudson Strait, "Sound of the Aurora," the "Unconscious Bias in Walking," "Right-Sidedness" and "Do Flying-fish Fly?"

I think you are better adapted for this work than most of the gentn. with whom I am acquainted."

Eager to begin, Rae first had to qualify as a surveyor. He walked out from the bay lowlands to Red River, only to find George Taylor, his would-be instructor, too ill to teach him. So Rae snowshoed 1,200 miles eastward, plodding past Rainy River and the Grand Portage to Sault Ste Marie through the drifting early winter snows. His only companion on this exhausting journey lost twenty-six pounds, but Rae managed to put two pounds more muscle on his 174-pound frame. Shortly afterward he walked to Toronto to study map-making with Lieutenant John Lefroy of the Observatory there.

As the HBC surgeon was about to launch himself on the prodigious Arctic voyages that would claim his attention for the next nine years, Rae's presence in York Factory was noted by Letitia Hargrave, the outpost's busy Boswell. "Dr. Rae came out with Dugald [Mactavish] to Moose," she wrote. "He had got his diploma unusually early and has not been home since nor (he says) opened a medical book for seven years. He is very good-looking and can walk 100 miles easily in two days. He has got a small observatory where he works away." Another contemporary witness was popular adventure writer R.M. Ballantyne, author of the 1848 story *Hudson's Bay*, who met Rae while travelling from York Factory to Norway House. "He was very muscular and active, full of animal spirits, and had a fine intellectual countenance. He was considered, by those who knew him well, to be one of the best snowshoe walkers in the service, was also an excellent rifle shot, and could stand an immense amount of fatigue.... He does not proceed as other expeditions have done – namely, with large supplies of provisions and ten or twelve men.... The party are to depend almost entirely on their guns for provisions, ... and penetrate into these unexplored regions on foot."

RAE'S ASSIGNMENT was to complete the surveys begun a decade earlier by Thomas Simpson and Peter Warren Dease, who in 1836 had been directed by the Hudson's Bay Company to examine the unexplored sections of the North American coastline. Thomas Simpson (a younger cousin of Sir George), who had earned a Master's degree at Aberdeen University before joining the company, had flourished in the HBC's service. He commanded brigades of canoes on the gruelling journeys from Montreal to Fort Garry and regularly snowshoed the seven hundred miles from Fort Garry to York Factory. When the London Committeemen reminded their Canadian viceroy that the time was opportune to resume the quest for the North West Passage so prominently mentioned in the HBC's original charter, Simpson detailed Thomas for the search. The younger Simpson applied his mixture of swashbuckling romanticism and Scottish toughness to make the most of his opportunity. After travelling down the Mackenzie River with Dease and a group of voyageurs, he turned west and marched to Point Barrow, the northernmost tip of what is now Alaska. He spent two winters frozen in at Fort Confidence on Great Bear Lake, then charged off down the Coppermine and turned east this time to explore past the Adelaide Peninsula and the desolate south coast of King William Land to the Gulf of Boothia.* He finally had to return without outlining

---

*By the end of 1839, anxious for orders to go north again, Simpson walked 1,910 miles in sixty-one days to the Red River settlement, where he arrived on February 2, 1840. The Arctic experiences had worked a strange alchemy on him. "I feel an irresistible presentment that I am destined to bear the Honourable Company's flag fairly through and out to the Polar Sea," he commented in his letters. "Fame I must have, but it must be alone." Good Company men do not write – or even think – like that. George Simpson had requested permission from London for Thomas to continue his search but when

the small but vital body of water later known as Rae Strait. This left unanswered two points that had to be resolved if a ship were to traverse the passage: whether or not Boothia was a peninsula, and whether or not King William was an island.

Rae proposed to resolve these riddles by sailing from Churchill to Repulse Bay; he would then sweep north and west to explore the Boothia land structure, as far as Fury and Hecla Strait. This, with the Thomas Simpson discoveries, would complete charting of the North West Passage.

The HBC explorer hand-picked a dozen Orkneymen to accompany him and on July 5, 1846 set sail northward out of Churchill in two twenty-foot dinghies named *Magnet* and *North Pole*, loaded to their gunwales. That first wintering near Repulse Bay remains a classic in the mastery of the Arctic. Rae and his brave band were among the first white men to sustain themselves through a dark Arctic winter entirely by their own exertions, although Rae found himself "very much reduced in flesh" and had to bring his belt in six inches. Nearly all Rae's wilderness survival techniques were tested on that journey.

The novelty of Europeans being self-sufficient in the Arctic was such that Rae's feat was not paralleled during the balance of the nineteenth century. The explorers and anthropologists who followed him (Charles Francis Hall, Frederick Schwatka and William H. Gilder, among

---

no immediate answer arrived, the dispirited explorer decided he would return to England to plead his cause in person. While travelling east through the Sioux country, on June 14, 1840, he was shot. (The presiding American Justice of the Peace who examined the death pronounced it a suicide, but the circumstances remain unexplained.) He missed by a few days learning that the HBC board had approved his next trip north, and that he had been awarded the Queen's Arctic Medal as well as a life pension of £100 per year.

others) depended for their sustenance on hired Eskimos. As well as Rae's unyielding conviction that the expedition leader must also be its chief hunter, his survival edicts called for strict simplicity of equipment, the first use of igloos by any European and the first reliance on Arctic peat and reindeer moss rather than imported coal or wood as chief wintering fuels.

On that faraway shore of Repulse Bay in 1846, Rae built a primitive fourteen-foot by thirty-foot stone abode which he dignified with the title Fort Hope.* Then he set out to prepare for the winter by shooting "120 deer, 62 caribou" and scores of ducks and geese. There being no room to store the meat, crypts consisting of a ton of rocks each had to be built around every shot animal to keep nomadic bears and wolves at bay. Deer blood was used to make soup, which was stored inside the animals' stomachs, the pouch being prepared by being turned inside out and rubbed with snow. "I have often seen our Hunter, Nibitabo," Rae noted, "when he had shot a deer, cut open the stomach and sup the contents with as much relish as a London alderman would a plate of turtle soup." The stone house, though ramshackle by southern standards, was solid enough and similar to the rustic country shelters he had visited in Orkney. Its loose slate slabs were held together by clay brought from the nearby estuary of the North Pole River; marine shells gave the mud an unusually high lime content. The clay never actually

---

*The Bay men who travelled above the treeline competed in the bravado with which they named the tiny huddles of rock where they endured the long winters. As well as Fort Hope, there was Fort Reliance, Fort Confidence, Fort Good Hope, Fort Defiance and Fort Resolution. Fort Hope survived remarkably well; when the site was visited by Major L.T. Burwash of Canada's Department of the Interior in late May 1926, part of Rae's 7-½-foot wall was still upright and the window apertures were still in place.

dried, but it froze soon enough. Rae was so well prepared that he had even brought four small double-pane windows with him. Moss was assembled for fuel; a roof was built using the dinghies' spars and oars, and the group settled in for the fearsome winter. The stone hut was quickly covered by permanent snow drifts and Rae recorded average daily *inside* temperatures of -13°F. He had meant to organize a school for his companions, but no one was really up to it. Rae whiled away the winter with the Malone edition of the complete plays of Shakespeare. The only way to keep it from freezing was to take the volume into bed with him each night, so that his body heat would thaw the pages.

The tiny fort's major failing was that it had no chimney; the belching smoke emitted by the cooking stove could escape only through the door, which consisted of a caribou skin stretched on boards. This meant that the door had to be kept open during cooking hours, allowing so much polar air to rush in that it was actually warmer when the stove was *not* in use. It took two hours to heat a kettle, and the cold grew so pervasive that the shivering men preferred to gnaw at raw or semi-cooked foods.

Rae was astoundingly inventive. When the expedition's pocket watches froze into uselessness and the one remaining timepiece suffered a broken mainspring, he ingeniously fashioned a replacement from a hacksaw blade. One craving he could not improvise on was his crew's addiction to tobacco. As supplies ran out, the smokers and chewers ate the linings of their coat pockets to taste that last grain of nicotine. But he did manage to celebrate Christmas with a dinner of "excellent venison steaks and plum-pudding," sips of brandy and a game of football. "Short as it was," he later noted about that most northern of football matches, "it was sufficiently amusing, for our faces were every moment getting frost-bitten, so as to require the continual application of the hand; and the rubbing, running about, and kicking the ball at the same time produced a very ludicrous effect. On the whole, I do not believe that a more happy company could have been found in America, large as it is."

The Company surgeon also taught his men to build igloos for exploration trips out from Fort Hope. The shape was that of a beehive, with spiralling walls six inches thick at the peak. Properly built, snow houses were so translucent that one could read and write inside under strong moonlight. The passage to the door was made very low and the bed placed four inches above the level of the top of the opening, so that it was out of the frigid draught. Once inside, the men slept under one reindeer skin, with Rae taking the outside berth, so he could make weather observations without waking the others. Any sleeper who wanted to turn had to notify all the others, in order that the troop could twist in unison – but gradually they became so accustomed to this manoeuvre that they could perform it without waking. Doing away with blankets, tents and furs (Rae wore only mole-skin drawers under his deerskins) reduced each man's travelling pack to thirty-five pounds from the ninety pounds carried by most Royal Navy expeditions. Any animal shot or caught was consumed in its entirety, right down to sucking the flavour out of a ptarmigan's claws and beak.

His devotion to exploration seldom distracted Rae from witnessing the small miracles of nature. At Repulse Bay, for example, he took time to note the camouflage methods of young seal: "It was interesting to watch the smaller kind of seal whilst the ice is forming, keeping breathing holes open ... by popping up their heads, and then throwing water and broken ice on the surface of the floe with their 'flippers,' where it freezes, and thus makes the ice after a time much thicker round the edge of the hole than elsewhere, raising it above the water level to the height of six or eight inches.... The advantage to the seal of the ice thus thickened ... is that, when the first fall of snow takes place, however slight, it drifts over and covers the opening … and acts the double part of concealing him from his enemies and of preventing the cold from freezing the opening."

Rae could be tough with his Orcadian subordinates. In the 1851 boat voyage from Coppermine to Victoria Land, he fired his second-in-command, Hector Aeneas Mackenzie, and packed him off back to Bear Lake "in consequence of his carelessness and inattention." But he was more than considerate in the way he dealt with the people already living on the land at a time few HBC traders recognized them as individual personalities. Thomas Misteagun, a bull-necked Ojibway from Norway House who acted as steersman on several Rae expeditions, was a special favourite. Rae was the first to defend the Eskimo way of life to the Foreign and Colonial Section of the Society of Arts in London. "The Eskimos," drawled Rae, "are said to be a diminutive race, but I have studied the true Londoner, and, without actual measurement of either, I am inclined to think that the Eskimos are as tall as the natives of our great city, and much heavier. When sitting, an Eskimo does not look short; the defect of stature is probably due to the shortness of the lower limbs…. I also tested their strength in lifting weights; some of my fellows I knew could lift 400 or 500 lbs. I found that the difference of strength between the two races was very slight, and in some cases so close that, fearing that some one might come who would excel my men or myself, I closed the competition.

"The Eskimos have a tradition that they came from the setting sun and that they crossed water, probably Bering Strait. They certainly, to my mind, give the idea of a former more civilized condition. They treat their wives kindly, are grateful for kindness, which they showed in a very delicate and pleasing manner, by bringing us seal's fat when we required it, and taking no pay, because, as they said, we had been kind to some of their old people who encamped near us, and were under our care when the younger persons were away hunting. The old folks left in our care never begged; and it was only by sending my servant to their tents that I found they were out of food. During the two seasons, the value of a sixpence was never stolen from us; on the contrary, we could with safety leave our tents in charge of some of the older people."

To outfox the elements, Rae freely copied Eskimo ways, adopting various of their survival techniques but also innovating for his own purposes. When he used dogs, for instance, it was in the forest-Indian tandem formation rather than the fan system preferred by the Eskimos of the Eastern Arctic. His affection for the northern people was returned. A century after his time in the Arctic, Eskimo elders clearly recalled their fathers' descriptions of the prolific feats of *Meeteelik* –"one who has a duck's spirit"– a reference to Rae's waddling gait as he marched northward in his skin outfit.

During that memorable first expedition to Repulse Bay, Rae set off on half a dozen probes north and west, tracing 655 miles of unmapped coastline. He proved conclusively that Boothia was a peninsula, thereby establishing that no North West Passage existed south of the 68th parallel. Although he remarked in his notes on the "celebrated navigator and discoverer, Sir John Franklin, whose protracted absence in the Arctic Sea is at present exciting so much interest and anxiety throughout England," he could not know that at one point in his travels he had been less than 150 miles from the inlet where Franklin's ships had been beset and held by a frozen sea. For the next seven years, John Rae's life and reputation would become intimately interwoven with the fate of that unlucky knight whose disappearance set off a series of the most dramatic rescue missions in northern exploration history.

JOHN RAE RETURNED to an England obsessed with the North West Passage. The expenditure of so much money, energy and human life was only vaguely connected with discovering a usable seaway across the top of the world. Each new voyage only helped confirm that the North West Passage was no passage at all, but a twisting, nigh-impassable furrow of glacial sea between bleak juts of land.

It was the mystical quest for glory that impelled nineteenth-century navigators to try to scrape their way through the white nightmare of heaving seas and grinding ice ridges, some the height of their ships' masts. They sailed on, praying to the leaden sky, mindful of Adam of Bremen's eleventh-century admonition of having ventured beyond "the darksome bounds of a falling world."

Captain James Cook's 1778 attempt to push into the Passage from the Pacific, halted by mountains of floating ice just three hundred miles east of Bering Strait, had eliminated the plausibility of easy commercial transit. But as J.J. Shillinglaw accurately observed in his *Narrative of Arctic Discovery*, the Polar Seas were "too eminently a theatre of British enterprise and daring to be long deserted." A less romantic reason was the mundane fact that the Royal Navy, in this hiatus between the Napoleonic and Crimean wars, did not have much to occupy its energies. The battle-hardened captains of Trafalgar were reaching out for flag rank and knighthoods, and the Arctic was a popular arena in which they could advance their individual causes.

They found an ally in Sir John Barrow, F.R.S., the crusty Secretary of the Admiralty, who was an ardent patron of Arctic expeditions. When William Scoresby, the leading whaler of his day, reported that the waters around Greenland had in the late summer of 1817 been virtually ice-free, Sir Joseph Banks, president of the Royal

Society, took up the call for northern discovery. (Scoresby also reported whales in both Pacific and Atlantic oceans with distinctive harpoons embedded in their blubber – weapons shot by whalers from opposite seas – thus proving to his satisfaction the existence of a North West Passage.) Banks began to press for a revision in the rules of the yet-unclaimed £20,000 reward (established in 1745) for discovery of the Passage, urging that £1,000 be awarded for every degree of latitude mapped beyond the 81st parallel. The combined lobbying talents of Banks and Barrow swayed Viscount Melville, First Lord of the Admiralty, to budget funds, ships and crews for a renewed assault on the Arctic.

Geographical knowledge of the far north had not advanced a great deal since Samuel Hearne had completed his epic trek down the Coppermine. There now followed an Admiralty-sponsored flotilla, including several historic voyages by Captain John Ross, who found a private patron in Felix Booth, the distiller of Booth's Gin. Ross turned back from exploring Lancaster Sound when he mistook a fog bank miasma for a mountain range. William Parry in a lucky season got as far as gravelly Banks Island, just 250 miles from the Beaufort Sea and the Passage's western outlet. By the end of these and other journeys, most of the northern coast had been charted, and the Arctic was revealed as a land-engirdled, ice-choked sea with narrow exits. But no one had yet braved the Passage itself.

Early in 1845, the Admiralty set its sights on one final onslaught. Britain was at peace; there were ample funds available to choreograph such an enterprise, and it seemed only fitting, after all the effort, that discovery of the North West Passage should not be left to some "foreigner." The ships selected were two stout bomb-ketches, *Erebus* and *Terror*. Barque-rigged three-masters displacing more than three hundred tons each, they were among the first Arctic ships equipped with curved copper hulls and steamdriven propellers. To command the voyage, which turned out to be both the greatest tragedy in the history of Polar exploration as well as its greatest catalyst, the Admiralty picked Sir John Franklin.

One of those full-faced professional sailors who cheerfully presided over England's dash for Empire, Franklin had joined the Royal Navy at fourteen as a cabin boy and survived shipwreck on Australia's coral reefs at sixteen. He had served under Nelson at Copenhagen and Trafalgar (as signals officer aboard *Bellerophon*), had had his ship sunk beneath him in the South Seas and had been wounded during the unsuccessful siege of New Orleans during the War of 1812. He had commanded the *Trent* in a futile attempt to reach a North East Passage by way of Spitzbergen and had completed land explorations down the Coppermine and Mackenzie rivers a half-century after Samuel Hearne's odyssey. With no naval assignments suitable to his seniority, Franklin had spent seven unhappy years as Governor of Van Diemen's Land (Tasmania), and even though he was by then fifty-nine years old, florid under his cocked hat and in far from perfect health, he was eager to sail north again. In 1845, the Admiralty gave him that chance. On May 19, manned by 139 officers and men and carrying a three-year food supply, the *Erebus* and *Terror* tacked carefully down the Thames. Fluttering her handkerchief at dockside was the captain's strong-willed wife, Lady Franklin. Seventeen years earlier, when his first wife Eleanor lay dying, Sir John had fallen in love with the beautiful Jane Griffin, a determined young Londoner. They were a perfect Victorian couple, theatrical and given to great gestures, happy to be extras in the extravaganza of Empire. Theirs was a conjugal love-pact of confluent ambitions. During their temporary absences from each other, the aching pair exchanged effusive love letters: "When all the latest energies of your nature are elicited," Jane wrote John on one occasion, "not I only, but all the world (most proudly I say even literally *all the world*) knows what you can do and England acknowledged with shouts which almost drowned the declaration, that: 'In the proud memorials of her fame/ Stands, linked with deathless glory/ Franklin's name.'"

Before leaving, Franklin and the Admiralty had agreed that search parties would be sent out only if no news of his whereabouts had reached England after two years. The only warning of imminent danger came from Dr Richard King, a maverick explorer-scientist who prophetically warned Barrow at the Admiralty that he was dispatching Franklin "to form the nucleus of an iceberg." After putting in at Stromness, the ships met in brief rendezvous with the whaler *Prince of Wales* on July 13, 1845 at Melville Bay just north of the 74th parallel. Then Franklin and his crew vanished into the polar mists.

By February 1847, when no word of the explorer's whereabouts had been received, the Admiralty arranged four search parties, including one headed by Sir John Richardson, who had accompanied Franklin on his two previous land trips into the Arctic. The expedition, which was to follow the Mackenzie to the sea and search eastward, brought Rae back into active service. He was loaned to the venture by the HBC and named second-in-command. Instead of his Orkney cronies from York Factory, Rae's fellow travellers this time were naval ratings and army sappers, whom he described as "the most awkward, lazy, careless set I ever had anything to do with." Richardson and Rae more than fulfilled their mandate, but raised no trace of Franklin. Sledding eastward from the mouth of the Mackenzie to Coronation Gulf, they were blocked by the hummocks of ice jamming Dolphin and Union Strait. After wintering at Great Bear Lake, Rae made another attempt, by himself, to reach Victoria Land, but got only as far as Cape Krusenstern.

The two men had an uneasy alliance. Richardson, then in his sixties and hardly in shape for Arctic expeditions, had nothing but kind words for his HBC colleague; Rae, on the other hand, ridiculed his elder companion at every turn. "My worthy Superior," he wrote sarcastically to Sir George Simpson on November 4, 1848, "has an excellent appetite and has filled out amazingly since the fatigues of his journey from the Coppermine. He had a habit of saying that everything in this country was conducted on the makeshift plan.... I made it pretty apparent that almost everything connected with the Expedition was a makeshift for such work – the men included."

At the end of these unsuccessful ventures, Rae was placed in charge of the HBC's Mackenzie River district, where the company ran into yet another round of disputes with the Admiralty. To Rae's dismay, as well as having to take care of the remaining members of the Richardson expedition, he was saddled with a posse of British tars under Lieutenant W.J.S. Pullen and his mate William Hooper of HMS *Plover*, a Franklin search team seeking winter shelter. Since the HBC posts were themselves critically short of supplies, the fourteen sailors had to be distributed among several outposts as much as eight hundred miles apart. "Although Pullen and Hooper are *vastly* civil to me," Rae complained to Simpson, "yet for some cause or another which I cannot divine, and which they themselves would probably be at a loss to explain, they have an evident dislike to the Company."

Then Rae cast his barb: "These self-sufficient donkies come into the country, see the Indians sometimes miserably clad and half-starved, the causes which they never think of inquiring into, but place it all to the credit of the Company quite forgetting that 10 times as much misery occurred in Ireland during the last few years, at the very door of the most civilized country in the world, than has happened in the Hudson's Bay Cos. Territories during the last 1/4 of century."

As usual, Letitia Hargrave had the last word. Writing from York Factory on March 29, 1849, her tone of decorous condescension reflected the HBC's view of the glory-seekers. "Dr. Rae & Sir John Richardson have come from the 'Sea' and did not see nor hear any thing of Captain Franklin. The Gentlemen in the Country all looked very polite as if Sir John's expedition was a very feasible exploit, but among themselves they either laughed at the whole turn out or seemed astonished that rational beings should undertake such a useless search."

BY THE SPRING of 1850, alarm over Sir John's fate had ricocheted from Admiralty memos to buskers' songs. Franklin had left England provisioned for three winters and had been gone for five. The Navy dispatched an Arctic armada led by its ablest captains (Richard Collinson, Robert McClure, Leopold McClintock and Horatio Austin, among them) to take up the search in earnest. Late summer of 1850 saw nine rescue vessels butting into the maze of pack ice in Lancaster Sound at the eastern end of the North West Passage, hooting their mournful foghorns into the impenetrable mists. Only McClure was at all successful. He spent the next four winters in the Arctic and, after abandoning his foundering ship in Mercy Bay, walked the North West Passage to Beechey Island – earning a £10,000 consolation prize. But apart from evidence of Franklin's first wintering at the entrance to Wellington Channel, the Royal Navy found nothing but clouds of ravenous sea birds and a lacy labyrinth of ice.

Franklin's disappearance had become a national preoccupation and, to some, an obsession. The mystery gained a new edge when the energetic Lady Franklin found solace with Joseph-René Bellot, the twenty-five-year-old son of a French blacksmith. London wags insisted that there was more to their tête-à-têtes than commiseration for the absent Sir John. Lady Franklin regally commanded the young Bellot to go forth on a mission north of the Boothia Peninsula. There he discovered the hellish strait that now bears his name, but not Sir John. Two years later, the gallant Bellot set off again but drowned en route to Lancaster Sound.

At this point, Rae was recruited by the Admiralty for yet another search. "The two journeys to Wollaston Land and Victoria Land, both made in one season, the first on foot and the second by boat, have ... never been equalled," wrote Professors J.M. Wordie and R.J. Cyriax in the introduction to their collection of Rae's correspondence. Travelling light and averaging 27 miles a day, Rae charged out on foot, deep into the still-blank Victoria sector, reaching to within 40 miles of Franklin's abandoned ships. He found only a bleached chunk of pinewood and an oak stanchion believed to have come from the *Erebus*. But during his journey, Rae mapped 725 miles of new coastline. When he returned to England, even the grumblers at the Royal Geographical Society were impressed and voted him their Founders' Gold Medal, then exploration's highest award. Rae stayed away from the ceremony, finding urgent business in the Orkneys on the day his medal was presented. Having made his declaration of independence, he promptly redesigned the medal to include special "clasps" commemorating each of his Arctic journeys – a move that hardly served to reduce his reputation for conceit.

Within half a year of his return, Rae had submitted a memorandum to the Hudson's Bay board, outlining his plan for a "survey of the northern shores of America, a small portion of which, along the west coast of Boothia, is all that now remains unexamined." He had in mind establishing, once and for all, whether King William Land was an island, and if there were a navigable channel east of it. Curiously, he did not even pretend that he was looking for Franklin, but in a letter to *The Times* on November 27, 1852, wrote guardedly: "I do not mention the lost navigators, as there is not the slightest hope of finding any trace of them in the quarter to which I am going." (Between 1847 and 1859, thirty-two expeditions searched for but did not find Franklin.)

By August 15, 1853 Rae was back in Repulse Bay, where he had spent his first Arctic season. With seven men, including two Eskimo interpreters, he wintered there, this time hunkered down in his own snowhut, reading Shakespeare by seal oil lamp in happy hibernation. He preferred suffering the tranquil cold of lone occupancy to inhaling the tobacco smoke of his wheezing companions. Retracing the steps of his previous winter, he easily found his old campsite, with his path worn into the lichens on the rocks where "it had been my habit to run and walk smartly up and down of a night to warm my feet before going to bed." March saw him restless; anticipating spring breakup of the ice, Rae set off to the northwest, and on April 21, near Pelly Bay (one of the two southern outcrops of the Gulf of Boothia), he met In-nook-poo-zhee-jook, an Eskimo of the Ilivilermiut group. At first the man shook his head when Rae asked him the standard queries whether he had seen any white men before. But when Rae persisted, In-nook-poo-zhee-jook revealed some spine-chilling news.

The explorer's field notes of that incident read: "Met a very communicative and apparently intelligent Esquimaux; had never met whites before, but said that a number of Kabloonans (white men), at least 35 or 40, had starved to death west of a large river a long distance off. Perhaps about 10 or 12 days' journey? Could not tell the distance, never had been there, and could not accompany us so far. Dead bodies seen beyond two large rivers; did not know the place. Could not or would not explain it on chart. Had seen a pillar of stones that had been built by whites near a small river. Top of pillar had fallen down ..."

Rae, noticing a gold-braid naval capband around In-nook-poo-zhee-jook's head, bought it from him and asked that he and his companions bring similar items to the wintering quarters at Repulse. Rae continued westward and northward into the empty muskox plains, establishing that King William Land was indeed an island and that Boothia was a peninsula; and he discovered Rae Strait. When he returned to Repulse, the Eskimos were waiting for him, and he learned for the first time that the estuary near which the rag-tag band of Franklin's men had perished must have been that of the Great Fish River, now named the Back River. In his subsequent reconstruction of these conversations, Rae reported:

In the spring, four winters past (1850), whilst some Eskimo families were killing seals near King William Land, forty white men were seen travelling in company southward over the ice and dragging a boat and sledges with them – None of the party could speak the Eskimo language so well as to be understood; but by signs the natives were led to believe the ship or ships had been crushed by the ice, and they were then going to where they expected to find some deer to shoot – They purchased a small seal from the natives ... At a later date the same season, but previous to the disruption of the ice, the corpses of some thirty persons and some graves were discovered on the Continent, and five dead bodies on an island near it, about a long day's journey to the north west of the mouth of a large stream, which can be no other than [Back's] Great Fish River... Some of the bodies were in a tent or tents; others were under the boat which had been turned over to form a shelter, and some lay scattered about in different directions. Of these seen on the Island, it was supposed that one was an officer (chief) as he had a telescope strapped over his shoulders, and his double barrelled gun lay underneath him ... There appears to have been an abundant store of ammunition ... a number of telescopes, watches, guns, compasses, etc., all of which seem to have been broken up, as I saw pieces of these different articles with the natives, and I purchased as many as possible, together with some silver spoons and forks, an Order of Merit in the form of a star, and a small plate engraved "Sir John Franklin, K.C.B."

It was at this meeting that Rae also heard evidence from the Eskimos that the last survivors had been forced to resort to cannibalism before themselves dying of hunger. "From the mutilated state of many of the bodies," he wrote, "and the contents of the kettles, it is evident that our wretched countrymen had been driven to the dread alternative of cannibalism as a means of sustaining life."

He now faced the dilemma of whether he should return north to check the truth of the Eskimos' story. Since the Franklin expedition had been gone nine years, Rae doubted that any of its members could possibly be alive. The Eskimos unanimously assured him that the last white man had died four years before. Rae knew he could not now reach the Great Fish River because the thaw had ruled out sledding and he did not have an appropriate boat. At the same time, he was keenly aware that a dozen search parties were about to head for the wrong area. He took the fateful decision to return immediately to York Factory so that he could embark on the HBC's supply ship, *Prince of Wales*, and return to England on her September sailing. His mission was complete. The northern mainland had been mapped; the mystery of the vanished Franklin had been solved.

JOHN RAE CARRIED WITH HIM TO ENGLAND forty-five relics that included personal belongings such as Sir John's monogrammed cutlery and a gold watch engraved with the name of *Erebus*'s ice-master, James Reid. Instead of being praised for resolving the Franklin riddle, he ran into a jangling chorus of abuse from a public recently unnerved by the news of the bloody charge of the Light Brigade.

One problem was that in his anxiety to document the evidence of the Franklin explorers' demise, Rae did not simultaneously stress the reasons why he had decided against going back north to validate the find. Letter-writers to *The Times*, soap-box orators at Hyde Park, strident parliamentarians, Cockney kitchen maids and parlour-bound explorers all began to question Rae's motives and tactics. Why had he not tried to confirm the Eskimo tales by exploring the Great Fish River where Franklin's men were supposed to have perished? Was it not possible that the aboriginal natives were protecting themselves or "other tribes" who might have killed, or even eaten, the Franklin survivors? And the ugliest question of all: had Dr Rae perhaps been in such a hurry to return so that he could be first to claim the £10,000 reward offered for news of Franklin's fate?

The good doctor answered these and other charges in his customary forthright style, pointing out that by the time he had taken possession of the relics at Repulse Bay, "it was too late to travel to the spot, as in the months of June and July it is all but impossible to travel across that country. In consequence of the melting of the snows, the low lands are perfectly flooded, and every little stream is converted into a torrent, shut in on each side by drift banks of snow, with perpendicular sides, so that there is no crossing them even with Halkett's* admirable little boats. Therefore having gained what I thought conclusive information, I came home to stop farther expeditions rather than wait a year to visit the spot."

This decision was applauded by the Admiralty, then preoccupied with the Crimean War. It decided to strike Franklin off the Navy List as officially dead, assuaging its collective conscience by posthumously promoting him to Rear-Admiral. But public suspicion was kept boiling by Rae's cool insistence on the veracity of the Eskimo reports of cannibalism among the members of the Franklin crew. Where was the proof? Surely, it was said, the piety, the courage, the *Britishness* of the men would never have permitted such an outrage. The integrity of these distinguished gentlemen-explorers, so went public opinion, ought not to be besmirched by "wild tales from a herd of savages."

Rae's credibility was somewhat weakened by the vehemence with which he claimed the £10,000 reward offered by the Admiralty "to any Party who shall by virtue of his efforts first succeed in ascertaining" the Franklin expedition's fate. Rae quite correctly pointed out that he could have known nothing of such a reward while isolated in Repulse Bay, but Lady Franklin voiced her opposition to giving him this impressive sum. She claimed that the truth about her husband's whereabouts had not been definitely resolved. In the United States, Chief Justice Charles Patrick Daly, president of the American Geographical Society, waded into the controversy with the charge that "Franklin had been murdered by the Indians,

---

*An early, rubber inflatable boat that could be rolled up flat and back-packed, it was designed by Lieutenant Peter Halkett, R.N.

who had already imbrued their hands in the blood of white travellers." In the popular press, the spectre of an Arctic tribe of man-eaters proved irresistible.

Charles Dickens, then editor of the popular weekly journal *Household Words*, sanctimoniously condemned the character of Canada's northern natives: "We believe every savage to be in his heart covetous, treacherous, and cruel; and we have yet to learn what knowledge the white man – lost, houseless, shipless, apparently forgotten by his race, plainly famine-stricken, weak, frozen, helpless, and dying – has of the gentleness of Esquimaux nature." A group of distinguished petitioners, supported by most of the principal British explorers of the day, implored the Prime Minister, Lord Palmerston, to finance one final expedition to clear up the mystery. But on June 19, 1856 the Admiralty awarded the £10,000 to Rae, who promptly doled out £2,000 to the members of his expedition.

It was Lady Franklin herself who pieced together the enduring puzzle of her husband's disappearance, with an expedition she financed in 1857, under Captain Leopold McClintock. At the mouth of the Great Fish River, in a rock cairn on Victory Point, McClintock and a companion found a document describing Franklin's last days. Sir John had died suddenly of natural causes on June 11, 1847 aboard his flagship; but scurvy had become epidemic, and seven hundred big tins of bully beef taken on in Greenland had gone rotten. The crew had panicked and abandoned their vessels, embedded in ice off the northernmost tip of King William Island. They then set off on their desperate journey by whaleboat and sled up the Great Fish River, aiming for the HBC post at Fort Reliance, 870 miles to the south. Without fur-lined jackets and wearing only regulation navy blue serge, they piled their sleds with a burdensome ten tons of dead weight, including a heavy cook stove, curtain rods, bedroom slip-

pers, silver polish and, of course, dress swords for the officers. By autumn they were in deep trouble. Finding their fowling pieces ineffective for shooting caribou, they resorted to hacking half-frozen limbs off their companions as they died and attempted to cook them in boots over open fires. By the time the snow geese flew north on their spring migration, the last of the Franklin survivors had the strength to shoot only half a dozen straggling birds; scattered feathers specked with blood were mute testimony to the men's final agony.

Documentation of the cannibalism first reported by Dr Rae came as the result of research done in the early 1980s by Dr Owen Beattie, a University of Alberta physical anthropologist. During expeditions to the south coast of King William Island, Beattie studied skeletal remains still recognizable as belonging to Franklin's sailors. As well as evidence of scurvy and lead poisoning (possibly due to faulty canning of meat carried by the ships), he found human bones that represented "a portable food supply ... and evidence of bone alteration (e.g., saw marks) due to human activity." The skulls and arm and leg bones, preserved by the Arctic cold, showed marks of having been sawn or hacked off human bodies and were found long distances from corresponding pelvic girdles and rib cages. Beattie theorized that the skulls were carried along as a portable delicacy: the panicked survivors must have supped on the brains of their fallen comrades.

DESPITE ITS GRISLY ENDING, the Franklin tragedy only helped stimulate the quest for the North West Passage. Almost forty expeditions had been mounted. But nobody won the great geographical prize until 1906, when the *Gjoa*, a tiny forty-seven-ton Oslo herring smack skippered by the great Norwegian explorer Roald Amundsen, finally bunted its way across in three winters. As a young man,

Amundsen had been thrilled by the accounts of the Franklin search and had hardened himself by sleeping with the windows open, even in winter. It was another thirty-six years before the next vessel, the eighty-ton RCMP schooner *St Roch*, navigated the whole Passage.* Both ships had utilized the tiny strait that Rae had discovered, east of King William Island.

In that sense at least, Rae had been the explorer who made possible the transit of North America's Arctic shore, the dream of adventure-bound navigators since John Cabot's second voyage nearly four centuries earlier.

It was unfortunate that Rae became so firmly connected in the public mind with his discovery of the Franklin relics. As Prof. H.B. Neatby has pointed out: "The man who perhaps ought to rank highest in the roll of the great discoverers from the Bay is chiefly remembered as playing a minor part in the tragedy of the *Erebus* and *Terror*."

HALFWAY THROUGH HIS LIFE and at the top of his form, John Rae uncharacteristically opted for retirement. Whether this was the result of physical exhaustion from his adventures or was simply a planned, gradual retreat is a matter of conjecture. He was only forty-three when he resigned from the HBC in 1856, having paid £2,000 for a Canadian-built schooner which he vaguely thought might be used for northern exploration. The vessel

---

*Two startling crossings of the North West Passage were the 1969 voyage of the giant U.S. oil tanker *Manhattan*, which had a hold large enough to accommodate all of the cargo carried by all of the ships used in Arctic exploration since Sir Martin Frobisher's great gold hunt, and the 1984 trip by the Swedish cruise ship *Lindblad Explorer*, which took ninety-eight sightseers across the Passage, at $22,000 per ticket, and completed the journey that had tormented so many explorers in just twenty-two uneventful, luxurious days.

foundered in a Great Lakes storm and except for a brief jaunt up a glacier in Greenland, Rae never went north again. He did take part in a survey for a telegraph land-line from Winnipeg to the Pacific Coast in 1864 and tested the challenges of the Fraser River canyons in a small dugout canoe.

Strikingly handsome, he married in 1860 Catharine Jane Alicia, the third daughter of Major George Ash Thompson of Ardkill, County Londonderry. Thus began his senatorial phase. He collected honorary degrees, was elected to the Royal Society, the British Association for the Advancement of Science and similar august bodies; he lectured, hacked away at chess, made stabs at an autobi-ography.* Except for one brief bit of mischief, he spent the last four decades of his life in self-satisfied hibernation, dividing his time between London and his shooting grounds at Westhill in the Orkneys. The only spark of his former venturesome self flared up in 1883 when, at the age of seventy, the old maverick full of Victorian vigour unexpectedly volunteered for the Orkney Artillery, listing himself incongruously as "Private J. Rae, M.D., F.R.S." He promptly won a rifle-shooting prize at Wimbledon.

The last of the HBC's great pathfinders, Rae died a decade later and was buried in the slate-walled churchyard of St Magnus' Cathedral in Kirkwall, capital of the Orkneys. The pettifogging pashas at the Royal Geo-graphical Society whose honour he had insulted by rejecting their boarding-school view of Arctic exploration did not forgive him, even in death. He had been a gargoyle on the cathedral of Empire. The Geographers were not officially represented at his funeral, and it was a full

---

*The manuscript came to light in 1967. It ends in mid-sentence just as Rae is about to describe his April 1854 discovery of the Franklin fragments.

four years before a brief and condescending obituary appeared in the Society's journal.

The measure of Rae's contempt for such hide-bound dithering has been caught by the sculptor who fashioned the effigy atop his tomb. Dressed in fringed buckskin and wrapped in a buffalo sleeping robe, he clutches a hunter's stone rifle in his lifelike hand. John Rae's bearded face is set in confident repose – the proud look of a man who managed to prosper where trees cannot live and quaffed more than his share of deer-blood soup.

EPILOGUE

BY THE END OF THE EIGHTEENTH CENTURY, *the Company of Adventurers could look back on the conquest of Hudson Bay and salute the successful launch of a reassuringly profitable commercial enterprise. The tentative probes by Groseilliers, Radisson, Bayley, Knight, Kelsey, Henday and Hearne had been amply rewarded. What was now emerging on their parchment maps was the outline of a great inland trapping preserve, all theirs, but increasingly menaced by the freebooters from Montreal.*

The pioneering traders who sat out their lives in the forts around the bay may have been unremarkable men, castaways in a tight-fisted land, yet they achieved something truly magnificent.

They endured.

Although colonies are founded as fragments of the mother societies from which they spring, a scarcely perceptible sea-change took place on the shores of Hudson Bay that transformed the early squatters and their spartan ethic. Despite the Company's rigid control, their individual attachments to their motherland eroded. To survive, they began to borrow from native lore, becoming more attuned to the cadence of their self-imposed exile, growing in confidence and sense of purpose as their mission expanded to the taming of a sub-continent.

The sleep by the frozen sea and its haunting, ice-bound serenity was over. From among the ranks of the Bay men in the next century would spring a dynasty of merchant princes who gave voice and deed to transforming these first awkward stirrings into the world's largest commercial empire – and, eventually, into a new nationality.

APPENDICES

The Charter

This is the full text of the original charter, now housed in the Company's boardroom in Toronto, that Charles II granted to Prince Rupert and his seventeen fellow investors on May 2, 1670. The wording is reproduced from *Charters, Statutes, Orders in Council, &c, relating to the Hudson's Bay Company*, published by the Company in London, 1949.

THE ROYAL CHARTER for incorporating
The Hudson's Bay Company, A.D. 1670.

CHARLES the SECOND By the grace of God King of England Scotland France and Ireland defender of the faith &c

To ALL to whome these presentes shall come greeting

WHEREAS Our Deare and entirely Beloved cousin Prince Rupert Count Palatyne of the Rhyne Duke of Bavaria and Cumberland &c Christopher Duke of Albemarle William Earle of Craven Henry Lord Arlington Anthony Lord Ashley Sir John Robinson and Sir Robert Vyner Knightes and Baronettes Sir Peter Colliton Baronett Sir Edward Hungerford Knight of the Bath Sir Paul Neele Knight Sir John Griffith and Sir Phillipp Carteret Knightes James Hayes John Kirke Francis Millington William Prettyman John Fenn Esquires and John Portman Cittizen and Goldsmith of London have at theire owne great cost and charge undertaken an

EXPEDICION for Hudsons Bay in the North west part of America for the discovery of a new Passage into the South Sea and for the finding some Trade for Furrs Mineralls and other considerable Commodityes and by such theire undertakeing have already made such discoveryes as doe encourage them to proceed further in pursuance of theire said designe by meanes whereof there may probably arise very great advantage to us and our Kingdome

AND WHEREAS the said undertakers for theire further encouragement in the said designe have humbly besought us to Incorporate them and grant unto them and theire successors the sole Trade and Commerce of all those Seas Streightes Bayes Rivers Lakes Creekes and Soundes in whatsoever Latitude they shall bee that lye within the entrance of the Streightes commonly called Hudsons Streightes together with all the Landes Countryes and Territoryes upon the Coastes and Confynes of the Seas Streightes Bayes Lakes Rivers Creekes and Soundes aforesaid which are not now actually possessed by any of our Subjectes or by the Subjectes of any other Christian Prince or State

NOW KNOW YEE that Wee being desirous to promote all Endeavours tending to the publique good of our people and to encourage the said undertakeing HAVE of our especiall grace certaine knowledge and meere mocion Given granted ratifyed and confirmed And by these Presentes for us our heires and Successors

DOE give grant ratifie and confirme unto our said Cousin Prince Rupert Christopher Duke of Albemarle William Earle of Craven Henry Lord Arlington Anthony Lord Ashley Sir John Robinson Sir Robert Vyner Sir Peter Colleton Sir Edward Hungerford Sir Paul Neile Sir John Griffith and Sir Phillipp Carterett James Hayes John Kirke Francis Millington William Prettyman John Fenn and John Portman That they and such others as shall bee admitted into the said Society as is hereafter expressed shall bee one Body Corporate and Politique in deed and in name by the name of the Governor and Company of Adventurers of England tradeing into Hudsons Bay and them by the name of the Governor and Company of Adventurers of England tradeing into Hudsons Bay one Body Corporate and Politique in deede and in name really and fully for ever for us our heirs and successors

WEE DOE make ordeyne constitute establish confirme and declare by these Presentes and that by the same name of Governor

& Company of Adventurers of England Tradeing into Hudsons Bay they shall have perpetuall succession And that they and theire successors by the name of the Governor and Company of Adventurers of England tradeing into Hudsons Bay bee and at all tymes hereafter shall bee persons able and capable in Law to have purchase receive possesse enjoy and reteyne Landes Rentes priviledges libertyes Jurisdiccions Franchyses and hereditamentes of what kinde nature and quality soever they bee to them and theire Successors And alsoe to give grant demise alien assigne and dispose Landes Tenementes and hereditamentes and to doe and execute all and singuler other thinges by the same name that to them shall or may apperteyne to doe   And that they and theire Successors by the name of the Governor and Company of Adventurers of England Tradeing into Hudsons Bay may pleade and bee impleaded answeare and bee answeared defend and bee defended in whatsoever Courtes and places before whatsoever Judges and Justices and other persons and Officers in all and singuler Accions Pleas Suitts Quarrells causes and demandes whatsoever of whatsoever kinde nature or sort in such manner and forme as any other our Liege people of this our Realme of England being persons able and capable in Lawe may or can have purchase receive possesse enjoy reteyne give grant demise alien assigne dispose pleade defend and bee defended doe permitt and execute   And that the said Governor and Company of Adventurers of England Tradeing into Hudsons Bay and theire successors may have a Common Seale to serve for all the causes and busnesses of them and theire Successors and that itt shall and may bee lawfull to the said Governor and Company and theire Successors the same Seall from tyme to tyme at theire will and pleasure to breake change and to make a new or alter as to them shall seeme expedient

AND FURTHER WEE WILL And by these presentes for us our Heires and successors

WEE DOE ordeyne that there shall bee from henceforth one of the same Company to bee elected and appointed in such forme as hereafter in these presentes is expressed which shall be

called The Governor of the said Company   And that the
said Governor and Company shall or may elect seaven of
theire number in such forme as hereafter in these presentes is
expressed which shall bee called the Comittee of the said
Company which Comittee of seaven or any three of them
together with the Governor or Députy Governor of the said
Company for the tyme being shall have the direcion of the
Voyages of and for the said Company and the Provision of the
Shipping and Merchandizes thereunto belonging and alsoe the
sale of all merchandizes Goodes and other things returned in
all or any the Voyages or Shippes of or for the said Company
and the mannageing and handleing of all other business affaires
and thinges belonging to the said Company

AND WEE WILL ordeyne and Grant by these presentes for us
our heires and successors unto the said Governor and Company
and theire successors that they the said Governor and Company
and theire successors shall from henceforth for ever bee ruled
ordered and governed according to such manner and forme as is
hereafter in these presentes expressed and not otherwise And
that they shall have hold reteyne and enjoy the Grantes
Libertyes Priviledges Jurisdiccions and Immunityes only hereafter
in these presentes granted and expressed and noe other And for
the better execucion of our will and Grant in this behalfe

WEE HAVE ASSIGNED nominated constituted and made And by
these presentes for us our heires and successors

WEE DOE ASSIGNE nominate constitute and make our said
Cousin PRINCE RUPERT to bee the first and present Governor of
the said Company and to continue in the said Office from the
date of these presentes untill the tenth of November then next
following if hee the said Prince Rupert shall soe long live
and soe until a new Governor bee chosen by the said Company
in forme hereafter expressed

AND ALSOE WEE HAVE assigned nominated and appointed And
by these presentes for us our heires and Successors

WEE DOE assigne nominate and constitute the said Sir John
Robinson Sir Robert Vyner Sir Peter Colleton James Hayes
John Kirke Francis Millington and John Portman to bee the

seaven first and present Committees of the said Company from the date of these presentes until the said tenth Day of November then alsoe next following and soe untill new Committees shall bee chosen in forme hereafter expressed

AND FURTHER WEE WILL and grant by these presentes for us our heires and Successors unto the said Governor and Company and theire successors that itt shall and may bee lawfull to and for the said Governor and Company for the tyme being or the greater part of them present at any publique Assembly commonly called the Court Generall to bee holden for the said Company the Governor of the said Company being alwayes one from tyme to tyme to elect nominate and appoint one of the said Company to bee Deputy to the said Governor which Deputy shall take a corporall Oath before the Governor and three or more of the Committee of the said Company for the tyme being well truely and faithfully to execute his said Office of Deputy to the Governor of the said Company and after his Oath soe taken shall and may from tyme to tyme in the absence of the said Governor exercize and execute the Office of Governor of the said Company in such sort as the said Governor ought to doe

AND FURTHER WEE will and Grant and by these presentes for us our heires and Successors unto the said Governor and Company of Adventurers of England tradeing into Hudsons Bay and theire Successors That they or the greater part of them whereof the Governor for the Tyme being or his Deputy to bee one from tyme to tyme and at all tymes hereafter shall and may have authority and power yearely and every yeare betweene the first and last day of November to assemble and meete together in some convenient place to bee appointed from tyme to tyme by the Governor or in his absence by the Deputy of the said Governor for the tyme being And that they being soe assembled itt shall and may bee lawfull to and for the said Governor or Deputy of the said Governor and the said Company for the tyme being or the greater part of them which then shall happen to bee present whereof the Governor of the said Company or his Deputy for the tyme being to bee one to elect and

nominate one of the said Company which shall bee Governor
of the same Company for one whole yeare then next following
which person being soe elected and nominated to bee Governor
of the said Company as is aforesaid before hee bee admitted to
the Execucion of the said Office shall take a Corporall Oath
before the last Governour being his Predecessor or his Deputy
and any three or more of the Committee of the said Company
for the tyme being that hee shall from tyme to tyme well and
truely execute the Office of Governor of the said Company in
all thinges concerneing the same and that Ymediately after the
same Oath soe taken hee shall and may execute and use the
said Office of Governor of the said Company for one whole
yeare from thence next following and in like sort Wee will
and grant that as well every one of the above named to bee of
the said Company or fellowshipp as all other hereafter to bee
admitted or free of the said Company shall take a Corporall
Oath before the Governor of the said Company or his Deputy
for the tyme being to such effect as by the said Governor and
Company or the greater part of them in any publick Court to
bee held for the said Company shall bee in reasonable and
legall manner sett down and devised before they shall bee
allowed or admitted to Trade or traffique as a freeman of the
said Company

AND FURTHER WEE WILL and grant by these presentes for us
our heires and successors unto the said Governor and Company
and theire successors that the said Governor or Deputy Governor
and the rest of the said Company and theire successors for the
tyme being or the greater part of them whereof the Governor or
the Deputy Governor from tyme to tyme to bee one shall and
may from tyme to tyme and at all tymes hereafter have power
and authority yearely and every yeare betweene the first and
last day of November to assemble and meete together in some
convenient place from tyme to tyme to be appointed by the
said Governor of the said Company or in his absence by his
Deputy and that they being soe assembled itt shall and may
bee lawfull to and for the said Governor or his Deputy and the
Company for the tyme being or the greater part of them which

then shall happen to bee present whereof the Governor of the said Company or his Deputy for the tyme being to bee one to elect and nominate seaven of the said Company which shall bee a Committee of the said Company for one whole yeare from thence next ensueing which persons being soe elected and nominated to bee a Committee of the said Company as aforesaid before they bee admitted to the execucion of theire Office shall take a Corporall Oath before the Governor or his Deputy and any three or more of the said Committee of the said Company being theire last Predecessors that they and every of them shall well and faithfully performe theire said Office of Committees in all thinges concerneing the same And that imediately after the said Oath soe taken they shall and may execute and use theire said Office of Committees of the said Company for one whole yeare from thence next following

AND MOREOVER Our will and pleasure is And by these presentes for us our heires and successors

WEE DOE GRANT unto the said Governor and Company and theire successors that when and as often as itt shall happen the Governor or Deputy Governor of the said Company for the tyme being at any tyme within one yeare after that hee shall bee nominated elected and sworne to the Office of the Governor of the said Company as is aforesaid to dye or to bee removed from the said Office which Governor or Deputy Governor not demeaneing himselfe well in his said Office

WEE WILL to bee removeable at the Pleasure of the rest of the said Company or the greater part of them which shall bee present at theire publick assemblies commonly called theire Generall Courtes holden for the said Company that then and soe often itt shall and may bee lawfull to and for the Residue of the said Company for the tyme being or the greater part of them within convenient tyme after the death or removeing of any such Governor or Deputy Governor to assemble themselves in such convenient place as they shall thinke fitt for the eleccion of the Governor or Deputy Governor of the said Company and that the said Company or the greater part of them being then and there present shall and may then and there before theire departure from the said place elect and nominate one other of the said Company to bee Governour or Deputy Governor for the said Company in the place and stead of him that soe dyed or was removed which person being soe elected and nominated to the Office of Governor or Deputy Governor of the said Company shall have and exercize the said Office for and dureing the residue of the said yeare takeing first a Corporall Oath as is aforesaid for the due execucion thereof And this to bee done from tyme to tyme soe often as the case shall soe require

AND ALSOE Our Will and Pleasure is and by these presentes for us our heires and successors

WEE DOE grant unto the said Governor and Company that when and as often as itt shall happen any person or persons of the Committee of the said Company for the tyme being at any tyme within one yeare next after that they or any of them shall bee nominated elected and sworne to the Office of Committee of the said Company as is aforesaid to dye or to be removed from the said Office which Committees not demeaneing them-selves well in theire said Office Wee will to be removeable at the pleasure of the said Governor and Company or the greater part of them whereof the Governor of the said Company for the tyme being or his Deputy to bee one that then and soe often itt shall and may bee lawfull to and for the said Governor and the rest of the Company for the tyme being or the greater part of them whereof the Governor for the tyme being or his Deputy to bee one within convenient tyme after the death or removeing of any of the said Committee to assemble themselves in such convenient place as is or shall bee usuall and accustomed for the eleccion of the Governor of the said Company or where else the Governor of the said Company for the tyme being or his Deputy shall appoint And that the said Governor and Company or the greater part of them whereof the Governor for the tyme being or his Deputy to bee one being then and there present shall and may then and there before theire Departure from the said place elect and nominate one or more of the said Company to bee of the Committee of the said Company in the place and stead of him or them that soe died or were or was soe removed which person or persons soe elected and nominated to the Office of Committee of the said Company shall have and exercize the said Office for and dureing the residue of the said yeare takeing first a Corporall Oath as is aforesaid for the due execucion thereof and this to bee done from tyme to tyme soe often as the case shall require And to the end the said Governor and Company of Adventurers of England Tradeing into Hudsons Bay may bee encouraged to undertake and effectually to prosecute the said designe of our more especial grace certaine knowledge and meere Mocion

WEE HAVE given granted and confirmed And by these presentes for us our heires and successors

DOE give grant and confirme unto the said Governor and Company and theire successors the sole Trade and Commerce of all those Seas Streightes Bayes Rivers Lakes Creekes and Soundes in whatsoever Latitude they shall bee that lie within the entrance of the Streightes commonly called Hudsons Streightes together with all the Landes and Territoryes upon the Countryes Coastes and confynes of the Seas Bayes Lakes Rivers Creekes and Soundes aforesaid that are not already actually possessed by or granted to any of our Subjectes or possessed by the Subjectes of any other Christian Prince or State with the Fishing of all Sortes of Fish Whales Sturgions and all other Royall Fishes in the Seas Bayes Isletes and Rivers within the premisses and the Fish therein taken together with the Royalty of the Sea upon the Coastes within the Lymittes aforesaid and all Mynes Royall aswell discovered as not discovered of Gold Silver Gemms and pretious Stones to bee found or discovered within the Territoryes Lymittes and Places aforesaid And that the said Land bee from henceforth reckoned and reputed as one of our Plantacions or Colonyes in America called *Ruperts Land*

AND FURTHER WEE DOE by these presentes for us our heires and successors make create and constitute the said Governor and Company for the tyme being and theire successors the true and absolute Lordes and Proprietors of the same Territory lymittes and places aforesaid And of all other the premisses

SAVING ALWAYES the faith Allegiance and Soveraigne Dominion due to us our heires and successors for the same

TO HAVE HOLD possesse and enjoy the said Territory lymittes and places and all and singuler other the premisses hereby granted as aforesaid with theire and every of theire Rightes Members Jurisdiccions Prerogatives Royaltyes and Appurtenances whatsoever to them the said Governor and Company and theire Successors for ever

TO BEE HOLDEN of us our heires and successors as of our Mannor of East Greenwich in our County of Kent in free and common Soccage and not in Capite or by Knightes Service

YEILDING AND PAYING yearely to us our heires and Successors for the same two Elkcs and two Black beavers whensoever and as often as Wee our heires and successors shall happen to enter into the said Countryes Territoryes and Regions hereby granted

AND FURTHER our will and pleasure is And by these presentes for us our heires and successors

WEE DOE grant unto the said Governor and Company and to theire successors that itt shall and may be lawfull to and for the said Governor and Company and theire successors from tyme to tyme to assemble themselves for or about any the matters causes affaires or buisnesses of the said Trade in any place or places for the same convenient within our Dominions or elsewhere and there to hold Court for the said Company and the affaires thereof   And that alsoe itt shall and may bee lawfull to and for them and the greater part of them being soe assembled and that shall then and there bee present in any such place or places whereof the Governor or his Deputy for the tyme being to bee one to make ordeyne and constitute such and soe many reasonable Lawes Constitucions Orders and Ordinances as to them or the greater part of them being then and there present shall seeme necessary and convenient for the good Government of the said Company and of all Governors of Colonyes Fortes and Plantacions Factors Masters Mariners and other Officers employed or to bee employed in any of the Territoryes and Landes aforesaid and in any of theire Voyages and for the better advancement and contynuance of the said Trade or Traffick and Plantacions and the same Lawes Constitucions Orders and Ordinances soe made to putt in use and execute accordingly and at theire pleasure to revoake and alter the same or any of them as the occasion shall require   And that the said Governor and Company soe often as they shall make ordeyne or establish any such Lawes Constitucions Orders and Ordinances in such forme as aforesaid shall and may lawfully impose ordeyne limitt and provide such paines penaltyes and punishmentes upon all Offenders contrary to such Lawes Constitucions Orders and Ordinances or any of them as to the said Governor and Company for the tyme being or the greater part of them then and there being present the said Governor or his Deputy being alwayes one shall seeme necessary requisite or convenient for the observacion of the same Lawes Constitucions Orders and Ordinances   And the same Fynes and Amerciamentes shall and may by theire Officers and Servantes from tyme to tyme to bee appointed for that purpose levy take and have to the use of the said Governor and Company and theire successors without the impediment of us our heires or successors or of any the Officers or Ministers of us our heires or successors and without any accompt therefore to us our heires or successors to bee made   All and singuler which Lawes Constitucions Orders and Ordinances soe as aforesaid to bee made WEE WILL to bee duely observed and kept under the paines and penaltyes therein to bee conteyned soe alwayes as the said Lawes Constitucions Orders and Ordinances Fynes and Amerciamentes bee reasonable and not contrary or repugnant but as neare as may bee agreeable to the Lawes Statutes or Customes of this our Realme

AND FURTHERMORE of our ample and abundant grace certaine knowledge and meere mocion

WEE HAVE granted and by these presentes for us our heires and successors DOE grant unto the said Governor and Company and theire Successors That they and theire Successors and theire

Factors Servantes and Agentes for them and on theire behalfe and not otherwise shall for ever hereafter have use and enjoy not only the whole Entire and only Trade and Traffick and the whole entire and only liberty use and priviledge of tradeing and Trafficking to and from the Territory Lymittes and places aforesaid but alsoe the whole and entire Trade and Trafficke to and from all Havens Bayes Creekes Rivers Lakes and Seas into which they shall find entrance or passage by water or Land out of the Territoryes Lymittes or places aforesaid and to and with all the Natives and People Inhabitting or which shall inhabit within the Territoryes Lymittes and places aforesaid and to and with all other Nacions Inhabitting any the Coaste adjacent to the said Territoryes Lymittes and places which are not already possessed as aforesaid or whereof the sole liberty or priviledge of Trade and Trafficke is not granted to any other of our Subjectes

AND WEE of our further Royall favour And of our more especiall grace certaine knowledge and meere Mocion

HAVE granted and by these presentes for us our heires and Successors DOE grant to the said Governor and Company and to theire Successors That neither the said Territoryes Lymittes and places hereby Granted as aforesaid nor any part thereof nor the islandes Havens Portes Cittyes Townes or places thereof or therein conteyned shall bee visited frequented or haunted by any of the Subjectes of us our heires or successors contrary to the true meaneing of these presentes and by vertue of our Prerogative Royall which wee will not have in that behalfe argued or brought into Question

WEE STREIGHTLY Charge Command and prohibitt for us our heires and Successors all the subjectes of us our heires and Successors of what degree or Quality soever they bee that none of them directly or indirectly doe visit haunt frequent or Trade Trafficke or Adventure by way of Merchandize into or from any the said Territoryes Lymittes or Places hereby granted or any or either of them other then the said Governor and Company and such perticuler persons as now bee or hereafter shall bee of that Company theire Agentes Factors and Assignes unlesse itt bee by the Lycence and agreement of the said Governor and

Company in writing first had and obteyned under theire Common
Seale to bee granted upon paine that every such person or
persons that shall Trade or Trafficke into or from any the
Countryes Territoryes or Lymittes aforesaid other then the said
Governor and Company and theire Successors shall incurr our
Indignacion and the forfeiture and the losse of the Goodes
Merchandizes and other thinges whatsoever which soe shall
bee brought into this Realme of England or any the Dominions
of the same contrary to our said Prohibicion or the purport or
true meaneing of these presentes for which the said Governor
and Company shall finde take and seize in other places out of
our Dominions where the said Company theire Agentes Factors
or Ministers shall Trade Traffick inhabitt by vertue of these our
Letters Patente As alsoe the Shipp and Shippes with the Furniture
thereof wherein such goodes Merchandizes and other thinges
shall bee brought or found the one halfe of all the said
Forfeitures to bee to us our heires and successors and the other
halfe thereof

WEE DOE by these Presentes cleerely and wholly for us our
heires and Successors Give and Grant unto the said Governor
and Company and theire Successors

AND FURTHER all and every the said Offenders for theire said
contempt to suffer such other punishment as to us our heires or
Successors for soe high a contempt shall seeme meete and
convenient and not to bee in any wise delivered untill they
and every of them shall become bound unto the said Governor
for the tyme being in the summe of one thousand Poundes at
the least at noe tyme then after to Trade or Traffick into any of
the said places Seas Streightes Bayes Portes Havens or Territoryes
aforesaid contrary to our Expresse Commandment in the behalfe
herein sett downe and published

AND FURTHER of our more especiall grace

WEE HAVE condiscended and granted And by these presentes
for us our heires and Successors DOE grant unto the said Governor
and Company and theire successors That Wee our heires and
Successors will not Grant liberty lycence or power to any
person or persons whatsoever contrary to the tenour of these

our Letters Patente to Trade trafficke or inhabit unto or upon any the Territoryes lymittes or places afore specifyed contrary to the true meaneing of these presentes without the consent of the said Governor and Company or the most part of them

AND of our more abundant grace and favour to the said Governor and Company

WEE DOE hereby declare our will and pleasure to bee that if it shall soe happen that any of the persons free or to bee free of the said Company of Adventurers of England Tradeing into Hudsons Bay who shall before the goeing forth of any Shipp or Shippes appointed for

A VOYAGE or otherwise promise or agree by Writeing under his or theire handes to adventure any summe or Sumes of money towardes the furnishing any provision or maintainance of any voyage or voyages sett forth or to bee sett forth or intended or meant to bee sett forth by the said Governor and Company or the more part of them present at any Publick Assembly commonly called theire Generall Court shall not within the Space of twenty Dayes next after Warneing given to him or them by the said Governor or Company or theire knowne Officer or Minister bring in and deliver to the Treasurer or Treasurers appointed for the Company such summes of money as shall have been expressed and sett downe in writeing by the said Person or Persons subscribed with the name of the said Adventurer or Adventurers that then and at all Tymes after itt shall and may bee lawfull to and for the said Governor and Company or the more part of them present

WHEREOF the said Governor or his Deputy to bee one at any of theire Generall Courtes or Generall Assemblyes to remove and disfranchise him or them and every such person and persons at their wills and pleasures and hee or they soe removed and disfranchised not to bee permitted to trade into the Countryes Territoryes and Lymittes aforesaid or any part thereof nor to have any Adventure or Stock goeing or remaineing with or amongst the said Company without the speciall lycence of the said Governor and Company or the more part of them present at any Generall Court first had and obteyned in that behalfe

Any thing before in these presentes to the contrary thereof in any wise notwithstanding

AND OUR WILL AND PLEASURE is And hereby wee doe alsoe ordeyne that itt shall and may bee lawfull to and for the said Governor and Company or the greater part of them whereof the Governor for the tyme being or his Deputy to bee one to admitt into and to bee of the said Company all such Servantes or Factors of or for the said Company and all such others as to them or the most part of them present at any Court held for the said Company the Governor or his Deputy being one shall be thought fitt and agreeable with the Orders and Ordinances made and to bee made for the Government of the said Company

AND FURTHER Our will and pleasure is And by these presentes for us our heires and Successors

WEE DOE grant unto the said Governor and Company and to theire Successors that itt shall and may bee lawfull in all Eleccions and By-Lawes to bee made by the Generall Court of the Adventurers of the said Company that every person shall have a number of votes according to his Stock that is to say for every hundred poundes by him subscribed or brought into the present Stock one vote and that any of these that have Subscribed lesse then one hundred poundes may joyne theire respective summes to make upp one hundred poundes and have one vote joyntly for the same and not otherwise

AND FURTHER of our expeciall grace certaine knowledge and meere mocion

WEE DOE for us our heires and successors grant to and with the said Governor and Company of Adventurers of England Tradeing into Hudsons Bay that all Landes Islandes Territoryes Plantacions Fortes Fortificacions Factoryes or Colonyes where the said Companyes Factoryes and Trade are or shall bee within any the Portes and places afore lymitted shall bee ymediately and from henceforth under the power and command of the said Governor and Company theire Successors and Assignes

SAVING the faith and Allegiance due to bee performed to us our heires and successors as aforesaid and that the said Governor and Company shall have liberty full Power and authority to appoint and establish Governors and all other Officers to governe them And that the Governor and his Councill of the severall and respective places where the said Company shall have Plantacions Fortes Factoryes Colonyes or Places of Trade within any the Countryes Landes or Territoryes hereby granted may have power to judge all persons belonging to the said Governor and Company or that shall live under them in all Causes whether Civil or Criminall according to the Lawes of this Kingdome and to execute Justice accordingly And in case any crime or misdemeanor shall bee committed in any of the said Companyes Plantacions Fortes Factoryes or Places of Trade within the Lymittes aforesaid where Judicature cannot bee executed for want of a Governor and Councill there then in such case itt shall and may bee lawfull for the chiefe Factor of that place and his Councill to transmitt the party together with the offence to such other Plantacion Factory or Fort where there shall bee a Governor and Councill where Justice may bee executed or into this Kingdome of England as shall bee thought most convenient there to receive such punishment as the nature of his offence shall deserve

AND MOREOVER Our will and pleasure is And by these presentes for us our heires and Successors

WEE DOE GIVE and grant unto the said Governor and Company and theire Successors free Liberty and Lycence in case they conceive it necessary to send either Shippes of War Men or Amunicion unto any theire Plantacions Fortes Factoryes or Places of Trade aforesaid for the security and defence of the same and to choose Commanders and Officers over them and to give them power and authority by Commission under theire Common Seale or otherwise to continue or make peace or Warre with any Prince or People whatsoever that are not Christians in any places where the said Company shall have any Plantacions Fortes or Factoryes or adjacent thereunto as shall bee most for the advantage and benefitt of the said Governor and Company and of theire Trade and alsoe to right and recompence themselves upon the Goodes Estates or people of those partes by whome the said Governor and Company shall susteyne any injury losse or dammage or upon any other People whatsoever that shall any way contrary to the intent of these presentes interrupt wrong or injure them in theire said Trade within the said places Territoryes and Lymittes granted by this Charter and that itt shall and may bee lawfull to and for the said Governor and Company and theire Successors from tyme to tyme and at all tymes from henceforth to Erect and build such Castles Fortifications Fortes Garrisons Colonyes or Plantacions Townes or Villages in any partes or places within the Lymittes and Boundes granted before in these presentes unto the said Governor and Company as they in theire Discrecions shall thinke fitt and requisite and for the supply of such as shall bee needefull and convenient to keepe and bee in the same to send out of this Kingdome to the said Castles Fortes Fortifications Garrisons Colonyes Plantacions Townes or Villages all Kindes of Cloathing Provision of Victuales Ammunicion and Implementes necessary for such purpose paying the Dutyes and Customes for the same As alsoe to transport and carry over such number of Men being willing thereunto or not prohibited as they shall thinke fitt and alsoe to governe them in such legall and reasonable manner as the said Governor and Company shall thinke best and to inflict punishment for misdemeanors or impose such Fynes upon them for breach of theire Orders as in these Presentes are formerly expressed

AND FURTHER Our will and pleasure is And by these presentes for us our heires and Successors

WEE DOE grant unto the said Governor and Company and to theire Successors full Power and lawfull authority to seize upon the Persons of all such English or any other our Subjectes which shall saile into Hudsons Bay or Inhabit in any of the Countryes Islandes or Territoryes hereby Granted to the said Governor and Company without theire leave and Licence in that Behalfe first had and obteyned or that shall contemne or disobey theire Orders and send them to England and that all and every Person and Persons being our Subjectes any wayes Imployed by the said Governor and Company within any the Partes places and Lymittes aforesaid shall bee lyable unto and suffer such punnishment for any Offences by them committed in the Partes aforesaid as the President and Councill for the said Governor and Company there shall thinke fitt and the meritt of the offence shall require as aforesaid. And in case any Person or Persons being convicted and Sentenced by the President and Councill of the said Governor and Company in the Countryes Landes or Lymittes aforesaid theire Factors or Agentes there for any Offence by them done shall appeale from the same That then and in such Case itt shall and may be lawfull to and for the said President and Councill Factors or Agentes to seize upon him or them and to carry him or them home Prisoners into England to the said Governor and Company there to receive such condigne punnishment as his Cause shall require and the Law of this Nacion allow of and for the better discovery of abuses and injuryes to bee done unto the said Governor and Company or theire Successors by any Servant by them to bee imployed in the said Voyages and Plantacions itt shall and may be lawfull to and for the said Governor and Company and theire respective Presidentes Chiefe Agent or Governor in the partes aforesaid to examine upon Oath all Factors Masters Pursers Supra Cargoes Commanders of Castles Fortes Fortificacions Plantacions or Colonyes or other Persons touching or concerning any matter or thing in which by Law or usage an Oath may bee administered soe as the said Oath and the matter therein conteyned bee not repugnant but agreeable to the Lawes of this Realme

AND WEE DOE hereby streightly charge and Command all and singuler our Admiralls Vice-Admiralls Justices Mayors Sherriffs Constables Bayliffes and all and singuler other our Officers Ministers Liege Men and Subjects whatsoever to bee ayding favouring helping and assisting to the said Governor and Company and to theire Successors and to theire Deputyes Officers Factors Servantes Assignes and Ministers and every of them in executeing and enjoying the premisses as well on Land as on Sea from tyme to tyme when any of you shall thereunto bee required

ANY STATUTE Act Ordinance Proviso Proclamacion or restraint heretofore had made sett forth ordeyned or provided or any other matter cause or thing whatsoever to the contrary in any wise notwithstanding

IN WITNES WHEREOF we have caused these our Letters to bee made Patentes WITNESS OURSELF at Westminster the second day of May in the two and twentieth yeare of our Raigne

By Writt of Privy Seale

The First Adventurers

Eighteen men and one woman joined Prince Rupert as early investors in the Hudson's Bay Company. They were worldly wise risk-takers and connected to the very top of contemporary English society.

SIR GEORGE CARTERET

Samuel Pepys reckoned him the richest man in England, and it was Carteret's personal credit, based on his hoard of bullion safely secured in continental vaults, that rescued the Royal Navy after Charles II had exhausted his treasury. A bold acquisitor who turned piracy into a superbly organized enterprise, Sir George was an intensely loyal monarchist of serious mien who alone dared openly challenge Charles's morals. When Charles and a party of dissolute hangers-on visited Sir George's Cranborne Lodge after a day's hunt in Windsor Forest – and, according to Pepys, "all fell a-crying for joy, being maudlin and kissing one another, in such a pickle as never people were" – Carteret sternly warned his monarch "of the necessity of having a show of Religion in the Government, and sobriety …"

Patriotically and personally proud of his fiscal indispensability to the Stuarts, Sir George confided to Pepys: "I have almost brought things to such a pass as I mean to do, that the King will not be able to whip a cat, but that I will be at his tail."

A tough-and-tumble man of action, Carteret had been bred a sea-boy, one of the hereditary rulers of Jersey and Sark in the Channel Islands. As a young commander in Charles I's navy, he took his six-hundred-ton gunship, the *Antelope*, on a punitive expedition against the Barbary pirates at Salee, blockaded their harbours and sank their galleys by boarding them at night with crews from small shallops. He eventually forced the Sultan of Morocco to sue for peace and give up 270 captives he had been holding for ransom. It was the treasure from this expedition that formed the foundation of Carteret's fortune. Only two years later (in 1639), having demonstrated a talent for accounting – and having proved his loyalty by sharing his booty with the Stuart treasury – he was made Comptroller of the Royal Navy. Wooed by the Parliamentarians, he stayed loyal to the king and spent the early part of the Civil War organizing ordnance and munition supplies for Rupert and the Royalists in the west of England from his cross-Channel base at St Malo.

As Lieutenant-Governor of Jersey, Carteret had easily recaptured his family's rockbound island from the Parliamentarians, and when the Stuarts were driven out of England, he welcomed the royal retinue-in-exile to Jersey. On February 16, 1649, only seventeen days after his father's execution, Charles II was proclaimed king of England in one of several such ceremonies, and Carteret was waving his hat in the air and urging his ragtag corps of drummers to roll their snares with regal resonance.

Until he was again driven off Jersey to seek refuge in France, Carteret used his strategically located little realm as a base for some highly creative privateering, picking off fat Round-head merchantmen to harvest funds for the Stuart cause as well as his own coffers. Even as a pirate, Carteret was superbly organized, using swift schooner-rigged galleys specially built to his design at St Malo; equipped with cannon, each was manned by a crew of thirty-six marines at the oars. These lean marauders preyed on the rotund Dutch three-masters rolling home along the Channel from the colonies and on lumbering coasters delivering salt, grain, sugar and timber to Cromwell's England. The captured goods were sold to France. The loyal but unsentimental Carteret then turned most of the funds over to the exiled court, always being careful to track the precise value and making sure he received red-sealed pledges of prime Crown real estate in return.

After the Restoration, Carteret was rewarded with the

promised acreage. He was appointed Vice-Chamberlain of the King's Household (in effect, manager of Charles II's finances), a member of the Privy Council, Treasurer of the Royal Navy and Commissioner of the Board of Trade. Elected Member of Parliament for Portsmouth, he spent most of his energies priming the financial pumps to keep the Royal Navy afloat. Pepys, who served as the Admiralty's overworked under-secretary and often felt the sting of his temper, described Carteret as "the most passionate man in the world." Carteret tried valiantly but unsuccessfully to keep Charles II solvent, though he had few such problems himself. He built a magnificent country retreat near the gates of Windsor Castle, where Prince Rupert was Warden, and the two aging former pirates joined forces in such commercial ventures as exploiting a local coal mine, manufacturing cannon and founding the Royal African and Hudson's Bay companies.

After helping introduce Radisson and Groseilliers to the British Court, Sir George maintained his interest in the fur venture and was its first recorded investor, subscribing an initial £20 on December 10, 1667. Because at the time he was being investigated by Parliament for irregularities in naval accounts and there had been a public outcry about the extent of his private holdings, Carteret placed the HBC stock in the name of his son, Philip.*

One of the HBC's original Committeemen, Sir George took over the Company's direct management as Deputy Governor in 1674, at Rupert's request. The combination of Rupert and Carteret was the source of court favour and of the managerial impetus that allowed the fledgling Hudson's Bay Company to overcome its initial growing pains.

---

*The younger Carteret was an awkward young man whom Pepys had to coach in the arts of matrimony, and whose young bride the busybody chronicler kissed in her matrimonial bed before drawing the curtains on her wedding night. Philip lost his life on May 28, 1672 in the sea battle of Solebay, off Suffolk, and the HBC stock was transferred back to his father.

ANTHONY ASHLEY COOPER, LORD ASHLEY, EARL OF SHAFTESBURY

A permanently stooped aristocrat with a polio-crippled body and a festering ulcer that had to be drained through a silver tap implanted in his side, Shaftesbury shifted political allegiance with the frequency and subtlety of the hue changes in a pigeon's iridescent neck feathers. Gilbert Burnet, a contemporary cleric who mapped his transferences of loyalty, marvelled: "I never saw any man equal to him in the art of governing parties, and of making himself part of them." What deflected Shaftesbury from fast-footed opportunism to luminous statemanship – he is recognized as the father of modern liberalism – was his stubborn and, for his time, heretic insistence that political parties must rule with the consent of their subjects and that civil and religious liberties were a right rather than a privilege.

He was orphaned and succeeded to his father's baronetcy before he was ten. Although his inheritance was plundered by lawyers and administrators, Shaftesbury clawed his way back, and the shrewd management of his remaining assets made him immensely wealthy. His estates earned an annual income at the peak of his success of more than £23,000. A gentleman-commoner at Oxford, the future Earl of Shaftesbury was admitted to Lincoln's Inn and at nineteen won election as M.P. for Tewkesbury, but he could not assume his seat because he was under age. Initially committed to the standard of Charles I, he went over to the Parliamentarians to be commander-in-chief of the forces in Dorset. A firm believer in religious tolerance and constitutional monarchy, he was a political pragmatist who loved to quote Sir Walter Raleigh's admonition, "Whosoever shall follow truth too near the heels, it may haply strike out his teeth." Shaftesbury was one of the twelve commissioners appointed by the House of Commons to journey to Breda and invite Charles II back to England. Created a peer as Lord Ashley, appointed Chancellor of the Exchequer and named to the Privy Council after the Restoration, he became one of the leading English expansionists of his day. Senior member of the Council of Trade and Plantations, he was a proprietor in the

1663 Carolina grant and helped develop British claims in Barbados, the Bahamas and Guinea, investing his personal funds heavily in the Royal African and Royal Fisheries companies. In most of these ventures, Shaftesbury was a close partner of Rupert.

Shaftesbury had purchased his first HBC stock at Rupert's behest on August 22, 1668 and eventually owned one-tenth of the Company. The two men were natural allies, partly because Shaftesbury's staunch Presbyterianism was closely allied to Rupert's religious leanings and partly because each recognized in the other a compulsion to promote England's naval and commercial supremacy by circumventing the pettiness of court life. Both men came under the influence of Shaftesbury's physician and private secretary, the eminent scientist-philosopher John Locke.*

Shaftesbury, a member of Charles II's infamous cabal from 1670, was appointed Lord Chancellor of England, the highest secular office in the land. He supported the liberal Declaration of Indulgence on the grounds that trade flourished where merchants were not subjected to interference because of religious affiliation, but later appeared to contradict his stand by sponsoring measures to exclude Roman Catholics from public office. Shaftesbury spent the rest of his life struggling to survive this dilemma, caused in large part by his growing conviction that the Catholic Duke of York's succession to England's throne was against the national interest.

Despite these travails, which saw Shaftesbury eventually deprived of his high office and incarcerated three times in the Tower of London, he spent a year managing the HBC as Deputy Governor, and between 1673 and 1676 was one of the

---

*Locke, who spent fifteen of his most productive years on Shaftesbury's staff, helped draft charters for the exploitation and colonization of the Carolinas, Jamaica, Barbados and the Bahamas while working on his famous *Essay Concerning Human Understanding*. There is circumstantial but not documentary evidence that he also had a hand in preparing the royal charter for the Hudson's Bay Company.

Company's most active Committeemen. As president of the Council of Trade and Plantations, the last important post he held under Charles II, Shaftesbury was able to provide frequent support to the young enterprise.

Prince Rupert was one of the few members of the Royal entourage who did not abandon Shaftesbury, but in 1679, when the Duke of York was named to the Company's Committee, the Earl sold all his HBC stock. On Rupert's death three years later, he quietly slipped away into exile.

GEORGE MONCK, DUKE OF ALBEMARLE

At the time of the Hudson's Bay Company's founding, George Monck, the first Duke of Albemarle, was a Privy Councillor and Lord of Trade and Plantations. He was a tough old professional soldier who had served with Rupert at the Siege of Breda and, with the collapse of Cromwell's Protectorate, had marched slowly towards London at the head of his Coldstream Guards, testing the national mood but refusing supreme military power, giving way instead to Parliament and the Restoration. Co-admiral with Rupert in the second war with the Dutch, he took the British fleet to sea* before the plague swept London and returned as the city's military ruler. A Lord Proprietor of the Carolinas, the Royal African and Royal Fisheries companies, he invested in Groseilliers's first voyage into Hudson Bay but had died and passed on his shares to his son, Christopher, by the time the HBC was incorporated. The second duke was a wastrel, taking no part in Company affairs or much else, ending his days as governor of Jamaica, where he expired in 1688 from the effects of too much rum.

---

*The Duke fought the Dutch in three great naval engagements but could never shed his army origins, issuing orders in the heat of battle to his captains to wheel their ships to the "left" or "right" instead of "port" and "starboard."

SIR JAMES HAYES

Unlike most of the other HBC Adventurers, who had either died or parted with their holdings by the time the first dividend was declared, Hayes turned a tidy profit on the risky enterprise – though at least some of it seems to have come under, rather than across, the boardroom table. A barrister-at-law and Member of Parliament, Hayes had a personal fortune founded on his marriage to Rachel, the wealthy widow of Henry Cary, the fourth Viscount Falkland.

Through Rupert, Hayes had attempted several entrepreneurial ventures such as purchasing for a seven-year term the revenue of Ireland, subject to an annual rent to the Crown of £75,000. But his main occupation was secretary and investment counsellor to the Prince, and his chief private investment was in the Hudson's Bay Company. On the books as its largest shareholder (at one time owning more than 20 percent of the Company), he held on to his financial interest until 1688 and served eight crucial years as Deputy Governor. In his pivotal position as Rupert's brisk and officious *chef de cabinet*, Hayes made his contribution by maintaining a healthy and mutually productive liaison among the Court, the Company and the City. It was Hayes who arranged for the loan of the *Eaglet* from the Admiralty and drafted the sailing instructions for the *Nonsuch*. Hayes successfully petitioned the King in Council to prohibit the illegal importation of beaver fur and made certain that pressure was placed on the New England colonial administration to prevent interlopers from sailing north into Hudson Bay. For these and many other interventions Hayes was rewarded with cash bonuses, gifts of silver plate and fur pieces for his wife. The Deputy Governor's last years in office were clouded by scandal. The Company's disbursement books showed a long series of expenditures in Hayes's name, listed vaguely in the "miscellaneous" category. When his audit-conscious fellow Committeemen stiffly requested a detailed accounting, Sir James retreated to Great Bedgebury, his stately mansion in Kent, and refused to indulge their pointed curiosity.

SIR ROBERT VYNER

Prince of the Goldsmiths, Controller of the Mint, Sheriff and Lord Mayor of London, Sir Robert was the leading merchant banker of his day. He first placed Charles II in his debt when he financed the royal regalia required for the king's coronation, replacing the crown jewels pawned by Charles I. He quickly became a royal banker, borrowing money at 6 percent and lending it to the Crown at higher rates, and appropriating excise and customs duties as his collateral. When Sir Robert was appointed Lord Mayor in 1674, Charles II broke precedent by attending his inaugural banquet; when the king tried to sneak away early to visit Nell Gwyn, Sir Robert stumbled after him and drunkenly commanded his sovereign: "Sir, you shall stay and take t'other bottle." Charles, regarding his tipsy host with benign tolerance, quoted the old song: "He that is drunk is as great as a king." Then, linking arms with his banker, he walked back into the hall.

Vyner was the Company's first treasurer and remained active until ill health and impending bankruptcy forced him to sell his stock in 1681.

SIR JOHN ROBINSON

Samuel Pepys dismissed him as a "talking, bragging bufflehead," but he was one of the HBC's early mainstays, having participated in financing the *Nonsuch* expedition, guaranteeing the Company's original underwriting and acting as its first Deputy Governor (1670–73). A commanding figure in Restoration London, Robinson spent most of his energy commuting among his many bailiwicks. He was a great City man – at one and the same time, a Committeeman of the East India Company, Court Assistant (chief lobbyist) for the Levant Company, Lord Lieutenant of the Tower of London (then an important military position), a Member of the House of Commons and Colonel of the Green Regiment, and he had preceded Sir Robert Vyner as Lord Mayor of London. The largest founding shareholder of the HBC, Sir John enlisted his considerable administrative talents in the Company's behalf.

SIR WILLIAM CRAVEN,
EARL OF CRAVEN

This generous and romantic nobleman had grown grey in the service of Prince Rupert's mother, Elizabeth, the Winter Queen of Bohemia, helping finance her enforced sojourn in Holland and sponsoring her post-Restoration return to England. His estates had been confiscated by Cromwell when he rashly donated £50,000 to help Charles II during the Continental exile. Restored to glory by the Stuart succession, the faithful Earl was appointed a Privy Councillor, Tangier Commissioner, Master of Trinity House, one of the Lord Proprietors of the Carolinas and a patentee of the Royal Fisheries Company. He was an original HBC investor. He courted Rupert's sister, the pious Elizabeth, but she opted for a convent instead, and there were whispers that the Earl had secretly married her mother, the Bohemian Queen. (She bequeathed all her private holdings to him.) This loyal old family retainer was chief mourner at Rupert's funeral, executor of his will and the guardian of his illegitimate daughter, Ruperta.

SIR PETER COLLETON

The eldest son of a prominent Barbadian sugar planter, Colleton was a leading Restoration imperialist whose overseas interests included promotion of the Carolinas and Bahamas colonies as well as charter ownership in the HBC. Immensely wealthy, he served a term as Governor of Barbados and introduced the magnolia tree to England. A Royalist during the Civil War, he served in government circles as the keeper of Public Accounts, and even though the Company was far from his major preoccupation, it was at Colleton's London house that Radisson and Groseilliers found comfortable shelter while waiting to sail for Hudson Bay.

SIR JOHN KIRKE

The third son of a Huguenot merchant who had captured Quebec City in 1628 and had brought Samuel de Champlain to London as his prisoner, Kirke was the only Adventurer with first-hand knowledge of the American fur trade, a keen understanding of Europe's fur markets and an appreciation of French trading goods and methods. He helped publicize the Hudson's Bay Company by presenting beaver hats to London bigwigs but was less than ecstatic when his daughter married the new man in town, Pierre Radisson.

SIR PAUL NEILE

A natural philosopher and founding member of the Royal Society, Sir Paul held various royal sinecures, expending most of his energies in the dissipation of a large inherited fortune. His HBC founding stock was mysteriously transferred to "Faith Read of London, widow" on March 19, 1674 and was just as mysteriously returned to his ownership seven months later.

SIR EDWARD HUNGERFORD

Created a Knight of the Bath at Charles II's coronation, and brother-in-law of Sir James Hayes, Sir Edward richly earned his reputation as the Restoration's most recklessly extravagant spendthrift, but he also had a practical side. When his ungainly town mansion, Hungerford House (near present-day Charing Cross station), burned down, he had market stalls set up on the site and turned many a penny and pound on the emergency venture. Elected to the House of Commons a dozen times, Sir Edward was associated more with self-serving amendments than with any new legislative initiatives. An HBC Committeeman for only one season (1674–75), he failed to distinguish himself in this or any other capacity and died penniless.

JOHN PORTMAN

The Hudson's Bay Company's first Treasurer, Portman was a London goldsmith and banker, working out of the Unicorn on

Lombard Street. Also treasurer of the Carolinas and New Providence (Bahamas) companies, he participated in so many dubious investments that when he died in 1683 he was occupying a cell for bankrupts deep in the Fleet prison for debtors.

FRANCIS MILLINGTON

A Puritan London businessman, Millington made a small fortune as a successful draper, brewer and Commissioner of Customs. Married to the fifteen-year-old niece of Sir Robert Vyner, he owned HBC stock worth £300 at incorporation.

SIR JOHN GRIFFITH

The only one of the original Adventurers who was a professional soldier, Captain Griffith had served Charles II during his exile in Holland and was later granted the offices of Keeper at the Blockhouses of West Tilbury and at Gravesend.

WILLIAM PRETYMAN

An ardent royalist and merchant adventurer to India who had served as the Stuarts' London agent during Charles II's exile, he afterward bore the proud title "King's Remembrancer of the First Fruits" and held a sinecure in the Treasury. His role with the HBC was limited to being the first subscriber – he acquired his original stock on February 10, 1667.

JOHN FENN

The Paymaster of the Admiralty, Fenn held £250 in HBC stock at incorporation but immediately assigned all his shares to Sir James Hayes.

SIR CHRISTOPHER WREN

The stellar Oxford-educated astronomer, Wren turned to architecture and was eventually named Surveyor-General to Charles

II. After the Great Fire of London, he drafted a grandiose plan for the city's rebuilding. When it was rejected because of cost, Wren had to content himself with a grand new St Paul's Cathedral, fifty-two parish churches, thirty-six livery companies' halls, the London Custom House, Greenwich Hospital and dozens of private residences. He collected healthy fees from some clients but charged the state a modest £300 for creating the magnificent cathedral, an obsession that occupied his talents for thirty-five years. He regarded this labour as so sacred that workers were dismissed if overheard using swear words. Hounded by jealous colleagues, Wren was forced out of all his professional involvements and died of a chill at the age of ninety. He was buried under a simple slab of black marble on which his son carved the immortal epitaph: *SI MONUMENTUM REQUIRIS, CIRCUMSPICE* –"If you seek a monument, look around."

Wren was no impractical dreamer, having invented the blood transfusion process* and finding time to serve as a Member of Parliament for four different constituencies. England's busiest architect, he invested his fees wisely, mainly in the Hudson's Bay Company. Not among the original partners, Wren invested £200 in the Company's stock on June 5, 1679. Three other lot purchases over the next four years brought his holdings to £1,200. He sold the stock at a profit, but while he held it, Wren was no nominal investor. Elected four times to serve as an HBC Committeeman (between 1679 and 1683), he chaired meetings whenever Rupert or his Deputy Governor was absent. At one such gathering on September 19, 1682, the Committee passed a resolution "that shutters, bolts and locks be made to the warehouse as Sir Christopher Wren shall judge fit to be done …"

---

*Dr Thomas Sprat's 1667 History of the Royal Society credits Wren with "inventing the practice of injecting into the blood stream" which led to blood transfusions and, in recent years, the blood bank. Wren's first experiments were made with opium introduced by means of a syringe attached to a quill and

ROBERT BOYLE

Less active in the Company's affairs but an early investor (1675), the father of modern chemistry retained his stock and even willed it to his heirs. A pious natural philosopher, Boyle not only formulated the laws of physics that led to the invention of the steam engine but had a lively interest in overseas development, including the New England Company, established "for the propagation of the Gospel in New England and the adjoining parts of America."

LADY DRAX

The first woman stockholder of the HBC, Margaret Drax was the second wife of James Drax of York and London, a financier who made his fortune in the sugar plantations of Barbados. She acquired shares worth £300 in June 1670 and doubled her holdings seven years later but took no part in the Company's affairs.

---

injected into "divers creatures" which were "thereby intoxicated, killed or revived according to the quality of the liquor injected." Wren amazed his fellow members at a Royal Society meeting on June 29, 1681 by revealing that Hudson Bay natives "live to the great age of 130 or 140 years without the use of spectacles."

London Homes
of the HBC

From its beginning, the Hudson's Bay Company enjoyed the considerable advantage of serving a market able to absorb all the fur its expanding network of trading posts could harvest. Except for the occasional period of over-production when imports were stored in anticipation of improved markets, the London auctions (and more recently, the Canadian auctions) have been comfortably successful in turning pelts into cash during the more than three centuries of the Company's operations. But as the enterprise evolved from a primitive barter house into a major multinational corporation, the venue of the HBC's London headquarters changed in both character and geography.

During the first dozen years after its incorporation, the Adventurers held their General Courts (annual meetings) wherever it was convenient, usually at Prince Rupert's in Whitehall, at his lodgings in Spring Gardens or at office quarters in The Tower. The Excise Office in Broad Street (later the old South Sea House and the site occupied by the City of London Club), the Golden Anchor Tavern in Cornhill, the home of Mr Letten in Turnwheel Lane and Garraway's Coffee House were favourite gathering points from 1679 to 1682, when the Company leased Scriveners' Hall at the corner of Noble Street and Oat Lane, in Aldersgate Ward. This was the first official Hudson's Bay House, initially mentioned in Committee Minutes for December 30, 1682. In a letter to Edward Randolph, Collector of H. M. Customs in New England, Sir Christopher Wren and some of his colleagues then in charge of the Company requested that replies to all correspondence be addressed to: "The Governor and Company of Adventurers of England Trading into Hudsons Bay, Hudson Bay House, Noble Street, London."

A decade later, the Company moved its premises to the upper end of Culver Court in Fenchurch Street, across the road from the Elephant Inn, where the painter William Hogarth in his apprentice years, paid his rent with four murals in the tap-room – one of his subjects being "The Hudson's Bay Company's Porters Going to Dinner." In 1794 the Company acquired the freehold on the south-west end of Nos. 3 and 4 Fenchurch Street, near the Church of St Benedict. Built of Georgian red brick, with rough stucco in the lower façade and columned doorways flanking the arched main entrance, this riverbank edifice was the Company's head office for much of the next century. The auctions at this location listed many items apart from furs, including bird feathers, moose skins, goose quills and whale fins.

Five years before the sale of Rupert's Land to the newly created Dominion of Canada, the HBC moved to the former silk warehouse of the East India Company at No. 1 Lime Street. Sales were first held in a commercial sales room and later at the auction hall of C. M. Lampson & Co., while administrative offices were moved to Threadneedle House, No. 34 Bishopsgate, and later to Nos. 52–68 on the same street.

During the early 1920s the Company decided to erect its first London headquarters, Beaver House, in Great Trinity Lane over the Mansion House Station on Garlick Hill, in the City. The new building was opened with great fanfare in 1925 on the Company's 255th birthday by Governor Sir Robert Kindersley.

Over the main doorway was the coat of arms carved in low relief, and on the front of the building, facing west, the keystone of the centre window contained a maple leaf signifying Canada and an oak leaf symbolizing England, both intertwined with the HBC's initials. The keys were presented to Kindersley by the Company's warehousekeeper, James H. Rendall, whose forty-six-year service completed a century and a half of consecutive HBC employ by himself, his father and grandfather.

The building was used as the HBC's headquarters until the Company's head office was transferred to Canada in 1970. The London fur auction rooms were abandoned in 1982, and the property was transferred to the HBC's Markborough Properties subsidiary, which tore down the building to erect an office tower jointly financed by the Royal Bank of Canada. Hudson's Bay and Annings Ltd., a subsidiary company, is located at Hudson's Bay House on Upper Thames Street, but Winnipeg, not London, is the Company's home now.

Governors and Deputy Governors (1670–1985)

GOVERNORS

His Highness Prince Rupert	1670–1682
H.R.H. James, Duke of York (King James II)	1683–1685
John, Lord Churchill (Duke of Marlborough)	1685–1692
Sir Stephen Evans	1692–1696
Right Honourable Sir William Trumbull	1696–1700
Sir Stephen Evans	1700–1712
Sir Bibye Lake, Bart.	1712–1743
Benjamin Pitt	1743–1746
Thomas Knapp	1746–1750
Sir Atwell Lake, Bart.	1750–1760
Sir William Baker	1760–1770
Bibye Lake	1770–1782
Samuel Wegg	1782–1799
Sir James Winter Lake, Bart.	1799–1807
William Mainwaring	1807–1812
Joseph Berens, Jr.	1812–1822
Sir John Henry Pelly, Bart.	1822–1852
Andrew Colvile	1852–1856
John Shepherd	1856–1858
Henry Hulse Berens	1858–1863
Right Honourable Sir Edmund Walker Head, Bart., K.C.B.	1863–1868
Right Honourable The Earl of Kimberley	1868–1869
Right Honourable Sir Stafford Northcote, Bart., M.P., Earl of Iddesleigh	1869–1874
Right Honourable George Joachim Goschen, M.P.	1874–1880
Eden Colvile	1880–1889
Donald A. Smith, Baron Strathcona and Mount Royal, G.C.M.G.	1889–1914

Sir Thomas Skinner, Bart.	1914–1915
Sir Robert Molesworth Kindersley, G.B.E.	1915–1925
Charles Vincent Sale	1925–1931
Sir Patrick Ashley Cooper	1931–1952
William Johnston Keswick	1952–1965
Right Honourable Derick Heathcoat Amory, Viscount Amory	1965–1970
George T. Richardson	1970–1982
Donald Scott McGiverin	1982–

DEPUTY GOVERNORS

Sir John Robinson	1670–1673
Lord Shaftesbury	1673–1674
Sir George Carteret	1674–1676
Sir James Hayes	1676–1685
The Honourable Sir Edward Dering	1685–1691
Samuel Clarke	1691–1701
John Nicholson	1701–1710
Thomas Lake	1710–1711
Sir Bibye Lake, Bart.	1711–1712
Captain John Merry	1712–1729
Samuel Jones	1729–1735
Benjamin Pitt	1735–1743
Thomas Knapp	1743–1746
Sir Atwell Lake, Bart.	1746–1750
Sir William Baker, Bart.	1750–1760
John Merry, Jr.	1760–1765
Bibye Lake	1765–1770
Robert Merry	1770–1774
Samuel Wegg	1774–1782
Sir James Winter Lake, Bart.	1782–1799
Richard Hulse	1799–1805
Nicholas Caesar Corsellis	1805–1806
William Mainwaring	1806–1807
Joseph Berens, Jr.	1807–1812
John Henry Pelly	1812–1822

Nicholas Garry	1822–1835
Benjamin Harrison	1835–1839
Andrew Colvile	1839–1852
John Shepherd	1852–1856
Henry Hulse Berens	1856–1858
Edward Ellice, M.P.	1858–1863
Sir Curtis Miranda Lampson, Bart.	1863–1871
Eden Colville	1871–1880
Sir John Rose, Bart., G.C.M.G.	1880–1888
Sir Donald A. Smith, K.C.M.G.	1888–1889
The Earl of Lichfield	1889–1910
Sir Thomas Skinner, Bart.	1910–1914
Leonard D. Cunliffe	1914–1915
Charles Vincent Sale	1915–1926
Sir Frederick Henry Richmond	1926–1931
Sir Alexander Murray	1932–1946
William Johnston Keswick	1946–1952
Eric O. Faulkner	1952–1955
Sir Henry Alexander Benson	1955–1963
Right Honourable Lord Cobbold	1963–1964
Right Honourable Derick Heathcoat Amory, Viscount Amory	1964–1965
Office Unoccupied	1965–1970
Alexander J. MacIntosh	1970–1985

Record of Dividends

The financial records for the Company's first fourteen years are based on four Grand Ledgers and two Grand Journals which have survived, covering the period 1676 to 1684 but incorporating earlier figures that had been in records subsequently lost. It is generally understood that there were no dividend payouts recorded before 1684. Between 1910 and 1965 a separate dividend was paid on account of land sales which was not subject to income tax. It is included in the yearly totals below. The repayment of several issues of preferred shares was completed in 1945. At the time of the head office transfer from London to Winnipeg, dividends were declared in cents per share instead of as a percentage of the £1 par value of the stock, since market value no longer had any relationship to par value. The substantial 1978 increase in shares outstanding was due to special issues in connection with the purchases of Zellers and Simpsons. As of June 30, 1985, Lord Thomson owned 76.4 percent of the HBC's issued shares through private holding companies.

The following list of annual capitalization and dividend payments provides important clues to both how profitable the Company has been for its proprietors through the centuries – with some tight spots – and how much mark-up it charged its customers. The change in calculations in 1970 reflects the Company's patriation to Canada and the 1982–84 accounts document the HBC's current difficulties.

DATE	CAPITAL	DIVIDEND
1670	Original stock of £10,500	No dividend
1671	,,	,,
1672	,,	,,
1673	,,	,,
1674	,,	,,
1675	,,	,,
1676	,,	,,
1677	,,	,,
1678	,,	,,
1679	,,	,,
1680	,,	,,
1681	,,	,,
1682	,,	,,
1683	,,	,,
1684	,,	50%
1688	,,	50%
1689	,,	25%
1690	£31,500	74%*
1691	,,	No dividend
1692	,,	,,
1693	,,	,,
1694	,,	,,
1695	,,	,,
1696	,,	,,
1697	,,	,,
1698	,,	,,
1699	,,	,,
1700	,,	,,
1701	,,	,,
1702	,,	,,
1703	,,	,,
1704	,,	,,
1705	,,	,,
1706	,,	,,
1707	,,	,,
1708	,,	,,
1709	,,	,,

*The dividend of 74 percent was actually a 25 percent dividend which was based on increased stock of £31,500.

DATE	CAPITAL	DIVIDEND
1710	,,	,,
1711	,,	,,
1712	,,	,,
1713	,,	,,
1714	,,	,,
1715	,,	,,
1716	,,	,,
1717	,,	,,
1718	,,	10%
1719	,,	6%
1721	£103,950	5%
1722	,,	10%
1723	,,	8%
1724	,,	12%
1725	,,	10%
1726	,,	10%
1727	,,	10%
1728	,,	10%
1729	,,	10%
1730	,,	10%
1731	,,	10%
1732	,,	10%
1733	,,	10%
1734	,,	10%
1735	,,	10%
1736	,,	10%
1737	,,	8%
1738	£103,950	8%
1739	,,	10%
1740	,,	10%
1741	,,	10%
1742	,,	10%
1743	,,	10%
1744	,,	10%
1745	,,	10%
1746	,,	8%
1747	,,	8%
1748	,,	8%
1749	,,	7%
1750	,,	7%

DATE	CAPITAL	DIVIDEND
1751	,,	8%
1752	,,	8%
1753	,,	8%
1754	,,	8%
1755	,,	8%
1756	,,	8%
1757	,,	8%
1758	,,	8%
1759	,,	8%
1760	,,	8%
1761	,,	8%
1762	,,	8%
1763	,,	10%
1764	,,	10%
1765	,,	10%
1766	,,	10%
1767	,,	10%
1768	,,	10%
1769	,,	10%
1770	,,	10%
1771	,,	10%
1772	,,	10%
1773	,,	10%
1774	,,	10%
1775	,,	10%
1776	,,	10%
1777	,,	10%
1778	,,	10%
1779	,,	8%
1780	,,	8%
1781	,,	8%
1782	,,	8%
1783	,,	No dividend
1784	,,	,,
1785	,,	,,
1786	,,	5%
1787	£103,950	5%
1788	,,	5%
1789	,,	5%
1790	,,	6%

DATE	CAPITAL	DIVIDEND
1791	,,	7%
1792	,,	8%
1793	,,	8%
1794	,,	8%
1795	,,	6%
1796	,,	6%
1797	,,	6%
1798	,,	6%
1799	,,	6%
1800	,,	6%
1801	,,	4%
1802	,,	4%
1803	,,	4%
1804	,,	4%
1805	,,	4%
1806	,,	4%
1807	,,	4%
1808	,,	4%
1809	,,	No dividend
1810	,,	,,
1811	,,	,,
1812	,,	,,
1813	,,	,,
1814	,,	,,
1815	,,	4%
1816	,,	4%
1817	,,	4%
1818	,,	4%
1819	,,	4%
1820	,,	4%
1821	,,	4%
1822	,,	4%
1823	,,	4%
1824	,,	4%
1825	£400,000	10%
1826	,,	10%
1827	,,	10%
1828	,,	20%
1829	,,	20%
1830	,,	20%

DATE	CAPITAL	DIVIDEND
1831	,,	20%
1832	,,	20%
1833	,,	16%
1834	,,	10%
1835	,,	15%
1836	,,	23%
1837	,,	10%
1838	,,	25%
1839	£400,000	23%
1840	,,	15%
1841	,,	15%
1842	,,	15%
1843	,,	10%
1844	,,	10%
1845	,,	15%
1846	,,	10%
1847	,,	10%
1848	,,	10%
1849	,,	10%
1850	£440,000	10%
1851	,,	10%
1852	£462,000	10%
1853	,,	10%
1854	£500,000	10%
1855	,,	10%
1856	,,	10%
1857	,,	10%
1858	,,	10%
1859	,,	10%
1860	,,	15%
1861	,,	10%
1862	,,	10%
1863	,,	11.94%
1864	£2,000,000	4.50%
1865	,,	4.50%
1866	,,	5.50%
1867	,,	4.50%
1868	,,	3%
1869	,,	3.50%
1870	,,	1%

DATE	CAPITAL	DIVIDEND
1871	£1,700,000	3.53%
1872	,,	5%
1873	,,	5.88%
1874	,,	5.88%
1875	,,	6.76%
1876	,,	4.41%
1877	,,	No dividend
1878	,,	,,
1879	,,	,,
1880	,,	,,
1881	,,	4.11%
1882	,,	4.11%
1883	£1,500,000	4%
1884	£1,400,000	7.86%
1885	,,	No dividend
1886	£1,300,000	5.77%
1887	,,	6.54%
1888	,,	No dividend
1889	,,	5.38%
1890	,,	5.38%
1891	£1,300,000	2.50%
1892	,,	2.50%
1893	,,	4.61%
1894	,,	3.84%
1895	,,	4.61%
1896	,,	5%
1897	,,	5%
1898	,,	5%
1899	,,	7.69%
1900	,,	9.61%
1901	,,	5.77%
1902	,,	8.65%
1903	,,	8.65%
1904	£1,100,000	15.91%
1905	£1,000,000	29%
1906	,,	40%
1907	,,	42.50%
1908	,,	30%
1909	,,	25%
1910	,,	40%

DATE	CAPITAL	DIVIDEND
1911	,,	40%
1912	,,	40%
1913	,,	50%
1914	,,	40%
1915	,,	No dividend
1916	,,	20%
1917	,,	30%
1918	,,	40%
1919	,,	45%
1920	,,	40%
1921	,,	40%
1922	,,	45%
1923	,,	19.50%
1924	,,	20%
1925	,,	20%
1926	,,	23.50%
1927	£1,500,000	20%
1928	£2,000,000	25%
1929	,,	25%
1930	,,	17.50%
1931	,,	No dividend
1932	,,	,,
1933	,,	,,
1934	,,	,,
1935	,,	,,
1936	,,	,,
1937	,,	,,
1938	£2,492,224	4%
1939	,,	3.50%
1940	,,	2.50%
1941	,,	2.50%
1942	£2,492,224	5%
1943	,,	5.50%
1944	,,	10%
1945	,,	10%
1946	,,	12%
1947	,,	13%
1948	,,	13%
1949	,,	13%
1950	,,	13%

DATE	CAPITAL	DIVIDEND
1951	,,	17%
1952	,,	20%
1953	£4,984,448	6.50%
1954	,,	15%
1955	£5,607,504	17.50%
1956	,,	17.50%
1957	,,	17.50%
1958	,,	22.50%
1959	,,	31%
1960	,,	29%
1961	£6,138,000	29%
1962	£13,553,428	14.50%
1963	,,	16.50%
1964	,,	17.50%
1965	,,	18.25%
1966	,,	19.50%
1967	,,	19.50%
1968	,,	19.50%
1969	,,	20%
1970	,,	31%

DATE	NUMBER OF SHARES OUTSTANDING	DIVIDEND PER SHARE (C$ cents)	NET EARNINGS (C$ millions)
1970	13,553,428	22	11.0
1971	,,	52	13.3
1972	,,	52	15.6
1973	13,809,000	56	17.6
1974	13,936,000	60	18.4
1975	13,985,000	60	22.0
1976	14,096,000	60	24.8
1977	14,155,000	65	29.9
1978	23,092,000	91	44.6
1979	23,712,000	110	80.3
1980	,,	120	54.5
1981	23,777,000	120	3.7
1982	23,870,000	75	− 122.2
1983	23,728,000	60	− 17.9
1984	23,787,166	60	− 107.4

Chronology

1610
Henry Hudson enters the strait and the bay which now bear his name and trades for furs with one Indian on the shores of James Bay.

1611
Henry Hudson's crew mutinies aboard the *Discovery* and set him and several others adrift in Hudson Bay in a sailing dinghy; their fate is unknown.

1613
Prince Rupert's parents, Frederick and Elizabeth, are married.

1612–1632
Exploration of Hudson Bay by Thomas Button (1612–13), William Baffin (1615), Jens Munk (1619–20), Luke Foxe (1631-32) and Thomas James (1631–32) shows it to be landlocked.

1619
Frederick and Elizabeth are crowned in Prague Cathedral; Prince Rupert is born.

1630
Charles II is born in England; will live through tumultuous times before he becomes king of England at thirty.

1631
British navigator Luke Foxe explores Hudson Bay and reports dramatic tide differentials.

1636
Sixteen-year-old Rupert and his brother Carl Louis travel to London in February for the first time and join court life.

1649
Charles I is tried and beheaded, and Charles II is proclaimed king on February 5 in Edinburgh, again in a small ceremony in Jersey on February 16 and yet again on June 24 when he lands in Scotland – but must wait until 1660 to claim his throne; late in the year, Rupert becomes a privateer to bolster family finances.

1651
English Parliament passes the first of several Navigation Acts at the urging of the East India, Levant and Eastland companies, reserving foreign trade to English ships; Pierre Radisson settles in Trois Rivières.

1654–56
Médard Chouart, Sieur Des Groseilliers, is trading among the "Far Indians."

1659
Radisson and Groseilliers embark in August on a private trading expedition west of Lake Superior to the upper Missouri and Mississippi.

1660

Radisson and Groseilliers travel among the tribes of the Great Lakes, returning to Montreal on August 20 with a rich load of furs; they propose exporting pelts via Hudson Bay but are arrested and fined because their journey had been "unauthorized"; with Charles II's coronation on May 8, the Stuarts are restored to the English throne; Pepys begins his diary; the population of England is $5\frac{1}{4}$ million, one quarter of that of France.

1662

Rupert returns to settle in London, involved with the newly chartered "Royal Adventurers trading into Africa"; Charles II marries Catherine of Braganza, whose £800,000 dowry is a stimulus to national trade; Charles sells Dunkirk to the French for £400,000; the Royal Society is incorporated; Radisson and Groseilliers announce their departure for Hudson Bay from Quebec but sail to New England instead.

1665

Bubonic plague sweeps London (one hundred thousand out of a population of six hundred thousand succumb, and many flee); Radisson and Groseilliers meet Colonel George Cartwright in Boston, are in London by December, and arrive at the beleaguered royal court at Oxford shortly afterward.

1666

Radisson and Groseilliers meet Charles II, then stay at Rupert's Windsor Castle apartments until April; French spies try to lure Groseilliers to the Netherlands; on September 2, the commercial city of London is swept by fire.

1667

The Hudson Bay adventurers are organizing their first test voyage, but the war with the Dutch prevents any trip to Hudson Bay; Sir George Carteret buys £20 worth of stock in the new venture on December 20, becoming the first recorded investor.

1668

A preliminary trade syndicate is formed; Radisson, on the *Eaglet*, is forced back to Plymouth on August 5; the *Nonsuch* reaches Hudson Bay; on the east coast of James Bay, the *Nonsuch* crew builds the first fort in the region; while Capt. Zachariah Gillam and Groseilliers trade for pelts, Radisson spends the winter in England writing his travel accounts.

1669

On June 14, the *Nonsuch* leaves Rupert River for England with a cargo (£1,380) of furs, which induces Charles II to prepare a royal charter for the founding of the Company of Adventurers.

1670

The charter of the Governor and Company of Adventurers is signed by Charles II on May 2, with Prince Rupert as first Governor, a post he holds until his death in 1682.

1671

The *Wivenhoe* and the *Prince Rupert* return from Hudson Bay to London with holds full of furs, thus confirming the feasibility of the new trade venture.

1672

Twenty-seven lots of furs are offered in the company's first public sale, at Garraway's Coffee House on January 24; Moose Factory is established by Radisson and Groseilliers for the HBC; Prince Rupert is appointed Admiral of the Fleet on the resignation of the Duke of York, who is excluded from the job by the Test Act.

1673

King Charles presents Radisson with a gold chain and medal on his return to England.

1674

In October, Radisson shifts his allegiance to New France.

1675

The Jesuit priest Father Albanel, in prison in England, persuades Radisson and Groseilliers to work for France.

1676

The HBC exports British goods

of £650 and returns a profit of £19,000.

1679

John Nixon replaces Charles Bayley as Governor at the bay.

1681

Rupert negotiates customs privileges for the HBC similar to those enjoyed by the Royal African Co.; Radisson goes to Canada under instruction from the French government.

1682

Prince Rupert dies on November 29 at sixty-two of pleurisy (his friend Shaftesbury flees to the Netherlands) and is succeeded the next year as Governor by James, Duke of York (later King James II); the HBC, with five forts on the bay, loses four to the French, retaining only Fort Albany.

1684

Radisson deserts from the Compagnie du Nord and travels to London to rejoin the HBC for £50 per year and £200 worth of stock.

1685

John, Lord Churchill (Duke of Marlborough), is appointed HBC Governor.

1686

The main struggle for possession of the tiny forts on Hudson Bay begins with the expedition of Chevalier de Troyes from Montreal.

1687

Marlborough petitions James II

to argue that the HBC had spent £200,000 on forts and factories destroyed by the French and should be compensated.

1690

Henry Kelsey begins a series of explorations for the company to the prairie lands, penetrating the interior to southeastern Saskatchewan; HBC stock trebles in value (a 200 percent stock bonus) to reflect the value of fortifications and establishments; the "Great Dividend" of 74 percent (actually a 25 percent dividend based on increased stock of £31,500) is declared and paid; HBC is called the only flourishing company in the kingdom, but no dividends are paid out again until 1718; with little opposition Parliament passes a private bill confirming the HBC's monopoly for another seven years.

1692

The goldsmith-banker Sir Stephen Evans replaces Marlborough as HBC Governor.

1694

Governor Sir Stephen Evans is ejected from the Customs Board for poor attendance; Radisson sues the HBC for back pay by filing a suit in Chancery Court.

1696

The English, with four ships, recover all the James Bay forts, and the men of the captured garrisons are taken prisoner to England.

1697

On September 5, the French fleet of four warships under d'Iberville on the *Pélican*, off the mouth of the Nelson River, inflicts defeat on the HBC ships *Hudson's Bay*, *Hampshire* and *Dering*; Fort Nelson is burned; the Treaty of Ryswick, signed in September, leaves the French in possession of all the settlements along the bay (except Fort Albany) for seventeen years; Thomas Lake buys his first HBC stock on May 13 during a drop in the market and becomes a dominant shareholder.

1700

Sir William Trumbull retires as Governor of the HBC after four years and Sir Stephen Evans takes the post for the second time; Radisson's application for the job of warehouse-keeper is not accepted by the company.

1710

Radisson dies in England; his widow Elizabeth (his third wife) is given £6 by the Company for his funeral expenses.

1712

Sir Bibye Lake is appointed HBC Governor.

1713

By the signing of the Treaty of

Utrecht, France relinquishes all claims to Hudson Bay, which again becomes a British possession.

1714
James Knight reclaims York Factory; William Stewart explores north of York Factory this summer and next.

1730
HBC critic Arthur Dobbs begins a twenty-year attack on the HBC, accusing the company of failing to explore its granted territories and of reaping great profits.

1731
Construction on new Prince of Wales's Fort begins at mouth of the Churchill River.

1743
Benjamin Pitt is appointed HBC Governor; Joseph Isbister opens Henley House at the junction of the Albany and Kenogami rivers.

1745
The Jacobite rising is led by the twenty-five-year-old Bonnie Prince Charlie; the British Parliament offers a reward of £20,000 for discovery of a North West Passage, and adds an award of £5,000 for reaching the North Pole.

1749
British House of Commons Committee is appointed to consider the trade and territory of the HBC; report favours the

HBC and disallows Dobbs's petition.

1750
Sir Atwell Lake is appointed HBC Governor.

1752
The HBC London Committee approves a proposal by James Isham, Factor at York, to move inland from the bay to counter French competition.

1754
Anthony Henday, starting from York Factory, traces the Saskatchewan River for the Company.

1755
Woudbee and his sons Snuff-the-Blanket and Sheanapp are hanged by the HBC after Henley House massacre.

1756
The Seven Years' War begins.

1761
The HBC dispatches Captain William Christopher to examine Chesterfield Inlet; New York fur traders continue to move into New France.

1763
On February 10, the Treaty of Paris ends the Seven Years' War, resulting in the withdrawal of French government from Quebec; Henley House is opened for trade for the third time.

1765
Bibye Lake is appointed HBC Deputy Governor; the Stamp

Act, put into effect March 22, aggravates the economic depression in the American colonies; the HBC starts a whale fishery on Marble Island, 250 miles north of Prince of Wales's Fort.

1767

The East India Co., debilitated by years of war taxation, bribery and political subsidies to maintain its charter, runs into severe financial difficulties; Hearne finds the remains of the James Knight expedition on Marble Island.

1768

Imperial regulations are relaxed to promote Quebec trade, and Montreal merchants are allowed to trade in the "North West" but not in Rupert's Land; huge decline in HBC trade due to the competitiveness of the Montreal-based "pedlars."

1769

Samuel Hearne sets out on his first journey to the Coppermine River but is forced back short of his goal.

1770

Hearne sets off again on February 23, travels about three hundred miles but is compelled to return to the fort yet again.

1771

Hearne finally reaches the Coppermine River on July 12, is shaken by the massacre at Bloody Fall on July 17 and reaches the Arctic at Coronation Gulf on July 18.

1772

The HBC sends Matthew Cocking from York Factory to check on the pedlars dominating the fur trade by using tobacco and liquor as trade items; Hearne arrives back at Prince of Wales's Fort on June 30.

1774

Hearne builds the first inland HBC post at Cumberland House, near Pine Island Lake on the Saskatchewan River.

1775

Thirty-year-old Hearne is appointed to command Prince of Wales's Fort.

1778

Peter Pond, exploring the Athabasca Delta for the North West Co., spots oil sands and rich furs and establishes a post.

1779

The North West Co. coalesces in earnest.

1780

Thomas Empson makes the first point blankets for the HBC, each "point," a small, dark mark woven into the wool, representing the value of one beaver pelt (a made-beaver); both the HBC and NWC begin establishing inland posts in fierce competition for the fur trade.

1782
Prince of Wales's Fort at Churchill River is captured by Admiral La Pérouse on August 9 and is destroyed; York Factory surrenders on August 25; Samuel Hearne is taken prisoner.

1786
HBC appoints William Tomison its first inland governor.

1799
Despite rapid expansion, the HBC has only 498 men posted in North America.

Resource People

Although there is a rich and varied lode in the published information on the HBC, it has been the interviews with people who have an interest in the Company's history or activities that have sparked and maintained the creative impulse behind this book. Talking to these men and women has provided the incentive and determination to "get things right" as the tale moves towards events within living memory.

In most cases when titles are given, they are those held by the individuals at the time of our meeting. The listings give the connection of the interviewee with the Company, with some exceptions, and where that person lives now.

The Rt. Hon. Lord Adeane
Director, The Royal Bank of Canada
(Financial adviser to Her Majesty the Queen)
London

Claus Aeschlimann
Fur broker
Frankfurt

The Rev. Jeremiah Albany
Former trapper
(Now Anglican priest)
Fort Severn, Ont.

Manasseh (Munzie) Albany
Former hunter and ship's pilot, HBC
(Now aged ninety-seven)
Fort Severn, Ont.

George Alexander
Manager, HBC store
Broughton Island, Baffin Island, N.W.T.

Elizabeth Allakariallak
Social welfare officer
Resolute Bay, N.W.T.

Denis Allen
Pensioner
Norway House, Man.

The Rt. Hon. Lord Amory
Governor, HBC, 1965–70
London

Del Anaquod
President, Saskatchewan Indian Federated College
Regina

Denyse Angé
Executive Director,
Fur Council of Canada
Montreal

Winnifred M. Archer
Former secretary to Philip
Chester, Managing Director for
Canada, HBC, 1946–59
Brantford, Ont.

Arthur Arthurson
Pensioner
Norway House, Man.

Michael I. Asch
Department of Anthropology
University of Alberta
Edmonton

Rosamond A. Austin
Reference Department,
Legislative Library
Queen's Park
Toronto

Jocelyn Baker
Daughter of George Allan of
Winnipeg, Chairman, Canadian
Committee, HBC, 1925–40
Now residing in Victoria

Timothy Ball
Department of Geography
University of Winnipeg
Winnipeg

Owen Beattie
Department of Anthropology
University of Alberta
Edmonton

Sir Henry Benson
Director, HBC, 1953–63
(Senior consultant, Bank of
England; Partner, 1934–75,
Cooper Bros. & Co., London,

later Coopers & Lybrand)
London

Bertrand Biron
Assistant Manager, HBC
Fort Rupert, Que.

Abel Bluecoat
Former freighter, HBC
Fort Severn and Trout Lake,
Ont.

Malvina Bolus
Editor, *The Beaver*, 1958–72
Now residing in Victoria

Mary Bonnycastle
Widow of R.H.G. (Dick)
Bonnycastle, Secretary of the
Canadian Committee, HBC,
1939–45
Toronto

Tom Boreskie
Historian, Historic Resources
Branch,
Manitoba Department of
Culture, Heritage & Recreation
Winnipeg

Ed Bovey
Director, Norcen Energy
Resources Ltd.
Toronto

John Bovey
Chief Archivist, British
Columbia Provincial Archives
Victoria

Hartwell Bowsfield
Former (and last) General
Editor, The Hudson's Bay
Record Society
(Now Archivist and member of
Department of History, York
University) Toronto

Dr Oliver Brass
Professor, Department of
Indian Studies
Saskatchewan Indian Federated
College
Regina

Sterling Brass
Vice-chairman, Federation of
Saskatchewan Indian Nations
Saskatoon

Jennifer S.H. Brown
Department of History
University of Winnipeg
Winnipeg

P.A.T. Brown
District Manager, HBC
Fort Severn, Ont.

Ben Brumer
Fur broker
Montreal

John M. Bumsted
Department of History
St John's College
University of Manitoba
Winnipeg

G. Allan Burton
Former Chairman and Chief
Executive Officer, Simpson's
Ltd.
Toronto

Bob Chessire
Former General Manager, Fur
Trade Department, HBC
Now residing in Victoria

Isabel Chester
Widow of Philip Chester,
former Managing
Director, HBC
Toronto

Helen Cheung
Librarian, Hudson's Bay
House
Winnipeg

J.B. Clark
Manager, Central Region, HBC
Winnipeg

Margaret E. Clarkson
Toronto

Alf Cleaven
Former Manager, HBC Fur
Sales Ltd. Montreal
Now residing in
Knowlton, Que.

R. Kirk Coates
Manager, HBC store
Norway House, Man.

W.L. (Bill) Cobb
Former Assistant General
Manager, Northern Stores
Department, HBC
Now residing in Shediac Cape,
N.B. and Victoria, B.C.

The Rt. Hon. Lord Cobbold
Director, HBC, 1962–75
(Governor, Bank of England)
Hertfordshire, England

The Rev. Jim Collins
St Thomas Anglican Church
Moose Factory, Ont.

J.E.H. Collins
Director, HBC, 1957–74
(Chairman, Morgan, Grenfel &
Co. Ltd.)
London

Lady Ashley Cooper
Widow of Sir Patrick Ashley
Cooper, Governor, HBC,
1931–52

Hexton Manor, Hertfordshire, England

Barry Cooper
Department of Political Science
University of Calgary
Calgary

Jim Cooper
Son of Sir Patrick Ashley Cooper
Hexton Manor, Hertfordshire, England

Dudley Copland
Former Manager, Western Arctic, Fur Trade Department, HBC
Now residing in Ottawa

George S. Cotter
Filmmaker
Cotter Wildlife Productions
Winnipeg

Brian Craik
Department of Anthropology
University of Guelph
Guelph

Diana M. Crosbie
Senior consultant
S.A. Murray Consulting Inc.
Toronto

George Currie
Former President
FP Publications
Toronto

Dr Stan Cuthand
Assistant Head, Department of Indian Studies
Saskatchewan Indian Federated College
Regina

The Rev. Jack Dangerfield
Wholesale Department, HBC
(Resigned in 1957 after 35 years of service to become an Anglican priest)
Now residing in Victoria

Dora F. Darby
Former secretary to Governors Sir Patrick Ashley Cooper and William Keswick
(Retired from HBC London in 1969 after 41 years of service)
Now residing in Beckenham, Kent, England

Peter Darling
Vice-president, S.G. Warburg & Co.
(The Warburg firm raised the capital for Kenneth R. Thomson to buy the HBC)
London

Lila Davis
Librarian
Parks Canada, Prairie Region
Winnipeg

Paul Davoud
Chief Pilot, HBC
Kingston, Ont.

Susan Demay
Coordinator, Indian Journalism & Communications Program
Federation of Saskatchewan Indian Nations
Regina

James G. Deyell
Manager, Ungava District, HBC
Chisasibi (Fort George), Que.

Chief Billy Diamond
Grand Chief of the Grand
Council of the Crees (of
Quebec)
Val d'Or, Que.

Adam Dick
Chief, War Lake Indian Band
Ilford, Man.

Ron Dick
Filmmaker
(Researcher/writer for *The
Other Side of the Ledger*,
produced by the National Film
Board of Canada)
Now residing in Chapel Hill,
North Carolina

C.H. (Punch) Dickins
Former General Manager,
Canadian Pacific Air Lines
Now residing in Victoria

Bruce F. Donaldson
Historian, Historic Resources
Branch,
Manitoba Department of
Culture, Heritage & Recreation
Winnipeg

Ian Dowling
Manager, HBC store
Chisasibi (Fort George), Que.

Sir Eric Drake
Director, HBC
London

Paul Dudgeon
Vice-president, Academic Affairs
Saskatchewan Indian Federated
College
Regina

Hugh M. Dwan
Managing director, Hudson's
Bay and Annings Ltd.
London

Fredrik Eaton
President, Eaton's of Canada
Toronto

Tex Enemark
President, B.C. Mining
Association
Vancouver

Aksayook Etoangat
Pangnirtung, Baffin Island,
N.W.T.

Sir Eric Faulkner
Deputy Governor, HBC,
1952–55, Director, HBC,
1950–72
(Former Chairman, Glyn, Mills
& Co., now at Finance for
Industry Ltd.)
London

Quinton J. Finlay
General Merchandise Manager,
Inuit Art and Blanket Division,
HBC
Toronto

Robin Fisher
Department of History
Simon Fraser University
Burnaby, B.C.

Irene Flett
Pensioner
Norway House, Man.

Ken Foley
Manager, HBC store
Moosonee, Ont.

John E. Foster
Department of History
University of Alberta
Edmonton

Arthur Frayling
General Manager, Fur Sales,
HBC
London

Gayle Friesen
Librarian
Hudson's Bay House
Winnipeg

Owen Funnell
Manager, HBC Calgary store,
1958–66
Now residing in Calgary

Michel Gagné
Manager, HBC store
Fort Rupert, Que.

John S. Galbraith
Department of History
University of California at Los
Angeles
Los Angeles

E.J. (Scotty) Gall
Head of transport, Western
Arctic, HBC, 1923–66
Now residing in Victoria

Don Galloway
Manager, HBC store
Resolute Bay, N.W.T.

Richard and Connie Glover
Victoria

David B. Greenspan, Q.C.
Partner, Thomson, Rogers
Toronto

A.G.S. Griffin
Director, S.G. Warburg &
Co. Ltd.
Toronto

Henry Grunfeld
Chairman, S.G. Warburg &
Co. Ltd.
London

David G. Guest
Blake, Cassels & Graydon
(Lawyer involved in transfer of
HBC from London to
Winnipeg)
Toronto

Jocelyn O. Hambro
Chairman, Phoenix Assurance
Co. Ltd.
London

C.R. Harington
Chief, Paleobiology Division,
National Museum of Natural
Sciences
Ottawa

Frank Helden
Secretary, Royal Marines
Association
Burnaby, B.C.

H. Albert Hochbaum
Delta, Man.

Stuart Hodgson
Chairman, British Columbia
Ferry Corp.
Former commissioner, North-
west Territories
Victoria

Leslie Hoffman
Historian, Hudson's Bay
House
Winnipeg

Archdeacon R.B. Horsefield
(Formerly of Northern
Manitoba)
Now residing in Sidney, B.C.

A. Rolph Huband
Vice-president and Secretary,
HBC
Toronto

M.W. Jacomb
Director, HBC, 1971–
(Vice-president, Kleinwort,
Benson, Ltd.)
London

Bob Janes
Manager, HBC store
Clyde River, Baffin Island,
N.W.T.

N.I. Jones
District Manager, National
Stores Department, HBC
Montreal

Sir William Keswick
Governor, HBC, 1952–65
(Chairman, Matheson & Co.
Ltd., London)
Now residing in Theydon Bois,
Essex, England

Barbara Kilvert
Public Relations, Canadian
Head Office, HBC, 1957–70
(Now Director, Public Relations,
Canadian Cancer Society)
Toronto

Les Kingdon
Manager, HBC store
Nanisivik, Baffin Island,
N.W.T.

Shirley Kovak
Member, Federation of
Saskatchewan Indian Nations
Regina

R. Brian Land
Director, Legislative Library
Queen's Park
Toronto

L.A. Learmonth
Manager, HBC Arctic stores
(Now in his nineties and
residing in
Georgetown, Ontario)

George S. Levin
Fur broker, The Canada
Traders Corp.
Toronto

Allan G. Levine
Historian
Winnipeg

J.G. Links
Director, HBC, 1950–75
(Calman Links Ltd., London,
Furrier to Her Majesty the
Queen)
London

L.F. McCollum
Director, Hudson's Bay
Oil & Gas Co.
(Former Chairman,
Continental Oil Co.;
Chairman emeritus,
MercantileTexas)
Dallas, Texas

Ian McDonald
Master's candidate concentrating
on Orkney surnames in Canada
University of Manitoba
Winnipeg

Donald McGiverin
Governor, HBC, 1982–
Toronto

Alexander J. MacIntosh
Deputy Governor, HBC,
1970–85
(Blake, Cassels & Graydon)
Toronto

Les R. McIntosh
Marketing Manager, Fur,
National Stores Department,
HBC
Winnipeg

Donald A. McIvor
Fur trader (Now retired)
Norway House, Man.

Malcolm H. MacKenzie
Corporate vice-president,
Personnel, HBC
Now residing in Toronto

Jocelyn McKillop
Former historian, Hudson's
Bay House
Winnipeg

Angus MacKinnon
Manager, HBC store
Churchill, Man.

Doug MacLachlan
Guardian,
York Factory, Man.

Hugh MacLennan
Author
Montreal

Jim McMillan
Manager, HBC store
Rankin Inlet, N.W.T.

Dan D. McTavish
General Manager, TASH Inc.
Toronto

Brig. Richard S. Malone
Former Chairman, FP
Publications
Toronto

Jacques Marchand
Manager, James Bay District,
HBC
Fort Rupert, Que.

Hubert G. Mayes
Department of French
University of Winnipeg
Winnipeg

Herbert J. Mays
Department of History
University of Winnipeg
Winnipeg

Fred Mehmel
Mehmel Fur Brokers Inc.
Toronto

Eric Mitchell
Post Manager, Fur Trade
Department, Arctic Division,
HBC
Now residing in Kleinburg,
Ont.

W.L. Morton
Historian
Winnipeg

James Richard (Dick) Murray
Managing Director, HBC,
1959–72
Now residing in Victoria

Keith Nordon
Trinity,
Jersey, Channel Islands, U.K.

S.M. (Mike) Norgrove
Manager, Materials Handling,
Northern Stores Department,
HBC
Winnipeg

Robert V. Oleson
Historian, HBC, 1973–79
(Now with Government of
Manitoba)
Winnipeg

The Rt. Hon. Lord O'Neill of
the Maine
London

Paul J. O'Pecko
Librarian, Mystic Seaport
Museum
Mystic, Connecticut

William Palk
Former Managing Director,
Eaton's of Canada Winnipeg
store
Now residing in Toronto

Frits Pannekoek
Director, Historic Sites Service
Historical Resources, Alberta
Culture
Edmonton

Phillip Patterson
Manager, Raw Fur Department,
HBC,
North Bay, Ont.

John de B. Payne,
Senior Assistant to the
Managing Director, HBC,
Winnipeg, c. 1947–57,
Now residing in Montreal

Neil Pearson
Fur broker
Oakville, Ont.

David Perks
Former Vice-president,
FP Publications
Toronto

James B. Pitblado
Chairman, Dominion Securities
Toronto

Michael Pitfield
Clerk of the Privy Council
during negotiations and
transfer of HBC Archives from
London to Winnipeg
Now residing in Ottawa

Reuben H. Ploughman
Pensioner
Moosonee, Ont.

Carol Preston
Librarian, Hudson's Bay
House
Winnipeg

Arthur J. (Skip) Ray
Department of History,
University of British Columbia;
also Amisk Heritage Planning
and Research
Vancouver

Gordon Rennie
Manager, HBC store
Frobisher Bay, Baffin Island,
N.W.T.

David Richardson,
James Richardson & Sons Ltd.
Winnipeg

George Richardson
Governor, HBC, 1970–83
(President, James Richardson &
Sons Ltd.)
Winnipeg

The Rt. Hon. Lord Robbins
Chairman, London School of
Economics
London

Michael Roberts
Editor, *Caribou News*
Nortext Information Design
Ltd.
Ottawa

Mr and Mrs John Robertson
Pensioners
Norway House, Man.

William A. Rose
Manager, Wholesale
Department, HBC, 1955-59
Winnipeg

Abraham Rotstein
Department of Political
Economy
University of Toronto
Toronto

Dennis Ryan
Manager, HBC store
Arctic Bay, Baffin Island,
N.W.T.

Isaiah Salt
Pensioner
Fort Rupert, Que.

Fred Scott
Manager, HBC store
Cape Dorset, Baffin Island,
N.W.T.

Bruce Sealey
Department of Education

University of Manitoba
Winnipeg

Joseph Segal
Kingswood Capital Corp.
Vancouver

Alex Shieff
Manager, Ontario Trappers
Association and Fur Sales
Service
North Bay, Ont.

George Shulof
Juliette Shulof Furs
New York

Mary Jane Sinclair
Pensioner
Norway House, Man.

Jack Skolnick
Fur broker
New York

Marsha G. Smoke
Executive assistant, Grand
Council of the Crees (of
Quebec)
Val d'Or, Que.

Glen R. Speers
Relief Manager, HBC store
Fort Severn, Ont.

Dr Ahab Spence
Department of Languages,
Literature and Linguistics
Saskatchewan Indian Federated
College
Regina

E.J. Spracklin
Former District Manager,
Keewatin District,
Northern Stores Department,
HBC
Winnipeg

Irene Spry
Former professor of economics,
University of Ottawa
(Author of numerous fur trade
studies)
Ottawa

John Stoddart
Manager, HBC store
Moose Factory, Ont.

Dr Blair Stonechild
Head, Department of Indian
Studies
Saskatchewan Indian Federated
College
Regina

H.W. Sutherland
Former Senior Vice-president,
HBC
Winnipeg

Eseas Thomas
Trapper and former HBC
freighter, York Factory and
Oxford House
Now residing in
Fort Severn, Ont.

Stanley Thomas
Interpreter, born in York
Factory
Now residing in
Fort Severn, Ont.

The Rt. Hon. Lord Thomson
of Fleet (Kenneth R. Thomson)
Chairman, President and CEO,
Thomson Newspapers Ltd.
Toronto

W.L. Tolboom
Accountant, National Stores
Department, HBC
Winnipeg

John Tory
President and Director,
Thomson Corp. Ltd.
Toronto

Liz Tory
Governor, Shaw Festival,
Niagara-on-the-Lake
(Animator *extraordinaire*)
Toronto

A.G. Towlson
Property Manager, Hudson's
Bay and Annings Ltd.
London

J. Raymond Tremblay
Les Fourrures J.R. Tremblay
Inc.
Montreal

Garth Turner
Business editor
The Toronto Sun
Toronto

The Rt. Hon. John N. Turner
Leader of the Opposition
Son-in-law of David Kilgour,
former head of the HBC
Canadian Committee
Now residing in Ottawa

The Rt. Hon. Lord
Tweedsmuir
Council on Tribunals
London

Luc Vachon
Manager, HBC store
Fort Albany, Ont.

Sylvia Van Kirk
Department of History
University of Toronto
Toronto

S.D. Vigod
Fur broker
Reliable Fur Dressers & Dyers
Ltd.
Toronto

Henry Voisey
Factor, HBC, 1965
Repulse Bay, N.W.T.

Leslie Walford
Manager, HBC store
Pond Inlet,
Baffin Island, N.W.T.

Frank Walker
Executive assistant to Philip
Chester of the Canadian
Committee, HBC, 1951-59
Now residing in Montreal

Sir Siegmund Warburg
Vaud, Switzerland

J.C. Warren
Former Factor at York Factory
Now residing in
North Vancouver

Mel Watkins
Department of Political
Economy
University of Toronto
Toronto

Bernie Weston
Trader and retailer
Skin & Bones
Toronto

George A. Whitman
Director of External Relations,
HBC
Winnipeg

H. Richard Whittall
Vice-chairman, Richardson
Greenshields of Canada Ltd.
Vancouver

The Rev. Frances Joan
Whitting
Assistant to the treasurer, HBC
(Resigned in 1971 to become
an Anglican priest)
Winnipeg

William Wilder
Chairman of the board,
Consumers' Gas Co. Ltd.
Toronto

Glyndwr Williams
Department of History
Queen Mary College, University
of London
London

Peter Wood
Executive Vice-president, HBC
Toronto

Bob Young
Manager, HBC store
Pangnirtung,
Baffin Island, N.W.T.

David Philip Young
Teacher and researcher
Victoria

Chapter Notes

FOREWORD:

P. xv. *character and circumstance*: John S. Moir, *Character and Circumstance*, p. x.

P. xvi. *"a convincing version of events"*: A.J.P. Taylor. In Duncan Fallowell, "The view from Twisden Rd." *The Spectator* 250:8081 (28 May 1983): pp. 21–2.

P. xvi. *"Kipling's itinerant story-teller"*: Barbara Tuchman, *Practising History*, p. 69.

YORK FACTORY

P. xxix. *"I was much surprised"*: Letitia Hargrave. In Margaret Macleod, *Letters of Letitia Hargrave*, p. 62.

P. xxx. *"a monstrous blot on a swampy spot"*: Robert Ballantyne, *Hudson's Bay*, p. 129.

P. xxxi. *"nine months of winter"*: James Hargrave. In Margaret Macleod, *Letters of Letitia Hargrave*, p. 282.

P. xxxi. *"a humbling affair"*: Letitia Hargrave. In Margaret Macleod, *Letters of Letitia Hargrave*, pp. 94–5.

P. xxxi. *"In consequence of the breathing"*: Robert Ballantyne, *Hudson's Bay*, pp. 166–7.

CHAPTER 1 THE BAY MEN

P. 2. *"a kind of kingdom by itself"*: John Buchan to Philip Chester, 10 December 1938. In Lord Tweedsmuir II, letter to the author, 2 March 1985.

P. 3. *"recorded history begins with the fur trade"*: John Foster. In *Encyclopedia of Canada*.

P. 4. *"the HBC gave with one hand"*: Gabrielle Roy, "Windflower, Episode 7," *CBC Booktime*, CBC Radio, 9 January 1985.

P. 4. *"the difference between being in the fire and being in the frying pan"*: Blair Stonechild, interview, Regina, Sask., March 1985.

P. 4. *"our origin in the northern frontier"*: W.L. Morton. In William Kilbourn, *Canada: A Guide to the Peaceable Kingdom*, pp. 280–84.

P. 7. *"Upon Hay Island"*: J.A. Hayes. In E.E. Rich and A.M. Johnson, *Copy Book of Letters Outward*, p. 9.

P. 8. *"the expansion of the British Empire"*: John S. Galbraith, *The Hudson's Bay Company as an Imperial Factor, 1821–1869* (Berkeley: University of California Press, 1957), p. 3.

P. 9. *Marquis of Lorne at Rat Portage*: In W. Stewart Mac-Nutt, *Days of Lorne*, p. 86.

P. 9. *"Canadians like to see themselves"*: Ronald Bryden, "Northern Light," *New York Times*, 3 June 1984, sec. 7, p. 32.

P. 10. *"to live lovingly with one another"*: HBCA A.6/3, fo. 124d.

P. 11. *"you might break all the ten Commandments"*: N.M.W.J. Mackenzie, *Men of the Hudson's Bay Company*, p. 140.

P. 12. *"One night when wet and cold"*: John Crofton. In "The Little Emperor," *The Beaver*, Summer 1960, p. 58.

P. 14. *"Throughout the Company's history"*: K.G. Davies, *Letters from Hudson Bay*, p. x.

P. 15. *ice sales of the* HBC *in San Francisco*: W.L. Ostenstad, "A Lucrative Contract: The HBC and the Pacific Ice Deal," *The Beaver*, Winter 1977, pp. 36–40.

P. 15. *the* HBC *and its First World War supply role*: HBCA A.1/162, fo. 48.

P. 17. *"Even a casual observer"*: Michael Payne, *Social History of York Factory*, p. 54.

P. 17. *"I consider it quite unnecessary"*: Sir George Simpson. In Margaret Macleod, *Letters of Letitia Hargrave*, p. 159n.

P. 18. *if contracts for officers and men*: Sir George Simpson. In E.E. Rich, *Journal of Occurrences in the Athabasca Department*, p. 2.

P. 18. *"I had the honour of my neighbours company"*: John McKay. In Harvey Bassett, "Christmas in the Fur Trade," *The Beaver*, December 1941, pp. 18–22.

P. 18. *"This being Christmas Morning"*: Thomas Stagner. Ibid., pp. 18–22.

P. 18. *"The reason was that they didn't want"*: Stuart Hodgson, interview with the author, Sidney, B.C., 1984.

P. 19. *"I never encouraged"*: E.J. Gall, interview with the author, Victoria, B.C., 1984.

P. 20. *the continent can be crossed by water-routes*: John McPhee, "A Reporter at Large: The Survival of the Bark Canoe – II," *The New Yorker* 51:2 (3 March 1975), p. 41.

P. 20. *"Canada's almost total navigability"*: Eric W. Morse, *Fur Trade Canoe Routes*, pp. 27, 29.

P. 22. *"Canada emerged as a political entity"*: Harold A. Innis, *The Fur Trade in Canada*, p. 379.

P. 23. *"For the next half century"*: Pierre Berton, *The Great Railway*, vol. 2, *The Last Spike*, p. 6.

P. 23. *"the forces of American manifest destiny"*: Irene Spry, interview with the author, Ottawa, 1984.

P. 24. *"My country has no history"*: Alden Nowlan, "1914–1918," *Saturday Night* 98:2 (February 1983), p. 76.

P. 25. *"The shape of the indigenous Canadian imagination"*: Abraham Rotstein, interview with the author, Toronto, 1984.

P. 26. *"the garrison mentality"*: Northrop Frye, *The Bush Garden*, p. 226.

P. 26. *"business is the law of the jungle"*: Roy Thomson, interview with the author, Toronto, 1974.

P. 29. *"I regret that the recession took place"*: Donald McGiverin, interview with the author, Toronto, 1981.

P. 29. *"my only apple tree"*: Ibid.

CHAPTER 2 BEYOND THE WESTERING SEA

P. 31. *they came to claim a new world*: For general reference works on the exploration of North America, the reader is referred to: (1) Alan Cooke and Clive Holland, *The Exploration of Northern Canada: 500 to 1920. A Chronology* (Toronto: Arctic History Press, 1978); (2) Richard Hakluyt. *The Principall Navigations, Voiages and Discoveries of the English Nation ...* 3 vols. Hakluyt Society, Extra Series, no. 39. (London: George Bishop et al, 1589–1600). Reprint ed. (Cambridge: Cambridge University Press, 1965).

P. 31. *"On every side of us are men"*: Kenneth Roberts, *Northwest Passage*, p. 2.

P. 33. *"not just an oversized island"*: Daniel Francis, *Battle for the West*, p. 15.

P. 33. *"If you wish to know"*: In Frank Rasky, *Polar Voyagers*, p. 63.

P. 35. On the voyages of John Cabot see James A. Williamson, *The Cabot Voyages and Bristol Discovery under Henry VII.* Hakluyt Society, Second Series, no. 120 (Cambridge: Cambridge University Press, 1962).

P. 35. *"they even stayed the ship's passage"*: John Cabot. In Frank Rasky, *Polar Voyagers,* p. 79.

P. 37. *"as near heaven by sea as by land"*: Humphrey Gilbert. In Frank Rasky, *Polar Voyagers,* p. 137.

P. 38. *"Whosoever commands the seas"*: Sir Walter Raleigh. In Gerald S. Graham, *A Concise History of the British Empire*, p. 18.

P. 38. For further information on Sir Martin Frobisher, see Vilhjalmur Stefansson, *The Three Voyages of Martin Frobisher* (London: Argonaut Press, 1938).

P. 38. *"the only thing of the world"*: Sir Martin Frobisher. In Jeanette Mirsky, *To the North!,* p. 32.

P. 38. *"outrageous common and*

daily piracies": Richard Hakluyt. In Frank Rasky, *Polar Voyagers,* p. 92.

P. 40. *"Her Majesty beholding the same"*: Sir Martin Frobisher. In John E. Caswell, "Sponsors of Canadian Arctic Exploration," *The Beaver,* Spring 1969, pp. 4–13.

P. 40. *"this place he named Frobisher's Straits"*: George Best. In Frank Rasky, *Polar Voyagers,* p. 104.

P. 42. On John Davis see Albert H. Markham, ed., *The Voyages and Works of John Davis, the Navigator.* Hakluyt Society, First Series, no. 59 (London: Hakluyt Society, 1880).

P. 42. Regarding Henry Hudson see G.M. Asher, *Henry Hudson, the Navigator.*

P. 49. *"I do confidently believe"*: Thomas Button. In Frank Rasky, *Polar Voyagers,* p. 240.

P. 49. For further information on Jens Munk see C.C.A. Gosch, ed. *Danish Arctic Expeditions, 1605 to 1620. In two books … Book II. The Expedition of Captain Jens Munk to Hudson's Bay in search of a North-west Passage in 1619–20.* Hakluyt Society, First Series, no. 97 (London: Hakluyt Society, 1897).

P. 49. *"wine and strong beer"*: Jens Munk. In W.A. Kenyon, *The Journal of Jens Munk,* p. 25.

P. 49. *"great pains in the loins"*: Ibid., p. 34.

P. 50. *"I could no longer stand the bad smell"*: Ibid., p. 35.

P. 50. *"good-night to all the world"*: Ibid.

P. 51. On Luke Foxe see L. Foxe, *North-West Fox, or, Fox from the Northwest Passage* (London: B. Alsop and Tho. Fauvcet, 1635). Reprint ed. (New York: Johnson Reprint Corporation., 1965).

P. 51. *"Many a Storme"*: Thomas James, *Strange and Dangerous Voyage,* p. 3.

P. 52. *"there came a great rowling sea"*: Ibid., pp. 29–30.

P. 52. *"This delicate morning"*: Luke Foxe. In Frank Rasky, *Polar Voyagers,* p. 248.

P. 52. *"So long as I am sailing"*: Ibid., p. 249.

P. 53. *"I caused the surgeon"*: Thomas James. In Frank Rasky, *Polar Voyagers,* p. 257.

P. 53. *"that merely imaginary passage"*: Thomas James. In George Malcolm Thomson, *Search for the North-west Passage,* p. 119.

CHAPTER 3
A BOUNTY OF BEAVER

P. 55. *"The beaver, by its defencelessness"*: Eric W. Morse, *Canoe Routes,* p. 109.

P. 57. *"They made frequent signs"*: Jacques Cartier. In W.A. Mac-

Kay, *Great Canadian Skin Game*, p. 1.

P. 59. *"one of the most important manufactures"*: Samuel Smiles, *The Huguenots: Their Settlements, Churches, and Industries in England and Ireland*, 6th ed. (London: John Murray, 1889), pp. 267–268n.

P. 61. *"to own a fine beaver"*: Walter O'Meara, *Savage Country*, p. viii.

P. 62. *"Every major political upheaval"*: Murray G. Lawson, *Fur*, pp. 4–5.

P. 62. *"The beaver does everything perfectly well"*: In Chrestien Le Clerq. *New Relation of Gaspesia, with the Customs and Religion of the Gaspesian Indians*. Translated and edited by William F. Ganong, The Publications of the Champlain Society, vol. 5 (Toronto: The Champlain Society, 1910), p. 277.

P. 65. *"Castoreum does much good to mad people"*: Joanne Franco. In "The Beaver: A Cure for all Ills," *The Beaver*, September 1931, pp. 283–4.

P. 66. *"he removes his own testicles"*: In T.H. White, ed., *The Book of Beasts, being a translation from a Latin Bestiary of the Twelfth Century* (London: Jonathan Cape, 1954), pp. 28–9.

P. 67. *ten million beaver in 1670*: Robert J. Naiman to the author, 16 August 1983.

P. 68. *"lazy beavers" which lived on land*: Malachy Postlethwayt, *The Universal Dictionary of Trade and Commerce ...* 4th ed. (London: W. Strahan et al, 1774).

P. 70. *"I cannot refrain from smiling"*: Samuel Hearne, *A Journey from Prince of Wales's Fort*, pp. 149–50.

P. 70. *"In respect to the beaver dunging"*: Ibid., pp. 156–7.

P. 71. *"Anxious to learn more about their ways"*: Dr. John Knox, "Some of My Best Canadian Friends Are Beavers," *Maclean's*, 15 May 1965, pp. 24, 48–50.

P. 72. *"It does act intelligently"*: E.R. Warren, *The Beaver and its Works* (Baltimore: Williams & Wilkins, 1927), p. 24.

P. 74. *beaver can cut down trees as fast as a man with a dull hatchet*: Ernest Thompson Seton, *Lives of Game Animals* (Boston: Charles T. Branford, 1953), p. 459.

P. 75. *"the beaver is much given to jealousy"*: Alexander Henry, *Alexander Henry's Travels and Adventures in the Years 1760–1776*, ed. Milo Milton Quaife, The Lakeside Classics (Chicago: R.R. Donnelley & Sons Co. 1921), p. 127.

P. 78. *"the Indians who were my companions along the trap-line"*: Frank Conibear, "The Beaver's Lodge," *The Beaver*, September 1951, pp. 36–7.

P. 78. *"a demonstration of the*

highest skill": A. Radclyffe Dugmore, *The Romance of the Beaver: Being the History of the Beaver in the Western Hemisphere* (Philadelphia: J.B. Lippincott Co., n.d.), p. 66.

P. 79. *"The history of Canada"*: Harold A. Innis, *The Fur Trade in Canada*, p.1.

CHAPTER 4
MESSRS RADISHES & GOOSEBERRIES
P. 82. *"between the Sun King and his Britannic Majesty"*: Agnes C. Laut, *The "Adventurers of England" on Hudson Bay*, pp. xi–xii.

P. 83. *"a more daring pair"*: Douglas MacKay, *The Honourable Company*, p.16.

P. 88. *interchange between Earl of Rochester and Charles II*: In Antonia Fraser, *King Charles II*, pp. 340–41.

P. 88. *"the golden-hearted prostitute"*: Ibid., p. 289.

CHAPTER 5
A PRINCELY UNDERTAKING
P. 95. *"one of the most varied careers"*: John Buchan. In George Edinger, *Rupert*, p.5.

P. 96. *"How many towns hast thou fired?"* In Maurice Ashley, *Rupert of the Rhine*, p. 115. See also *A Dog's Elegy, or Rupert's Tears, for the late defeat given him at Marstonmoore, ...* (London: 1644).

P. 96. *"A man of intense loyalties"*: Hugh Trevor-Roper, "Prince Rupert, 1619–82," *History Today* 32:3 (March 1982): pp. 4–11.

P. 97. *"abreast of contemporary thought"*: George Edinger, *Rupert*, p. 14.

P. 98. *mezzotints of Prince Rupert*: See P.H. Hulton, "Prince Rupert: Artist and Patron of the Arts," *The Beaver*, Winter 1960, pp. 3–11.

P. 102. *"God damme, if they will turn out"*: Rupert to Samuel Pepys, Pepys's diary, vol. 7, p. 264.

P. 103. *"the most modest of the court"*: Duchess Sophia. In George Malcolm Thomson, *Warrior Prince*, p. 217.

P. 105. *"full complement of original investors"*: Fulmer Mood, "Hudson's Bay Company Started as a Syndicate," *The Beaver*, March 1938, pp. 52–8.

P. 107. *"civility and courtesy"*: J.A. Hayes et al. In Grace Lee Nute, "Radisson and Groseilliers' Contribution to Geography," *Minnesota History* 16 (1935), pp. 414–26.

P. 107. *"if by accident you meete"*: Ibid., pp. 414–26.

P. 107. *"discovery of the passage"*: Ibid., p. 420.

P. 108. *"This visit was different"*: Daniel Francis and Toby Morantz, *Partners in Furs*, p. 22.

P. 112. *"a voyage for Holland"*: Jan Van Heemskerk. In Grace Lee Nute, *Caesars of the Wilderness*, p. 126.

P. 112. *"a faire embroidered purse"*: In Agnes C. Laut, *Conquest*, p. 137.

P. 113. *"The granting of such wide territory"*: Arthur S. Morton, *History of the Canadian West*, p. 57.

P. 116. *"our Deare and entirely Beloved cousin"*: In *Charters, Statutes*, p. 3.

P. 117. *"you are to consider how"*: HBCA A. 37/7.

P. 118. *to yield and pay*: In *Charters, Statutes*, p. 12.

P. 118. *"In case she put down"*: Sir Eric Faulkner, interview with the author, London, 1980.

P. 118. *Lord Amory and Queen Elizabeth*: Ibid.

P. 120. *"the passing of the Navigation Act"*: Barry M. Gough, "The 'Adventurers of England Trading into Hudson's Bay': A Study of the Founding Members of the Hudson's Bay Company, 1665–1670," *Albion* 2:1 (1970), pp. 35–47.

P. 121. *"Profit and power"*: Sir Josiah Child, *A New Discourse of Trade*, 2nd ed. (1694), pp. 114–15. In Charles Wilson, *Profit and Power*, p. 1.

P. 124. *"Absolutism, pomp, formality"*: Agnes C. Laut, *The Adventurers of England*, p. 42.

P. 124. *gifts of the HBC in early years*: Agnes C. Laut, *Conquest*, vol. 1, pp. 137–8.

P. 124. *"I do swear"*: Ibid., vol. 1, p. 136.

P. 131. *"Friend, once 'twas Fame"*: John Dryden. In G.M. Thomson, *Warrior Prince*, p. 213.

P. 132. *"I strove as much as the winds would permit"*: Charles Duncan. In Alice M. Johnson, "The Mythical Land of Buss," *The Beaver*, December 1942, pp. 43–7.

P. 132. *"There were gentlemen"*: Thomas Babington Macaulay, *History of England*, vol. 1, p. 294.

P. 136. *"It cannot be my beauty"*: Catherine Sedley. In Thomas Babington Macaulay, *History of England*, vol. 2, p. 726.

P. 140. *"On this evidence"*: K.G. Davies. In Malvina Bolus, *People and Pelts*, p. 69.

CHAPTER 6
BATTLING FOR THE BAY

P. 145. *"the men in London"*: Grace Lee Nute, "The History of the Hudson's Bay Company, 1670–1870," *The Beaver*, Spring 1959, pp. 45–7.

P. 147. *"The* Compagnie du Nord's *fatal error"*: Edward Borins, *La Compagnie du Nord, 1682–1700*.

P. 148. *"all bachelors and very resolute fellows"*: HBC London

Committee. In E.E. Rich, *The History of the Hudson's Bay Company*, vol. 1, p. 135.

P. 150. *"could be brought over again"*: Sir James Hayes. In Beckles Willson, *Great Company* (Toronto: Copp, Clark Co., 1899), p. 112.

P. 150. *"more like a savage"*: Godey. In Beckles Willson, *Great Company*, p. 113.

P. 150. *"I yielded to these solicitations"*: Pierre-Esprit Radisson. In Beckles Willson, *Great Company*, p. 116.

P. 153. For more on the d'Iberville invasion, see: (1) Beckles Willson, *Great Company*, chap. 14; (2) Grace Lee Nute, "The French on the Bay." *The Beaver*, Winter 1957, pp. 32–7; (3) Nellis M. Crouse, *Lemoyne d'Iberville*.

CHAPTER 7
THE CENTURY OF THE LAKES

P. 168. *"the connivance of a bankrupt Governor"*: E.E. Rich, *Hudson's Bay Company*, vol. 1, pp. 461–8.

P. 170. *"There is nothing more persistent"*: Lord Bolingbroke. In Beckles Willson, *Great Company*, p. 203.

P. 170. *"The said most Christian King"*: In J.B. Tyrrell, *Documents relating to the early history of Hudson Bay*, p. 409.

P. 171. *"unobtrusive sanity"*:

E.E. Rich, *Hudson's Bay Company*, vol. 1, p. 660.

P. 172. *"the nature of a private copartnery"*: Adam Smith, *An Inquiry into the Wealth of Nations*, vol. 2, p. 231.

P. 174. *Canada and Guadeloupe*: In W.L. Grant, "Canada versus Guadeloupe, An Episode of the Seven Years' War," *American Historical Review* 17:4 (July 1912), pp. 735–43.

P. 177. *"What little exploration"*: Glyndwr Williams, "The Hudson's Bay Company and its Critics," pp. 149–71.

P. 177. *obscure financial dealings of HBC*: See ibid., which gives as source the Hudson's Bay Company Archives HBCA A.43/4 (Stock Transfer Book, 1730–60). On Bibye Lake, see *A Compleat Guide to London* (London, 1740), p. 134.

P. 177. For further information on the financial data of the HBC in this period, see: (1) E.E. Rich, *Hudson's Bay Company*, vol. 1, chap. 36; (2) K.G. Davies, "The years of no Dividend."

CHAPTER 8
ASLEEP BY THE FROZEN SEA

P. 186. *"a confused heap"*: James Knight. In Davies, *Letters from Hudson's Bay*, p. 38. Knight to Captain John Merry, HBCA B.239/a/1, fos. 5d.–6.

P. 187. *"There being no Towns"*: John Oldmixon, *British Empire in America,* (London, 1708), p. 382, in Glyndwr Williams, "The Hudson's Bay Company and its Critics," p. 150.

P. 187. *"The search for the North West Passage"*: Tim Ball, "Climatic Change in Central Canada," p. 51.

P. 188. *"countries bordering on Hudson Bay"*: "Remarks on the Fur Trade," *Gentleman's Magazine,* New Series 24 (1754), pp. 503–5.

P. 188. *"the most enormous and confirmed offenders"*: In Glyndwr Williams, "Hudson's Bay Company and its Critics," pp. 163–4. Castle Dobbs Papers (Public Record Office of Northern Ireland, Belfast), D.O.D. 162/60, p. 5.

P. 189. *the 1742 rebuke:* HBCA A. 6/7, fos. 17d–18d, 5 May 1743.

P. 190. *"Your general letter"*: HBCA A. 6/7, fo. 6d.

P. 191. *"at the edge of a frozen sea"*: Joseph Robson, *An Account of Six Years Residence,* p. 6.

P. 191. *"Rich as the trade"*: John Oldmixon. In Tyrrell, *Documents,* p. 373.

P. 192. *"the wine with which the officers drank"*: Christopher Middleton. In Glyndwr Williams, *British Search,* p. 62.

P. 192. *"The head of my bed-place"*: William Wales. In Richard Glover, "An Early Visitor," pp. 37–45.

P. 193. *factors' journal entries on weather*: Timothy Ball, "Climatic Change," pp. 369–467 *passim.*

P. 193. *"The winter in general"*: Samuel Hearne. In Timothy Ball, "Climatic Change," p. 439. HBCA B.42/a/94.

P. 194. *"painful, tender little pimples"*: Robert Ballantyne, *Hudson's Bay,* p. 129.

P. 194. *"such swarms of a small sand flyes"*: James Knight, *Founding of Churchill,* pp. 147–8.

P. 194. *"the summer never thaws"*: James Knight. In George Ingram, *York Factory,* p. 5. HBCA, York Factory Journal, B.239/ a/3, fo. 7, 10 October 1716.

P. 195. *"to leave the factory"*: James Knight. In George Ingram, *York Factory,* p. 3. HBCA, York Factory Journal, B.239/a/1, fos. 38–9, 7 May 1715.

P. 195. *"almost universal destruction"*: Joseph Colen. In George Ingram, *York Factory,* p. 36. HBCA, York Factory Journal, B.239/ a/88, fo. 42, 9 May 1788.

P. 198. *"list of ships sunk in the Bay"*: Alan Cooke and Clive Holland, *Exploration of Northern Canada.*

P. 199. *"on the basis of intelli-*

gence": Richard Glover. In E.E. Rich and A.M. Johnson, *Cumberland House Journals and Inland Journals, 1775–82. First Series: 1775–78*, p. lvii.

P. 200. *"more like beasts than men"*: James Isham. In E.E. Rich and A.M. Johnson, *James Isham's Observations*, p. 117.

P. 200. *"a beaver skin which comes down"*: William Wales, "Journal of a Voyage," p. xvi.

P. 200. *"a beard as long as Captain Teach's"*: James Isham. In E.E. Rich and A.M. Johnson, *James Isham's Observations*, p. 117.

P. 200. *"Teach allowed his beard to grow"*: Hugh Rankin, *Golden Age of Piracy*, p. 108.

P. 201. *"the water beats between the logs"*: Joseph Robson, *Account of Six Years' Residence*, p. 30.

P. 202. *"It is 310 feet long"*: Joseph Tyrrell, *A Journey from Prince of Wales's Fort*, pp. 21–2.

P. 203. *"the ships taking refuge"*: Arthur S. Morton, *History of the Canadian West*, p. 227.

P. 204. *"the major part of the people"*: Andrew Graham. In Glyndwr Williams, "The Hudson's Bay Company and the Fur Trade, 1670–1870," *The Beaver*, Autumn 1983, pp. 4–86.

P. 206. *"the cask of hogs' cheeks"*: Anthony Beale. In Michael Payne, *Prince of Wales' Fort*, p. 53. HBCA B.42/a/67, fo. 90.

P. 206. *"Such rich mould has laine fallow"*: A.M. Johnson, "Life on the Hayes," *The Beaver*, Winter 1957, pp. 38–43. HBCA A.6/4, fo. 82.

P. 208. *"Take whole salmons"*: HBCA B.42/a/1, fo, 33d.

P. 210. *"partridges strowed about in the dirt and gravel"*: Joseph Isbister. In Michael Payne, *Prince of Wales' Fort*, p. 56. HBCA B.42/a/94, fo. 24, 20 March 1777.

P. 210. *"always handsomely supplied"*: Andrew Graham. In Glyndwr Williams, *Andrew Graham's Observations*, p. 297.

P. 211. *"the healthiest part in the known world"*: Samuel Hearne. In Michael Payne, *Prince of Wales' Fort*, p. 91. HBCA B.42/1/94, fo. 24. 20 March 1777.

P. 213. *"a very large quantity of … brandy"*: HBC London Committee. In E.E. Rich and A.M. Johnson, *Hudson's Bay Copy Booke*, p. 143.

P. 213. *"Trade as little brandy as possible"*: HBC London committee. In K.G. Davies and A.M. Johnson, *Letters from Hudson Bay*, p. 29n. HBCA A.6/3, fos. 20d.–21d.

P. 213. *"in the medicine chest"*: HBC London Committee. In K.G. Davies and A.M. Johnson, *Letters from Hudson Bay*, p. 204n. HBCA A.6/5, fos. 93d–95.

P. 214. *"This evening James*

Robertson": HBCA B. 239/a/8, fo. 68d, 17 January 1726.

P. 215. *"To brew this beer"*: Michael Payne, *Prince of Wales' Fort*, pp. 74–5. HBCA B.42/a/50, fo. 9d., 28 October 1751.

P. 216. *"Vice and ignorance"*: Richard Staunton. In E.E. Rich, *The History of the Hudson's Bay Company*, vol. 1, p. 547.

P. 216. *"Many of the accidents"*: Frits Pannekoek, "Corruption," pp. 4–11.

P. 217. *"a nest of free and accepted Masons"*: James Duffield. In Frits Pannekoek, "Corruption," p. 9.

P. 217. *"ruled by a series of compromises"*: Glyndwr Williams, "Hudson's Bay Company and the Fur Trade, 1670–1870," *The Beaver*, Autumn 1983, pp. 4–86.

P. 218. *"I desired him not to be saucy"*: Henry Pollexfen. In E.E. Rich, *The History of the Hudson's Bay Company*, vol. 1, p. 547.

P. 220. *"I will with pleasure"*: Andrew Graham. In Glyndwr Williams, *Graham's Observations*, p. 344. HBCA A.11/115, fo. 144d.

P. 220. *"In regard to your request"*: HBC London Committee. In Glyndwr Williams, *Graham's Observations*, p. 345. HBCA A.5/1, fo. 152d.

P. 222. *"It should be remem-* bered"*: Michael Payne, *Prince of Wales' Fort*, pp. 100–101.

P. 223. *"hard-drinking but always alert"*: James Morris, "A View of the Royal Navy," *Encounter* 40:3 (March 1973), pp. 15–27.

P. 223. *"Gentlemen had to be just that"*: Philip Goldring, *Papers on the Labor System*, p. 38.

P. 225. *"In order to draw a line of distinction"*: HBCA B.239/k/1, fos. 55, 55d.

P. 227. *"To excite emulation and ambition"*: HBCA A.11/4, fos. 184, 184d.

P. 228. *Pro Pelle Cutem*: E.E. Rich, *"Pro Pelle Cutem,"* *The Beaver*, Autumn 1980, pp. 65–69.

P. 228. *"The day was arranged rather like watches"*: Glyndwr Williams, interview with the author, London, 1980.

P. 229. *"your impertinent and ridiculous note"*: Sir George Simpson. In E.E. Rich, *Journal of Occurrences*, p. 240.

CHAPTER 9
THE SALTY ORCADIANS

P. 232. *"our London born childring"*: John Nixon. In E.E. Rich and G.N. Clark, eds. *Minutes of the Hudson's Bay Company, 1679–1684. First Part, 1679–82*. The Publications of the Champlain Society, vol. 8. (Toronto: The Champlain Society, 1945), p. 280.

P. 234. *"I was surprised"*: Alexander Henry. In Elliott Coues, *Manuscript Journals*, vol. 1, p. 426.

P. 234. *"turned out to be a woman"*: John Kipling. In Malvina Bolus, "The Son of I. Gunn," *The Beaver*, Winter 1971, p. 24.

P. 234. *"many men have been sent out"*: HBC London Committee. In A.M. Johnson, *Saskatchewan Journals*, p. lxxxvii. HBCA A.5/4, fo. 159.

P. 235. *"The Orcadian was the perpetual immigrant"*: R. Glover. In E.E. Rich and A.M. Johnson, *Cumberland House Journals, Second Series, 1779–82*, p. xlviii.

P. 236. *"A bizarre occurrence"*: H. Lamb, *Climate*, p. 204.

P. 238. *"the quietest servants"*: Samuel Hearne. In E.E. Rich, *The History of the Hudson's Bay Company*, vol. 2, p. 128.

P. 239. *"slow, inanimate habits"*: Sir George Simpson. In E.E. Rich and Harvey Fleming, *Minutes of Council*, p. 349.

P. 239. *"if any person from the Orkney Isles"*: William Walker. In E.E. Rich and A.M. Johnson, *Cumberland House Journals, First Series*, p. xxxviii. HBCA A.11/116, fo. 19.

P. 239. *"a set of the best men"*: Philip Turnor. In J.B. Tyrrell, *Journals of Samuel Hearne*, p. 251.

P. 239. *"a close, prudent, quiet people"*: Edward Umfreville, vol. 5, *Canadian Historical Studies* (Toronto: Ryerson Press, 1954). *Present State of Hudson's Bay*, p. 109.

P. 239. *"It is not easy"*: Sir John Franklin. In E.E. Rich and A.M. Johnson, *Cumberland House Journals, Second Series*, p. xli.

P. 240. *"From the western Arctic to Red River"*: William T. Cutt. In John Shearer et al, *New Orkney Book*, pp. 63–9.

P. 240. *"pulled the wilderness round them like a cloak"*: Bernard de Voto, *Westward the Course of Empire* (London: Eyre & Spottiswoode, 1953).

CHAPTER 10
A SAVAGE COMMERCE
P. 243. *"The picture of the Indian"*: James W. St. G. Walker, "The Indian in Canadian Historical Writing," *The Canadian Historical Papers*, 1971, p. 22.

P. 245. *"When at the point of starvation"*: Robert Douglas and J.N. Wallace, *Twenty Years of York Factory*, p. 40.

P. 245. on Catlin's Indian guests in Paris. George Catlin, *Catlin's Notes of Eight Years' Travels*, vol. 2, pp. 220–1.

P. 248. *The Mandan were "a sensible people"*: Richard White. In Sylvia Van Kirk, "Many Tender Ties," p. 26.

P. 249. *"I have never seen a finer sense"*: Michael Asch, interview with the author, 1985.

P. 250. *"The Indians saw themselves as partners"*: Jennifer Brown, interview with the author, 1985.

P. 250. *"The Indian people inadvertently became dependent"*: Blair Stonechild, interview with the author, 1985.

P. 252. *"In Canada, the Indians were not directly shot at"*: Stan Cuthand, interview with the author, 1985.

P. 252. *"Indian treaties and sovreignty"*: Blair Stonechild, letter to the author, 1985.

P. 252. *"Military action was personal and vital"*: Barbara Tuchman, *Practising History*, p. 57.

P. 252. *on New Englanders and the Beothuk:* Harold Horwood, "The people who were murdered for fun," *Maclean's*, October 10, 1959, p. 36; and Ingeborg Marshall, "The Beothuk," *Horizon Canada* 2:14 (May 1985), pp. 326–331.

P. 253. *"Imagine its impact on a people"*: Chief Dan George, narration from the film. *The Magnificent Gift*, Peter Kelly, director; broadcast Nov. 4, 1970, CBC-TV.

P. 255. *"The Company exchanged as many furs"*: Carol Judd, letter to the author, 1984.

P. 255. *"equivalent to the way we think"*: Abraham Rotstein, interview with the author, 1985; and Abraham Rotstein, "Trade and Politics: An Institutional Approach," *The Western Canadian Journal of Anthropology*, 3:1 (1972), p. 14.

P. 255. *beaver skin prices on London market:* Harold A. Innis, *The Fur Trade in Canada*. pp. 254–5.

P. 256. *individual versus collective bargaining:* William Asikinack (Blackbird), in letter to the author from Blair Stonechild, 1985.

P. 257–260. Details and sequences of the trading ceremony are based on five main sources: "Visit of the Trading Indians" in Glyndwr Williams, *Andrew Graham's Observations*, pp. 315–24; E.E. Rich and Alice Johnson, *James Isham's Observations*, pp. 82–8 (re ceremony of the pipe and trade), pp. 47–54 (re sample conversations between Indians and trader); Arthur Ray and Donald Freeman, *Give Us Good Measure*, chapters 6 and 7; E.E. Rich, *The History of the Hudson's Bay Company*, vol. 1, pp. 597–602 (re credit system, standard of trade, etc.); Abraham Rotstein, "Fur Trade and Empire."

P. 257. *"takes the pipe in both hands"*: Edward Umfreville,

Present State, pp. 28–32.

P. 259. *"You told me last year"*: Ibid., pp. 28–32.

P. 262. *re battle lasting six hours*: Sir Charles Piers, "Fire-Arms of the Hudson's Bay Company," *The Beaver*, March 1934, p. 11.

P. 263. *furs for guns, "unhistorical rubbish"*: Glyndwr Williams, letter to the author, 1980.

P. 264. *"The official standard did remain unchanged"*: Glyndwr Williams, telegram to the author, 1985.

P. 264. *"You bought a gun with skins"*: Henry Simba, brief to the Mackenzie Valley Pipeline Enquiry, Kakisa Lake, N.W.T., July 17, 1976, community hearing before the Honourable Mr Justice Berger, Commissioner; vol. 69, S-692-C69, pp. 7932–33.

P. 264. *markup levels between 1725 and 1760s*: Public Archives of Canada, HBCA B. 239/d/1-72.

P. 265. *"The natives are our asset"*: HBCA DFTR/19, quoted in Arthur J. Ray, "Periodic Shortages, Native Welfare, and the Hudson's Bay Company 1670–1930." In Shepard Krech III, *The Subarctic Fur Trade*.

P. 266. *"If you look at the range"*: Mel Watkins, interview with the author, 1985.

P. 266. *"I must confess that such conduct"*: Samuel Hearne. In Gordon Speck, *Samuel Hearne*, p. 170–2.

P. 268. *"learn the grunts and twists"*: John Ewers, "The Influence of the Fur Trade upon the Indians of the Northern Plains." In Malvina Bolus, *People and Pelts*, p. 22.

P. 268. *Fink and Carpenter duel*: Walter O'Meara, *Daughters of the Country*, p. 140.

P. 269. *"Connubial alliances are the best security"*: Sir George Simpson, *Journal of Occurrences*, p. 392.

P. 270. *"About midnight we were awakened"*: Alexander Henry the Younger. In Elliott Coues, *Manuscript Journals of Alexander Henry*, vol. 1, p. 235.

P. 270. *"the women agreed to being offered"*: Sylvia Van Kirk, *Many Tender Ties*, pp. 78–9.

P. 270. *"the norm for sexual relationships"*: Ibid., p. 4.

P. 271. *"not for wives but use them as Sluts"*: George Nelson, Nelson Papers, Journal No. 5, June 1807–October 1809, p. 225.

P. 271. *"the worst brothel House in London"*: Ferdinand Jacobs. In Glyndwr Williams, "The Hudson's Bay Company and the Fur Trade, 1670–1870," *The Beaver*, Autumn 1983, pp. 4–86.

P. 271. *a mare for a girl*: Alexander Henry the Younger.

In Elliott Coues, *Manuscript Journals of Alexander Henry*, vol. 1, p. 235.

P. 272. *"female captives taken in slave raids"*: Walter O'Meara, *Daughters of the Country*, p. 130; Oscar Lewis, *The Effects of White Contact*, p. 150; and Agnes Laut, *Conquest*, vol. 1, p. 348.

P. 273. *"Your servants of every rank"*: William Auld to the HBC London Committee, HBCA A.11/118, 26 September 1811.

CHAPTER 11
PATHFINDERS

P. 279. *Isham on the fur trade in 1749*: E.E. Rich and Alice Johnson, *James Isham's Observations*, p. xcix. HBCA, Arthur Dobbs' Folder, Isham's Evidence, 4 May 1749.

P. 280. *John Butler's son being sent up-country*: K.G. Davies and A.M. Johnson, *Letters from Hudson's Bay*, p. 113n. HBCA A.6/4, fo. 98d. HBC London Committee to Richard Norton, 19 May 1725.

P. 280. *"the fog of war"*: Richard Glover. In E.E. Rich and Alice Johnson, *Cumberland Journals, First Series*, p. lviii.

P. 281. *"too unsubstantial"*: Lawrence J. Burpee. "York Factory," pp. 307–64.

P. 282. *"Because I was alone"*:

Henry Kelsey, *Kelsey Papers*, pp. 1–3 *passim*.

P. 282. *"What, if anything, the Company made"*: Glyndwr Williams, "The Hudson's Bay Company and the Fur Trade, 1670–1870," *The Beaver*, Autumn 1983, pp. 4–86.

P. 285. *"none but a Sott"*: James Knight. In E.E. Rich, *The History of the Hudson's Bay Company*, vol. 1, p. 439.

P. 289. *"made herself hoarse with her perpetual talking"*: James Knight. HBCA, B.239/a/2, fo. 27–27d.

P. 290. *"made them all stand in fear"*: Ibid., fo. 29.

P. 290. *"ketcht him by the nose"*: James Knight. In Sylvia Van Kirk, "Thanadelthur," pp. 40–45.

P. 290. *"She did rise in such a passion"*: Ibid., pp. 40–45.

P. 291. *"York Fort is badd"*: James Knight. In Kenney, *Founding of Churchill*, p. 60.

P. 291. *"Governor Knight knew the way"*: Joseph Robson, *Account*, p. 15.

P. 294. *"least concern"*: Glyndwr Williams, *British Search*, p. 20.

P. 294. *"Mr. Handcock tells me"*: HBCA, York Factory Journal, B.239/a/5, fo. 80v, 10 August 1720.

P. 295. *"I am heartily sorry"*:

John Scroggs. In Glyndwr Williams, *British Search*, p. 26. HBCA, Churchill Journal, B.42/a/2, fo. 51r, 25 July 1722.

P. 295. *"at the hazard of your life"*: HBC London Committee. In Joseph Robson, *Account*, Appendix, p. 32.

P. 295. "a piece of oak": T.S. Drage, *An account of a voyage*, vol. 1, p. 97.

P. 296. *"The total length of coastline"*: W. Gillies Ross and William Barr, "Voyages," pp. 28–33.

P. 296. *"Many days after the rest"*: Samuel Hearne, *Journey*, pp. lxiii–lxiv.

P. 298. *"Them natives to the Norward"*: James Knight. In E.E. Rich and Alice Johnson, *James Isham's Observations*, p. xl. HBCA A.11/114, fo. 15.

P. 298. *"the Company were against him going"*: Arthur Dobbs, *Remarks*, p. 9.

P. 298. *"some of the Company Committeemen"*: Joseph Robson, *Account*, p. 15.

P. 303. *"the discoverer of Western Canada"*: Lawrence J. Burpee, "La Verendrye – Pathfinder of the West," *Canadian Geographical Journal* 66:2 (February 1963), pp. 44–9.

P. 303. *on relative French and English prices*: Arthur J. Ray and Donald B. Freeman, *"Give Us Good Measure,"* p. 196.

CHAPTER 12
THE DOBBS INTERVENTION

P. 308. *"a fat, wealthy monopoly"*: Desmond Clarke, *Arthur Dobbs*, p. 204.

P. 311. *"to have any body interfere"*: Charles Wager. In Dobbs, *Remarks*, pp. 101–2. Wager to Dobbs, 4 March 1738.

P. 311. *Middleton on magnetic variations*: Christopher Middleton, "New and Exact TABLE Collected from several Observations, taken in four Voyages to *Hudson's Bay* … Shewing the Variation of the *Magnetic Needle* … from the Years 1721, to 1725 …" *Philosophical Transactions* (London) 34 (Spring 1726), pp. 73–6.

P. 311. *"no ship was ever pester'd"*: Middleton. In Glyndwr Williams, *British Search*, p. 68. Middleton to Admiralty, 16 October 1742, Adm I/2099.

P. 311. *Daily Post headline*: Glyndwr Williams, *British Search*, p. 58.

P. 312. *"by inevitable necessity"*: HBC London Committee. In Glyndwr Williams, *British Search*, p. 53. HBCA, Committee Minutes, A.1/35, fo. 190, 13 May 1741.

P. 312. *"very unbecoming"*: Sir Charles Wager. In Glyndwr

Williams, *British Search*, p. 55.
Wager to Newcastle, 17 May
1741. State Papers, Domestic
(Public Record Office), 42/81,
fo. 388.

P. 316. *"utmost penury and
distress"*: "Cook's Voyage to
the Pacific Ocean," *Monthly
Review* 70 (1784), pp. 460–74.

P. 316. *Dobbs' Account:* Arthur
Dobbs, *Account.*

P. 317. *"who, to deter others"*:
Arthur Dobbs, *Account*, p.2.

P. 320. *"any single Adventurer"*:
John or Robert Merry. In
Glyndwr Williams, "The
Hudson's Bay Company and
its Critics," p. 162.

P. 320. "a great number of
Larks": John Merry. In
Glyndwr Williams, *British
Search*, p. 117.

P. 321. *"some more happy
Adventurer"*: A. Dobbs, *A Short
Narrative and Justification of the
Proceedings of the Committee
Appointed by the Adventurers, to
prosecute the Discovery of the
Passage to the Western Ocean of
America* (London, 1749), p.
13. In Glyndwr Williams,
British Search, p. 121.

P. 321. *Williams on Dobbs and
the Robson critique:* Glyndwr
Williams, "Arthur Dobbs and
Joseph Robson: New Light on
the Relationship between Two
Early Critics of the Hudson's
Bay Company," *Canadian
Historical Review* 40 (1959), pp.
132–6.

P. 321. *"This fly-away River"*:
John Bean. In Glyndwr
Williams, *British Search*, pp.
125n, 126. HBCA B.42/a/45,
47.

P. 321. *"nothing more at heart"*:
HBC London Committee. In
E.E. Rich and Alice Johnson,
James Isham's Observations, p.
xxx. HBCA A.6/7, fo. 141d.

P. 323. *"the Cree of the
Mountains"*: La Vérendrye. In
Glyndwr Williams, "Puzzle,"
pp. 40–56.

P. 323. *"I don't very well like it"*:
Anthony Henday. In Glyndwr
Williams, "Puzzle," p. 54.

P. 323. *"my bed-fellow"*: Ibid.,
p. 53.

P. 324. *"Such remarks I thought
exceeding true"*: Lawrence J.
Burpee, "York Factory," p.
338.

P. 324. *"water . . . smells like
Brine"*: Henday. In Glyndwr
Williams, "Puzzle," p. 53.

P. 326. *"The French talk several
languages"*: Ibid., p. 48. HBCA
E.2/4, fos. 35–60.

P. 326. *"a dishonestly optimistic
light"*: Glyndwr Williams,
"Puzzle," p. 56.

CHAPTER 13
SAMUEL HEARNE'S
ODYSSEY

P. 330. *"The achievement of Samuel Wegg"*: Glyndwr Williams, "The Hudson's Bay Company and Its Critics," p. 171.

P. 330. *"an old experienced trader"*: [Anthony Cluny], *The American Traveller: or, Observations on the present state, culture and commerce of the British Colonies in America … By an old and experienced trader,* (London: n.p. 1769).

P. 331. *"far to the north"*: HBC London Committee. In Samuel Hearne, *Journey,* pp. lxiv–lxv n. Committee to Norton, 25 May 1769.

P. 332. *"a man of the least merit"*: Samuel Hearne, *Journey,* p. lxiii.

P. 333. *"greater probability of my making some returns"*: Samuel Hearne. In Joseph Tyrrell, *Journals of Hearne,* p. 27.

P. 333. *"one of the most debauched wretches"*: Samuel Hearne, *Journey,* p. 39n.

P. 333. *"it would be absolutely incomprehensible"*: Sylvia Van Kirk, "Moses Norton." In *Dictionary of Canadian Biography.* Vol. 4: *1771 to 1800,* pp. 583–5. Toronto: University of Toronto Press, 1979. p. 584.

P. 334. *"not to give the Indians any disgust"*: HBC London Committee. In E.E. Rich, *History of the Hudson's Bay Company,* vol. 2, p. 45.

P. 334. *"viewed by a summer traveller"*: Farley Mowat, *Top of the World* trilogy, vol. 3, *Tundra,* p. 18.

P. 336. *"fresh caribou meat"*: H. Albert Hochbaum, letter to the author, 1985.

P. 338. *"Their mutual hostility"*: Dr Robert McGhee, letter to the author, 1984.

P. 338. *"The actual violence took much less time"*: Lionel Tiger and Robin Fox, *Imperial Animal,* p. 214.

P. 341. *"maidens are very rare"*: James Isham. In E.E. Rich, *The History of the Hudson's Bay Company,* vol. 1, p. 604.

P. 341. *"many of them cohabit"*: Samuel Hearne, *Journey,* p. 84n.

P. 341. *"On these occasions"*: Ibid., pp. 68–9.

P. 342. *"Ask a northern Indian"*: Ibid., pp. 56–7.

P. 342. *"Chipewyan women ranked lower"*: Diamond Jenness, *Indians of Canada,* p. 386.

P. 342. *"Women were made for labour"*: Samuel Hearne, *Journey,* p. 35.

P. 343. *"porridge sown with razor blades"*: R.A.J. Phillips, *Canada's North,* p. 5.

P. 345. *"I never saw a set of people"*: Samuel Hearne, *Journey,* pp. 32–3.

P. 345. *"scrupulous adherence to truth and honesty"*: Ibid., p. 224.

P. 345. *"the vivacity of a Frenchman"*: Ibid., p. 225.

P. 346. *"Probably no Canadian explorer"*: Maurice Hodgson, "The Exploration Journal as Literature," *The Beaver,* Winter 1967, pp. 4–12.

P. 347. *"When I was on my passage"*: Samuel Hearne, *Journey,* pp. 165–6.

P. 348. *"to suckle a young Bear"*: Ibid., p. 238.

P. 348. *"For some inward complaints"*: Ibid., pp. 123–4.

P. 349. *"As I was the first"*: Ibid., p. 78.

P. 350. *"I must acknowledge"*: Ibid., p. 48.

P. 350. *"The instant, however, the poor woman"*: Ibid., p. 58.

P. 350. *"It is perhaps not generally known"*: Ibid., p. 111.

P. 351. *"When it perceives any people"*: Ibid., pp. 111–12.

P. 351. *"in so barbarous a manner"*: Ibid., p. 184.

P. 352. *Hearne among the Inuit of the Coppermine*: Robert McGhee, letter to the author, 1984.

P. 353. *"She fell down at my feet"*: Samuel Hearne, *Journey,* pp. 99–100.

P. 354. *"the brutish manner"*: Ibid., p. 100.

P. 354. *"body was like a cullender"*: Ibid., p. 102.

P. 354. *"I am confident"*: Ibid., p. 100.

P. 355. *"His descriptions of Coronation Gulf"*: Denis St-Onge, interview with the author, Ottawa, 1984.

P. 355. *"erected a mark"*: Samuel Hearne, *Journey,* p. 106.

P. 355. *"No small measure of mirth"*: George Vancouver, *A Voyage of Discovery to the North Pacific Ocean,* … 3 vols, Bibliotheca Australiana, no. 32. (London: G.G. Robinson et al, 1798). Reprint ed. (N. Israel, 1967), vol. 3, p. 285.

P. 356. *"Though my discoveries"*: Samuel Hearne, *Journey,* p. 195.

P. 358. *"this elegant apostrophe"*: Ibid., p. 40.

CHAPTER 14
THE BLOOD FEUD BEGINS

P. 359. *"The natives are very dilatory"*: Matthew Cocking. In Lawrence J. Burpee, "An Adventurer from Hudson Bay," 2, pp. 91–121.

P. 359. *"I get no rest at nights"*: Ibid., p. 110.

P. 360. *"laid out in gingerbread"*: Sylvia Van Kirk, *"Many Tender Ties,"* p. 97. HBCA B.239/b/79, fo. 28d.

P. 361. *"The Company's success"*: Richard Glover, "Cumberland House," pp. 4–7.

P. 362. *"both his Big Toes much froze"*: Samuel Hearne. In Joseph Tyrrell, *Journals of Samuel Hearne*, p. 139.

P. 364. *"seven lieutenants coats"*: Samuel Hearne. In Arthur Ray and Donald Freeman, *"Give Us Good Measure"*, pp. 199–200.

P. 365. *"in company with canary birds"*: Samuel Hearne, *Journey*, pp. 269–70.

P. 365. *"The beaver were so fond"*: Ibid., p. 157.

P. 365. *"they answered to their names"*: Ibid.

P. 365. *Mary Norton would "have shone with superior lustre"*: Ibid., pp. 81–2n.

P. 366. *"any sane strategical balance"*: Richard Glover. In E.E. Rich and Alice Johnson, *Cumberland House Journals, First Series*, p. lxxxiv.

P. 367. *"I burned with impatience"*: La Pérouse, in "Supplément à la Gazette du Mardi 29 Octobre 1782. Extrait de la lettre écrite au Marquis de Castries, Ministre & Secrétaire d'État au département de la Marine par le Sieur de la Pérouse, Capitaine de Vaisseau, commandant une Division de Roi; à bord du *Sceptre*, dans le détroit d'Hudson, le 6 Septembre 1782," *La Gazette de France* 87 (29 October 1782), pp. 413–15. (Author's translation.)

P. 368. *"mow down the French troops"*: David Thompson. In J.B. Tyrrell, *David Thompson's Narrative*, pp. 10–11.

P. 369. *tally of furs plundered*: Glyndwr Williams, *Hudson's Bay Miscellany*, p. 89.

P. 371. *"Their numbers appeared so formidable"*: Humphrey Marten. In Glyndwr Williams, *Hudson's Bay Miscellany*, p. 90.

P. 371. *"During their approach"*: Edward Umfreville, *Present State*, p. 67.

P. 372. *"politeness, humanity and goodness"*: Edward Umfreville, *Present State*, p. 68.

P. 372. *La Pérouse on the publication of Hearne's journal*: Edward Weber Allen, *The Vanishing Frenchman*, pp. 154–5.

P. 373. *"Indians lying dead about the Barren Ground"*: William Walker. In E.E. Rich and Alice Johnson, *Cumberland House Journals, Second Series*, p. xl.

P. 373. *"extended over all the Indians"*: David Thompson. In J.B. Tyrrell, *David Thompson's Narrative*, pp. 322–3.

P. 374. *"pleasing friend and faithful wife"*: Samuel Hearne, *Journey*, p. 82n.

P. 374. *"Poor man!"*: Samuel Hearne, *Journey*, p. 228.

P. 379. *"have you not always told me"*: D. Thompson. In R. Glover, *David Thompson's Narrative*. p. 109.

P. 380. *"The Hudson's Bay Traders"*: Edward Umfreville, *Present State*, p. 108–109.

P. 384. *"It has been my good fortune"*: J.B. Tyrrell, *Journey from Prince of Wales's*, pp. 4–5.

P. 385. *"critics of geography"*: Samuel Hearne, *Journey*, p. xlix.

P. 386. *"mixture of indecision and persistency"*: Gordon Speck, *Samuel Hearne*, p. 110.

CHAPTER 15
THE ARCTIC FOX
P. 390. *"the scientific point of view"*: Vilhjalmur Stefansson, "Rae's Arctic Correspondence," pp. 36–37.

P. 392. *"Lt. Franklin, the officer who commands"*: George Simpson. In Vilhjalmur Stefansson, "Arctic Controversy," pp. 486–93.

P. 392. *"A party situated as mine was"*: John Rae. In E.E. Rich and Alice Johnson, *John Rae's Correspondence*, p. xcvii.

P. 394. *"Rae was apparently considered"*: Vilhjalmur Stefansson, "Rae's Arctic Correspondence," p. 36.

P. 394. *"The prime objective of foxhunting"*: Vilhjalmur Stefansson, *Unsolved Mysteries*, p. 126.

P. 395. *"The (Royal Navy) Hydrographer"*: John Rae. "Letter to the Editor." *Nature* 27:694 (1883), p. 366.

P. 397. *"By the time I was fifteen"*: John Rae. In E.E. Rich and Alice Johnson, *John Rae's Correspondence*, p. xiv.

P. 397. *"double capacity of Clerk and surgeon"*: Sir George Simpson. In E.E. Rich and Alice Johnson, *John Rae's Correspondence*, p. xvi. HBCA D.4/20, fo. 4.

P. 398. *"An idea has entered my head"*: Ibid., p. 301. HBCA D.4/64, fo. 99–99d.

P. 399. *"He had got his diploma"*: Letitia Hargrave. In Margaret Macleod, *Letters of Letitia Hargrave*, p. 211.

P. 399. *"He was very muscular"*: Robert Ballantyne, *Hudson's Bay*, pp. 225–6.

P. 400. *"an irresistible presentiment"*: Thomas Simpson. In Alexander Simpson, *The Life and Travels*, p. 340.

P. 400. *"Fame I must have"*: Ibid., p. 339.

P. 402. *"I have often seen our Hunter"*: John Rae, *Narrative of an Expedition*, p. 150.

P. 403. *"Short as it was"*: Ibid., pp. 82–3.

P. 404. *"It was interesting to watch"*: John Rae. In Alan Cooke, "Autobiography," pp. 173–77.

P. 405: *"said to be a diminutive race"*: John Rae, "On the Conditions," pp. 38–41.

P. 406. *"celebrated navigator and discoverer"*: John Rae. In Ross Mitchell, "Physician, Fur Trader and Explorer," pp. 16–20, 65.

P. 407. *"a theatre of British enterprise"*: J.J. Shillinglaw, *A Narrative*, p. 342.

P. 409. *"all the latest energies of your nature"*: Jane Franklin. The last sentence quoted from this letter is taken from a Newdigate prize poem composed by Legh Claughton for the occasion of Franklin's honorary degree of doctor of civil law, awarded in July 1829. In Roderic Owen, *The Fate of Franklin*, p. 146.

P. 411. *"My worthy Superior"*: John Rae. In E.E. Rich and Alice Johnson, *John Rae's Correspondence*, pp. 91–2. Letter to Sir George Simpson, 4 November 1848.

P. 411. *"Pullen and Hooper are vastly civil"*: Ibid., p. 174. Rae to Simpson, 23 April 1851.

P. 411. *"These self-sufficient donkies"*: Ibid., pp. 175–6.

P. 412. *"Dr. Rae & Sir John Richardson"*: Letitia Hargrave. In Margaret Macleod, *Letters of Letitia Hargrave*, p. 242.

P. 413. *"two journeys to Wollaston Land"*: E.E. Rich and Alice Johnson, *John Rae's Correspondence*, p. xiii.

P. 414. *"I do not mention the lost navigators"*: John Rae. In E.E. Rich and Alice Johnson, *John Rae's Correspondence*, p. 222. Rae to Barclay (HBC Secretary), 1 May 1852.

P. 414. *"it had been my habit"*: John Rae. In Alan Cooke, "Autobiography," p. 176.

P. 414. *"apparently intelligent Esquimaux"*: John Rae. In E.E. Rich and Alice Johnson, *John Rae's Correspondence*, p. lxxix.

P. 415. *"In the spring, four winters past"*: John Rae. In Ross Mitchell, "Physician," p. 20.

P. 416. *"the mutilated state"*: John Rae. In E.E. Rich and Alice Johnson, *John Rae's Correspondence*, p. 276. Letter to Barclay, 1 September 1854.

P. 417. *"it was too late"*: Ibid., p. xcvi.

P. 419. *"We believe every savage"*: Charles Dickens, "The Lost Arctic Voyagers," pp. 361–65.

P. 421. *"a portable food supply"*: Owen Beattie and James M. Savelle, "Discovery of Human Remains," pp. 100–105.

P. 422. *"who perhaps ought to rank highest"*: H.B. Neatby, "History of Hudson Bay." In C.S. Beals, *Science, History*, vol. 1, pp. 69–125.

P. 425. *Louis Hartz on colonies as fragments*: Louis Hartz, *The Founding of New Societies*, p. 3.

Bibliography

This listing is a selection from the main texts and journal articles consulted during the writing of this volume. The Chapter Notes in Appendix 8 provide further information for those pursuing research, or for readers curious about the sources of the quotes used in the book.

Adams, Arthur T., ed. *The Explorations of Pierre Esprit Radisson.* Minneapolis, Minn.: Ross & Haines, 1961.

Adams, Gary. "Art and Archeology at York Factory." *The Beaver*, Summer 1982, 38–42.

Adams, Howard. *Prison of Grass: Canada from the Native Point of View.* Toronto: New Press, 1975.

———. "The Cree as a Colonial People." *The Western Canadian Journal of Anthropology*, 1, no. 1: 120.

Allen, Edward Weber. *The Vanishing Frenchman: The Mysterious Disappearance of La Pérouse.* Rutland, Vt.: Charles E. Tuttle Co., 1959.

Alwin, John A. "Colony and Company Sharing the York Mainline." *The Beaver*, Summer 1979, 4–11.

Armstrong, G.H. *The Origin and Meaning of Place Names in Canada.* Toronto: Macmillan of Canada, 1930.

Asher, G.M., ed. *Henry Hudson, the Navigator, The original documents* ... Hakluyt Society, 1st ser., no. 27. London: Hakluyt Society, 1860.

Ashley, Maurice. *Rupert of the Rhine.* London: Hart-Davis, MacGibbon, 1976.

Back, Captain George. *Narrative of the Arctic Land Expedition to the mouth of the Great Fish River, and along the shores of the Arctic Ocean, in the Years 1833, 1834, and 1835.* Edmonton: M.G. Hurtig, 1970.

Ball, Timothy F. "Climatic Change in Central Canada: A Preliminary Analysis of Weather Information from the Hudson's Bay Company Forts at York Factory and Churchill Factory, 1714–

1850." Ph.D. dissertation, University of London, 1983.

Ballantyne, Robert M. *Hudson's Bay, or, Every-day Life in the Wilds of North America, being six years' residence in the territories of the Honourable Hudson's Bay Company.* Edmonton: Hurtig Publishers, 1972.

Banfield, A.W.F. *The Mammals of Canada.* Published for the National Museum of Natural Sciences, National Museums of Man. Toronto: University of Toronto Press, 1974.

Barbeau, Marius. "Our Beaver Emblem." *Canadian Geographical Journal,* December 1957, 244–50.

Barbour, Violet. *Capitalism in Amsterdam in the 17th Century.* Ann Arbor, Mich.: University of Michigan Press, 1950.

Barger, W.K. "Inuit-Cree Relations in the Eastern Hudson Bay Region." *Arctic Anthropology,* 16, no. 2 (1979): 59–75.

Barnett, Correlli. *The First Churchill: Marlborough, Soldier and Statesman.* New York: G.P. Putnam's Sons, 1974.

Beals, C.S., ed. *Science, History and Hudson Bay.* 2 vols. Ottawa: Department of Energy, Mines and Resources, 1968.

Beattie, Owen B., and James M. Savelle. "Discovery of Human Remains From Sir John Franklin's Last Expedition." *Historical Archaeology,* 17, no. 2 (1983): 100–105.

Berry, Virginia G. *A Boundless Horizon: Visual Records of Exploration and Settlement in the Manitoba Region, 1624–1874.* Catalogue of exhibition, September 15–October 30, 1983. Winnipeg: The Winnipeg Art Gallery, 1983.

Berton, Pierre. *The Great Railway, 1881–1885.* Vol. 2, *The Last Spike.* Toronto: McClelland and Stewart, 1971.

Bindoff, S.T. *Tudor England.* Harmondsworth, Middx.: Penguin Books, 1950.

Bishop, Charles A. "Demography, Ecology and Trade Among the Northern Ojibwa and Swampy Cree." *The Western Canadian Journal of Anthropology,* 3, no. 1: 58–71.

———. *The Northern Ojibwa and the Fur Trade: An Historical and Ecological Study.* Toronto: Holt, Rinehart and Winston of Canada, 1974.

———. "York Factory Project Proposal." Unpublished paper, Parks Canada, Winnipeg, 1979.

Blanchet, Guy H. "Thelewayaza-yeth." *The Beaver,* September 1949, 8–11.

Bolus, Malvina, ed. *People and Pelts: Selected Papers of the Second North American Fur Trade Conference*. Winnipeg: Peguis Publishers, 1972.

———. "The Son of I. Gunn." *The Beaver*, Winter 1971, 23–26.

Borins, Edward H. *La Compagnie du Nord, 1682–1700*. Master's thesis, McGill University, 1968.

Brandt, G.W. "Note on Breeding of Beavers." *Journal of Mammology*, 21 (1941): 220–21.

Bredvold, Louis I., Alan D. McKillop and Lois Whitney, eds. *Eighteenth Century Poetry & Prose*. New York: Ronald Press Company, 1956.

Brown, George Mackay. *Portrait of Orkney*. London: Hogarth Press, 1981.

Brown, Jennifer S.H. "A Demographic Transition in the Fur Trade Country: Family Sizes and Fertility of Company Officers and Country Wives, ca. 1750–1850." *Western Canadian Journal of Anthropology*, 6, no. 1: 61.

———. *Strangers in Blood: Fur Trade Company Families in Indian Country*. Vancouver: University of British Columbia Press, 1980.

———. "Two Companies in Search of Traders: Personnel and Promotion Patterns in Canada's Early British Fur Trade." In *Proceedings of the Second Congress, Canadian Ethnology Society*, edited by Jim Freedman and Jerome H. Barkow. Ottawa: National Museum of Man, Mercury Series, Canadian Ethnology Service, Paper no. 28.

Bryce, George. *The Remarkable History of the Hudson's Bay Company*. London: Sampson, Low, Marston, 1910.

Buckle, Henry Thomas. *On Scotland and the Scotch Intellect*. Edited by H.J. Hanham. Chicago: University of Chicago Press, 1970.

Burpee, Lawrence J., ed., "An Adventurer from Hudson Bay: Matthew Cocking's Journal." *Proceedings and Transactions of the Royal Society of Canada*. 3rd ser., 2 (1908).

———. "York Factory to the Blackfeet Country: The Journal of Anthony Hendry [sic], 1754–55." *Proceedings and Transactions of the Royal Society of Canada*. 3rd ser., 1 (1907).

Campbell, Marjorie E. Wilkins. *The North West Company*. Toronto: Macmillan Co. of Canada, 1957.

Campbell, Walter Stanley. [Stanley Vestal, pseud.] *King of the Fur Traders: The Deeds and Deviltry of Pierre Esprit Radisson.* Boston: Houghton Mifflin Co., 1940.

Canadian Encyclopedia, 3 vols. Edmonton: Hurtig Publishers, 1985.

Cantwell, Robert. *The Hidden Northwest.* Philadelphia: J.B. Lippincott, 1972.

Carlyle-Gordge, Peter. "York Factory 1682–1982." *Manitoba Nature,* 23, no. 2 (Spring 1982): 10–18.

Caswell, John E. "The Sponsors of Canadian Arctic Exploration." *The Beaver,* Summer 1969, 38–45.

Catlin, George. *Catlin's Notes of Eight Years' Travels and Residence in Europe, with his North American Indian Collection, with Anecdotes and Incidents of the Travels and Adventures of Three Different Parties of American Indians Whom He Introduced to the Courts of England, France and Belgium.* 2 vols. Indian Collection, no. 6. Published by author, London, 1848.

Chamberlin, J.E. *The Harrowing of Eden: White Attitudes Toward Native Americans.* New York: Seabury Press, 1975.

Christenson, Deanna. *A General History of the Fort Carlton Area 1770–1900.* Regina: Saskatchewan Dept. of Culture & Youth, 1980.

Churchill, Winston S. *The New World.* New York: Dodd, Mead, 1956.

Clarke, Desmond. *Arthur Dobbs, Esquire, 1689–1765, Surveyor-General of Ireland, Prospector and Governor of North Carolina.* London: The Bodley Head, 1958.

Clouston, Joseph Storer. *A History of Orkney.* Kirkwall, Orkney Islands: W.R. Mackintosh, 1932.

———. "Orkney and the Hudson's Bay Company." *The Beaver,* Part 1, December 1936, 4–8. Part 2, March 1937, 38–43, 62. Part 3, September 1937, 37–39.

Cocking, Matthew. *An adventurer from Hudson Bay: Journal of Matthew Cocking from York Factory to the Blackfeet country, 1772–73.* London: Journal and Proceedings of the Royal Geographical Society, 1908.

Cooke, Alan. "The Autobiography of Dr. John Rae (1813–1893): A Preliminary Note." *The Polar Record,* 14, no. 89 (1968): 173–77.

Cooke, Alan, and Clive Holland. *The Exploration of Northern Canada, 500– 1920.* Toronto: Arctic History Press, 1978.

Coues, Elliott, ed. *The Manuscript Journals of Alexander Henry, Fur Trader of the North-*

west Company ... 2 vols. New York: Francis P. Harper, 1897.

Court, W.H.B. *A Concise Economic History of Britain from 1750 to Recent Times.* Cambridge: Cambridge University Press, 1965.

Cowles, Virginia. *The Great Marlborough and His Duchess.* London: George Weidenfeld and Nicolson, 1983.

Craig, Joan. "Three Hundred Years of Records." *The Beaver,* Autumn 1970, 65–70.

Cranston, Maurice. *John Locke.* London: Longmans, Green, 1957.

Crouse, Nellis M. *Lemoyne d'Iberville: Soldier of New France.* Toronto: Ryerson Press, 1954.

Crowe, Keith J. *A History of the Original Peoples of Northern Canada.* Montreal: McGill-Queen's University Press for Arctic Institute of North America, 1974.

Daniells, Roy. *Alexander Mackenzie and the North West.* Toronto: Oxford University Press, 1971.

Davies, K.G., and A.M. Johnson, eds. *Letters from Hudson Bay, 1703– 40.* The Publications of the Hudson's Bay Record Society, vol. 25. London: Hudson's Bay Record Society, 1965.

Davies, W.A. "A Brief History of the Churchill River." *The Musk-Ox.* Churchill River Special Issue, no. 15 (1975): 30–38.

Day, Martin S. *History of English Literature 1660–1837.* Garden City, N.Y.: Doubleday, 1963.

De Ford, Miriam Allen, and Joan S. Jackson. *Who Was When?* New York: H.W. Wilson, 1976.

d'Equilly, Pierre-Louis Morin. "York Factory to St. Boniface on Foot, 1836–37." Translated by Hubert G. Mayes. *The Beaver,* Winter 1979, 46–51.

Dickens, Charles. "The Lost Arctic Voyageurs." *Household Words,* no. 245, December 2, 1854, 361–65.

Dickson, Wendy. "Orcadians of the Bay." *Scotland's Magazine,* August 1969, 30–32.

Dictionary of Canadian Biography. Toronto: University of Toronto Press, (Vol. 1) 1966; (Vol. 2) 1969; (Vol. 3) 1974; (Vol. 4) 1979; (Vol. 6) 1983; (Vol. 9) 1976; (Vol. 10) 1972; (Vol. 11) 1982.

Dillon, Richard H. *Siskiyou Trail: the Hudson's Bay Company route to California.* American Trail Series, vol. 12. New York: McGraw-Hill, 1975.

Dobbs, Arthur. *An Account of the Countries Adjoining to Hudson's Bay.* London, 1774. Reprint ed., Toronto: Clarke Irwin, 1967.

———. *Remarks upon Capt. Middleton's Defence.* London: J. Robinson, 1744.

Dodge, Ernest S. *Northwest by Sea.* New York: Oxford University Press, 1961.

Donaldson, Bruce F. "York Factory: A Land-Use History." Parks Canada Manuscript Report Series, no. 444. Winnipeg: Parks Canada, August 1981.

———. "York Factory: An Overview, 1682–1982." Manitoba Dept. of Cultural Affairs and Historical Resources, Historic Resources Branch, Report no. 9. Winnipeg: Manitoba Dept. of Cultural Affairs and Historical Resources, June 1982.

Doughty, Arthur C., and Chester Martin, eds. *The Kelsey Papers.* Ottawa: Public Archives of Canada, 1929.

Douglas, Robert, and J.N. Wallace, eds. *Twenty Years of York Factory, 1694–1714: Jérémie's Account of Hudson Strait and Bay.* From the French edition, 1720. Ottawa: Thorburn and Abbott, 1926.

Dugmore, A. Radclyffe. *The Romance of the Beaver, Being the History of the Beaver in the Western Hemisphere.* London: William Heinemann, 1913.

Drage, T.S. *An account of a voyage for the discovery of a North-West Passage by Hudson Streights ... 2 vols.* London: Jolliffe et al, 1748. Reprint ed., New York: Johnson Reprint Corp., 1968.

"Dr. John Rae, FRS." *Geographical Journal,* 2, no. 3 (1893): 275–76.

Eccles, W.J. "A Belated Review of Harold Adams Innis, *The Fur Trade in Canada.*" *Canadian Historical Review,* 60, no. 4 (1979): 419–41.

———. *The Canadian Frontier, 1534– 1760.* Toronto: McClelland and Stewart, 1969.

Edinger, George. *Rupert of the Rhine, The Pirate Prince.* London: Hutchinson & Co, 1936.

Ellis, Henry A. *A Voyage to Hudson's Bay by the Dobbs Galley and California in the Years 1746 and 1747, for Discovering a Northwest Passage.* London: H. Whitridge, 1748. Reprint ed., New York: Johnson Reprint Corp., 1967.

Fellowes, W.D. *Historical Sketches of Charles the First, Cromwell, Charles the Second, and the Principal Personages of that*

Period. London: John Murray, 1828.

Fisher, Robin. *Contact and Conflict: Indian-European Relations in British Columbia 1774–1890.* Vancouver: University of British Columbia Press, 1977.

Forsyth, William. "The Hudson's Bay Company." *Good Words,* May 1, 1869, 358–65.

Foster, John E. "The Home Guard Cree and the Hudson's Bay Company: The First Hundred Years." In *Approaches to Native History in Canada,* edited by D.A. Muise. National Museum of Man, Mercury Series, Paper no. 25, 49–64. Ottawa: National Museum of Man, 1977.

———. "The Indian-Trader in the Hudson Bay Fur Trade Tradition." In *Proceedings of the Second Congress, Canadian Ethnology Society,* edited by Jim Freedman and Jerome H. Barkow. National Museum of Man, Mercury Series, Canadian Ethnology Service, Paper no. 28, 586–602. Ottawa: National Museum of Man, 1975.

Francis, Daniel. *Battle for the West: Fur Traders and the Birth of Western Canada.* Edmonton: Hurtig Publishers, 1982.

Francis, Daniel, and Toby Morantz. *Partners in Fur: A History of the Fur Trade in Eastern James Bay 1600–1870.* Montreal: McGill-Queen's University Press, 1983.

Fraser, Antonia. *King Charles II.* London: George Weidenfeld and Nicolson, 1979.

———. *The Weaker Vessel: Woman's Lot in Seventeenth-Century England.* London: Methuen, 1984.

Friedenberg, Edgar Z. *Deference to Authority: The Case of Canada.* White Plains, N.Y.: M.E. Sharpe, 1980.

Friesen, Gerald. *The Canadian Prairies: A History.* Toronto: University of Toronto Press, 1984.

Frye, Northrop. *The Bush Garden: Essays on the Canadian Imagination.* Toronto: Anansi, 1971.

Fumoleau, René. *As Long As This Land Shall Last: A History of Treaty 8 and Treaty 11, 1870–1939.* Toronto: McClelland and Stewart, 1973.

Galbraith, John Kenneth. *The Scotch.* Baltimore: Penguin Books, 1966.

Galbraith, John S. *The Hudson's Bay Company as an Imperial Factor, 1821–1869.* Berkeley: University of California Press, 1957.

George, M. Dorothy. *London Life in the XVIIIth Century*. London: Kegan Paul, Trench, Trubner & Co., 1925.

Getty, Ian A.L., and Antoine S. Lussier, eds. *As Long As The Sun Shines And Water Flows: A Reader in Canadian Native Studies*. Nadoka Institute Occasional Paper no. 1. Vancouver: University of British Columbia Press, 1983.

Gibbon, John Murray. "The Orkneymen in Canada." *Transactions of the Royal Society of Canada*, 3rd ser., 44 (1950).

———. *Scots in Canada: A History of the Settlement of the Dominion from the Earliest Days to the Present Time*. London: Kegan Paul, Trench, Trubner & Co., 1911.

Gillespie, Beryl C. "Changes in Territory and Technology of the Chipewyan." *Arctic Anthropology*, 8, no. 1 (1976): 6–11.

Gilman, Carolyn. *Where Two Worlds Meet: The Great Lakes Fur Trade*. St Paul, Minn.: Minnesota Historical Society, 1982.

Glazebrook, G.P. de T. *A History of Transportation in Canada*. Toronto: Ryerson Press, 1938.

Glover, Janet Reaveley. *The Story of Scotland*. London: Faber and Faber, 1960.

Glover, Richard G. "Andrew Graham, Thomas Hutchins, and the first record of Peary's caribou." *Arctic*, 13, no. 1; 2-4.

———. "Cumberland House." *The Beaver*, December 1951, 4–7.

———, ed. *David Thompson's Narrative, 1784–1812*. The Publications of the Champlain Society, vol. 40. Toronto: Champlain Society, 1962.

———. "An Early Visitor to Hudson Bay." *Queen's Quarterly*, 55 (Spring 1948): 37–45.

———. "The French Fleet, 1807–1814; Britain's Problem; and Madison's Opportunity." *Journal of Modern History*, 39, no. 3 (September 1967): 233–52.

———. "La Pérouse on Hudson Bay." *The Beaver*, March 1951, 42–46.

———. "Matonabbee (ca. 1736– 1782)" *Arctic*, 35, no. 3 (1983): 206–7.

———. "Sidelights on Sl Hearne." *The Beaver*, March 1947, 10–14.

———. "The Witness of David Thompson." *Canadian Historical Review*, 31, 1950: 25–38.

Goldring, Philip. "Papers on the Labor System of the

Hudson's Bay Company, 1821–1900." Parks Canada Manuscript Report Series, no. 412. Ottawa: Parks Canada, 1980.

Gosse, Philip. *The History of Piracy*. New York: Tudor Publishing, 1934.

Gough, Barry M. "The 'Adventurers of England Trading Into Hudson's Bay': A Study of the Founding Members of the Hudson's Bay Company, 1665–1670." Proceedings of the Conference on British Studies, Pacific Northwest Section, Elmira College, Washington State University, 1970. *Albion*, 2, no. 1

Graham, Gerald S. *A Concise History of the British Empire*. New York: Viking Press, 1970.

Gramont, Philibert, Comte de. *Memoirs of the life of Count de Grammont: Containing in Particular, the Amorous Intrigues of the Court of England in the Reign of King Charles II*. Translated by [Abel] Boyer. London: J. Round et al, 1714.

Grant, William L. "Canada versus Guadeloupe: An Episode of the Seven Years' War." *American Historical Review*, 17, no. 4 (July 1912): 735–43.

Gregor, Alexander. *Vilhjalmur Stefansson and the Arctic*.

Agincourt, Ont.: Book Society of Canada, 1978.

Hall, Eugene Raymond. *The Mammals of North America*. Vol. 2. 2nd ed. Toronto: John Wiley & Sons, 1981.

Hannon, Leslie F. *Forts of Canada: The Conflicts, Sieges and Battles That Forged a Great Nation*. Toronto: McClelland and Stewart, 1969.

Hartz, Louis. *The Founding of New Societies: Studies in the History of the United States, Latin America, South Africa, Canada, and Australia*. New York: Harcourt, Brace & World, 1961. [See also S.F. Wise.]

Hatton, Ragnhild. *Europe in the Age of Louis XIV*. London: Thames and Hudson, 1969.

Head, C. Grant. *Eighteenth Century Newfoundland: A Geographer's Perspective*. Carleton Library, no. 99. Toronto: McClelland and Stewart, 1976.

Hearne, Samuel. *A Journey from Prince of Wales's Fort in Hudson's Bay to the northern ocean undertaken by the order of the Hudson's Bay Company for the discovery of copper mines, a north west passage, etc., in the years 1769, 1770, 1771, and 1772*. Edited by Richard Glover. Toronto: Macmillan Co. of Canada, 1958.

Heidenreich, Conrad E., and Arthur J. Ray. *The Early Fur Trades: A Study in Cultural Interaction.* A Canada Studies Foundation/Canadian Association of Geographers Project. Toronto: McClelland and Stewart, 1976.

Henry, Alexander. *Travels and Adventures in Canada and the Indian Territories Between the Years 1760 and 1776.* Edmonton: Hurtig Publishers, 1969.

Herbert, J.D. "Fur Trade Sites: Canada." *Minnesota History,* 40, no. 4 (Winter 1966): 188.

"Historic Fort Closes." *The Bay News,* July 1957.

"Historic York Factory Century Ago Described." *Fort William* (Ont.) *Times-Journal,* December 20, 1939.

Horwood, Harold. *The Colonial Dream 1497/1760.* Canada's Illustrated Heritage. Toronto: Natural Sciences of Canada, 1978.

Houston, C. Stuart, ed. *To the Arctic by Canoe 1819–1821: The Journal and Paintings of Robert Hood, Midshipman with Franklin.* The Arctic Institute of North America. Montreal: McGill-Queen's University Press, 1974.

Hudson's Bay Company. *Charters, Statutes, Orders in Council, etc, relating to the Hudson's Bay Company.* London: Hudson's Bay Company, 1949.

"Hudson's Bay and Its Furs." *Chambers's Journal of Popular Literature, Science, and Art,* no. 132, May 12, 1860, 293–96.

Inglis, Alex. *Northern Vagabond: The Life and Career of J.B. Tyrrell.* Toronto: McClelland and Stewart, 1978.

Ingram, George. *Prince of Wales's Fort: A Structural History.* Parks Canada Manuscript Report Series, no. 297, Part 2. Ottawa: Parks Canada, 1979.

———. *York Factory: A Structural History.* Parks Canada Manuscript Report Series no. 297, Part 1. Ottawa: Parks Canada, 1979.

Inkyo [pseud.] *Reflections of Inkyo on the Great Company.* London: London General Press, 1931.

Innis, Harold A. *The Fur Trade in Canada: An Introduction to Canadian Economic History.* New Haven, Conn.: Yale University Press, 1930.

Irwin, Margaret. *The Stranger Prince.* London: Chatto and Windus, 1937.

Jackson, Henry F.J. "The Steward's Yarn." *The Beaver,* Spring 1978, 20–23.

James, Thomas. *The Strange and Dangerous Voyage of Captain Thomas James, in his intended Discovery of the Northwest Passage into the South Sea.* London: John Legatt, 1663. Reprint ed., Amsterdam: Theatrum Orbis Terrarum Ltd., 1968.

Jenness, Diamond. *The Indians of Canada.* 7th ed. Toronto: University of Toronto Press, 1977.

Jérémie, Nicolas. *Twenty Years of York Factory 1694–1714: Jérémie's Account of Hudson Strait and Bay.* Translated from the French edition of 1720. Edited by Robert Douglas and J.N. Wallace. Ottawa: Thorburn & Abbott, 1926.

Johnson, Alice M., ed. *Saskatchewan Journals and Correspondence: Edmonton House 1795– 1800, Chesterfield House 1800–1902.* The Publications of the Hudson's Bay Record Society, vol. 26. London: Hudson's Bay Record Society, 1967.

Johnston, Basil. *Ojibway Heritage.* Toronto: McClelland and Stewart, 1976.

Judd, Carol M., and A.J. Ray, eds. *Old Trails and New Directions: Papers of the Third North American Fur Trade Conference.* Toronto: University of Toronto Press, 1980.

Kelsey, Henry. *The Kelsey Papers.* Edited by Arthur G. Doughty and Chester Martin. Ottawa: King's Printer, 1929.

Kenyon, J.P. *Stuart England.* Harmondsworth, Middx.: Penguin Books, 1978.

Kilbourn, William, ed. *Canada: A Guide to the Peaceable Kingdom.* Toronto: Macmillan of Canada, 1970.

Kinder, Hermann, and Werner Hilgemann. *The Penguin Atlas of World History.* Vol. 1. Harmondsworth, Middx.: Penguin Books, 1974.

Klinck, Carl F., general ed. *Literary History of Canada: Canadian Literature in English.* Toronto: University of Toronto Press, 1965.

Knight, James. *The Founding of Churchill, Being the Journal of Captain James Knight, Governor-in-Chief in Hudson Bay from the 14th of July to the 13th of September, 1717.* Edited by J.F. Kenney. Toronto: J.M. Dent and Sons, 1932.

Krech, Shepard, III, ed. *Indians, Animals, and the Fur Trade: A Critique of "Keepers of the Game."* Athens, Ga.: University of Georgia Press, 1981.

———. *The Subarctic Fur Trade: Native, Social and Economic Adaptations.* Vancouver: University of British Columbia Press, 1984.

Lamb, H. *Climate, History and the Modern World.* London: Methuen, 1982.

La Pérouse. "Extract of a letter from the Sieur de La Pérouse, Capitaine de Vaisseau, commanding a division of the King's Fleet, to the Marquis de Castries, Minister and Secretary of State for the Marine Department, on board the *Sceptre,* in Hudson's Strait, September 6, 1782." *Supplément à la Gazette de France,* Paris, 1782.

Latham, Robert, ed. *The Illustrated Pepys: Extracts from the Diary.* Berkeley: University of California Press, 1978.

Laut, Agnes C. *The 'Adventurers of England' on Hudson Bay: A Chronicle of the Fur Trade in the North.* Toronto: Glasgow, Brook, 1914.

———. *The Conquest of the Great Northwest: Being the Story of the Adventurers of England known as The Hudson's Bay Company.* 2 vols. New York: Outing Publishing Co., 1908.

Lavender, David. *"The Hudson's Bay Company."* A Tricentennial Report. *American Heritage,* 21, no. 3 (April 1970): 5–10.

———. *Winner Take All: The Trans-Canada Canoe Trail.*

Toronto: McGraw-Hill, 1977.

Lawson, Murray G. *Fur: A Study in English Mercantilism 1700–1775.* University of Toronto Studies, History and Economics Series, vol. 9, Toronto: University of Toronto Press, 1943.

Lebhane, Brendan. *The Northwest Passage.* Seafarers Series. Alexandria, Va.: Time-Life Books, 1981.

Leveson-Gower, R.H.G. "The Archives of the Hudson's Bay Company." *The Beaver,* December 1933, 40–42, 64.

Lewis, Oscar. *The Effects of White Contact upon Blackfoot Culture, with special reference to the role of the fur trade.* Monographs of the American Ethnological Society, 6. New York: J.J. Augustin, 1942.

"Life in a Hudson Bay Company's Fort." *Chambers's Journal of Popular Literature, Science and Art,* no. 828, November 8, 1879: 705–7.

Lindsay, Jack. *The Monster City: Defoe's London, 1688–1730.* London: HartDavis, MacGibbon, 1978.

Linklater, Eric. *Orkney and Shetland: An Historical, Geographical, Social and Scenic Survey,* 3rd ed. London: Robert Hale, 1980.

MacAndrew, Craig, and Robert B. Edgerton. *Drunken Comportment: A Social Explanation.* Chicago: Aldine Publishing Co., 1969.

Macaulay, Thomas Babington. *The History of England from the Accession of James II.* vols. Edited by Charles H. Firth. London: Macmillan & Co., 1914.

MacDonald, Robert. *The Owners of Eden: The Life and Past of the Native People.* Calgary: Ballantrae Foundation, 1974.

McGowan, Alan. *The Ship: The Century before Steam – The Development of the Sailing Ship, 1700–1820.* National Maritime Museum Series. London: Her Majesty's Stationery Office, 1980.

MacKay, Douglas. *The Honourable Company: A History of the Hudson's Bay Company.* 2nd ed. Toronto: McClelland and Stewart, 1949.

MacKay, W.A. *The Great Canadian Skin Game.* Toronto: Macmillan of Canada, 1967.

Mackenzie, Alexander. *Voyages from Montreal on the River St. Laurence through the Continent of North America to the Frozen and Pacific Oceans in the Years 1792 and 1793.* The Publications of the Radisson Society of Canada. Toronto: Radisson Society of Canada, 1927.

Mackenzie, N.M.W.J. *The Men of the Hudson's Bay Company, 1670 A.D.– 1920 A.D.* Fort William, Ont.: Times-Journal Presses, 1921.

Macleod, Margaret Arnett, ed. *The Letters of Letitia Hargrave.* The Publications of the Champlain Society, vol. 28. London: Champlain Society, 1947.

MacNutt, W. Stewart. *Days of Lorne: From the Private Papers of the Marquis of Lorne, 1878–1883, in the possession of the Duke of Argyll at Inveraray Castle, Scotland.* Fredericton, N.B.: Brunswick Press, 1955.

Mahan, Alfred Thayer. *The Influence of Sea Power upon History, 1660–1805.* London: Bison Books, 1980.

"Manitoba's First Business Closing Shop." *Winnipeg Tribune,* June 15, 1957.

Manning, Brian. *The English People and the English Revolution.* Harmondsworth, Middx.: Penguin Books, 1976.

Martin, Calvin. *Keepers of the Game: Indian-Animal Relationships and the Fur Trade.* Berkeley: University of California Press, 1978.

Marwick, Hugh. *Orkney.* London: Robert Hale, 1951.

Merk, Frederick, ed. *Fur Trade and Empire: George Simpson's*

Journal ... 1824–25. Cambridge, Mass.: Harvard University Press, Belknap Press, 1968.

Mirsky, Jeannette. *To the Arctic! The Story of Northern Exploration from Earliest Times to the Present.* New York: Viking Press, 1934.

Mitchell, Ross. "Physician, Fur Trader and Explorer [John Rae]." *The Beaver,* September 1936, 16.

Moir, John S., ed. *Character and Circumstance: Essays in Honour of Donald Grant Creighton.* Toronto: Macmillan of Canada, 1970.

Morgan, Dale L. "The Fur Trade and Its Historians." *Minnesota History,* 40, no. 4 (Winter 1966): 151.

Morgan, Dale L., et al, eds. *Aspects of the Fur Trade: Selected Papers of the 1965 North American Fur Trade Conference.* St. Paul, Minn.: Minnesota Historical Society, 1967. [Also published as December 1966 issue of *Minnesota History.*]

Morris, James. *Heaven's Command: An Imperial Progress.* Harmondsworth, Middx.: Penguin Books, 1978.

Morris, Jan. *The Spectacle of Empire: Style, Effect, and the Pax Britannica.* London: Faber and Faber, 1982.

Morse, Eric W. *Fur Trade Canoe Routes of Canada – Then and Now.* 2nd ed. Toronto: University of Toronto Press, 1979.

———. "Modern Maps Throw New Light on Samuel Hearne's Route." *Cartographica,* 18, no. 4 (1981): 23–35.

Morton, Arthur S. *A History of the Canadian West to 1870–71: Being a History of Rupert's Land (The Hudson's Bay Company's Territory) and of the North West Territory (including the Pacific Slope).* 2nd ed. Edited by Lewis G. Thomas. Toronto: University of Toronto Press, 1973.

———. *Under Western Skies: being a series of pen-pictures of the Canadian West in early fur trade times.* Toronto: Thomas Nelson & Sons, 1936.

Morton, W.L. *The Kingdom of Canada: A General History from Earliest Times.* New York: Bobbs-Merrill Co., 1963.

Mountfield, David. *A History of Polar Exploration.* New York: Dial Press, 1974.

Mowat, Farley. *Coppermine Journey.* Toronto: McClelland and Stewart, 1958.

———. *The Top of the World.* Vol. 3, *Tundra: Selections from the Great Accounts of Arctic*

Land Voyages. Toronto: Mc-Clelland and Stewart, 1958.

Munk, Jens. *The Journal of Jens Munk, 1616–1620.* Edited by W.A. Kenyon. Toronto: Royal Ontario Museum, 1980.

Neatby, Leslie H. *In Quest of the North-west Passage.* Toronto: Longmans, Green & Co., 1958.

Nekich, Sandra. "The Feast of the Dead: The Origin of Indian-White Trade Ceremonies in the West." *The Western Canadian Journal of Anthropology,* , no. 1:1.

Nelson, George, *The Nelson Papers,* Baldwin Room, Metropolitan Toronto Library, Journal no. 5, June 1807–October 1809, 185–229

Novarkowski, N.S. "The Winter Bioenergetics of a Beaver Population in Northern Latitudes." *Canadian Journal of Zoology,* 45, no. 1107 (1967): 1115 ff.

Nute, Grace Lee. "Beaver Money." *Minnesota History,* 9 (September 1928): 287–88.

———. *Caesars of the Wilderness: Médard Chouart, Sieur des Groseilliers, and Pierre Esprit Radisson, 1618–1710.* New York: Appleton-Century Co., 1943.

O'Connor, D.J. *John Locke,* New York: Dover Publications, 1967.

Ogg, David. *Europe in the Seventeenth Century.* New York: Collier Books, 1960.

"Old York Factory A Century Ago." *Eganville* (Ont.) *Leader,* October 20, 1939.

O'Meara, Walter. *Daughters of the Country: The Women of the Fur Traders and Mountain Men.* New York: Harcourt, Brace & World, 1968.

———. *The Last Portage.* Boston: Houghton Mifflin Co., 1962.

———. *The Savage Country.* Boston: Houghton Mifflin Co., 1960.

Opekowkew, Delia. *The First Nations: Indian Government and the Canadian Confederation.* Saskatoon: Federation of Saskatchewan Indians, 1980.

Owen, Roderic. *The Fate of Franklin.* London: Hutchinson & Co., 1978.

Palmer, Tony. *Charles II: Portrait of an Age.* London: Cassell, 1979.

Pannekoek, Frits. "'Corruption' at Moose." *The Beaver,* Spring 1979, 4–11.

Patrick, A.J. *The Making of a Nation 1603–1789.* Harmondsworth, Middx.: Penguin Books, 1967.

Payne, Michael. *Prince of Wales' Fort: A Social History, 1717–1782*. Parks Canada Manuscript Report Series, no. 371. Ottawa: Parks Canada, 1979.

———. *A Social History of York Factory 1788–1870*. Parks Canada Microfiche Report Series, no. 133. Ottawa: Parks Canada, 1980.

Pelletier, Wilfred. "Some Thoughts About Organization and Leadership." In *Two Articles*, a paper presented to the Manitoba Indian Brotherhood, Neewin Publishing Co., 1967.

Peterson, Randolph L. *The Mammals of Eastern Canada*. Toronto: Oxford University Press, 1966.

Pethick, Derek. *First Approaches to the North-West Coast*. Vancouver: J.J. Douglas, 1976.

Phillips, Paul Chrisler. *The Fur Trade*. Volume 1. Norman, Okla.: University of Oklahoma Press, 1961.

Phillips, R.A.J. *Canada's North*. Toronto: Macmillan Co. of Canada, 1967.

Pinkerton, Robert. *The Gentlemen Adventurers*. Toronto: McClelland and Stewart, 1931.

Powys, Llewellyn. *Life of Henry Hudson*. London: John Lane The Bodley Head Ltd., 1927.

Prebble, John. *The Highland Clearances*. Harmondsworth, Middx.: Penguin Books, in association with Martin Secker & Warburg, 1963.

Preble, Edward A. *North American Fauna: A Biological Investigation of the Athabaska-Mackenzie Region*. U.S. Department of Agriculture Bureau of Biological Survey, no. 27. Washington, D.C.: U.S. Government Printing Office, 1908.

"Prince Rupert of Bohemia: The Immigrant Who Never Came." Encounters in History, part 1. *Nase Hlasy, Independent Czechoslovak Weekly*, Centennial Issue, 1967: 7.

Radisson, Pierre-Esprit. *Voyages of Peter Esprit Radisson, being an account of his travels and experiences among the North American Indians, from 1652 to 1684*. Research and Source Works Series, no. 131. New York: Burt Franklin, 1967.

Rae, John. "The Arctic Regions and Hudson's Bay Route." Lecture to the Historical and Scientific Society of Winnipeg, October 11, 1882. *Manitoba Free Press*: 1882.

———. *Correspondence with the Hudson's Bay Company on*

Arctic Exploration, 1844–1855. Edited by E.E. Rich and Alice M. Johnson. The Publications of the Hudson's Bay Record Society, vol. 16. London: Hudson's Bay Record Society, 1953.

———. Letter to the Editor, *Nature*, 27, no. 694 (1883): 366.

———. *Narrative of an Expedition to the Shores of the Arctic Sea in 1846 and 1847.* London: T. & W. Boone, 1850.

———. "On the Conditions and Characteristics of some of the Indian Tribes of the Hudson's Bay Company's Territories." 1882 Address to the Royal Society of Arts, London. Reprinted in "Rae on the Eskimoes." *The Beaver,* March 1954, 38–41.

Ralph, Julian. "Talking Musquash." *Harper's New Monthly Magazine,* 84, no. 140 (March 1892): 491–510.

Rankin, Hugh F. *The Golden Age of Piracy.* Williamsburg in America Series, no. 7. New York: Holt, Rinehart and Winston, 1969.

Rasky, Frank. *The Polar Voyagers.* Toronto: McGraw-Hill Ryerson, 1976.

Ray, Arthur J. "The Early Hudson's Bay Company Account Books as Sources for Historical Research: An Analysis and Assessment." *Archivaria,* 1, no. 1 (Winter 1975–76): 3–38.

———. "The Factor and the Trading Captain in the Hudson's Bay Company Fur Trade before 1763." In *Proceedings of the Second Congress, Canadian Ethnology Society,* edited by Jim Freedman and Jerome H. Barkow, National Museum of Man, Mercury Series, Canadian Ethnology Service, Paper no. 28. Ottawa: National Museum of Man., 1975.

———. *Indians in the Fur Trade: their role as trappers, hunters, and middlemen in the lands southwest of Hudson Bay, 1660–1870.* Toronto: University of Toronto Press, 1974.

Ray, Arthur J., and Donald B. Freeman. *'Give Us Good Measure': an economic analysis of relations between the Indians and the Hudson's Bay Company before 1763.* Toronto: University of Toronto Press, 1978.

Ray, Arthur J., and C. Heidenrich. *The Early Fur Trades: A Study in Cultural Interaction.* Toronto: McClelland and Stewart, 1976.

Ray, Mrs George. "York Factory to Red River by Dog Team." *The Beaver,* March 1941, 29.

"Regular Trappers." *Household Words*, no. 199, January 14, 1854: 471–76.

Reid, W. Stanford. *The Scottish Tradition in Canada*. History of Canada's Peoples Series. Toronto: McClelland and Stewart, 1976.

"Remarks on the Fur Trade." Reprinted from *The Evening Advertiser* in *The Gentleman's Magazine*, new series, no. 24, November 1754: 503–5.

Remington, Franklin. "Harvard to York Factory in 1888." *The Beaver*, December 1944: 8–12.

———. "York Factory to London, 1888." *The Beaver*, September 1943, 18–21.

Rich, E.E. *The Fur Trade and the Northwest to 1857*. Canadian Centenary Series. Toronto: McClelland and Stewart, 1967.

———. *The History of the Hudson's Bay Company, 1670–1870*. Vol. 1: *1670–1763*. The Publications of the Hudson's Bay Record Society, vol. 21. London: Hudson's Bay Record Society, 1958.

———. *The History of the Hudson's Bay Company, 1670–1870*. Vol. 2: *1763–1870*. The Publications of the Hudson's Bay Record Society, vol. 22. London: Hudson's Bay Record Society, 1959.

———, ed. *Journal of Occurrences in the Athabaska Department by George Simpson, 1820 and 1821, and Report*. The Publications of the Hudson's Bay Record Society, vol. 1. Toronto: Champlain Society, 1938.

———, ed. *Minutes of the Hudson's Bay Company 1671–1674*. The Publications of the Hudson's Bay Record Society, vol. 5. Toronto: Champlain Society, 1968.

———. "Trade Habits and Economic Motivation among the Indians of North America." *Canadian Journal of Economics and Political Science*, 26, (February 1960): 35–53.

Rich, E.E., and G.N. Clark, eds. *Minutes of the Hudson's Bay Company, 1679–1684. Part 1: 1679–82*. The Publications of the Champlain Society, vol. 8. Toronto: Champlain Society, 1945.

———. *Minutes of the Hudson's Bay Company, 1679–1684. Part 2: 1682–84*. The Publications of the Hudson's Bay Record Society, vol. 9. Toronto: Champlain Society, 1946. Reprint ed., Nendeln/Liechtenstein: Kraus Reprint, 1968.

Rich, E.E., and Harvey Fleming, eds. *Minutes of Council, Northern Department of Rupert Land, 1821–31*. The Publications of the Hudson's Bay Record Society, vol. 3. London: Hudson's Bay Record Society, 1940.

Rich, E.E., and Alice M. Johnson, eds. *Copy Book of Letters Outward & c – Begins 29th May, 1680; Ends 5 July, 1687.* The Publications of the Hudson's Bay Record Society, vol. 11. London: Hudson's Bay Record Society, 1948.

———. *Cumberland House Journals and Inland Journals, 1775–82. First Series, 1775–78.* The Publications of the Hudson's Bay Record Society, vol. 14. London: Hudson's Bay Record Society, 1951.

———. *Cumberland House Journals and Inland Journals, 1775–82. Second Series, 1779–82.* The Publications of the Hudson's Bay Record Society, vol 15. London: Hudson's Bay Record Society, 1952.

———. *Hudson's Bay Copy Booke of Letters, Commissions, Instructions Outward, 1688– 1696.* The Publications of the Hudson's Bay Record Society, vol 20. London: Hudson's Bay Record Society, 1957.

———. *James Isham's Observations on Hudsons Bay, 1743, and Notes and Observations on a Book Entitled 'A Voyage to Hudsons Bay in the Dobbs Galley, 1749.'* The Publications of the Champlain Society, vol. 12. London: Champlain Society, 1949. Reprint ed., Nendeln/ Liechtenstein: Kraus Reprint Ltd., 1968.

———. *John Rae's Correspondence with the Hudson's Bay Company on Arctic Exploration, 1844–1855.* Introduction by J.M. Wordie and R.J. Cyriax. The Publications of the Hudson's Bay Record Society, vol. 16. London: Hudson's Bay Record Society, 1953.

———. *Moose Fort Journals, 1783–85.* The Publications of the Hudson's Bay Record Society, vol. 17. London: Hudson's Bay Record Society, 1954.

Richards, R.L. "Dr. John Rae and the Hudson Bay Route." *The Musk-Ox,* no. 31 (1982): 60–70.

Ridington, Robin. "Beaver Dreaming and Singing." In *Pilot Not Commander: Essays in Memory of Diamond Jenness,* edited by Pat and Jim Lotz. Anthropologica, Special issue, new series, 13, nos. 1 and 2. (1971):115–28.

Roberts, Kenneth. *Northwest Passage.* Garden City, N.Y.: Doubleday & Co., 1946.

Robson, Joseph. *An Account of Six Years Residence in Hud-*

son's Bay from 1733 to 1736, and 1744 to 1747. London: J Payne et al., 1752. Reprint ed., New York: Johnson Reprint Corp., 1965.

Ross, W. Gillies, and William Barr. "Voyages in Northwestern Hudson Bay (1720–1772) and Discovery of the Knight Relics on Marble Island." The Musk-Ox, no. 11 (1972): 28–33.

Rotstein, Abraham. "Fur Trade and Empire: An Institutional Analysis." Ph. D. dissertation, University of Toronto: 1967.

———. "Innis: The Alchemy of Fur and Wheat." Journal of Canadian Studies, 12 (1977): 6–31.

———. "Trade and Politics: An Institutional Approach." Western Canadian Journal of Anthropology, 3, no. 1 (1972): 1–28.

Rousmanière, John. "The First Yachts and Yachtsmen." Nautical Quarterly, Winter 1982, 2–15.

Rowse, A.L. The Early Churchills: An English Family. London: Macmillan & Co., 1956.

Royal Commission on the Ancient Monuments of Scotland. Twelfth Report with an Inventory of the Ancient Monuments of Orkney & Shetland. Vol.1, Report and Introduction. Edinburgh: His Majesty's Stationery Office, 1946.

Rue, Leonard Lee, III. The World of the Beaver. Philadelphia: J.B. Lippincott, 1964.

"Sad News from Hudson's Bay: Two Vessels Lost, and 15 Men Die of Scurvy." Whalemen's Shipping List and Merchants' Transcript, September 9, 1873: 2.

Scott, Eva. Six Stuart Sovereigns 1512–1701. London: George Allen & Unwin, 1935.

Seton, Ernest Thompson. Lives of Game Animals. Vol 4. part 2, Rodents. Boston: Charles T. Branford, 1953.

Shaw, Bernard. In Good King Charles's Golden Days. London: Constable & Co., 1939.

Shearer, John W. Groundwater, and J.D. MacKay, eds. The New Orkney Book. London: Thomas Nelson and Sons, 1966.

Shepherd, John, John Westaway and Trevor Lee. A Social Atlas of London. Oxford: Clarendon Press, 1974.

Shillinglaw, J.J. A Narrative of Arctic Discovery: From the Earliest Period to the Present Time. London: William Shoberl, 1850.

Ship Registers of New Bedford, Massachusetts. Vol. III, 1866–1939. Survey of Federal Archives, Division of

Professional and Service Projects, Work Projects Administration. Boston: National Archives Project, 1940.

Simpson, Alexander. *The Life and Travels of Thomas Simpson, the Arctic Discoverer*. London: Richard Bentley, 1845.

Smith, Adam. *An Inquiry into the Wealth of Nations*. 2 vols. Everyman's Library. London: J.M. Dent & Sons, 1924.

Smith, James G.E., and Ernest S. Burch, Jr. "Chipewyan and Inuit in the Central Canadian Subarctic, 1613–1977." *Arctic Anthropology*, 16, no. 2 (1979): 76–101.

Smith, Ralph. "Discovery of One of James Knight's Ships at Marble Island: a preliminary report." *The Musk-Ox*, no 9. (1971): 12–14, 53.

"Some Account of the late Samuel Hearne." *European Magazine and London Review*, 31 (1797): 371–72.

Soper, J. Dewey. "Notes on the Beavers of Wood Buffalo Park, Alberta." *Journal of Mammalogy*, 18, no 1. (February 1937). [Reprinted as pamphlet.]

Speck, Gordon. *Breeds and Half-Breeds*. New York: Clarkson N. Potter, 1969.

———. *Northwest Explorations*. Portland, Ore.: Binfords & Mort, 1954.

———. *Samuel Hearne and the Northwest Passage*. Caldwell, Idaho: Caxton Printers, 1963.

Squadrito, Kathleen M. *John Locke*. Boston: Twayne Publishers, 1979.

Starbuck, Alexander. *History of the American Whale Fishery from its earliest inception to the year 1876*. Vol 2. First published 1878. Reprint ed., New York: Argosy-Antiquarian Ltd., 1964.

Stefansson, Vilhjalmur. "Arctic controversy: the letters of John Rae." *Geographical Journal*, 120, no. 4 (1954): 486–93.

———. "Rae's Arctic Correspondence." *The Beaver*, March 1954, 36–37.

———. *The Three Voyages of Martin Frobisher*. London: Argonaut Press, 1938.

———. *Unsolved Mysteries of the Arctic*. New York: Macmillan Co., 1939.

Stephen, Sir Leslie, and Sir Sidney Lee, eds. *Dictionary of National Biography*. London: Oxford University Press, 1921–22.

Strynadka, Arnold. " One Native Person's Comments on the Field of Anthropology." *The Western Canadian Journal of Anthropology*. 1, no. 3: 32.

Sturtevant, William C., general

ed. *Handbook of North American Indians*. Vol. 6, *Subarctic*, edited by June Helm. Washington, D.C.: Smithsonian Institution, 1981.

Tanner, Adrian. *Bringing Home Animals: Religious Ideology and the Mode of Production of the Mistassini Cree Hunters*. Social and Economic Studies no. 23. St. John's, Nfld.: Institute of Social and Economic Research, Memorial University, 1979.

———. "The End of the Fur Trade History." *Queen's Quarterly*, 90, no. 1 (Spring 1983): 176–91.

"The Stop the Way Company." *Household Words*, no. 198, January 7, 1854: 449–54.

Thomas, Lewis G. "Historiography of the Fur Trade Era." *In A Region of the Mind: Interpreting the Western Canadian Plains*, edited by Richard Allen. Regina: Canadian Plains Research Center, 1973. [Revision of earlier article "Historiography of the Fur Trade" in *Alberta Historical Review*, 17, no. 1 (Winter 1969): 21–27.]

Thompson, David. *David Thompson's Narrative 1784–1812*. Edited by Richard Glover. The Publications of the Champlain Society, vol. 40. Toronto: Champlain Society, 1962.

Thompson, George Malcolm. *The Search for the North-West Passage*. New York: Macmillan Publishing Co., 1975.

———. *Warrior Prince: Prince Rupert of the Rhine*. London: Secker & Warburg, 1976.

Tiger, Lionel and Robin Fox. *The Imperial Animal*. Toronto: McClelland and Stewart, 1971.

Trease, Geoffrey. *Samuel Pepys and his World*. New York: G.P. Putnam's Sons, 1972.

Trevelyan, G.M. *English Social History: A Survey of Six Centuries, Chaucer to Queen Victoria*. Harmondsworth, Middx.: Penguin Books, 1967.

Trudel, Marcel. *The Beginnings of New France 1542–1663*. The Canadian Centenary Series. Toronto: McClelland and Stewart Ltd., 1973.

Tuchman, Barbara W. *Practising History: Selected Essays*. New York: Alfred A. Knopf, 1981.

Tucker, Joseph. *A Selection from his Economic and Political Writings*. New York: Columbia University Press, 1931.

Turner, Raymond. "Notes and Suggestions: Charles II's Part in Governing England." *American Historical Review*, 34, no. 1 (October 1928): 44–47.

Tyler, T.E. "Early Days at York Fort." *The Beaver*, March 1954, 49–53.

———. "York Factory, 1714–1716." *The Beaver*, Summer 1955, 48–50.

Tyrrell, Joesph Barr. *David Thompson's Narrative of his Explorations in Western America, 1784–1812*. The Publications of the Champlain Society, vol. 12. Toronto: Champlain Society, 1916.

———. *Documents Relating to the Early History of Hudson Bay*. The Publications of the Champlain Society, vol. 18. Toronto: Champlain Society, 1931.

———, ed. *Journals of Samuel Hearne and Philip Turnor between the years 1774 and 1792*. The Publications of the Champlain Society, vol. 21. Toronto: Champlain Society, 1934.

———, ed. *A journey from Prince of Wales's Fort in Hudson's Bay to the Northern Ocean in the years 1769, 1770, 1771, and 1772, by Samuel Hearne*. The Publications of the Champlain Society, vol. 6. Toronto: Champlain Society, 1911.

Umfreville, Edward. *The Present State of the Hudson's Bay, containing a full description of that settlement, and the adjacent country: and likewise of the Fur Trade with hints for its improvement etc., etc.* Edited by W. Stewart Wallace. Canadian Historical Studies, vol. 5. Toronto: Ryerson Press, 1954.

———. *Nipigon to Winnipeg: a canoe voyage through Western Ontario by Edward Umfreville in 1784*. Edited and published by Robert Douglas. Ottawa: 1929.

Vachon, André. *Dreams of Empire Canada before 1700*. Public Archives of Canada, in collaboration with Victorin Chabot and André Desrosiers. Ottawa: Ministry of Supply and Services Canada, 1982.

Van Kirk, Sylvia. *"Many Tender Ties": Women in Fur-Trade Society in Western Canada, 1670–1870*. Winnipeg: Watson & Dwyer Publishing, 1981.

———. "Thanadelthur." *The Beaver*, Spring 1974, 40–45.

Wales, William. "Journal of a Voyage, made by Order of the Royal Society, to Churchill River, on the Northwest Coast of Hudson's Bay; of Thirteen Months Residence in that Country; and the Voyage back to England; in the years 1768 and 1769."

Philosophical Transactions of the Royal Society, vol. 60. London: Royal Society, 1771.

Warren, Edward Royal. *The Beaver: Its Work and its Ways*. Monographs of the American Society of Mammalogists, no. 2. Baltimore: Williams & Wilkins Co., 1927.

Washburn, Wilcomb E. "Symbol, Utility, and Aesthetics in the Indian Fur Trade." *Minnesota History*, 40, no. 4 (Winter 1966): 198.

Watkins, Mel. "The Staple Theory Revisited." *Journal of Canadian Studies*, 12, no. 5 (Winter 1977): 83–95.

Weis, Frank W. *Lifelines: Famous Contemporaries from 600 B.C. to 1975*. New York: Facts on File, 1982.

Wells, Eric. "Arctic Chess–White to Play." Unpub. paper on John Rae, 1983. [Copied by permission.]

Williams, Glyndwr, ed. *Andrew Graham's Observations on Hudson's Bay, 1767– 91*. The Publications of the Hudson's Bay Record Society, vol. 27. London: Hudson's Bay Record Society, 1969.

———. "Arthur Dobbs and Joseph Robson: New Light on the Relationship between Two Early Critics of the Hudson's Bay Company." *Canadian Historical Review*, 40, no. 2 (June 1959): 132–36.

———. *The British Search for the Northwest Passage in the Eighteenth Century*. Imperial Studies Series, no. 24. London: Longmans, Green 1962.

———. "Highlights of the First 2000 Years of the Hudson's Bay Company." *The Beaver*, Autumn 1970, 4–63. Reprint ed., Winnipeg: Peguis Publishers, 1976.

———. "The Hudson's Bay Company and its Critics in the Eighteenth Century." *Transactions of the Royal Historical Society* (London), 5th ser., 20 (1970).

———, ed. *Hudson's Bay Miscellany, 1670–1870*. The Publications of the Hudson's Bay Record Society, vol. 30. Winnipeg: Hudson's Bay Record Society, 1975.

———. "The Puzzle of Anthony Henday's Journal, 1754–1755." *The Beaver*, Winter 1978, 40–56.

Willis, Jane. *Geneish: An Indian Girlhood*. Toronto: New Press, 1973.

Willson, Beckles. *The Great Company, being a history of the Honourable Company of Merchants-Adventurers trading into Hudson's Bay*. Toronto: Copp, Clark Co., 1899.

Wilson, Charles. *Profit and Power: A Study of England*

and the Dutch Wars. London: Longmans, Green, 1957.

Wilson, Clifford, ed. *Northern Treasury: Selections from The Beaver*. Toronto: Thomas Nelson & Sons (Canada), n.d.

Wilson, J. Tuzo "New Light on Hearne." *The Beaver*, June 1949, 14–18.

Wise, S.F. "Liberal Consensus or Ideological Battleground: Some Reflections on the Hartz Thesis." In *Canadian Historical Association: Historical Papers*, 1–13. Toronto: Canadian Historical Association, 1974.

Woodcock, George. *The Hudson's Bay Company*. Toronto: Collier-Macmillan Canada Ltd., 1970.

Woods, Betty. "Must York Factory Become a Ruin?" *St. James* (Man.) *Leader*, August 4, 1960.

Woolhouse, R.S. *Locke*. Brighton, Sussex: Harvester Press, 1983.

Key to Illustrations

Courtesy Rare Books and Manuscripts Division; The New York Public Library; Astor, Lenox and Tilden Foundations.

p. 39

Englishman in a Skirmish with Eskimos

Pen and ink watercolour by John White, ca. 1590.

This sixteenth-century watercolour shows a number of similarities to Dionye Settle's account of a battle that occurred between Frobisher's crew and Eskimos in a Baffin Island bay during a 1577 prospecting voyage that preceded Frobisher's major mining expedition of 1578.

Courtesy The Trustees of the British Museum, London.

p. 46

Nineteenth-century portrayal of Henry Hudson cast adrift by his mutinous crew, with his son John and a few loyal sailors

Painting by the Honourable John Collier. First exhibited 1881.

Courtesy The Tate Gallery, London

p. 54

La caccia dei castori

Beaver hunting as depicted in an Italian engraving of 1760 published in Monaco. Engraver: Rossi.

Courtesy Hudson's Bay Company

p. 60

Modifications of the Beaver Hat

Taken from Horace T. Martin, *Castorologia* (London, 1892).

Courtesy Hudson's Bay Company

p. 69

An early, fantastic portrayal of a beaver colony

Published by Herman Moll (London, 1715).

Courtesy Public Archives of Canada. Neg. no. C16758.

p. 80

Radisson and Groseilliers (Radisson is standing.)

By Frederic Remington.

Photo courtesy of the Frederic Remington Art Museum, Ogdensburg, New York.

p. 90

King Charles II

(1630–1685)

Portrait by Sir Peter Lely.

Courtesy Hudson's Bay Company

p. 94

Prince Rupert

(1619–1682)

Portrait by Sir Peter Lely.

Courtesy Hudson's Bay Company

p. 106

The *Nonsuch*

Drawing by Adrian Small.

Courtesy Hudson's Bay Company

p. 113

The first page of the Hudson's Bay Company Charter

Courtesy Hudson's Bay Company

p. 115

The signing of the Hudson's Bay Company Charter by King Charles

Trading Territories

At the time that the Hudson's Bay Company was first setting up trading operations, territories overlapped and were shared by neighbouring tribes. In the mid-nineteenth century, with the signing of treaties and the restriction of tribal movement, boundaries became more distinct. (The tribal locations shown here are therefore based partly on mid-nineteenth century designations.)

p. 261

A hunter-family of Cree Indians at York Fort, drawn from nature
Watercolour by Peter Rindisbacher.
Courtesy Public Archives of Canada. Neg. no. C1917.

p. 267

Indians trading furs, 1785
Pen and ink drawing by C.W. Jefferys.
(Some artistic licence may have been taken in this drawing; trading actually took place through a trading window, not across a counter.)
Courtesy Public Archives of Canada. Neg. no. C73431.

p. 276

Map of Hudson's Bay, with "parts unknown"
Drawn by John Wigate, a clerk who sailed with Christopher Middleton, and dedicated to Arthur Dobbs. Published by John Bowles (London, 1746).
By permission of the British Library, London

p. 283

Kelsey sees the buffalo, August 1691
From the painting by C.W. Jefferys for the Hudson's Bay Company.
Courtesy Hudson's Bay Company

p. 287

Rival traders racing to the Indian camp
Print by Frederic Remington.
Courtesy Public Archives of Canada. Neg. no. C747.

p. 313

The Governor Arthur Dobbs
From the portrait by William Hoare.
Courtesy Duke University Library

p. 314

New Map of Part of North America
Drawn by Joseph La France, "a French Canadese Indian, who Traveled thro those Countries and Lakes for 3 Years from 1739 to 1742".
(The map appeared in Arthur Dobbs's critique of the Hudson's Bay Company monopoly.)
Courtesy Hudson's Bay Company

p. 325

Henday enters the Blackfoot camp, 1754
From the painting by Franklin Arbuckle for the Hudson's Bay Company.
Courtesy Hudson's Bay Company.

INDEX

Index

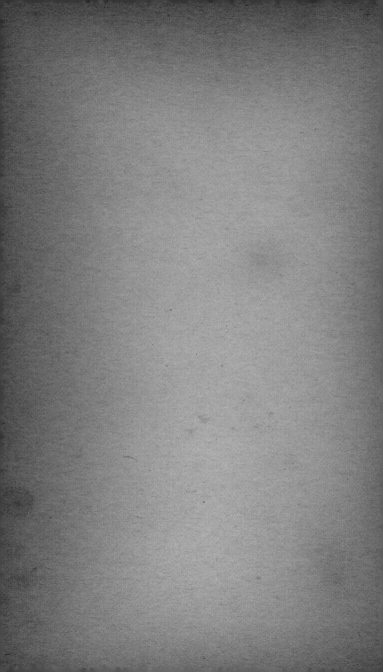

BY THE SAME AUTHOR: